ASYLUM – A RIGHT DENIED

This book is a thorough and incisive account of the flaws in the EU's Common European Asylum System, and is a must-read for anyone interested in the fate of refugees within the European Union.

Steve Peers, University of Essex, UK

This book constitutes an invaluable and enriching contribution to the literature on EU asylum law and policy capturing the dynamics and complexities of the evolving landscape of the Common European Asylum System. O'Nions deepens our understanding of the difficulties encountered in giving concrete meaning to the right of asylum and the problems concerning its full protection in practice.

Samantha Velluti, University of Lincoln, UK

This book makes a powerful argument that our present laws and structures actually undermine asylum rather than creating sanctuary. Grounded in an impressive breadth of scholarly research, the book is also highly readable, and offers a lively critique of the EU asylum system as well as a clarion call to a more effective system of protection. O'Nions weaves together carefully chosen detail from EU member states and institutions in service of the wider perspective which she develops. Her perspective is an important contribution to the effort to separate asylum from immigration control and the terrorism agenda, and she offers a vision which reinstates the grant of asylum as an act of international protection.

Gina Clayton, author of *Textbook on Immigration and Asylum Law*

AF696004

Law and Migration

Series Editor
Satvinder S. Juss, King's College London, UK

Migration and its subsets of refugee and asylum policy are rising up the policy agenda at national and international level. Current controversies underline the need for rational and informed debate of this widely misrepresented and little understood area.

Law and Migration contributes to this debate by establishing a monograph series to encourage discussion and help to inform policy in this area. The series provides a forum for leading new research principally from the Law and Legal Studies area but also from related social sciences. The series is broad in scope, covering a wide range of subjects and perspectives.

Other titles in this series:

Regional Approaches to the Protection of Asylum Seekers
An International Legal Perspective
Edited by Ademola Abass and Francesca Ippolito
978-1-4094-4297-4

Immigration, Integration and the Law
The Intersection of Domestic, EU and International Legal Regimes
Clíodhna Murphy
978-1-4094-6251-4

Migrants and the Courts
A Century of Trial and Error?
Geoffrey Care
978-1-4094-5196-9

Migration, Work and Citizenship in the Enlarged European Union
Samantha Currie
978-0-7546-7351-4

Refugee Law and Practice in Japan
Osamu Arakaki
978-0-7546-7009-4

Asylum – A Right Denied

A Critical Analysis of European Asylum Policy

HELEN O'NIONS
Nottingham Trent University, UK

Routledge
Taylor & Francis Group
LONDON AND NEW YORK

First published 2014 by Ashgate Publishing

Published 2016 by Routledge
2 Park Square, Milton Park, Abingdon, Oxfordshire OX14 4RN
711 Third Avenue, New York, NY 10017, USA

First issued in paperback 2016

Routledge is an imprint of the Taylor & Francis Group, an informa business

Copyright © 2014 Helen O'Nions

Helen O'Nions has asserted her right under the Copyright, Designs and Patents Act, 1988, to be identified as the author of this work.

All rights reserved. No part of this book may be reprinted or reproduced or utilised in any form or by any electronic, mechanical, or other means, now known or hereafter invented, including photocopying and recording, or in any information storage or retrieval system, without permission in writing from the publishers.

Notice:
Product or corporate names may be trademarks or registered trademarks, and are used only for identification and explanation without intent to infringe.

British Library Cataloguing in Publication Data
A catalogue record for this book is available from the British Library

The Library of Congress has cataloged the printed edition as follows:
O'Nions, Helen, 1971- author.
Asylum – a right denied : a critical analysis of European asylum policy / By Helen O'Nions.
pages cm. -- (Law and migration)
Includes bibliographical references and index.
ISBN 978-1-4094-0409-5 (hardback)
1. Asylum, Right of--Europe. I. Title.
KJC5202.O55 2014
342.2408'3--dc23

2013041500

ISBN 13: 978-1-138-24810-6 (pbk)
ISBN 13: 978-1-4094-0409-5 (hbk)

Contents

Introduction
Situating Asylum Law in Context

As a legal concept, asylum is ill-defined and poorly understood yet its meaning is typically assumed to be solid by those who make reference to it. When I asked a group of final year undergraduate law students back in 1999 about the difference between asylum seekers and refugees they were, without exception, baffled. Some believed the terms to be synonymous. Others, the majority, believed that an asylum seeker was a label denoting illegality, applied to those that had entered without correct documents who then tried to assert, illegitimately, that they were fleeing persecution. The term refugee was understood as comprising both a factual statement to identify a person fleeing persecution, and a legal status, afforded to those that had demonstrated to the host state that their fear was legitimate. One may question the reason for the apparent confusion over the label 'asylum seeker'. It is after all a rather straightforward statement of fact denoting a person who has left their country of origin and is seeking sanctuary elsewhere, ultimately through legal recognition as a refugee. The term asylum lacks a clear legal definition but established academic authority refers to durable international protection for refugees (as opposed to temporary or limited protection).[1] Yet, it is clear that the distinction between refugees, asylum seekers and other migrants has long been blurred in the public mind.[2]

Ten years later I asked the same question to a different group of final year undergraduates studying Immigration and Race Relations. Most of this group of 30 were from families with recent migratory histories, and one might therefore have anticipated a greater understanding of such terms. Yet the same misconceptions arose. Undergraduate law students, with no prior knowledge of the subject, simply did not understand the label 'asylum seeker' and in many cases it was again associated with notions of illegality.

The source of the students' confusion was not easy to pinpoint but the group generally agreed that media, politicians, family and friends played their part in reinforcing this negative perception. This is borne out by research into the British media's portrayal of asylum seekers in the early 1990s which concluded that the mainstream media played an intermediary role in an 'orchestrated government campaign to downgrade the public perception of refugees' which could then

1 Grahl-Madsen, A *The Status of Refugees in International Law* (AW Sitjhoff 1972) 6; Battjes, H *European Asylum Law and International Law* (M Nijhoff 2006).

2 Loescher, G 'The European Community and Refugees' (1989) 65 International Affairs 617.

justify tightening entry controls.[3] This may be attributable to the fact that as a 'figure whose characteristics are unknown',[4] the image of the asylum applicant is beset with uncertainty. There appears to be 'near consensus among experts' that politicians and the media dramatise the prospects of danger and threat to generate a feeling of being swamped which induces a general anxiety over immigration.[5] As Pécoud and Guchteneire recognise, there is a popular misconception that the majority of illegal migrants enter Europe through smuggling routes.[6] This allows additional resources to be deployed in tightening border control and intercepting smuggling operations. The reality is rather less threatening: many are actually over-stayers from student or visitor visas.

Thus we should not be surprised by this confusion. Media coverage stressing criminality or illegitimacy of the asylum applicant is supported by politicians who may use this representation as a convenient distraction in times of economic or political uncertainty. Of course there is an identifiable relationship between 'irregular' or undocumented immigration and asylum; the asylum-migration nexus,[7] but the conflation of immigration with asylum policy has generated a perception that an asylum applicant is little more than an economic migrant who would be unlikely to qualify for entry under the ordinary immigration rules. The 'illegitimate' asylum route is thus viewed as a way for entrants to avoid the strictures of immigration law. Moreno Lax argues that a control strategy has taken over the 'exigencies of refugee protection', a phenomenon she regards as 'particularly visible (and noxious at the point of entry'.[8] The students' confusion is

3 Kaye, R 'Redefining the Refugee: The Media Portrayal of Asylum Seekers' in Koser, K and Lutz, H *The New Migration in Europe: Social Constructions and Social Realities* (Palgrave 1998) 163.

4 El-Enany, N 'Who is the New European Refugee?' (2008) 33 EL Rev 3, 317.

5 Brochmann, G 'Controlling Immigration in Europe' in Brochmann, G and Hammar, T (eds) *Mechanisms of Immigration Control: A Comparative Analysis of European Regulation Policies* (Berg 1999) 330; Huysmans, J *The Politics of Insecurity: Fear, Immigration and Asylum in the EU* (Routledge 2006) 58; Beutin, R; Canoy, M; Horvath, A; Hubert; Lerais, F and Sochacki, M 'Reassessing the Link between Public Perception and Migration Policy' (2007) 9 Eur J Migration and L 394; Lewis, M *Warm Welcome? Understanding Public Attitudes to Asylum Seekers in Scotland* (Institute of Public Policy Research 2006).

6 Pécoud, A and Guchteneire, P 'Migration without Borders: An Investigation into the Free Movement of People' (2005) 27 Global Migration Perspectives.

7 Feller, E 'Asylum, Migration and Refugee Protection: Realities, Myths and the Promise of Things to Come' (2006) 18 Intl J Refugee l 509.

8 Moreno Lax, V 'Must EU Borders have Doors for Refugees? On the Compatibility of Schengen Visas and Carriers' Sanctions with EU Member States' Obligations to Provide International Protection to Refugees'(2008)10 Eur J Migration and L 315; Hathaway argues that refugee law should be seen fundamentally as an aspect of human rights protection rather than a mode of immigration. 'Why Refugee Law Still Matters' (2007) 8 Melb J Intl L 96.

reproduced in letters to British newspaper editors examined by Lynn and Lea.[9] The concept of the bogus 'asylum-seeker' has become naturalised within the UK. It is presented in many of the letters as a fact that requires no further substantiation:

> Exaggeration, distortion and a heavy reliance upon stereotypes provide the context in which politicians, legislator and law-enforcement agencies tighten social and legal controls. Meanwhile, refugees and asylum-seekers who as a group lack significant 'speaking rights' or 'voice' are more easily oppressed, discredited and stigmatized.[10]

This is further linked to the observation that asylum constitutes a particular threat to the national (in this case, British) way of life, a finding similarly seen in research undertaken in the Netherlands and Germany.[11]

Recent developments in refugee law including the attempted harmonisation of asylum policy in Europe, have failed to address this confusion. On the contrary, it is commonly suggested that cooperation has made matters worse by emphasising deterrence and the burden of protection at the expense of humanitarian duties.[12] Whilst it is tempting for lawyers to believe that public misunderstanding of such labels is of no real consequence, indeed it adds to the mystification of the legal process, this could not be farther from the truth in the context of refugee law and policy. As Hathaway reminds us, refugee law is a mechanism of human rights protection and it is therefore fundamentally erroneous to link policies of immigration and asylum.[13] The dramatic rise in violent attacks directed at those perceived to be foreigners in Greece, serves to remind us that public perception really matters.[14]

The law on asylum and refugees in Europe is complicated and intricate, juxtaposed uncomfortably between human rights law and immigration control

9 Lynn, N and Lea, S 'A Phantom Menace and the New Apartheid': Social Construction of Asylum Seekers in the UK' (2003) 14 Discourse Society 425–452.

10 Ibid 447; Van Dijk, T *Racism and the Press* (Routledge 1991); similar pictures emerge in other Europe countries, such as the Netherlands: Verkuyten, M 'Immigration Discourses and Their Impact on Multiculturalism: A Discursive and Experimental Study' (2005) 44 British J of Social Psychology 223 and France: Van der Valk 'Right-Wing Parliamentary Discourse on Immigration in France' (2003) 14 Discourse Society 309.

11 Verkuyten, M; De Jong, W and Masson, C 'The Construction of Ethnic Categories: Discourses of Ethnicity in the Netherlands' (1995) 18 Ethnic and Racial Studies 2, 265; Steiner, N *Arguing about Asylum: The Complexity of Refugee Debates in Europe* (St. Martin's Press 2000); Kaye, R 'Defining the Agenda: British Refugee Policy and the Role of Parties' (1994) 7 J Refugee Studies 2/3, 144.

12 See eg Dummett, A and Nicol, A *Subjects, Citizens, Aliens and Others* (Weidenfeld & Nicolson 1990) 256.

13 Hathaway, J 'Why Refugee Law Still Matters?' (2007) 8 Melb J Intl Law 89.

14 Cossé, E 'Greece's Epidemic of Racist Attacks' Human Rights Watch 26 January 2012.

and international and national law, with considerable implications for security and welfare policies. Similarly, the refugee sits outside a conception of the modern citizen which focuses on membership of a bounded territorial community.[15] Refugee law and the refugee are constructed as oppositional to the national interest. The popular press frequently reminds citizens that a generous asylum policy does not serve the national interest. The refugee presents a problem 'by lacking an effective state representation and protection; she is uprooted, dislocated and displaced'.[16]

Outside of academia, comparatively little attention is given to how well asylum law serves the needs of those who seek to benefit from it. Rising asylum numbers in the 1990s led to the emergence of asylum as a highly politicised European issue. The Amsterdam Treaty 1997 moved asylum from the third pillar to the first pillar of the European Community Treaty, resulting in a new body of secondary legislation based on 'minimum standards' and burden-sharing among the EU28.[17] Although the UK has opted out of recent amended directives and is not a member of the Schengen visa scheme, it is no longer possible to view asylum policy as a matter purely of national competence.

The EU's harmonisation focus has been on preventing irregular migration and on tightening Europe's borders. Simultaneously, there has been greater emphasis placed on equalising the burden of processing asylum claims, a process which is formally, albeit somewhat inaccurately described as 'burden-sharing'. Consequently, the EU position often appears to sit awkwardly against the views expressed by the United Nations High Commission for Refugees (hereafter 'UNHCR') the body entrusted with the guardianship of the 1951 Geneva Convention on the Status of Refugees (hereafter 'Refugee Convention').[18]

Further, EU asylum policy is grounded in some particular conceptions of the genuine refugee, as a result, European law absorbs and reflects many of the generalised misunderstandings surrounding the asylum applicant and their motivations. It will be argued that the translation of generalised misunderstandings into common standards inevitably deprives many refugees of the protection that they seek.[19] At the same time the difficulties experienced when seeking lawful access to Europe may encourage others to evade detection through unlawful means. In other words irregular immigration may in fact be created and stimulated

---

15 Soguk, N *States and Strangers: Refugees and Displacement of Statecraft* (University of Minnesota Press 1999) 9–10.

16 Haddad, E 'The Refugee: Forging National Identities' (2002) 2 Studies in Ethnicity and Nationalism 2, 32.

17 These obligations may also extend to the EEA states of Norway, Lichtenstein and Iceland. Similarly Switzerland (though not an EEA state) has aligned much of its asylum system with that of the EU.

18 See eg Executive Committee of the High Commissioner's Programme *Note on International Protection* 7th July 1994 A/AC 96/989 UN GA para 15 UNHCR.

19 Tuitt, P *False Images: The Law's Construction of the Refugee* (Pluto 1996).

by restrictive policies and the depiction of immigration as 'potentially dangerous' which has served to close off legal routes.[20] Any solution needs to address this virtualist argument whereby 'notions of immigration as potentially dangerous feed into policy and practice, which in turn create 'illegal 'immigration'.[21]

Although 2012 officially marked the end of the asylum harmonisation process, in many respects it is only the beginning as EU cooperation has led to the deepening of a European identity which is partly forged on restricting access to the 'privileged club'. Therefore the following analysis will examine the effect of harmonisation on the identification and protection of refugees. I will begin by considering the extent of obligations on the state to admit and protect refugees from a normative position. Chapter 2 will examine the *lex specialis* obligations of the 1951 Refugee Convention along with relevant international human rights instruments which compliment, and in some cases, extend refugee protections. This will enable a legal underpinning based on universal principles from which we can assess the approach and impact of the Common European Asylum System (CEAS). The direct and indirect motivations of the European legislators will be evaluated in Chapter 3, followed by a detailed analysis of the legislation concerning asylum procedures and reception conditions in Chapters 4 and 5 respectively. Chapter 6 will examine a variety of proposals and initiatives which deflect refugee movements and contract-out refugee determinations in ways that threaten the very foundations of international refugee law. The concluding chapter will assess the cumulative effects of such initiatives and consider alternative positions that could better advance the protection of refugees whilst responding to the resource and security concerns of States. The ultimate question is whether European law and policy is doing more than paying lip service to the fundamental right to seek and enjoy asylum as set out in the Universal Declaration of Human Rights.

---

20 Samers, M 'An Emerging Geopolitics of "Illegal" Immigration' (2004) 6 Eur J Migration & L 29.

21 Ibid at 43. Samers grounds his arguments in the work of Miller, D 'Conclusion: A Theory of Virtualism' in Carrier, J and Miller, D (eds) *Virtualism: A New Political Economy* (Berg 1998).

Chapter 1
Dimensions of Protection

Introduction

International law protects the dignity of all persons regardless of nationality, positing the human rather than the citizen at the centre of rights protection.[1] Yet human rights are not hermetically sealed from the politics of border control which seeks to define and exclude those who have no clear right of entry.[2] Border management itself results from a complex negotiation between different state actors and interests. The two most common justifications for tighter border controls relate to the financial costs of immigration and the preservation of national identity (including the culture and security of the national community). When considering the realisation of a right to seek and enjoy asylum, advocates of more generous admission policies must seek to overcome these justifications.

The Positivist Position of International Law

The right to seek and enjoy asylum was first accorded universal recognition in the Universal Declaration on Human Rights in 1948.[3] The initial proposal had placed the asylum seeker in a strong position by preferring a right to 'be granted' over a right to 'enjoy' asylum, but states were keen to prioritise their territorial sovereignty over any legal obligation to offer protection.[4]

Whilst the right to seek and enjoy asylum did not find expression in the subsequent human rights covenants, it had by then received *lex specialis* recognition in the 1951 Refugee Convention and subsequent New York protocol.[5]

---

1 Lauterpacht, H *International Law and Human Rights* (Stevens & Sons 1950) 72; Kesby, A *The Right to Have Rights* (OUP 2012) 101.

2 Kesby ibid 103.

3 UN GA *Universal Declaration of Human Rights*, General Assembly Resolution 217 (III) of 10 December 1948.

4 The detail of these negotiations is discussed by Goodwin-Gill, G and McAdam, J *The Refugee in International Law* (OUP 2007) 358.

5 The 1951 Convention was time limited geographically to European refugees and temporally to events occurring before the 1 January 1951. The protocol removed these limitations. 145 states are signatories to the 1967 protocol whereas 144 states are signatories to the 1951 Convention – Cape Verde, US and Venezuela are not party to the 1951 convention but are party to the protocol. For further details on ratification see UNHCR 2011. Available at: http://www.unhcr.org/3b73b0d63.html (accessed 7 July 2013).

The Convention emerged from a cautious climate in the early days of universal obligations where state sovereignty prevailed and this resulted, according to Goodwin-Gill, in an essentially reactive legal instrument.[6]

Whilst the Convention defines a refugee in international law, it does not place a legal obligation on any state to admit an asylum seeker to their territory for the purpose of seeking refugee status. However, once an asylum seeker arrives at the frontiers of the state, s/he is protected from return or 'refoulement', as discussed in Chapter 2. This guarantee derives from the 1933 Convention Relating to the International Status of Refugees.[7] It has special status in international law as an obligation *erga omnes*, and is regarded by many commentators as having the status of *jus cogens* and customary international law.[8] The UNHCR have confirmed that this obligation should apply to those seeking asylum and should not be limited to those formally recognised as refugees.[9]

The Ad Hoc Committee on Statelessness and Related Problems had initially proposed an absolute prohibition on refoulement, with no exceptions,[10] but the 1951 Conference of Plenipotentiaries qualified the principle by adding a paragraph denying its benefit to the refugee with regard to whom there are 'reasonable grounds for regarding as a danger to the security of the country … or who, having been convicted by a final judgment of a particularly serious crime, constitutes a danger to the community of that country'.[11] Thus international refugee law legitimises a public order argument for limiting state obligations to refugees who may pose a threat to state security.

The obligation of non-refoulement clearly encroaches on traditional notions of territorial sovereignty and some states have attempted to evade their legal responsibility through resort to interception strategies which prevent access to

---

6 Goodwin-Gill, G 'Convention Relating to the Status of Refugees, Geneva, July 1951' UN Audiovisual Library of Intl law. Available at: http://untreaty.un.org/cod/avl/ha/prsr/prsr.html (accessed 5 November 2012); The UN Charter Article 2(7) expressly prohibits the UN from interfering in the domestic affairs of states., June 26, 1945, 59 Stat 1031, TS 993, 3 Bevans 1153, entered into force 24 October 1945.

7 Convention Relating to the International Status of Refugees, Geneva, 28 October 1933, League of Nations, *Treaty Series*, vol 159, No 3663.

8 Declaration of State Parties to the 1951 Convention and/or its 1967 Protocol Relating to the Status of Refugees UN Doc HCR/MMSP/2001/09 (UNHCR 16 January 2002); Field, JRC 'Bridging the Gap Between Refugee Rights and Reality' (2010) 22 Int J Refugee L 4, 512; Coleman, N 'Non-Refoulement Revised: Renewed Review of Non-Refoulement as Customary International law' (2003) 5 Eur J Migration L 23.

9 UN EX Comm No. 6 XXVIII *On Non-refoulement* 1977 Office on the UNHCR.

10 United Nations Economic and Social Council, Summary Record of the Twentieth Meeting, Ad Hoc Committee on Statelessness and Related Problems, First Session, United Nations doc E/AC 32/SR 20 (1950), 11–12, paras 54 to 55.

11 Article 33(2) Refugee Convention.

their territory.[12] This practice has confronted the European Court of Human Rights (hereafter 'ECtHR') with the need to determine that a state's obligations under Article 3 of the European Convention on Human Rights (hereafter 'ECHR') may be applied to actions taken outside of that state's territory.[13] Article 3 contains an absolute prohibition of, inter alia, inhuman or degrading treatment or torture. As such it overlaps and expands the non-refoulement obligation by admitting no exceptions. As well as finding implied recognition in Article 3 of the ECHR, non-refoulement finds specific recognition in European Union law by virtue of Article 19 of the EU Charter of Fundamental Rights.[14]

Although the Refugee Convention lacks an enforcement mechanism, the UNHCR acts as its guardian, having been established to provide 'international protection to refugees and to assist governments in seeing 'permanent solutions for the problem of refugees'.[15] The UNHCR *Handbook on Procedures and Criteria for Determining Refugee Status*, published in 1979 provides authoritative guidance on the correct interpretation of the Convention. Whilst its Executive Committee Conclusions give further guidance which is increasingly cited as soft law in national refugee determinations.[16]

The Refugee Convention is merely a starting point in understanding international obligations to refugees. Due to its reactive nature, it does not oblige a state to provide asylum or deal with conditions of admission. It also neglects to address the causes of irregular migration, whilst its definition of the refugee as a person 'outside their country of origin' is inevitably construed as excluding internally displaced persons.[17] Notwithstanding these limitations, it remains the bedrock of international refugee protection and, along with *lex generalis* human rights principles, it is the legal standard against which European harmonisation and burden-sharing initiatives must be assessed.

---

12 In *Xhavara v Italy and Albania* App 39473/98 11 January 2001, it was held that interception methods id not breach the right of freedom of movement under Article 2(2) of Protocol 4 as they were aimed at preventing entry to Italy rather than preventing a right of exit from Albania.

13 *Hirsi Jamaa and Others v Italy* App No 27765/09 23 February 2012.

14 2000/C 364/01.

15 Statute of the Office of the United Nations High Commissioner for Refugees. General Assembly Resolution 428 (v) of 14 December 1950 para 8((a).

16 *Handbook on Procedures and Criteria for Determining Refugee Status Under the 1951 Convention and the 1967 Protocol Relating to the Status of Refugees* HCR/IP/4/Eng/REV 1Reedited, Geneva, January 1992, UNHCR 1979. (See also the website of the Office of the United Nations High Commissioner for Refugees for other handbooks and guidelines: http://www.unhcr.org).

17 The UNHCR estimates that there are some 26.4 million IDPs in the world, as of 2011: http://www.unhcr.org/pages/49c3646c146.html (accessed 2 July 2013). The number is likely to be significantly higher today due to the conflict in Syria.

Normative Arguments for Enhanced Protection

The universal and individualised approach of the Refugee Convention has long been under assault with some states questioning its relevance in the modern era and others arguing for protection in regions of origin.[18] For the purpose of expedited refugee determination, most European states have adopted lists of 'safe' countries from which there are presumed to be no genuine refugees.

On the other hand, there is an argument that European states *should* do much more to identify and protect refugees. Many in genuine need of protection are left with little option but to remain in the region or country of origin due to family responsibilities and resource constraints As a result, the European picture of the typical refugee as a young, single, male is distorted.[19] Any system of enhanced protection must extend to all those in fear of persecution or serious harm, not just those who can afford to make the journey.

Yet the prevalence of the statist paradigm where the sovereign power to protect borders from intrusion is universally supported by state practice[20] poses a significant obstacle when advancing refugee rights which directly challenge that paradigm. It is commonly asserted that the stability of the nation state and the tolerance of its citizens demands restrictive immigration policies.[21] Whilst it is evident that an emphasis on universal and transnational human rights calls into question the distinction between aliens and nationals which has characterised traditional statism,[22] international human rights norms 'cannot erase the spectre of the territorial border'.[23] This leaves non-citizens with a precarious, hybrid legal status, balanced between international, universal principles and territorially defined recognition.[24] For Benhabib, a person's right to exit a state would be

---

18 Phuong, C 'Protecting Refugees in the Context of Immigration Controls' in Shah, P (ed) *The Challenge of Asylum to Legal Systems* (Cavendish 2005); see for example the Bair vision discussion in Chapter 6.

19 Albertinelli, A 'Population and Social Conditions' (2010) Eurostat Statistics in Focus 27/2010 records that over 90 per cent of asylum seekers arriving in Europe from India, Bangladesh, Algeria, Somalia and Pakistan were male; El-Enany, N 'Who is the New European Refugee?' (2008) 33 EL Rev 313.

20 Dauvergne, C *Making People Illegal: What Globalization Means for Migration and Law* (CUP 2008) 44; Kesby supra n1, 15.

21 Dowty, A *Closed Borders* (Yale UP 1987) 14; Brochmann, G 'Controlling Immigration in Europe' in Brochmann, G and Hammar, T (eds) *Mechanisms of Immigration Control: A Comparative Analysis of European Regulation Policies* (Berg 1999) 23.

22 Jacobson, D contends that the state is turned on its head by international rules and institutions which impact on the sovereign body, *Rights across Borders* (Johns Hopkins 1996) 89.

23 Kesby supra n1, 116.

24 Kesby supra n1, 117; Bosniak, L *The Citizen and the Alien: Dilemmas of Contemporary Membership* (Princeton UP 2006) 38.

anomalous without a corollary right to enter in a world that is dominated by nation states.[25] Yet this is the anomaly presented by the legal position.

European states have been prepared to accept limitations to this sovereign right under European Union free movement laws which extend European movement and residence rights to all EU citizens and their family members.[26] Further, once an asylum seeker arrives at the state border, their legal status under international human rights law shifts to accommodate the non-refoulement obligation, even in cases where they have yet to be formally admitted. For Benhabib, 'The prerogative of democratic sovereigns to define criteria of political inclusion is not an unconditional right. Democratic sovereignty and human rights considerations must mutually limit and control each other'.[27] Whilst the state's executive agencies may attempt to limit their obligations by denying formal entry, national and regional judicial bodies are frequently called to plug this protection gap.[28] Asylum policy can be characterised as a 'tug of war' between international, universal norms and morals on the one hand and national, particularist interests on the other; effectively leaving lawyers with a choice between two 'foundational paradigms'.[29] The state's right to control its borders is clearly extensive but is certainly not unfettered.

The Liberal Case for Permissive Entry

For some scholars, state borders are arbitrary constructs which should be dismantled to generally enable entry for all.[30] According to John Rawls the original position of liberal democracy requires us to consider organisational principles of

---

25 Benhabib, S *The Claims of Culture: Equality and Diversity in the Global Era* (Princeton UP 2002) 172; see also Dummett, A 'The Transnational Migration of People Seen from within a Natural Law Tradition' in Barry and Goodin (eds) *Free Movement: Ethical Issues in the Transnational Migration of People and of Money* (Wheatsheaf 1992) 162. A right to exist and to return to one's own country is recognised by Article 13(2) Universal Declaration of Human Rights 1948.

26 Directive 2004/38 of the European Parliament and of the Council on *the Right of Citizens of the Union and Their Family Members to Move and Reside Freely within the Territory of the Member States* L 158/77 29 April 2004.

27 Supra n25.

28 Jacobson, D *Rights across Borders* (Johns Hopkins Press 1996) 75. The point is also made by Lillich, R *The Human Rights of Aliens in Contemporary International Law* (Manchester UP 1984) 3 and Thränhardt, D 'Germany's Immigration Policies and Politics' in Brochmann and Hammar supra n21, 48.

29 Steiner, N *Arguing about Asylum: The Complexity of Refugee Debates in Europe* (St. Martin's Press 2000) 7; Noll, G *Negotiating Asylum: The EU Acquis, Extraterritorial Protection and the Common Market of Deflection* (M Nijhoff 2000) 72; Pirjola, J 'European Asylum Policy – Inclusions and Exclusions under the Surface of Universal Human Rights Language' (2009) 11 Eur J Migration L 349.

30 Harris, N 'Migration without Borders: Economic Perspectives' UNESCO. Available at: www.unesco.org/most/migration/paper_n_harris.pdf.

justice behind a veil of ignorance.[31] For Carens this would extend to ignorance of our national origins, thus the right to migrate would necessarily be included as a fundamental human rights principle.[32] This right would impose corresponding obligations on the nation state to facilitate entry and any limitations on entry would be narrowly construed. Expulsion should never be predicated on the negative reaction of existing citizens as all human beings have equal moral worth as part of a global community.[33] Thus, Carens argues that as liberalism expresses general moral views in terms of universal principles, these principles cannot be legitimately restricted by national origins.[34] Consequently, he views border controls as illiberal, feudal barriers to mobility which protect unjust and arbitrary privileges.[35] On this reasoning, any moral argument to restrict entry would directly challenge the assumption that all individuals have equal moral worth.[36]

Walzer's Case for Border Control

The morally neutral principles underpinning the liberal democratic state are typified by notions of tolerance, equality and, to some extent, respect for difference. For Michael Walzer the survival of these values depends, paradoxically, on a degree of border control which helps to preserve national cultural identity. Walzer's *Spheres of Justice* begins with an account of membership which aims to promote communal cohesion in part through the demarcation of strangers from members.[37] Restricted group membership becomes essential for developing his principles of distributive justice which begins with membership rights, 'It must indicate a limited right of closure, without which there could be no community, and the political inclusiveness of the existing communities'.[38]

Thus when states restrict access to their borders, prioritising entry for those with kinship and family ties, they are defending liberty and the welfare of the national community by ensuring that its inhabitants are committed to one another and to their common life.[39]

---

31 Rawls, J *A Theory of Justice* (Harvard UP 1971).

32 Carens, J 'Aliens and Citizens: The Case for Open Borders' (1987) 49 The Rev of Politics 2, 256.

33 Carens supra n32, 265.

34 Ibid, 269; This is evidenced by the approach of universal human rights instruments which transcend state boundaries emphasising equal respect and non-discrimination, irrespective of national origins. Noll gives the example of the majority judgement of the ECtHR in *Chahal v UK* App 22414/93 15 November 1996; Noll supra n29, 75.

35 Carens supra n32, 271.

36 Ibid 269; Dummett, A and Nicol, A *Subjects, Citizens, Aliens and Others* (Weidenfeld & Nicolson 1990) 265.

37 Walzer, M *Spheres of Justice: A Defence of Pluralism and Equality* (Martin Robertson 1983).

38 Ibid, 62.

39 Ibid, 39.

Walzer compares affluent, liberal countries with elite universities which find themselves besieged by applicants. Entrance criteria based on certain common values are thus developed to determine who should be prioritised for admittance.[40] Allowances are made for refugees under the principle of mutual aid, provided that the risks and costs to the host state in providing such aid are relatively low.[41] The right to restrain the flow of refugees remains a feature of communal self-determination, 'The principle of mutual aid can only modify and not transform admissions policies rooted in a particular community's understanding of itself'.[42]

The cohesion of the national community is a common concern raised by politicians to justify restrictive entry policies which inevitably impacts on refugees along with other categories of migrant. Rarely is a political voice heard that presents refugee migration in a more positive light.[43] Hathaway challenges this, arguing that given the certainty of continuing irregular migratory movements, it is in the state's self-interest to provide favourable, managed migration channels for refugees. It is also in the interests of the global, human rights agenda and the principle of hospitality so essential to an enlightened, liberal tradition.[44] Arendt's one true human right, the 'right to have rights' depends on belonging to a political community.[45] Without this functioning political community, the individual is unable to develop their full potential and the realisation of all other rights is consequently jeopardised.

As a communitarian, Walzer rejects the position that a state can and should be neutral as to the common values it seeks to endorse. In the communitarian conception of justice, the state may seek to position itself by endorsing a particular vision of the good life and certain instrumental values, whilst simultaneously rejecting others. This contrasts with the traditional liberal model, characterised by John Rawls,[46] of a culturally and politically neutral state apparatus which encourages tolerance of difference by its rejection of a particular vision of the good life. Any suggestion that members 'must' adopt a particular cultural and political position is the antithesis of this neutrality agenda. We have seen that for Carens, immigration restrictions within liberal democratic states are a paradox in that they deny to some the liberal values of the culture they are supposed to preserve. Border controls arguably feed intolerance by suggesting that foreigners

40 Ibid, 32.

41 Ibid, 33.

42 Ibid, 51.

43 The European Green movement is a notable exception: europeangreens.eu.

44 Hathaway, J 'Why Refugee Law Still Matters' (2007) 8 Melb J Intl L 96; Noll, G 'Why Refugees Still Matter: A Response to Hathaway' (2007) 8 Melb J Intl L 546.

45 Arendt, H *Origins of Totalitarianism* (Harcourt 1966).

46 Young, S *Beyond Rawls: An Analysis of the Concept of Political Liberalism* (UP of America, 2002) 44.

are undesirable and this in turn impacts inwards to generate internal boundaries which damage social cohesion.[47]

A weak point in Walzer's position centres on the extent to which immigration impacts on national culture. Given the size and diversity of migrant populations in Europe, the cultural erosion argument may be overstated. Dummett and Nicol posit that mass-tourism might have a bigger effect than migration on the national culture, 'the claim that immigration controls are needed to protect culture is hollow *unless* immigration is either so massive that the resident population's culture cannot be maintained, or the immigrants, though few in number, actively destroy it'.[48] Almost certainly, cultural erosion resulting from the presence of refugees in European states is marginal. Interview-based research suggests that most seek integration and membership in the national community.[49]

It may further be suggested that some of the arguments against widening community membership have racial as well as cultural overtones. Certainly, the European expansion project has enabled a divide between third country migrants and European migrants which is just as much about culture as economics and, for writers such as Pieterse and Sivandan, racism plays a large part in fortifying these borders.[50] There is certainly a question over how cultural erosion is measured in the absence of quantifiable and morally valid indicators and care must be taken to ensure that such assessments do not 'give undue weight to the vociferous objections of small but organised political groups that do not reflect the general tolerance of the majority of citizens'.[51]

47 Pécoud, A and Guchteneire, P 'International Migration, Border Controls and Human Rights: Assessing the Relevance of a Right to Mobility' (2006) 21 Journal of Borderlands Studies 1, 79; Hayter, T *Open Borders: The Case against Immigration Controls* (Pluto 2000).

48 Dummett and Nicol supra n36, 277.

49 See for example Ager, A and Strang, A 'Indicators of Integration: Final Report' Home Office Development and Practice Report 28 (Home Office 2004); 'The Experience of Integration: A Qualitative Study of Refugee Integration in Local Communities of Pollokshaws and Islington' Home Office Online Report 55 2004; Vrecer, N 'Living in Limbo: Integration of Forced Migrants from Bosnia and Herzegovina in Slovenia' (2010) 23 J Refugee Studies 4, 484; Losi, N and Strang, *Intagraref: Local Communities and Refugees, Fostering Social Integration.* Project Report (Institute for International Health and Development 2008) Available at: http://eresearch.qmu.ac.uk/1240 (accessed 18 June 2013).

50 Pieterse, JN 'Fictions of Europe' (1991) 32 Race and Class 3, 3; Sivandan, A *Communities of Resistance – Writings on Black Struggles for Socialism* (Verso 1990). Elspeth Guild observes how European immigration policy has divided the world's population into two halves: those within the external border and those without, *Security and Migration in the 21st Century* (Polity 2009).

51 Anker, D; Fitzpatrick, J and Shacknove, A 'Crisis and Cure: A Reply to Hathaway/ Neve and Schuck' (1998) 11 Harvard Human Rights J 306l.

Walzer gives no justification for prioritising the communal interest over the rights of refugees when determining membership.[52] It could certainly be argued that the distinct identity of the political community that Walzer seeks to preserve is an imaginary community, maintained in part through its differentiation from external communities.[53] This maintenance comes at a price, namely the promotion of insecurity and intolerance. It might be countered that intolerance could be more effectively countered through policies of inclusion, breaking down rather than fortifying these imaginary barriers.[54]

Walzer argues that to demolish these walls would 'create a thousand petty fortresses'.[55] This echoes a common argument in political discourse justifying restrictive controls as essential to harmonious race relations.[56] It further lends support to arguments rejecting multiculturalism.[57] Yet one may respond that a world with such walls is by its nature already a world of petty fortresses. It would seem that the constitutive dialectic, which requires separation from strangers and the external world, is largely based on insecurity and fear. This in turn necessitates a protective obligation on the sovereign state, maintained through a variety of legal instruments such as detention and expulsion of outsiders.[58] In this respect, deference to a meta-right of security on which all other rights depend becomes a

52 Singer, P and Singer, R 'The Ethics of Refugee Policy' in Gibney, M (ed.) *Open Borders? Closed Societies?* (Greenwood 1988) 121.

53 Anderson, B *Imagined Communities: Reflections on the Origin and Spread of Nationalism* (Verso 1983); Balibar, E 'The Nation Form: History and Ideology' in Balibar, E and Wallerstein, I *Race, Nation, Class: Ambiguous Identities Politics* (Verso 1991) 86.

54 Haddad, E 'The Refugee: Forging National Identities' (2002) 2 Studies in Ethnicity and Nationalism 2, 24; Hollifield notes that the anti-immigration Pasqua law introduced in France in 1993 may have reduced immigration but it also 'fanned the flames' of xenophobia by giving the impression that immigration was a threat to French identity, Hollifield, J 'Ideas, Institutions and Civil Society: On the Limits of Immigration in France'; see also Brochmann supra n21, 4–8; 329 who observes how the Front Nationale continued to gain in popularity after the legislation.

55 Walzer supra n37, 39.

56 This has been well documented in the political debates of both right and left in the UK. See for example Back, L; Keith, M; Khan, A; Shukra, K and Solomos, J 'The Return of Assimilationism: Race, Multiculturalism and New Labour' (2002) 7 Sociological Research Online 2. Available at: http://www.socresonline.org.uk/7/2/back.html (accessed 5 November 2012). The association between restrictive border controls and harmonious race relations is typically presented as axiomatic; see for example Brochmann and Hammar supra n21, 24.

57 Cohen, R 'The Free Movement of Money and People: Debates before and after 9/11' CSGR Working Paper No. 160/05 (University of Warwick 2005). Kymlicka argues that rejecting immigrant multiculturalism is a high-risk strategy in such a climate: Kymlicka, W *Multiculturalism: Success, Failure and the Future* Migration Policy Institute February 2012.

58 Huysmans, J *The Politics of Insecurity: Fear, Immigration and Asylum in the EU* (Routledge 2006) 51.

means of securitising rights.[59] As a result, Huysmans argues that the freedom of the political community whose membership Walzer seeks to protect is predicated on insecurity, 'securing thus works on the basis of insecuring'.[60] Walzer modifies his approach when it comes to those migrants already admitted into the territory to which the state has a moral obligation to ensure full participation in the national community, through naturalisation and integration.[61] To hold otherwise would allow tyranny to prevail where denizens are excluded from full assimilation into the dominant culture. The Refugee Convention certainly supports an obligation to assist those recognised as refugees to integrate into the dominant society, for example through access to public education and the right to work.[62] This position implicitly challenges state mechanisms of temporary protection which offer a short-term solution to large-scale asylum demands.[63] Such initiatives leave the refugee in a precarious position, unable to take root in the new state.

A lack of opportunity for integration is likely to generate feelings of alienation among denizens which, if allowed to continue, could present a threat to state stability. Aleinikoff agrees that there is 'something distasteful, if not unconstitutional, about inflicting harm solely to make the non-afflicted feel special'.[64] As migrant populations grow so too will the demand for civil rights, equality and non-discrimination, prompting Legomsky to predict that immigration will become *the* civil rights issue of the twenty-first century.[65]

---

59 Lazarus, L 'Securing Rights of Securitising Rights?' in Dickinson, R; Katselli, E; Murray, C and Pedersen, O *Examining Critical Perspectives on Human Rights* (CUP 2012) 87.

60 Husymans supra n58, 61; Arendt, H *On Violence* (Harcourt, Brace & World 1970); Lazarus ibid, 103.

61 Walzer supra n38, 62.

62 The various sources of this obligation are examined by Da Costa, R *Rights of Refugees in the Context of Integration: Legal Standards and Recommendations* POLAS/2006/02 (UNHCR 2006).

63 Fitzpatrick, J 'Flight from Asylum: Trends towards Temporary 'Refuge' and Local Responses towards Forced Migrations (1994–5) 35 Va J Intl Law 13; Hathaway supra n44; Price also rejects temporary protection in cases concerning Convention Refugees supra n66, 166; for full discussion see Ch 6.

64 Aleinikoff, A 'Citizens, Aliens, Membership and the Constitution' (1990) 7 Const Commentary 9, 28.

65 Legomsky, S 'Immigration, Minorities and Pluralism: What Kind of Society Do We Really Want?' (1998) 6 Willamette Journal of Intl and Dispute Resolution 153–161; 'Immigration, Equality and Diversity' (1993) 31 Colum J Transitional L 319. It is worth considering the potential impact of climate change in this respect.

A Way Forward for Refugee Protection?

In order to navigate these contrasting positions we need to distinguish asylum from the broader issues of immigration and migration control. That is not to deny that this can be an awkward distinction (particularly as it is not uncommon for the asylum system to be used by those who have failed in their quest to remain in other capacities).[66] However, a separation is crucial to fully appreciate our humanitarian obligations, particularly in times of economic strain when resource arguments are frequently deployed to restrict general immigration.[67] Persecution is a particular kind of harm which repudiates a person's claim for political membership, undermining the realisation of all other human rights. Asylum thus provides a distinctive remedy in situations of forced migration by offering surrogate political membership.[68] It is the unequal distribution of this surrogacy arrangement, otherwise known as 'burden-sharing', which worries many governments and has prompted concerns that states are engaged in a competition to dilute standards in order to deter asylum seekers.[69]

When considering a normative basis for the obligation to admit refugees, a claim to protection may be stronger where the receiving state has some pre-existing relationship with the applicant or where the action or inaction of that state may have somehow contributed to the refugee's position.[70] Yet the influence of Western governments on the political affairs of many of the main refugee producing countries would make this obligation extensive.[71] In his attempt to reorganise the priorities for US immigration policy, Gibney argues that the first priority of entry policy should be based on the 'harm principle', where a special duty is owed to those migrants to whom the receiving state has done some past harm. This is followed by a basic rights principle which is based on broader protectionism and would cover obligations to refugees. Other migration, such as family reunion, would then be demoted from a first consideration in order to prioritise where moral

---

66 Price, M *Rethinking Asylum: History, Purpose and Limits* (CUP 2009) 204.

67 Caution needs to be exercised with this simplistic definition as many forced migrants do not satisfy the definition of refugee under the Refugee Convention: Cohen, R 'Response to Hathaway' (2007) 20 J Refugee Studies 370.

68 Price supra n66, 13; Arendt supra n45.

69 Toshkov and de Haan argue that harmonisation in European asylum laws has prevented this 'race to the bottom': Toshkov, D and de Haan, L 'The Europeanization of Asylum Policy: An Assessment of the EU Impact on Asylum Applications and Recognitions Rates'(2013) 20 J of Eur Public Policy 5, 661.

70 For example, in the case of Vietnamese refugees who had typically been Americanised before arriving in the US.

71 Carens supra n32 at 269; Robinson and Segrott cite the example of a Sri Lankan refugee in the UK who claimed that the UK Government were directly responsible for her treatment due to their failure to protect minority rights following independence, *Understanding the Decision-making of Asylum Seekers* (Home Office Research Study 243 2002).

responsibility is greatest.[72] This reorganisation would enable the state to preserve the identity of its national community whilst reinforcing the liberal values of tolerance and hospitality.

Whether a moral obligation towards asylum seekers derives from a state's previous involvement in foreign policy or simply from a recognition of our global interconnectedness depends on how we define equality: either as a political virtue that only applies among people who are bound by the same political path or as a pre-political virtue that applies between human beings that do not share membership of the same polity.[73] There is no moral justification within the liberal framework to use national origins as a basis to restrict basic rights. For Noll, each person is part of a global community which must secure a minimum level of protection where a local community, such as the nation state, fails to do so.[74] This position is the basic underpinning of international refugee protection. Without this recognition the equal worth of all human beings becomes a question of luck rather than right and universalism is little more than empty rhetoric.[75]

Carens and Walzer do agree that there is a moral responsibility owed to refugees, but for Walzer this obligation is dictated by pragmatism as, given countervailing factors, the claim for asylum may simply not be strong enough to require admission. A strong moral obligation certainly arises where a refugee risks being refouled as a consequence of physical rejection from a state border.[76] This is supported by international law which makes a state responsible for the consequences of its decision to refuse entry or to expel in so far as this action directly or indirectly results in refoulement.[77] Once an asylum seeker reaches the jurisdictional boundary of the state, the legal obligation prohibiting refoulement cannot be ignored. However, this obligation is not commensurate with an obligation to authorise entry or grant asylum. These decisions have largely been left to the public policy of individual states and here, Walzer's countervailing factors have come to dominate.[78]

---

72 Gibney, M *Strangers or Friends: Principles for a New Alien Admission Policy* (Greenwood Press 1986).

73 White, S *Equality* (Polity 2007) 12.

74 Noll, G *Negotiating Asylum: The EU Acquis, Extraterritorial Protection and Common Market of Deflection* (M Nijhoff 2000), 75.

75 See also Singer and Singer supra n52.

76 Carens, J 'Who Should Get In? The Ethics of Immigration Admissions' (2003) 17 Ethics and Internal Affairs 1, 101.

77 See decisions of the ECtHR including *Soering v UK* 161 Eur. Ct. H.R. Series A (1989) paras 90–91; *Vilvarajah and Others v UK* App ٢٦ ٣٠٦–٣٠٢/٢٣٦/١٩٩٠/٤٥ September ١٩٩١, para 103; *Hirsi Jamaa and Others v Italy* supra n13, para 115; *MSS v Belgium and Greece* App 30696/09 21 January 2011; also see decisions of the UN Committee Against Torture discussed in Chapter 2.

78 Singer and Singer accuse Walzer of relying on the political status quo to legitimise his argument in the absence of a clear theoretical underpinning which can prioritise membership over individual rights, supra n52.

The Introduction of the Security Paradigm

Carens argues that limitations on the admission rights of all migrants should be the exception rather than the rule. For Walzer however, such limitations can be more readily justified by countervailing factors in the interests of defending the national community. It is the latter position which typifies the politics of migration in the developed world as states make frequent reference to economic and security factors when justifying restrictive policies.

One view, originally promulgated by far-right political parties and commentators which has increasingly filtered into mainstream European politics, argues that borders should be closed with the nation state having absolute discretion to determine admissions.[79] This discretion will be generally exercised so as to preserve national identity from immigrants who are viewed as causing lasting damage to the national culture.[80] Holders of this view tend to reject arguments for admitting refugees in favour of their relocation to countries in the region of origin. For others, a limited number of refugees can be admitted if they are genuinely in need and are willing to assimilate into the dominant culture. The inhabitants of this camp typically stress the dangers of multiculturalism and view the host country as under threat from alien cultures and values.[81] Refugee protection is thus bound up with questions of nationalism and the preservation and defence of national identity.

Zolberg identifies an emergency mentality in Western politics over the last 30 years which has resulted in immigration and asylum being identified as primary security concerns.[82] The fear generated by this threat is exploited by some politicians in order to expose opposition parties as soft on crime and security.[83] Huysmans

---

79 See for example the influential campaigning and lobbying of the right-wing think-tank 'Migration Watch' in the UK: http://www.migrationwatchuk.co.uk/what-is-the-problem and the mainstreaming of anti-immigration policies in the Netherlands, Van Amersfoot, H 'Migration Control and Minority Policy: The Case of the Netherlands' in Brochmann and Hammar, supra n21, 159.

80 This is particularly, but not exclusively, seen in Europe where the immigrants are non-Christian (specifically Muslim) as evidenced in Dummett and Nicol's findings on the effect of increased refugee rates (from 1,000 to 6,000 acceptances in 1985–86) in Denmark which were depicted as causing a crisis for Danish homogeneity supra n36, 262.

81 See for example the prolific campaigning activity of Migration Watch in the UK, http://news.migrationwatch.org.uk/refugees (accessed 2 March 2013) and the discussions surrounding the new Integration Bill proposed by the centre right government in the Netherlands: Kern, S 'The Netherlands to Abandon Multiculturalism' Gatestone Institute, 23 June 20011. Available at: http://www.gatestoneinstitute.org/2219/netherlands-abandons-multiculturalism.

82 Zolberg, A and Benda, P *Global Migrants, Global Refugees* (Berghahn Books 2001).

83 O'Nions, H 'What Lies Beneath: Exploring Links Between Hate Crime and Asylum Policy in the UK' (2011) 31 Liverpool Law Review 3, 233; Pugh, M 'Drowning

views insecurity as a politically and socially constructed phenomenon: 'Even if one accepts that the arrival of a large group of outsiders can be disruptive for a community, the definition of the situation and the way one governs it is dependant on social and political processes'.[84] Through these processes and frameworks emphasising security, policing and defence, asylum becomes embedded in a security problematic.[85]

A distinct security discourse has emerged in European politics which offers a useful diversion in times of economic uncertainty and soaring unemployment. Migrant workers have been presented as threats to the native workforce and asylum seekers as threats to the welfare system of host states.[86] Unfortunately, the influence of extremist politics in shaping immigration and asylum policy has become ever more evident, having been given fresh vigour following the terrorist attacks of 11 September 2001 which appeared to confirm a link between immigration and security.[87] This perceived link is all the more surprising given that none of the hijackers were asylum seekers. In her exploration of the links between articulated politics and anti-immigrant attitudes in Europe, Bohman found that the real danger of encouraging extremist views came from mainstream political parties when they absorbed the language and policies of extremist right-wing parties.[88] Further research suggests that such policies receive wider public acceptance when couched in terms of cultural identity rather than simply racist rhetoric.[89]

Not Waving: Boat People and Humanitarianism at Sea' (2004) 17 J Refugee Stud 66, 50–69.

84 Huysmans supra n58, 2.

85 Ibid 4.

86 Heisler, M and Layton-Henry, Z 'Migration and the Nexus between Social and Societal Security' in Weaver et al *Identity, Migration and The New Security Agenda in Europe* (Pinter 1993) 158.

87 See for example French policy and the Pasqua law in the early 1990s, discussed by Hollifield, J 'Ideas, Institutions and Civil Society: On the Limits of Immigration in France' and by Brochmann supra n21, 4–8, 329; Geddes, A *The Politics of Migration and Immigration in Europe* (Sage 2003); Marr, D and Wilkinson, M *Dark Victory* (Allen & Unwin 2003); Lahav, G 'Migration and Security: The Role of Non-State Actors and Civil Liberties in Liberal Democracies' United Nations, Population Division, New York: UN/Pop/Mig/2003. Available at: http://www.un.org/esa/population/publications/secoord2003/secoord.htm.

88 Bohman, A 'Articulated Antipathies: Political Influence on Anti-Immigrant Attitudes' (2011)52 IJCS 6 457; the influence of far-right extremist parties is explored by Thrändhart, D 'The Political Uses of Xenophobia in England, France and Germany' (1995) 1 Party Politics 3 323. This is seen clearly in the Netherlands, van Amersfoot supra n79 and, more recently, with respect to the influence of the far-right Freedom Party on the Integration Bill.

89 Wilkes R, Guppy N and Farris L 'Comment on Semyonov, Raijman, and Gorodzeisky, SR, June 2006: Right-Wing Parties and Anti-Foreigner Sentiment in Europe' (2007) 72 American Sociological Rev 5, 831.

Penelope has demonstrated an association between terrorism and asylum in the deliberations of the UN Security Council, culminating in its 2001 resolution establishing the Counter-Terrorism Committee. The resolution explicitly links asylum to the prevention of terrorism by suggesting that before granting refugee status, states should ensure that the asylum seeker had not planned, facilitated or participated in the commission of terrorist acts.[90] A similar position was adopted by the Council of the EU in its Common Position on Combating Terrorism whilst the European Commission urged Member States to apply the exclusion clauses in the Refugee Convention to prevent suspected terrorists from claiming refugee status.[91] Thus asylum has become part of a security continuum through practical and institutional policy framing.[92] A general societal unease can be dramatised by security language so that it becomes an existential security threat.[93] This security threat helps to promote unity amongst the polity and is thus self-justifying as society *appears to* be more united and less unstable. For Huysmans 'In the pursuit of freedom from threat it is the rendition of dangerous life that makes the judgement of the good life possible'.[94] In the EU this has exposed contradictions and tensions which challenge the image of a liberal democratic regime.[95]

The Introduction of the Economic Paradigm

The perceived danger of asylum and immigration to the national interest further intensifies during periods of economic uncertainty. The former British prime minister Gordon Brown sparked a furore with his public pledge in 2007 that British jobs should be given to British workers.[96] No doubt Brown was aware that the pledge was legally untenable due to the UK's membership of the EU, but this rhetoric enabled him to appear tough on immigration and fuelled the debate

---

90 Penelope, M 'Resolution 1373: A Call to Pre-Empt Asylum Seekers? (or 'Osama' the Asylum Seeker) in McAdam, J (ed) *Forced Migration, Human Rights and Security* (Hart 2008) 22.

91 Council Common Position of 27 December 2001 On Combating Terrorism (2001/930/CFSP) L344/90 OJ 28 December 2001; COM (2001) 743 Final, The relationship between safeguarding internal security and complying with international protection obligations and instruments' Commission Working Paper Brussels 5 December 2001, 6.

92 Huysmans, J *The Politics of Insecurity: Fear, Immigration and Asylum in the EU* 4; See Also Walters, W 'The Power of Inscription: Beyond Social Construction and Deconstruction' (2002) 31 Millenium Eur Integration Studies 1, 81; and discussion of securitisation in Chapter 3; see also Cholewinski, R *EU Policy on Irregular Migration: Human Rights Lost* Paper submitted to Conference on Irregular Migration and Human Rights, University of Leicester 28–29 June 2003.

93 Huysmans supra n92, 47.

94 Huysmans supra n58, 47.

95 Levy, C 'The European Union after 9/11: The Demise of a Liberal Democratic Asylum Regime?' (2005) 40 Government and Opposition 1, 31.

96 BBC News 'What Does "British Jobs" Pledge Mean?' 16 November 2007 BBC.

over tighter border control. In a similar vein, recent policy announcements have been published in the UK favouring reduced welfare payments and health care to migrants following a surge in popularity for the right-wing UK Independence Party.[97]

The unpredictable financial cost of irregular migration is an understandable concern to states in uncertain economic times. Given the legal obligations deriving from the free movement of European citizens, EU Member States are restricted in terms of what measures they can legitimately impose to restrict entry. Concern over the lifting of entry restrictions on nationals from Romania and Bulgaria led several EU states to tighten entry policies for third country nationals, inevitably impacting on asylum seekers.[98]

Carens accepts that open borders may be limited in the interests of public order, which may be adversely affected by conflict over the allocation of limited national resources, particularly in cases of large-scale arrival.[99] But, like Benhabib, he rejects any argument that places a state's economic interest as a 'moral trump' above a commitment to fundamental rights.[100] Thus the financial cost of asylum becomes relevant only where it is so great as to promote public disorder. For this reason, cost emerges as a relevant factor in the normative debate; demanding, as far as possible, an economic assessment of the impact of asylum.

There are clear indications that the financial cost of asylum is frequently exaggerated for political purposes. Typically, the enormous costs of interception and deflection strategies, such as Frontex, the Schengen Information Scheme and EuroSur are calculated within the costs of refugee determination.[101] This results in a significant but misleading figure as their ultimate value is disputed by many commentators.[102]

A cost analysis of asylum rarely considers the positive cost benefits of migration.[103] Research on migrant integration in Canada, the US and the UK typically found a beneficial effect on economic growth which outweighed any loss of jobs, wages or welfare costs.[104] Similar findings have emerged from more recent

---

97 See announcements in the Queen's speech, 8 May 2013 BBC News.

98 Birrell, I 'The Immigration Debate: Evidence-Free and More Rancid than Ever' (Guardian Online 25 March 2013). Available at: http://www.guardian.co.uk/commentisfree/2013/mar/25/immigration-debate-evidence-free-rancid (accessed 25 March 2013).

99 Singer and Singer make a similar concession but only when the damage done to the national community outweighs the damage done to the refugee who is denied entry, supra n52, 125.

100 Carens supra n32, 174.

101 For further details on these costs see Chapter 3.

102 See for example Andreas, P and Snyder, T *The Wall around the West* (Rowman & Littlefield, 2000).

103 Boswell, C *The Political Uses of Expert Knowledge* (CUP 2009).

104 Studies cited from Canada and the US in Dowty supra n21, 238; Teitelbaum, M 'Rights versus Right: Immigration and Refugee Policy in the United States' (1980) 59 Foreign Affairs, 39; UK Cabinet Office *Migration: An Economic and Social Analysis* 1999

European research.[105] The informal economy certainly benefits from the lower-wages paid to those with uncertain and temporary immigration status, although this leaves many migrants vulnerable to exploitation.[106] Harris has argued that, contrary to the popular view, there is actually an economic imperative for open borders.[107] Prior to the events of 11 September 2001 the EU had recognised an urgent demand for non-EU labour migration arising from demographic changes.[108] Refugees are often highly skilled and could make a valuable contribution to the host economy. Further, remittances sent back by migrants can make a considerable difference to the reduction of poverty in countries of origin which in turn can help to reduce irregular migration and its associated costs.[109]

The number of persons seeking asylum in the European Union has steadily declined from its first peak of 675,460 at the time of the Bosnian war in 1992 to the present day, with a spike in 2001–02.[110] The European Commission reported that applications for asylum in the EU were down 45 per cent over a four-year period from 2003 yet the costs of preventing irregular migration rose exponentially during the same period.[111] Peaks in arrivals have coincided with the collapse of the former Yugoslavia, the deployment of armed forces in Afghanistan and Iraq and, in 2011, the regime changes of the Arab Spring.[112] Thus patterns in asylum seeking

---

cited in Boswell, 151 ibid. For a more recent endorsement of this view see Riley, J *Let Them In: The Case for Open Borders* (Penguin Group 2008).

105 European Migration Network *Impact of Immigration on Europe's Societies* (European Commission, March 2006).

106 De Haas, H 'The Myth of Invasion: The Inconvenient Realities of African Migration to Europe' (2008) 29 3rd World Q 7, 1305.

107 Harris, N *The New Untouchables* (Penguin 1996); *Thinking the Unthinkable: The Immigration Myth Exposed* (I.B. Tauris 2001); see also Rodrik, D 'Feasible Globalisations' (Faculty Research Working Papers Series RWP02029 John F Kennedy School of Government, Harvard University, 2002).

108 Levy supra n95 at 59; Heisler, M and Layton-Henry, Z 'Migration and the Links between Social and Societal Security' in Weaver, O; Buznan, B; Kelstrup, M and Lemaitre, P *Identity, Migration and the New Security Agenda in Europe* (Pinter 2003) 152; Brochmann, G 'Controlling Immigration in Europe' in Brochmann and Hammar supra n21, 299.

109 Zolberg, A 'The Next Waves: Migration Theory for a Changing World' (1989) 23 International Migration Rev 3, 424; Bright, M 'Asylum Crisis Hyped in Europe, says UN' (Observer 2 June 2002) 5; Guild supra n50, 137–9.

110 The number of asylum seekers arriving in the EU was 5 per cent lower in 2010 than the previous year, UNHCR 'Asylum levels and trends in industrialized countries 2010' (UNHCR 2011). It should also be remembered that the EU was notably smaller in 1991–92 with only 15 Member States.

111 This is notwithstanding some particularly high increases in some states, Greece (105 per cent), Sweden (37 per cent), Hungary (62 per cent) and Cyprus (49 per cent): European Commission *Staff Working Document. Impact Assessment* COM (2008) 815 Final, SEC (2008) 2944 Brussels 3 December 2008, 6.

112 UNHCR 'Asylum Claims in Industrialized Countries up Sharply in 2011' (27 March 2012). Available at: http://www.unhcr.org/4f7063116.html (accessed 7

strongly correlate to instability in regions of origin and this in turn suggests that tightening borders is at best going to have a marginal impact on numbers. A much more cost-effective strategy would focus on the causes of conflict and migration, but such efforts are likely to be counter-productive if the rationale is ultimately to combat irregular migration.[113]

The costs of refugee support could be significantly reduced if asylum seekers were permitted to work pending the outcome of their applications. Refusing or delaying permission to work forces asylum applicants into a welfare-trap which is damaging to future integration and is unlikely to be cost effective to the host state.[114] The reformed EU Reception Directive, discussed in Chapter 5, enables states to refuse permission to work for nine months from the date of the initial asylum application.[115] Yet, applicants can be left waiting much longer due to administrative delays and legal technicalities.[116]

A further cost which has risen significantly despite falling asylum applications is the cost of detention and reception facilities.[117] Several states have expanded their detention estates to provide for detention in expedited procedures with no justification beyond administrative convenience. As the prison system has been deemed unsuitable for administrative detention by the UNCHR and Council of Europe,[118] states have funded purpose-built centres with the requisite medical and legal support. The huge cost of immigration detention, estimated at £22 million per annum in the UK alone, is difficult to justify in the absence of imminent removal or a clear risk that an applicant will abscond.[119]

November 2012).

113 Gent, S *The Root Causes of Migration: Criticising the Approach and Finding a Way Forward* (Sussex Migration Working Paper No 11 2002, University of Sussex).

114 Jesuit Refugee Service, Europe 'Dublin II: A Summary of JRS Experiences in Europe' (JRS 2008) 6.

115 The initial position was 12 months under Council Directive 2003/9/EC of 27 January 2003 *Laying Down Minimum Standards for the Reception of Asylum Seekers*, OJ L31 6 February 2003, Article 11. This position will be reduced to nine months once the recast directive, adopted in June 2013, enters into force – see Chapter 5 for full discussion.

116 *R (on the application of ZO (Somalia) and others) (Respondents) v Secretary of State for the Home Department,* [2010] UKSC 36; see also *Tekle v Secretary of State for the Home Department* [2008] EWHC 3064 (Admin) in which the applicant had waited over four years for permission to work having made a fresh asylum claim.

117 For further discussion see Chapter 5. This practice was endorsed by the decision of the ECtHR in *Saadi v UK* App 13229/03 ECHR 29 January 2008.

118 UNHCR *Guidelines on Applicable Criteria and Standards Relating to the Detention of Asylum Seekers* 1999 UNCHR Guideline 10; CE Parliamentary Assembly *The Detention of Asylum Seekers and Irregular Migrants in Europe* Res 1707 (2010)1 para 9.2.2.

119 Home Office, response to a request under the Freedom of Information Act, January 2007, quoted by Information Centre about Asylum Seekers and Refugees (ICAR)

In terms of refugee protection, it may conceded that short-term costs outweigh the benefits to the state but this position is likely to shift in the longer term as refugees are able to contribute more to the host society.[120] The option of ignoring the plight of refugees will surely be more cost-intensive in the long-term, as regions of origin become destabilised by large displaced populations with limited resources and security.

The Symbolism of Crisis and Control

The unpredictable nature of refugee movements and the demands on host states mean that such migration is difficult to manage. In this respect control strategies come to have a symbolic value.[121] Brochmann observes how individual stories are merged into *flows* with metaphors such as 'invasion' and 'flood' frequently deployed to add to the symbolism of control.[122] Laws are subsequently tightened to respond to the demand for increasing restriction.[123]

This perception of an 'international migration crisis' has dominated much of the political debate on managing migration, resulting in the present emergency mentality which 'leads to breathless responses that are deeply counterproductive'.[124] The existence of such a crisis has been strongly disputed by Zolberg and Schmeidl who point to declining refugee movements since the end of the Cold War.[125] It is further clear that the vast majority of the world's refugees are in the developing regions of the global South.[126] This attracts the condemnation of Hathaway who accuses governments in the developed world of contributing to a global apartheid

Detention of Asylum Seekers in the UK (ICAR 2007) 6; see more recently Question by Baroness Warsi HL1462 Hansard 4 February 2010 Col WA67.

120 Noll, G 'Risky Games? A Theoretical Approach to Burden-Sharing in the Asylum Field' (2003) 16 J Refugee Studies 237.

121 Brochmann supra n21, 329.

122 Brochmann supra n21, 330.

123 The rise of extreme right politics in Germany is identified as key motivation in the tightening of German asylum laws in 1993, with German foreign minister Klaus Kinkel warning that immigration was threatening the stability of German democracy; *The Economist* 'Refugees Keep Out' (19 September 1992) 4.

124 Sen, A 'Population: Delusion and Reality' (1994) New York Review of Books 22 September 1971; Zolberg, A and Benda, P (eds) *Global Migrants, Global Refugees: Problems and Solutions* (Berghahn Books 2001). This view is challenged by the findings of Kritz, M 'Population Growth and International Migration: Is there a Link?' in Zolberg and Benda (eds) ibid.

125 Zolberg, A 'Introduction. Beyond the Crisis' and Schmeidl, S 'Conflict and Forced Migration: A Quantitative Review 1964–1995' in ibid.

126 US Committee for Refugees and Migrants *Word Refugee Survey 2006* (2006). According to the survey, the refugee to citizen ratio in Europe is 1:2000 compared to 1:100 in Lebanon, Chad, Tanzania and Iran – the figure in Jordan due to the Syrian refugee crisis is greater still.

'under which most refugees not only remain in the less developed world, but remain there under conditions which are generally rights-abusive and often literally life-threatening'.[127] Yet it is the cost of irregular migration to the developed world that is repeatedly stressed as demanding immediate, preventative action.

A significant amount of time has been taken up during negotiations between the EU and third countries on the subject of security. Much of this is attributable to the role of the European Council's High Level Working Group on Asylum and Immigration which formulates the policy of the 'external dimension'.[128] Its mandate to 'help reduce the influx of asylum seekers and migrants' by analysing and combating the reasons for flight' is indicative of a restrictive, prevention-focused agenda that has come to characterise the Council's position.[129] Whilst security concerns dominate the external dimension they are also accused of influencing the direction of European integration and subsequent enlargement.[130]

The security prism allows human rights to be side-lined when formulating policy on irregular migration. Hamood gives the example of a European Community seminar in 2005 promisingly entitled 'Saving life at sea and in the desert' which centred almost entirely on the subject of border surveillance. She concludes that 'overall the EU appears to be pushing forward a security agenda without insisting on corresponding action on other aspects, especially human rights and refugee protection'.[131] There can be little doubt that strategies aimed at interception and diversion risk refoulement contrary to international law. The humanitarian story is simply lost within a security and deterrence rhetoric.

Remote control migration measures serve to shift the locus of control outside the region, making it easier to distance the problem.[132] This is evidenced by the plight of sub-Saharan refugees who travel by truck on long, treacherous journeys

---

127 Hathaway supra n44, 89.

128 Discussed further in Chapter 6.

129 European Council *Responsibilities of Council Bodies in the Field of Justice and Home Affairs Following Entry into Force of the Treaty of Amsterdam* 6166/1/99 Rev 1 (Council of the EU 1999); Discussed by Chou, M-H 'The European Security Agenda and the "External Dimension" of EU Asylum and Migration Cooperation' (2009) 10 Perspectives on European Politics and Society, 4, 551.

130 Waever, O; Buznan, B; Kesltrup, M and Lemaitre, P *Identity, Migration and the New Security Agenda in Europe* (Pinter 1993) 195.

131 Hamood, S 'EU–Libya Cooperation on Migration: A Raw Deal for Refugees and Migrants?' (2008) 21 J Refugee Studies 1, 34; Cholewinski, R 'The Criminalisation of Migrants' in Baldaccini, A; Guild, E and Toner, H (eds) *Whose Freedom, Security and Justice: EU Immigration and Asylum Law and Policy* (Hart 2007) 326.

132 Zolberg, A 'The Archaeology of Remote Control' in Fahrmeir, A; Faron, O and Weil, P (eds) *Migration Control in the North Atlantic World: The Evolution of State Practices in Europe and the US: From the French Revolution to the Inter-War Period* (Berghahn Books, 2003) 195.

across the desert at the mercy of Sudanese and Libyan smugglers.[133] Humanitarian organisations have repeatedly reported cases of Libyan officials summarily removing migrants by escorting them into the desert.[134] Yet, if we discount the concerns expressed by some members of the European Parliament, they rarely feature in European Council discussions and have had little influence on European readmission negotiations. Whilst the EU does not wish to encourage this route it is surprising that the carrot of EU funding and trade initiatives have not been more effectively applied to capacity building in neighbouring regions.

The image of a European fortress is particularly vivid when migrants at sea are forcibly returned to their embarkation points without any attempt to identify protection needs.[135] Recent interceptions have drawn on the heavily criticised Australian precedent commonly referred to as the 'Pacific solution', in order to abdicate state responsibility.

The 'Pacific solution' In August 2001 the spotlight was turned on Australian refugee policy during the Tampa incident in which the Australian government refused permission for the captain of a Norwegian freighter to disembark 438 refugees (including 36 children) who had been recovered from a damaged fishing boat in international waters near the Australian territory of Christmas Island. The captain, under threat of prosecution, was instructed to return the passengers to Indonesia. Fearing for the health of the passengers and the safety of his crew the captain eventually proceeded to enter Australian coastal waters resulting in an acrimonious and protracted dispute in which the government authorised SAS commandos to board the Tampa.[136] The passengers were eventually transported by the Australian navy to the sovereign state of Nauru where their claims for refugee status could be processed in detention centres.[137] During the transfer, the government attempted to legislate retrospectively in order to prevent the passengers from claiming asylum and to remove any element of Australian liability.[138] The

133 Hamood, supra n131, 31. She quotes the Sudanese popular Congress who identified 486 Sudanese migrant deaths between 2004 and 2007 on the journey to Libya, 32; Young, H; Osman, A; Aklilu, Y; Dale, R and Badri, R *Darfur: Livelihoods under Siege* (Finstein International Famine Centre 2005) 89.

134 Interview reported in Human Rights Watch *Pushed Back, Pushed Around: Italy's Forced Return of Boat Migrants and Asylum Seekers, Libya's Mistreatment of Migrants and Asylum Seekers* (Human Rights Watch 2009).

135 See *Hirsi Jamaa* supra n13.

136 In a further embarrassment to the Howard Government, Captain Arne Rinnan was awarded a series of awards and accolades for his humanitarian actions, including the Norwegian King's medal of honour.

137 Goodwin-Gill, G and McAdam, J *The Refugee in International Law* (OUP 2007) 385 note that the Australian government justified the policy by arguing that it was saving lives by deterring people from resorting to dangerous methods of travel. All those rescued from the sea were subsequently recognised as refugees.

138 Border Protection Act (Validation and Enforcement Powers) Act 2001.

liberal government of John Howard was widely condemned outside Australia for elevating the problem of undocumented boat arrivals as a threat to national identity and Australian sovereignty.[139]

Subsequent Australian migration policy involved the excision of up to 5,000 Australian islands and ports, removing them from Australian migration control and thereby preventing unauthorised arrivals from having any claim to protection visas in Australia.[140] The policy ended in 2008 by which time the number of arrivals by boat had decreased markedly from 5,516 in 2001 to fewer than 100 per year.[141] In a convenient and contested interpretation of the non-refoulement obligation, the 'Pacific solution' narrowed the scope of the obligation to actions brought within the state's territorial borders.[142] This interpretation was subsequently rejected by the ECtHR when raised as a defence to interceptions in the Mediterranean by the Italian authorities in the *Hirsi Jamaa* case (discussed below).[143]

Following an Australian High Court decision in 2008, condemning the processing of applicants on the territory of Christmas Island,[144] the distinction between off-shore and on-shore applicants in Australian law has been eradicated and the primacy of the Refugee Convention has been re-asserted.[145] Yet, like its European counterparts, the Australian government continues to intercept asylum seekers at overseas airports and works closely with third countries in order to prevent the arrivals of undocumented migrants, many of whom are protection seekers.[146]

---

139 Maley, W 'Asylum-Seekers in Australia's International Relations' (2003) 57Aust J Intl Affairs 1, 192; Pugh supra n83, 52. Nevertheless, Howard received a more positive response from the Australian public and was elected for a second term shortly after.

140 Woods, T and McAdam, J 'Australian Asylum Policy All at Sea: An Analysis Of *Plaintiff M70/2011 v Minister for Immigration and Citizenship* and the Australia–Malaysia Arrangement' (2012) 61 ICLQ 1, 276; Taylor, S 'Offshore Barriers to Asylum Seeker Movement: The Exercise of Power without Responsibility' in McAdam, J (ed) *Forced Migration, Human Rights and Security* (Hart 2008) 94.

141 Phillips, J and Spinks, H 'Background Note: Boat Arrivals in Australia since 1976' Dept of Parliamentary Services, Parliament of Australia (15 July 2011). The most recent figure for 2011 was 1675 undocumented boat arrivals, UNHCR 'Fewer Asylum Claims in Australia' (UNHCR 18 October 2011).

142 Kneebone, S 'Outing Off-Shore Processing: The High Court of Australia Defines the Role of the Refugee Convention' (2012) 26 J IANL 2, 156; Goodwin-Gill and McAdam supra n137, 244–253; Taylor supra n140, 118. The EU's recast Procedures Directive, discussed in Chapter 4, now explicitly applies the non-refoulement obligation to territorial waters and transit zones.

143 Supra n135, see also the rejection by the UN Committee against Torture in the Marine 1 case: *P.K. et al v Spain*, Communication No. 323/2007, U.N. Doc. CAT/C/41/D/323/2007 (2008).

144 *Plaintiff M61/2010e V the Commonwealth Office* (2010) 85 ALJR 133.

145 Kneebone supra n142, 159.

146 Australia received 2.5 per cent of asylum claims across 44 industrialised countries in 2011, UNHCR supra n141.

In 2011, the Australian government announced an agreement with Malaysia to return the next eight hundred asylum seekers travelling by boat from Malaysia in exchange for some 4,000 UNHCR-recognised refugees.[147] Malaysia has not ratified the Refugee Convention and asylum seeking is considered a crime which is not distinguished from other types of migration.[148] The Australian Senate Committee urged the government to abandon the arrangement, finding that the conditions faced by refugees were appalling, with violence and harassment a daily occurrence.[149] The High Court subsequently declared the transfer of two Afghan refugees to Malaysia unlawful due to the risk of subsequent refoulement, notwithstanding the inability of the Australian courts to directly apply the Refugee Convention.[150]The agreement has now been abandoned in favour of fresh negotiations.[151]

The factors resulting in Australia's restrictive position are very different to those facing states in Southern Europe. The Australian government appears to be trying to appease a largely conservative electorate in a region where few other states offer any refugee protection. Additionally there is a comparative weakness in positive human rights obligations as there is no regional human rights instrument comparable to the ECHR. Yet, despite the more entrenched position of human rights norms in Europe, there are obvious parallels with the Australian experience, such that the European judiciary have been compelled to defend the human rights of asylum seekers against unfettered executive power.

Interception and interdiction in the Mediterranean Most irregular migratory movement into Europe occurs at Europe's southern borders. According to a study carried out by the UNHCR in 2011, more than 1,400 people lost their lives in the Mediterranean after leaving North Africa for Europe in the first eight months of the

147 *Arrangement between the Government of Australia and the Government of Malaysia on Transfer and Resettlement* 25 July 2011, discussed at length by Woods and McAdam supra n140.

148 UNHCR Country Operations Profile – Malaysia 2013. Available at: http://www.unhcr.org/pages/49e4884c6.html.

149 Discussed by Woods and McAdam supra n140, 299.

150 *Plaintiff M70/2011 and Plaintiff M106/2011 v Minister for Immigration and Citizenship* [2011] HCA 32 31 August 2011. As in the UK, Australia has a dualist constitutional system where international law is not directly applicable in domestic courts unless first enacted by statute. The government subsequently tried and failed to introduce legislative amendments to the Migration at 1958 in order to circumvent this court's ruling.

151 ABC News 'Immigration Minister Tony Burke Admits Malaysia Asylum Seeker Swap Deal No Longer Viable' (ABC News Australia, 6 July 2013). Available at: http://www.abc.net.au/news/2013-07-06/government-admits-malaysia-asylum-seeker-deal-no-longer-viable/4803756 (accessed 4 September 2013). The new Australian Government under the direction of Kevin Rudd has expressed a desire to revisit the Refugee Convention with a view to further restricting its obligations to asylum seekers.

year.[152] Both Italy and Malta have been implicated in the interception and return of migrants on the high seas in an effort to control and reduce these movements. Spain has constructed border fences to prevent access to Spanish territory in Morocco and has lobbied the European Commission for assistance in preventing arrivals in the Canary Islands.[153] More than 50 per cent of the irregular crossings into Europe in 2012 occurred at the border between Turkey and Greece which has led to the deployment of some 1,800 Greek border guards and the construction of several detention centres around Evros.[154]

Following the adoption of the 'Treaty on Friendship, Partnership and Cooperation' between Italy and Libya in 2009,[155] Italian vessels carried out nine interception operations (with a further two interceptions and returns to Algeria), resulting in the forced return of 834 migrants, including many asylum seekers, to the Libyan coast.[156] Libya has not ratified the Refugee Convention and migrants

---

152 UN Office of High Commissioner for Human Rights 'Crossing Borders: For Millions of People on the Move, Borders Can Be a Dangerous Space' (UNHCHR 13 April 2012) Available at: http://www.december18.net/article/crossing-borders-millions-people-move-borders-can-be-dangerous-space (accessed 3 July 2012). Most recently, 360 North Africa migrants died off the coast of the Italian island of Lampedusa, BBC News 'Italian Police Arrest Somali over Lampedusa Boat Tragedy'8th Nov. 2013. Available at: http://www.bbc.co.uk/news/world-europe-24865115 (accessed 20 November 2013)

153 In April 2013, a group of African migrants attempted to climb the fence at Mellila and several were badly injured. The previous week several Spanish police had been injured in a clash with migrants at the same position. In March three migrants were killed when attempting to climb the fence: Beating Borders '3 Dead and 15 Wounded at Melilla Border Fence' 2013 Available at: http://beatingborders.wordpress.com/2013/03/26/3-dead-and-15-wounded-at-melilla-border-fence (accessed 10 13 May). The budget for Frontex operations Hera 1 and Hera II concerning the detection and interception of irregular migration on route to the Canary Islands was €3.5 million. Hera III has since been commenced. For details see Frontex information: http://www.frontex.europa.eu/news/hera-iii-operation-It9SH3 (accessed 16 July 2013).

154 Pro Asyl *Walls of Shame: Accounts from the Inside. The detention Centres of Evros* (April 2012). Available at: http://infomobile.w2eu.net/files/2012/04/Evros-Bericht_12_04_10_BHP.pdf (accessed 10 July 2013).

155 Ratification Law No. 2009/7. See Ronzitti, N 'The Treaty on Friendship, Partnership and Cooperation between Italy and Libya: New Prospects for Cooperation in the Mediterranean?' (2009) 1 *Bulletin of Italian Politics* 1, 125; it was widely reported that the Italian government had paid €5 billion to the Gaddafi regime in order to assist with interception and processing.

156 Details were provided by Tondini, M 'Fishers of Men? The Interception of Migrants in the Mediterranean Sea and Their Forced Return to Libya' (INEX Paper October 2010 Ministry of Interior, Italian Initiatives: Security, Immigration, Asylum, Rome, 14 April 2010) 27. Available at: http://www.interno.it/mininterno/export/sites/default/it/assets/files/19/0844_opuscolo_engl_def.pdf. Other Official Sources Confirm That, from 6 May to 7 September 2009, 1,005 Migrants Have Been Returned to Libya: 833 by Italian Vessels and 172 by Libyan Patrol Boats (see the speech of the Italian ambassador

face harsh detention conditions and summary removal without a full determination of their protection needs.[157] In the Siracusa incident of August 2009, 75 Somali migrants (including three children) were forcibly handed over to the Libyan authorities by an Italian coastal patrol boat. Charges of abuse of office filed by a group of MP's against the Italian Minister of Interior were rejected by a tribunal on the basis that the minister had not intended to cause harm and lacked legal culpability.[158] The effect of these interceptions is significant as during the first quarter of 2010 only 170 migrants landed on the Italian coast, marking a 96 per cent reduction in undocumented arrivals.[159] The Council of Europe's Committee for the Prevention of Torture recognised that interception and return strategies seriously undermined the legal principle of non-refoulement.[160]

More recently, 63 Libyan migrants died of starvation in the presence of NATO ships after their calls for rescue to Maltese and Italian coastguards were ignored.[161] Their small rubber boat was left drifting in the sea for 16 days before being washed back to the Libyan coast where the 10 surviving inhabitants were duly imprisoned. A report into the incident was subsequently adopted by the Council of Europe's Parliamentary Assembly Migration Committee.[162] The surviving witness testimonies indicate that food had been dropped from a military helicopter following the first distress call. A military vessel and several fishing boats had passed by in full view of the occupants but there had been no attempt to rescue its passengers despite their obvious distress. The report concluded that there was 'a failure to react to distress calls and a "vacuum of responsibility" for search and rescue' which had undoubtedly contributed to the deaths.

EU migration policies may have augmented this vacuum as it was pressure from the EU to stem the flow of migrants that caused Libya to tighten its own borders, arresting and returning thousands of migrants, including refugees and asylum seekers.[163] Pursuant to this agenda, the European Commission offered grants to

---

to Tripoli, Francesco Paolo Trupiano, before the Italian Parliament's 'Schengen Committee' (Rome, 13 October 2009). Available at: http://www.camera.it/_dati/leg16/lavori/stenbic/30/2009/1013/s000r.htm?campo=/_bicamerali/leg15/schengen/resoconti/leg15fr.htm.

157 UNHCR Interview 'Asylum Seekers Pushed Back to Libya' Briefing Paper (UNHCR 14 July 2009); supra n.

158 Italian Criminal Code, Art 323 reported by Tondini supra n156.

159 Italian Minister of Interior, Roberto Maroni supra n156.

160 Council of Europe Committee for the Prevention of Torture and Inhuman or Degrading Treatment or Punishment 28 April 2010 Cpt/Inf (2010) 14. Available at: http://www.cpt.coe.int/documents/ita/2010-inf-14-eng.htm (accessed 11 July 2012).

161 Strik, T 'Lives Lost in the Mediterranean Sea: Who is Responsible?' Council of Europe Parliamentary Assembly Migration Committee 29 March 2012 (Council of Europe 2012).

162 Ibid.

163 Human Rights Watch *Libya-Stemming the Flow: Abuses against Migrants, Asylum Seekers and Refugees* 18, 5(E) (Human Rights Watch September 2006).

secure Libyan assistance with border controls despite Libya's persistent refusal to recognise the competence of the UNHCR and to apply the Refugee Convention.[164] The Libyan authorities have continued to repatriate refugees to Eritrea without any examination of their claim for refugee status, despite evidence of widespread human rights abuses in Eritrea, including secret-detention and kidnapping of dissidents.[165] Numerous reports from human rights agencies have condemned the refugee protection system in Libya and many refugees have experienced gross violations of their human rights.[166] In short, the protection of the human rights of refugees is unlikely in Libya.[167] This remains the position despite the downfall of the Gaddafi regime in 2011.[168] The European institutions cannot claim to be unaware of the situation but continue to take an 'out of sight, out of mind' approach.

Pugh has explored the reasons why a comparatively small number of boatpeople seeking entry to Australia became the focus of a security rhetoric which enabled draconian policies to dominate.[169] The reasons are equally evident in the Mediterranean example. Many of the metaphors used to condemn irregular arrivals are common to both situations.[170] Pugh's analysis suggests that the economic opportunism of the arrivals and their lack of a specific common point of origin allow politicians to dehumanise them, often through metaphors of the sea.[171] Paradoxically, securitisation inverts the risks; the immediate danger to the boatpeople is overlooked in the face of the state battling to preserve its sovereignty and national security.[172]

---

164 Middle East Online 'UN Refugee Agency Ordered to Leave Libya' 8 June 2010.

165 For an updated position see UNHCR *Freedom in the World 2012-Eritera* Available at: http://www.unhcr.org/refworld/docid/4fb6139da.html (accessed 21 March 2013); BBC News 'Eritreans in Plane Hijack Drama' BBC 27 August 2004; Human Rights Concern – Eritrea 'Secret Detention of 12 Eritreans from Libya' 19 February 2010 Available at: http://asmarino.com/press-releases/559-secret-deportation-of-12-Eritreans-from-Libya- (accessed 11 July 2012); Human Rights Watch *Service For Life – State Repression and Indefinite Conscription in Eritrea* (Human Rights Watch May 2009).

166 US Committee for Refugees and Immigrants *World Refugee Survey 2008.* Available at: http://www.refugees.org/resources/refugee-warehousing/archived-world-refugee-surveys/2008-world-refugee-survey.html (accessed 2 July 2012); Human Rights Watch supra n163; Amnesty International Visit 15–23 May 2009.

167 Statement by Antonio Guterres, UN High Commissioner for Refugees in Jesuit Refugee Service 'Do They Know? Asylum Seekers Testify to Life in Libya' (JRS December 2009) 18.

168 France24 'Stranded Immigrants Detained in "Racist" Libyan Camps' 25 June 2012. Available At: http://observers.france24.com/content/20120625-stranded-without-papers-immigrants-detained-libyan-camps-tripoli-benghazi-detention-migrant-workers-africans (accessed 20 July 2012).

169 Pugh supra n83 at 54–5.

170 Dummett, M *On Immigration and Refugees* (Routledge 2001) 133.

171 Pugh supra n83, 54.

172 Ibid, 55.

According to the UNHCR, 75 per cent of the undocumented arrivals in Italy claimed asylum and at least half of those applicants were subsequently recognised as refugees. This route can thus be characterised as an asylum route.[173] Many of those forcibly intercepted and returned were denied the most basic fundamental right, 'the right to have rights'.[174]

The Hirsi Jamaa judgement The protection vacuum resulting from bilateral migration arrangements can be seen clearly in the Hirsi Jamaa case which examined the first joint return of a group of Somali and Eritrean refugees intercepted in May 2009. In a unanimous judgement, the Grand Chamber of the ECtHR placed the responsibility firmly at the door of the Italian authorities, who had intercepted the three vessels 35 nautical miles from the Lampedusa coast (an area of Maltese responsibility).[175] The occupants had been transferred by Italian Revenue Police and the coastguard to Italian military ships with joint Italian-Libyan crews and were then transported to Tripoli. On arrival they were disembarked and detained. Crucially, their identities and claims for refugee status were not examined at any point prior to their return, despite the fact that the majority were subsequently recognised as refugees.

The ECtHR found two violations of Article 3 ECHR concerning the prohibition of inhuman or degrading treatment, as the applicants had been exposed to the foreseeable risk of ill-treatment in Libya and of subsequent repatriation to Somalia or Eritrea (in contravention of the principle on non-refoulement). The Court further found violations of Article 4 of Protocol No. 4 (the prohibition of collective expulsions) and Article 13 (the right to an effective remedy) taken in conjunction with Article 3 and Article 4 of Protocol No.4.[176] The Italian government argued that the prohibition on collective expulsion only applied to exclusions from the state's national territory, a view firmly rejected by the court which reasoned that 'whenever the State through its agents operating outside its territory exercises control and authority over an individual, and thus jurisdiction, the State is under an obligation under Article 1 to secure to that individual the rights and freedoms under Section 1 of the Convention'.[177]

The ruling makes it clear that the ECtHR will scrutinise state attempts to avoid international obligations through the denial of a jurisdictional link, and will reject the traditional stance that responsibility for human rights breaches is territorially

173 JRS supra n167, 19.

174 Arendt supra n45; Kesby supra n1.

175 Lauterpacht, E and Bethlehem, D 'The Scope and Content of the Principle of Non-Refoulement: Opinion' in Feller, E; Türk, V and Nicholson, F (eds) *Refugee Protection in International Law: UNHCR's Global Consultations on International Protection* (CUP 2003).

176 *Hirsi Jamaa* supra n135.

177 *Hirsi Jamaa* supra n135 para74.

defined.[178] The need to establish a jurisdictional link does remain crucial as a necessary condition to state liability but states cannot avoid their responsibility simply by contracting with third countries.[179]

The Council of Europe's Parliamentary Assembly has addressed the issue of interception at sea in a strongly worded resolution.[180] It notes that Member States disagree over the interpretation of international obligations, including the relevance of the non-refoulement principle in interception cases and criticises the lack of human rights protection in interception operations whilst raising concern over the disproportionate burden that continues to be placed on southern EU states.[181] The Assembly calls on states to place humanitarian concerns at the forefront of border and surveillance activities, which includes: enabling access to a fair and effective asylum procedure, guaranteeing the prohibition of refoulement (including indirect refoulement, which may take place at sea), and ensuring that detention excludes vulnerable people (including minors) and is always authorised by a judicial authority.[182] Bilateral readmission arrangements are seen as posing particular problems for the protection of human rights and there is a call for greater monitoring in order to ensure that the principle of non-refoulement is respected in all cases.[183]

Yet whilst the status of the rule is regarded as a fundamental norm, the Parliamentary Assembly's report noted that some states continue to contest its scope and application. The *pacta sunt servanda* and good faith provisions in the Vienna Convention on the Law of Treaties require states to interpret treaties in line with their object and purpose.[184] The latter can be identified by taking account of any subsequent practice and international rules.[185] Good faith requires states to obey the letter of the law and to abstain from acts which would inevitably affect their ability to perform their treaty obligations.[186] It is certainly arguable

---

178 A move in this direction had also come in a case concerning British responsibility under Article 2 for actions committed by British forces in Iraq, *Al-Skeini and Others v UK* 55721/07 7 July 2011.

179 See also *Medvedyev and Others v France* [2010] 51 EHRR 39.

180 Res 1821 (2011) *Resolution on the Interception and Rescue at Sea of Asylum Seekers, Refugees and Irregular Migrants*.

181 Ibid para 5.1.

182 Para 9 contains 12 specific measures that states are asked to guarantee.

183 Ibid para 9.9.

184 Vienna Convention on The Law of Treaties 23 May 1969. United Nations, Treaty Series, vol 1155, p. 331, Article 31(1).

185 Goodwin-Gill, G 'The Right to Seek Asylum: Interception at Sea and the Principle of Non-Refoulement' in Jesuit Refugee Service *Safe and Secure: How Do Refugees Experience Europe's Borders?* (JRS-Europe 2011) 6; JRS 'Do They Know? Asylum Seekers Testify to Life in Libya' (JRS December 2009) 19.

186 *Yearbook of International Law Commission* 1964 vol 1 Summary Records of the 16th Session 727th Meeting A/CN 4/SERA/1964 20 May 1964, 70.

that lawful deterrence measures are delimited by the requirement for good faith.[187] Nevertheless, the European Commission has not decisively condemned measures which effectively undermine the principle. Jacques Barrot, Vice President of the Commission, has stated that the asylum *acquis* only applies to applications made within the territory of Member States and therefore 'it is clear from a legal standpoint that the Community *acquis* in the field of asylum does not apply to situations on the high seas'.[188] This position is now doubtful following the *Hirsi* ruling and amendments to the EU Procedures Directive.[189]

Above all, the interception cases serve to demonstrate two important lessons. States at the borders of the EU cannot be relied upon to assist refugees to access safe territory and refugee determination procedures in the absence of legal intervention and wider European support. Secondly, refugees continue to seek access to these states despite enormous personal risks. Refugee movements may be temporarily reduced or, more likely, displaced by such measures but they will not cease until the risks presented are greater than the risks faced by remaining at home. Thus state resources aimed at preventing irregular migration are unlikely to succeed in their objective unless they begin to address root causes and conditions in countries of origin.

Concluding Observations

Whilst there may be a legitimate concern behind the states right to de-limit entry to its national community, this argument is problematic from both legal and moral perspectives when extended to refugees.

The resources allocated to the management of irregular migration are significant, yet the effect on asylum migration is likely to be temporary at best, whilst penalising those genuinely in need. Closed borders do not solve the problem of irregular migration, as Dowty recognises 'The flow is an expression of human needs and aspirations ... any effort to control illegal immigration without addressing its source will be futile'.[190] Those determined to enter Europe by circumventing border controls will continue to search for undetected travel routes which will be increasingly dangerous whilst traffickers and smugglers profit in a

187 Goodwin-Gill and McAdam supra n137, 389; UNHCR 'Maritime Interception Operations and the Processing of International Protection Claims: Legal Standards and Policy Considerations with respect to Extraterritorial Processing' Protection Policy Paper (UNHCR November 2010) para 49.

188 Letter from Mr Jacques Barrot to the President of the European Parliament Committee on Civil Liberties, Justice and Home Affairs 15 July 2009 included in *Hirsi* supra n13, para 34.

189 This position is echoed in the obiter statement of the Permanent Court of International Justice in *SS 'Lotus' (France v Turkey)* PCIJ 1928 Series A, 10, 18–19. Article 3 of the recast EU Procedures Directive 2013/32 EU, discussed in Chapter 4, has been amended to specifically include actions taken by contracting states on the high seas.

190 Dowty supra n21, 245.

'sellers' market'. The closure of the primary migration routes for third country nationals in most European states will inevitably mean that migrants in search of a better life will resort to unorthodox methods of travel, clearly complicating the asylum-immigration nexus.[191]

In 2006 the European Parliament acknowledged the failure of European migration policy, citing the number of migrants that had died in the Mediterranean whilst seeking entry to the EU.[192] Since the ECtHR's judgement in *Hirsi Jamaa* it is irrefutable that this migration route is also a significant asylum route.[193] Thus the failure of migration policy also marks a failure in refugee protection.

In order to address the protection needs of those who most require it, the issue of asylum must be decoupled from immigration. Rather than bending refugee law to fit a restrictive migration policy objective, decoupling will enable policy-makers to ground asylum in fundamental universal principles, such as non-refoulement and non-discrimination.[194] The search for practical and durable solutions is supported rather than diminished by this grounding. Durable solutions will inevitably require European states to do more to protect refugees, honouring their commitments in international law. Despite falling asylum numbers in Europe since the end of the Yugoslavian conflict, there are huge refugee communities in countries neighbouring conflict zones in developing regions, including Chad, Iran, Pakistan and Jordan.[195]

European cooperation presents an opportunity to improve the global prevention and protection system At the very least the EU can assist neighbouring states by genuinely sharing the obligation to protect though the development of asylum systems, resources and expertise. The necessary resources could be purposefully diverted from the plethora of prevention and deflection mechanisms.[196]

In the next chapter the legal foundations of refugee protection will be considered in an effort to understand the prescriptive content of the right to seek and enjoy asylum. The following chapter examines the driving forces and governing principles behind the Common European Asylum System which lays the foundations for a

---

191 Chou supra n129, 554.

192 European Parliament *Resolution on the Common Immigration Policy* B6–0508/2006 26 September 2006 para L.

193 *Hirsi Jamaa* supra n13.

194 Goodwin-Gill makes a similar point in relation to the policy of interception at sea, supra n185, 443.

195 The World Bank 'Refugee Population by Country of Asylum' (World Bank 2011) Available at: http://data.worldbank.org/indicator/SM.POP.REFG (accessed 7 November 2012). The Syrian conflict has created enormous pressure on neighbouring states and many now fear that this could destabilise the entire region.

196 Pécoud, A and Guchteneire, P also suggest that resources could be better devoted to improve opportunities for integration 'Migration without Borders: An Investigation into the Free Movement of People' *Global Migration Perspectives* No 27, 2005, 81; Leitner, H 'Reconfiguring the Spatiality of Power: The Construction of a Supranational Migration Framework for the European Union' (1997) 16 Political Geography 2, 123; Mitsilegas, V 'Border Security in the EU' in Baldaccini supra n131, 370.

focused analysis of asylum procedures and reception conditions in Chapters 4 and 5 respectively. The external dimension of European asylum policy and its influence on neighbouring states will be explored in Chapter 6 where strategies such as readmission, resettlement and external processing will be assessed in a quest to find workable durable solutions. Finally, the conclusion will measure the effect of European harmonisation in light of international standards and will consider whether the right to seek and enjoy asylum is now illusory. Notwithstanding Tuitt's concern that there is a growing 'conflict between international refugee law and the refugee',[197] a reaffirmation of the Refugee Convention is the platform on which to renew a European commitment to refugee protection with 'protection-sharing' standards negotiated and applied equitably. If Europe fails to honour its international commitments the price will surely be high: greater global inequality, increased irregular migration and less security for all.

197 Tuitt is less optimistic, regarding this conflict as 'irreparable', supra n197, 19.

Chapter 2
International Foundations of Protection

Introduction

Any legal critique of asylum law and policy needs to be framed in terms of current international legal obligations which stem from the universalist position of international refugee and human rights law. The former is governed by the 1951 Convention on the Status of Refugees (the 'Refugee Convention') and its 1967 protocol which extended the territorial and temporal application of the Convention.[1] The origins of this document can be traced back to the League of Nations' 1933 Refugee Convention which was one of the first universal human rights instruments.[2] The Refugee Convention has 145 state parties and most developed states now have a de facto system of refugee protection.[3] Yet there has been mounting pressure to revisit these obligations, some of which questions the ethos and relevance of the Convention itself.

Any analysis of the obligations imposed by international law in a statist paradigm necessarily requires an exploration of the particularist claims of state parties. These claims are generally advanced to justify limiting obligations towards incomers and are centred on two related objectives; namely, maintaining public order (the security argument) and reducing cost (the economic argument). This chapter will consider the extent of these universal legal obligations and the legitimacy of state actions which seek to reduce and deflect these obligations.

From *Lex Generalis* to *Lex Specialis* Obligations

The Human Right to 'Seek' and 'Enjoy' Protection

It has been noted that the law on refugees should be situated in the context of human rights rather than immigration law. It has more similarities with the former as the obligations owed to refugees are in fact obligations deriving from a failure to respect basic human rights. As Hathaway contends, 'refugee law is therefore

1 189 UNTS 2545 28 July 1961.

2 League of Nations, *Convention Relating to the International Status of Refugees*, 28 October 1933, League of Nations, Treaty Series vol CLIX No 3663, although it received comparatively few signatures.

3 Hathaway, J *The Rights of Refugees under International Law* (CUP 2005) 3.

a remedial or palliative branch of human rights law'.[4] The inclusion of a right to asylum in the Universal Declaration of Human Rights, confirms this approach.[5] Although declaratory rather than legally binding, the Declaration forms the basis of the two universal covenants on human rights.[6] Article 14 consists of a 'strongly compressed formulation' proclaiming the right 'to seek and enjoy asylum', thus affirming refugee protection as an essential element of human rights law.[7]

The Declaration does not afford a right to be granted refugee status and for the detail of how this determination should be made one needs to examine the Refugee Convention.[8] A consideration of the latter's drafting process indicates that many states were uncomfortable with accepting an obligation to provide asylum.[9] The 1967 Declaration on Territorial Asylum exhibited similar caution.[10] The position remains that there is no international, substantive right to be granted asylum, although there is an international procedural right to 'seek' protection.[11]

At the European level there is no express right to seek asylum included in the ECHR. By contrast, the ratification of the Treaty on the Functioning of the European Union has seen legal status afforded to the EU's Charter on Fundamental Rights which has wider coverage than the ECHR, including many second generation rights deriving from social equality. However, it should be noted that the Charter consolidates existing fundamental rights and is not seen as creating new actionable rights.[12] Article 18 of the Charter refers to a substantive 'right to asylum' based on the principles in the Refugee Convention and Protocol.[13] This right, along with other Charter rights, is enforceable against the actions of the EU institutions but not those of Member States.[14]

---

4 Ibid at 5.

5 UDHR UNGA Res 217A (III) 10 December 1948.

6 The International Covenant on Civil and Political Rights and the International Covenant on Economic, Social and Cultural Rights, both adopted in 1966 by the UN General Assembly.

7 Gammeltoft-Hansen, T and Gammeltoft-Hansen, H 'The Right to Seek-Revisited: On the UN Human Rights Declaration Article 14 and Access to Asylum Procedures in the EU' (2008) 10 Eur J Migration & L 441; Edwards, A 'Human Rights, Refugees and the Right "to Enjoy" Asylum' (2005) 17 I J Refugee L, 297.

8 Stevens, D *UK Asylum Law and Policy* (Sweet & Maxwell 2004) 136.

9 Gammeltoft supra n7, 445.

10 UN GA Res 2312 (XXII), 14 December 1967.

11 Gammeltoft supra n7, 446; for discussion on the right 'to seek' compared to the right 'to be granted' see Goodwin-Gill, G and McAdam, J *The Refugee in International Law* (OUP 2007) 359–366.

12 Goodwin-Gill, G and McAdam, J *The Refugee in International Law* (OUP 2007) 367.

13 Charter of Fundamental Rights of the European Union 18 December 2000 C 364/01 'Charter of Fundamental Rights'.

14 Charter of Fundamental Rights Article 51(1); Lenart, J 'Fortress Europe': Compliance of the Dublin II Regulation with the European Convention for the Protection

Once a person exercises their right to 'seek' asylum and arrives at the frontier of a state requesting sanctuary, human rights law supplements this procedural right providing additional protection.[15] However, the right of entry itself has been fiercely resisted by states that perceive it as an unwelcome interference in state sovereignty. The term 'enjoy' indicates that such a right it entirely based on state acceptance.[16] Yet when Article 14 UDHR is coupled with the prohibition of refoulement in Article 33 of the Refugee Convention, the right has more depth than initial analysis reveals. The UN Sub-Commission on Human Rights has affirmed the significance of this right and highlighted concern that state policies, particularly detention, could be incompatible with international human rights and refugee law.[17] It is thus important that Article 14 be read together with other international refugee and human rights obligations.

The Refugee Convention and the Role of the UNHCR

The Refugee Convention and Protocol set out who qualifies for refugee status and provide that those satisfying the definition should not be treated less favourably than citizens in a variety of contexts, including: freedom of religion, freedom of movement and the right to an elementary education. In addition there are certain services which the state is obliged to provide to the refugee, including administrative assistance, identity papers and travel documents and the opportunity for naturalisation.

Many states have issued reservations against the freedom of movement provision which effectively allows them to provide designated residence on the grounds of public order or national security. Further, there are many different reservations against the right to work in Article 17(1) which provides that refugees should be given 'most favoured nation treatment' when accessing the labour market.[18]

The Conference of Plenipotentiaries, responsible for drafting the Refugee Convention, recommended, inter alia, that: 'Governments continue to receive refugees in their territories and that they act in concert in a true spirit of international cooperation in order that these refugees may find asylum and the possibility of

---

of Human Rights and Fundamental Freedoms' (2012) 28 Merkourios - International and Eur Migration L 75, 10.

15 Harvey, C 'The Right to Seek Asylum in the European Union' [2004] EHRLR 23.

16 Ibid, 50.

17 UNHCR Sub-commission on Human Rights Resolution 2000/20 *The Right to Seek and Enjoy Asylum* UNHCR 27th Meeting. 18 August 2000.

18 UN Convention Relating to the Status of Refugees Geneva, 28 July 1951 United Nations, *Treaty Series*, vol 189, 137. For full list of Reservations see: http://www.unhcr.org/cgibin/texis/vtx/search?page=search&docid=3d9abe177&query=1951%20refugee%20convention (accessed 12 March 2013).

resettlement'.[19] Despite numerous challenges, the continuing relevance of the Refugee Convention and the commitment of the signatory states was affirmed by state parties in a Declaration of 2001.[20] This period saw the biggest rise in refugee numbers in Europe, largely as a consequence of the dissolution of the former Yugoslavia. Yet, far from retracting from their international obligations, states reaffirmed:

> that the 1951 Convention, as amended by the 1967 Protocol, has a central place in the international refugee protection regime, [] believing also that this regime should be developed further, as appropriate, in a way that complements and strengthens the 1951 Convention and its Protocol.[21]

Guidance on the interpretation of the Refugee Convention is provided by the UNHCR's *Handbook on Procedures and Criteria for Determining Refugee Status* ('The Handbook').[22] The Handbook is not specifically covered by the Vienna Convention on the Law of Treaties[23] and is thus not legally binding on state parties. But it is submitted that the Vienna Convention's requirement that international rights obligations be interpreted in good faith may require a more nuanced approach, allowing the law to be interpreted 'reasonably' and thus in line with the Handbook provisions.[24] Article 31(3)b of the Vienna Convention requires consideration of the context of the treaty as well as any agreement between the parties regarding the interpretation of the treaty or the application of its provisions; any subsequent practice in the application of the treaty which establishes the agreement of the parties regarding its interpretation; and any relevant rules of international law applicable in the relations between the parties.

---

19 Final Act of the UN Conference of Plenipotentiaries on the status of Refugees and Stateless Persons, Geneva 25 July 1951, D. Available at: http://www.unhcr.org/40a8a7394.html (accessed 12 March 2013).

20 Declaration of States parties to the 1951 Convention and/or its 1967 Protocol Relating to the Status of Refugees, Ministerial Meeting of States Parties, Geneva, Switzerland, 12–13 December 2001, UN Doc HCR/MMSP/2001/09, 16 January 2002. The Declaration was welcomed by the UN General Assembly in resolution A/RES/57/187, para 4, adopted on 18 December 2001.

21 Ibid, para 7.

22 UNHCR *Handbook on Procedures and Criteria for Determining Refugee Status Under the 1951 Convention and the 1967 Protocol Relating to the Status of Refugees* HCR/IP/4/Eng/REV 1Reedited, Geneva, January 1992 (UNHCR 1979).

23 Vienna on 23 May 1969. Entered into force on 27 January 1980. United Nations, Treaty Series, vol 1155, 331.

24 Goodwin-Gill, G and Lambert, H *The Limits of Transnational Law* (CUP 2010) 217. The authors cite the *Barcelona Traction Case* 1970 ICJ Reports 3, 48, para 3 as authority for this proposition.

The consultative and supervisory role of the UNHCR is expressly provided for in EU law[25]and the Handbook has been afforded highly persuasive authority in judgements of national courts.[26] Yet, there is some concern that the agency's supervisory role is being marginalised by the EU processes.[27] For example, Hurwitz notes that the Advocate General's opinion in the recent *Elgafaji* case made no reference to the UNHCR's interpretation of international refugee standards.[28]

The Status of the Asylum Applicant

The Refugee Convention itself predicates entitlements on de facto status; those lawfully staying in the host state are entitled to rights which are greater than those afforded to new arrivals and those whose status has not been finally determined. At the same time it is vital to appreciate that basic Convention obligations, including the prohibition of refoulement, must be respected by the host state until a negative decision is reached on the applicant's status.

The asylum seeker is thus not ignored altogether by the Refugee Convention, but questions do arise as to whether an asylum applicant who has availed themselves of the refugee determination procedure should be regarded as lawfully present in the host state. The consequences of this 'intermediate' status are considerable and include protection from expulsion. The UN position has appeared reasonably solid in this respect following the Human Rights Committee's decision in *Celepli v Sweden*[29] which ruled that an illegal entrant subject to expulsion but who was not removed on humanitarian grounds was lawfully present as their status had effectively been regularised. The Australian authority of *Rajendran* similarly suggests that applicants who avail themselves of the domestic law on refugee determination should be viewed as lawfully present.[30] Hathaway argues that if the applicant has provided all the information requested and has complied with the determination procedures they should be viewed as lawfully present.[31] It is submitted that this is a logically sound approach; to decide otherwise would encourage states that are reluctant to provide protection to delay and prolong the

25 Article 21(1)c Council Directive on Minimum Standards of procedures in Member States for granting and withdrawing refugee status 2005/85/EC 'Procedures Directive' 13 December 2005 OJ L 326/13.

26 See the UK House of Lords decision in *R v SSHD ex p Adan and Aitseguer* [2001] UKHL 2 AC 477 per Lord Steyn 477; *R v SSHD ex p Robinson* [1998] QB 929 per L Woolf, 938.

27 See further discussion in Chapter 6.

28 Hurwitz, A *The Collective Responsibility of States to Protect Refugees* (OUP 2009) 238.

29 CCPR/C/51/D/456/1991, 26 July 1994, para 9.2.

30 *Karthigesu Rajendran v Minister for Immigration & Multicultural Affairs* [1998] 1085 FCA, 1085 FCA, Australia: Federal Court, 4 September 1998, available at: http://www.unhcr.org/refworld/docid/3ae6b7638.html (accessed 4 December 2012).

31 Hathaway supra n3, 80.

determination process and thereby deny essential protection to the applicant. Yet the ECtHR has ruled in the context of detention, that an asylum seeker is not 'lawfully present' until their status has been formally authorised by the host state.[32] Consequently states may impose measures on asylum applicants that could not be imposed on recognised refugees or other categories of lawful migrants.

The Prohibition of Refoulement

International Formulations

The obligation of non-refoulement demands that the neither an asylum applicant nor refugee should be returned ('refouled') in any manner whatsoever, to a territory where their life or freedom would be threatened. It is the basic underpinning of refugee law which, it is argued, has become a peremptory norm of international human rights law.[33] However this assessment is problematic as the status of *jus cogens* requires consistent state practice and evidence of *opinio juris sive necessitatis* (i.e. an acceptance of its legally binding nature).[34] The lack of uniform state practice and attempts to delimit the obligation means that it is not possible to conclusively establish this status.[35] Further, Hathaway disputes that non-refoulement can be regarded as a customary principle of international law as interstate practice does not demonstrate near-universal respect for the principle.[36]

Nevertheless, the principle is well-established in many states, having emerged from the 1933 Refugee Convention.[37] Article 33(1) of the Refugee Convention provides:

> 1 No contracting state shall expel or return ('refouler') a refugee in any manner whatsoever to the frontiers of territories where his life or freedom would be threatened on account of his race, religion, nationality, membership of a social group or political opinion.

---

32 *Saadi v UK* App 13229/03 29 January 2008 discussed further in Chapter 5; see also *Bugdaycay v SSHD* [1987] 1 AC 514.

33 Lambert, H 'Protection Against Refoulement from Europe: Human Rights Law Comes to the Rescue' (1999) 48 Intl & Comp L Q 518.

34 Hurwitz, A *The Collective Responsibility of States to Protect Refugees* (OUP 2009) 204.

35 Noll, G *Negotiating Asylum: The EU Acquis, Extraterritorial Protection and the Common Market of Deflection* (M Nijhoff 2000) 359. For a summary of the different arguments on the customary status see Hurwitz supra n28, 206 and Hathaway supra n3, 363–370.

36 Hathaway supra n3, 364.

37 Art 3 *Convention Relating to the International Status of Refugees* 1933 159 LNTS No 3663 provides the obligation that states would not expel or reject the entry of refugees unless dictated by national security or public order.

This is a negative formulation and, as with Art 14 UDHR, there is no corresponding duty on the state to officially recognise the applicant as a refugee.

The Refugee Convention is unclear when it comes to rejection at the border. Indeed it has been suggested that the non-refoulement obligation as originally conceived did not provide protection in such situations. Kälin applies a contextual and teleological construction to the right and argues that an inclusionary reading is demanded.[38] Davy draws a similar conclusion from her application of the Vienna Convention.[39] She notes that whilst the drafters may have intended to exclude border rejection, the use of the French term 'refouler' complicates this position as its ordinary meaning includes rejection at the frontier. A clear interpretation based on the language and context precludes the need to adopt a teleological approach. Noll concurs, 'the question whether non-rejection at the border is embraced by Article 33 GC must be answered in the affirmative'.[40] Thus there appears to be a legal obligation derived from Article 33 at least to admit the asylum applicant to a fair and effective procedure in order to determine their needs.[41]

Chapter 1 considered the argument, advanced by Walzer, that obligations owed to refugees might be restricted in the interests of maintaining and protecting the national community. The Refugee Convention provides for exclusions from refugee status as well as exceptions to the principle of non-refoulement. Article 33(2) provides that the latter may not apply where the individual is a danger to the security of the country, or, having been convicted of a particularly serious crime, the refugee constitutes a danger to the community of that country. The same approach is found in the EU Qualification Directive.[42]

These exceptions may be justified from a Walzerian perspective as the refugee's need for protection may be limited in the interests of community safety. However, it is essential to the goal of protection that a serious, discernible risk to the country of refuge is identified. According to leading authorities, the danger envisaged must be interpreted as a 'very serious danger' which encompasses 'an appreciation of a *future* threat from the person concerned rather than on the commission of some act in the past'.[43] The UNHCR's advisory opinion makes it clear that the danger to

38 Kälin, W *Das Prinzip des Non-Refoulement: Das Verbot der Zurückweisung, Ausweisung und Auslieferung von Flüchtingen, den Verfolgerstaat im Völkerrecht und im schweizerischen Landesrecht* (Peter Lang 1982) 107.

39 Davy, U *Asyl und Internationales Flüchtingrecht, Band I: Völkerrechtlichter Rahmen* Verlag Österreich 1996) 101–103.

40 Noll supra n35, 431.

41 UNHCR Ex Committee Conclusions No 85 *On International Protection* (1998) and No 99 *On International Protection* (2004).

42 Article 21(2) 2011/95/EU On standards for the qualification of third-country nationals or stateless persons as beneficiaries of international protection, for a uniform status for refugees or for persons eligible for subsidiary protection, and for the content of the protection granted. L 337/6 Official Journal of the European Union 20 December 2011.

43 Lauterpacht, E and Bethlehem, D 'The Scope and Content of the Principle of *Non-Refoulement*: Opinion' in Feller, E Türk, V and Nicholson, F (eds) *Refugee Protection in*

security must relate to the country of refuge rather than other countries.[44] In order to satisfy the requirement of reasonableness, the assessment of risk must be based on credible evidence. Furthermore, to ensure proportionality, there must be a rational connection between the removal of the refugee and the elimination of the danger; *refoulement* must be the last possible resort to eliminate the danger; and the danger to the country of refuge must outweigh the risk to the refugee upon *refoulement*.[45] It is worth noting that this position is not reflected in current UK legislation which specifically provides that no assessment of proportionality will take place when assessing security risks under Article 33 or Article 1F Refugee Convention.[46]

In terms of the second exception which relates to the commission of a particularly serious crime, the position has largely been governed by domestic reference points. In the UK, for example, there is a statutory presumption that imprisonment for at least two years would be 'particularly serious' to justify the exception.[47] In addition, the assessment of dangerousness to the community will require other factors to be considered including mitigating factors, prospects of recidivism and any history of offending.[48]

The UNHCR's position reflects that of Carens who argues that limits on the entry of refugees should only be applied sparingly and proportionately.[49] As these exceptions contradict a fundamental human rights norm, namely the prohibition of torture or inhuman and degrading treatment, it is essential that they should only be deployed in exceptional circumstances.[50]

The non-refoulement obligation is confirmed by the UN Convention Against Torture ('CAT') 1984:

International Law: UNHCR's Global Consultations on International Protection (CUP 2003) para 169; see also Grahl-Madsen, A *Commentary on the Refugee Convention 1951: Article* 2–11, 13–37 (1963, published by UNHCR, 1997) 236.

44 UNHCR Advisory Opinion from the Office of the United Nations High Commissioner for Refugees (UNHCR) on the Scope of the National Security Exception under Article 33(2) of the 1951 Convention Relating to the Status of Refugees, 6 January 2006, available at: http://www.unhcr.org/refworld/docid/43de2da94.html (accessed 10 December 2012).

45 UNHCR ibid.

46 s34(1) Anti-Terrorism, Crime and Security Act 2001, see discussion in Symes, M and Jorro, P *Asylum Law and Practice* (Bloomsbury Professional 2010), 450.

47 Symes and Jorro ibid 444.

48 Symes and Jorro supra n46, 447.

49 See discussion in Chapter 1.

50 Mink, J 'EU Asylum Law and Human Rights Protection: Revisiting the Principle of *Non-Refoulement* and the Prohibition of Torture and Other forms of Ill-treatment' (2012) 14 Eur J Migration L 147.

> No state party shall expel, return ('refouler') or extradite a person to another state where there are substantial grounds for believing that he would be in danger of being subjected to torture.[51]

The Committee Against Torture considers this to be an absolute, non-derogable provision which, unlike the Refugee Convention, permits no exceptions. In *Mutombo v Switzerland* the Committee established that expulsion to Zaire could violate Article 3 if 'there are substantial grounds for believing' the applicant would be in danger of being subject to torture and that this consequence was 'foreseeable and necessary' taking into account all the relevant circumstances.[52] The Committee has found many violations of Article 3, demonstrating its continued relevance, particularly in cases where states attempt to raise the exceptions under the Refugee Convention.[53]

The use of diplomatic assurances in the interests of political expediency was condemned by the Committee Against Torture in the case of *Agiza v Sweden*.[54] The complaint concerned two Egyptian asylum seekers who had been removed from Sweden following diplomatic assurances from the Egyptian authorities. Both men subsequently claimed to have been tortured. The Committee found a violation of Article 3 on the basis that the Swedish authorities should have known that torture of political opponents was widespread and further, that the giving of assurances could not obviate the respondent states obligations.

Similar facts occurred in the British case of *Youseff v Home Office* but, in the event, removal was not actioned as assurances from the Egyptian authorities were not forthcoming.[55] Nevertheless, Prime Minister Tony Blair plainly regarded the Egyptian signature to the CAT as determinative, stating: 'Given that torture is banned under Egyptian law, it should not be difficult for the Egyptians to give

---

51 Article 3 Convention against Torture and Other Cruel, Inhuman or Degrading treatment of Punishment UN Treaty United Nations, Treaty Series, vol. 1465, 85 (26 June 1987).

52 Communication No13/1993 27 April 1994 para 9.3. The Committee has found numerous violations of Article 3 including *Alan v Switzerland* Communication No 21/1995; *Tala v Sweden* Communication No 41/1996; *Kisoki v Sweden* Communication 41/1996; *Paez v Sweden* Communication 39/1996; *A v the Netherlands* Communication No 91/1997 and *Aydin v Sweden* Communication No101/1997; *Kalonzo v Canada* CAT/C/48/D/343/2008 Communication No 343/200; *M.A.M.A et al v Sweden* CAT/C/48/D/391/2009 Communication No 391/2009; *Gbadjavi v Switzerland* CAT/C/48/D/396/2009 Communication No 396/2009; *Abdussamatov et al v Kazakhstan* CAT/C/48/D/444/2010 Communication No 444/2010.

53 Such as *M.A.M.A v Sweden* ibid where the applicant and his family argued that return would be likely to lead to their torture on account of, inter alia, familial links with Al Qaida.

54 CAT/C/34/D/233/2003 20 May 2005; see discussion in Guild, E *Security and Migration in the 21st Century* (Polity 2009) 91–103.

55 [2004] EWHC 1884.

such an undertaking'.[56] UN rapporteurs have consistently maintained that such assurances cannot be legitimately used to avoid the obligations of humanitarian and refugee law.[57]

The CAT as a whole lacks an effective mechanism of legal enforcement, although analysis of state practice does suggest that the Committee's views are complied with.[58] Article 3 also has some contextual limitations leaving it with a comparatively narrow application: it is only concerned with actions constituting return, it does not extend to other types of inhuman or degrading treatment falling short of torture, and it only applies where the acts of torture are perpetrated or acquiesced in by the state.[59]

The UN Human Rights Committee has additionally implied non-refoulement into Article 7 of the International Covenant on Civil and Political Rights which extends the obligation to protection from cruel, inhuman and degrading treatment.[60] In *Byahuranga v Denmark* the Human Rights Committee found that a violation of Article 7 would occur if the applicant, a Ugandan national who had been tortured by the Ugandan military, was returned to Uganda following the commission of a drugs related offence.[61] The competence of the Committee to adjudicate in such disputes depends on whether signatory states have signed the first Optional Protocol.[62]

The Prohibition of Refoulement in Europe

There is no specific right to seek asylum contained in the ECHR. However, the prohibition of torture and inhuman or degrading treatment in Article 3 (which is similar to Article 7 of the ICCPR),[63] has frequently been interpreted by the ECtHR

56 Home Office Memo February 1999, 8jn.

57 For example, Special rapporteur Manfred Nowak speaking on BBC Radio 4's Today Programme 4 March 2005.

58 Andrysek, O 'Gaps in International Protection and the Potential for Redress through Individual Complaints Procedures' (1997) 9 Int J Refugee L 402.

59 Goodwin-Gill and McAdam supra n12, 302; Lambert supra n33.

60 General Comment No 31 (1984) para. 12 Nature of the General Legal Obligation on States Parties to the Covenant, UN Doc CCPR/C/21/Rev1/Add 13 (2004). See for example *C v Australia* No 900/1999 UN Doc CCPR/C/76/D/900/1999 13 November 2002.

61 *Byahuranga v Denmark* HRC 9 December 2004 CCPR/C/82/D/1222/2003.

62 UN Office of the Human Rights Commissioner Optional Protocol to the International Covenant on Civil and Political Rights Adopted and opened for signature, ratification and accession by General Assembly Resolution 2200A (XXI) of 16 December 1966 entry into force 23 March 1976, 144 ratifications including all EU states, except the UK.

63 Article 7 is also absolute and non-derogable, see UN Office of the High Commissioner for Human Rights *General Comment* 20 10 March 1992; Joseph, S; Mitchell, K and Gyorki, L *Seeking Remedies for Torture Victims: A Handbook on the Individual Complaints Procedures of the UN Treaty Bodies* (OMCT Series Handbook, UN 2006).

to prevent expulsion when a person will suffer torture or inhuman or degrading treatment on their return.[64] Unlike the Refugee Convention, Article 3 ECHR is absolute and non-derogable; it cannot be restricted in the interests of national security or otherwise.[65] Consequently, Lambert concludes that Article 3 offers the best hope for refugees and asylum seekers.[66] Indeed, in the 12 years since Lambert's analysis there has been greater reliance on Article 3 in European removal cases. The recent decisions of the Court's Grand Chamber in *MSS v Belgium and Greece* and *Hirsi Jamaa v Italy* demonstrate its continuing importance.[67] Moreover, for those asylum applicants challenging removal from the UK, it is the only source of enforceable international human rights protection against refoulement as the UK has not recognised the competence of either the UN Committee Against Torture or the Human Rights Committee to investigate individual complaints. All Council of Europe states are signatories to the Council of Europe's Convention for the Prevention of Torture and Inhuman or Degrading Treatment or Punishment. Its Committee complements the work of the ECtHR by providing a non-judicial approach consisting of periodic state visits and reports.[68]

Despite the absence of a specific prohibition of refoulement in the ECHR, Article 3 offers extensive protection in removal situations. It is not limited to conduct amounting to torture (unlike the CAT); it is absolute (unlike the Refugee Convention) and the ECHR enables applicants to mount a legal challenge which is binding on the state parties.[69] The decision in *Soering v UK* established that state liability for the prohibited treatment could arise from removal actions where the ill-treatment would be suffered post removal.[70] The seminal ruling in *Chahal v UK* went further in establishing that Article 3 applies to all people within the state's jurisdiction (ie within the control of the state)[71] including illegal entrants and those whose conduct may endanger national security.[72] This position echoes that of UN Human Rights Committee and Committee Against Torture.[73]

---

64 See for example: *Chahal v UK* (1996) 23 ECtHR 413; *Soering v UK* (1989) 11 EHRR 439.

65 *Chahal v UK* supra n64.

66 Lambert supra n33, 543.

67 App 30696/09 21 January 2011; App 27765/09 23 February 2012 respectively.

68 For the work of the Committee for the Prevention of Torture and Inhuman or Degrading Treatment or Punishment, see http://www.cpt.coe.int/en/about.htm.

69 All 47 Council of Europe states are parties to the ECHR, including the 28 EU Member States.

70 *Soering v UK* 1989 Series A No 161, 11 ECtHR 439.

71 *Al-Skeini and Others v UK* App 55721/07 7 July 2011.

72 *Chahal v UK* supra n64.

73 Wouters, K *International Legal Standards for the Protection from Refoulement* (Intersentia 2009) 372, 435 Bruin, R 'Border Control: Not a Transparent Reality' in Goudappel, F and Raulus, H (eds) *The Future of Asylum in the European Union* (TMC Asser 2011) 30.

Non-refoulement is further prohibited by Article 19(2) of the EU Charter of Fundamental Rights:

> No one may be removed, expelled or extradited to a State where there is a serious risk that he or she would be subjected to the death penalty, torture or other inhuman or degrading treatment or punishment.[74]

Although the Charter only creates obligations on the European institutions, the inclusion of the non-refoulement obligation demonstrates its importance as a fundamental, if not customary, international legal rule.[75]

The development of the obligation in human rights instruments beyond the Refugee Convention means that it should not be narrowly construed to apply only to those who are formally recognised as Convention refugees. Its inclusion in the scope of Article 3 ECHR means that it will be difficult for European states to reply on the exemptions in the Refugee Convention when there is a possibility that torture or inhuman treatment that will occur following removal.

However, whilst the obligation operates to prevent removal, this position is not synonymous with the grant of refugee status and does not create a clear legal basis for a claim to entry. Whilst an inclusionary reading requires that a protection seeker should not be rejected at the border, it is altogether less clear that s/he has a legal right of entry.

Non-discrimination as a ground for entry The right of non-discrimination is found in most international human rights instruments but the scope of the right can rarely be deployed to argue a case for entry. The UN Convention on the Elimination of All Forms of Discrimination prohibits discrimination based on national origins but specifically excludes 'distinctions, exclusions, restrictions or preferences made by a state party to the Convention, between citizens and non-citizens'.[76] Its impact will therefore be minimal in the field of refugee protection. Discrimination based on race, religion or country of origin, is prohibited under Article 3 of the Refugee Convention but only as far as the provisions of the Convention apply, i.e. when the person has been formally recognised as a refugee.

Article 26 ICCPR establishes a free-standing non-discrimination provision which includes discrimination based on nationality.[77] For the discriminatory treatment to be considered lawful it needs to be based on reasonable and objective criteria:

---

74 2000/C 364/01 Official Journal C364/1 18 December 2000.

75 Declaration of state parties to the 1951 Convention and/or its 1967 Protocol relating to the status of refugees UN Doc HCR/MMSP/2001/09 16 January 2002.

76 Noll supra n35, 546.

77 *Ibrahima Gueye et al v France*, Communication No 196/1985, UN Doc CCPR/C/35/D/196/1985 (1989).

> The right to equality before the law and to equal protection of the law without any discrimination does not make all differences of treatment discriminatory. A differentiation based on reasonable and objective criteria does not amount to prohibited discrimination within the meaning of Article 26.[78]

On this basis it is generally considered that Article 26 will not enable the assertion of a right of entry.

Under the ECHR the parasitic nature of the non-discrimination provision in Article 14 requires that the applicant must demonstrate that the discriminatory treatment has occurred in relation to one of the substantive Convention rights (although no breach of that substantive right needs to be proven).[79] Article 14 does not require identical treatment in every situation and the state will most likely defend any allegation on the basis that they are pursuing an objective and reasonable justification by maintaining strong border controls. It is thus difficult to argue for any right to enter based on Article 14.[80] Although once a person enters the state it will be more difficult for the state to justify discriminatory treatment.[81] Whilst Protocol 12 to the ECHR establishes a free-standing non-discrimination provision it has yet to be ratified by most Council of Europe states and there has been no case-law on its application to asylum.[82]

The Treaty on the Functioning of the EU ('TFEU') prohibits 'any discrimination on grounds of nationality'.[83] The development of EU citizenship law clearly prohibits discrimination on the grounds of nationality between EU and national citizens and this has been extended by the CJEU to encompass social rights and benefits.[84] However, most commentators agree that this provision does not apply

78 *Zwaan – de Vries v the Netherlands* Communication No 182/1994 UN Doc CCPR/C/OP/2 at 209 (1990) para 13.

79 *Abdulaziz, Cabales and Balkandali v UK* App 9214/80, 9473/81, 9474/81 28 May 1985.

80 Goldston, J 'Fighting Terrorism While Fighting Discrimination: Can Protocol No 12 Help?' in *Non-Discrimination as a Human Right* Seminar to mark the entry into force on Protocol 12 (Council of Europe, 2006).

81 *Koua Poirrez v France* (2003), para 49; Lambert, H 'The European Convention on Human Rights and the Protection of Refugees: Limits and Opportunities' (2005) 4 Refugee Studies Q 2.

82 Council of Europe *Protocol No 12 to the Convention for the Protection of Human Rights and Fundamental Freedoms* CETS No: 177 4 November 2011; Mole, N 'Asylum and the European Convention on Human Rights' (2007) 9 Human Rights Files 12 http://www.unhcr.org/refworld/pdfid/4ee9b0972.pdf (accessed 16 November 2012).

83 Article 18 (ex 12) TFEU.

84 See for example *Grzelczyk v Centre Public d'aide Sociale d'Ottignies-Louvain-la-Neuve* 2001 Case C-184/99.

to third country nationals.[85] This view is supported by the Court of Justice in the *Vatsouras and Koupatantze* judgement.[86]

Article 10 TFEU identifies non-discrimination as one of the fundamental principles of the Union. However, the absence of national origins as a prohibited ground for discriminatory treatment means that these provisions have little value in the current discussion. The various asylum directives do not include a specific right which would enable asylum seekers to ground a non-discrimination claim in order to assist entry. The Equal Treatment Directive makes a specific exception for differences of treatment based on nationality and 'is without prejudice to provisions and conditions relating to the entry into and residence of third country nationals and stateless persons … and to any treatment which arises from the[ir] legal status'.[87]

Thus the right to enter a state to request asylum is not provided by international human rights or refugee law. This omission leaves a significant protection gap in terms of accessing sanctuary which may consequently encourage applicants to resort to illegitimate means of entry.

Defining a Convention Refugee

Whilst Article 3 ECHR may assist an applicant in an argument against expulsion, it has been noted that there is no requirement on states to formally recognise an individual at risk of refoulement as a refugee. Recognition is governed by the Refugee Convention which bestows refugee status on a person who:

> owing to well-founded fear of being persecuted for reasons of race, religion, nationality, membership of a particular social group or political opinion, is outside the country of his nationality and is unable or, owing to such fear, is unwilling to avail himself of the protection of that country; or who, not having a nationality and being outside the country of his former habitual residence as a result of such events, is unable or, owing to such fear, is unwilling to return to it.[88]

The interpretation of these grounds, as well as the evidence required to demonstrate a 'well-founded fear', has been largely left to individual states with the assistance

85 Zahn, R The EU Lisbon Treaty: What Implications For Anti-Racism? (European Network Against Racism 2009) 13; Peers, S *EU Justice and Home Affairs Law* (OUP 2011) 177.

86 *Athanasios Vatsouras* (C-22/08) and *Josif Koupatantze* (C-23/08) v *Arbeitsgemeinschaft (ARGE) Nürnberg 900*. Joined cases C-22/08 and C-23/08. European Court Reports 2009 Page I-04585 paras 51–53.

87 Council Directive 2000/43/EC of 29 June 2000 implementing the principle of equal treatment between persons irrespective of racial or ethnic origin *Official Journal L 180, 19/07/2000 0022 – 0026*, Article 3(2).

88 Article 1A Refugee Convention.

of the UNHCR Handbook and Executive Committee Conclusions.[89] It is well-documented that the absence of definitional precision has led to inconsistent interpretations, for example involving persecutory actions perpetrated by non-state agents.[90] It has also left a significant protection gap to be filled by subsidiary protection when an applicant's fear arises from generalised violence, such as that occurring in civil war situations.[91]

The EU Qualification Directive

EU harmonisation has enabled many of these inconsistencies to be revisited and ironed out on the European stage. The Qualification Directive specifically includes persecution by non-state actors.[92] It has also extended subsidiary protection when there are substantial grounds for believing that a person would suffer 'serious harm'.[93] This is defined, inter alia, to encompass situations where a person may be returned to a country in which there is a threat to life or person due to violence in situations of armed conflict.[94] It is worth noting that protection under the Qualification Directive is subject to a number of exclusions similar to those in the Refugee Convention.[95] The recast directive which must be implemented by Member States by 21 December 2013, maintains this position. The Qualification Directive has also helped to clarify what treatment can constitute persecution and has included prosecution or punishment for refusal to perform military service in a conflict and acts of a gender-specific or child-specific nature.[96]

89 UNHCR supra n22.

90 Lambert supra n33, 534.

91 See for example *R v SSHD Exp Adan* (1998) 37 ILM 1090.

92 Council Directive 2004/83/EC of 29 April 2004 as amended by Directive 2011/95/ supra n42, Article 6.

93 Ibid, Article 15; Storey, H 'Legislative Comment. EU Refugee Qualification Directive: A Brave New World?' (2008) 20 Int J Refugee L 1,1; Gil-Bazo, M 'Refugee Status and Subsidiary Protection under EC Law: The Qualification Directive and the Right to be Granted Asylum' in Baldaccini, A et al (eds), *Whose Freedom, Security and Justice? EU Immigration and Asylum Law and Policy* (Hart 2007) 236.

94 Qualification Directive, Article 15.

95 Qualification Directive, Article 12.

96 Qualification Directive, Articles 9(2)(e) and 9(2)(f). Although concerns have been expressed about the provisions protecting refusal to perform military service which arises from conscientious military objection (see for example ECRE *Comments From The European Council On Refugees And Exiles on the European Commission Proposal to recast the Qualification Directive* March 2010, ECRE.

Exceptions to the Obligation to Protect

In addition to the noted exceptions to the non-refoulement obligation, Article 1F Refugee Convention allows for the exclusion of refugee status to a person against whom there are serious reasons for considering that:

> (a) He has committed a crime against peace, a war crime, or a crime against humanity, as defined in the international instruments drawn up to make provision in respect of such crimes;
>
> (b) He has committed a serious non-political crime outside the country of refuge prior to his admission to that country as a refugee;
>
> (c) He has been guilty of acts contrary to the purposes and principles of the United Nations.

The EU Qualification Directive extends the scope of these exclusions by including instigation or other participation in such crimes or acts.[97] This provision also applies to those applying for subsidiary protection with one notable addition:

> 3. Member States may exclude a third country national or a stateless person from being eligible for subsidiary protection, if he or she prior to his or her admission to the Member State has committed one or more crimes, outside the scope of paragraph 1, which would be punishable by imprisonment, had they been committed in the Member State concerned, and if he or she left his or her country of origin solely in order to avoid sanctions resulting from these crimes.[98]

Whilst the exclusions require more than mere suspicion, the standard of proof falls short of the criminal standard as prosecution would then be more appropriate.[99] The UNHCR again stress the importance of proportionality, where the risk to the applicant on return is balanced against the type of act that has been committed.[100] However, this assessment has been questioned by some commentators who point to its absence in common law jurisdictions, including the UK.[101]

---

97 Qualification Directive, Article 12(2) and 12(3).

98 Qualification Directive, Article 17(3).

99 Symes and Jorro supra n46, 392–394.

100 UNHCR Background Note on the Application of the Exclusion Clauses: Article 1F of the 1951 Convention relating to the Status of Refugees' 4 September 2003. Available at: http://www.unhcr.org/refworld/docid/3f5857d24.html (accessed 7 December 2012).

101 Symes and Jorro supra n46, 395; see Weis, P *The Refugee Convention, 1951: The Travaux Préparatoires Analyzed with a Commentary by Dr. Paul Weis* (CUP 1995) 342 and Lauterpacht and Bethlehem supra n43, 140 who argue that the state's margin of appreciation should be circumscribed in these cases.

Bond highlights the problems that may arise from the application of Article 1F in situations of conflict and mass influx. She advocates a criminal law standard which would pay greater respect to the applicant's fundamental rights through a binary culpability assessment. The assessment would consider the situational nuances which may determine the level of individual blameworthiness, the degree of liability and the personal circumstances of the offender.[102]

In the Council of Europe, the effect of these exclusions will be limited in practice by the absolute prohibition on torture, inhuman and degrading treatment or cruel and unusual punishment in Article 3 ECHR. This extraneous interference in national security matters is of considerable concern to many Council of Europe states. In the *Chahal* case the British Government wished to deport a Sikh nationalist to India where he would face charges of terrorist activity. The deportation was planned notwithstanding substantiated allegations that during a previous period of incarceration, Chahal had been tortured at the hands of state officials. Whilst the state could rely on the exception in Article 33(2) of the Refugee Convention it could not avoid the absolute prohibition on torture and inhuman and degrading treatment under Article 3 of the European Convention on Human Rights:

> The prohibition provided by Article 3 against ill-treatment is equally absolute in expulsion cases ... the activities of the individual in question, however undesirable or dangerous, cannot be a material consideration. The protection afforded by Article 3 is thus wider than that provided by Article 32 and 33 of the United Nations 1951 Convention on the Status of Refugees.[103]

The ECtHR's approach constitutes a significant limitation on state sovereignty in an area of enormous political sensitivity. The applicant will have to show that there are substantial grounds for believing that s/he will be at risk of such treatment on return but this does not require definitive proof. In *Saadi v Italy* the ECtHR held that there would be a violation of Article 3 if the applicant, a Tunisian man convicted in abstentia of terrorism offences in Tunisia, was removed from Italy.[104] The ruling emphasised that paper commitments to human rights norms were not by themselves sufficient guarantees of protection.[105]

Article 3 ECHR has also been deployed to argue against return where an applicant would suffer health consequences due to the scarcity of national resources, particularly medical treatment. The authority of *D v UK*[106] must now be considered as limited to its specific facts following a series of subsequent cases which have

---

102 Bond, J 'Excluding Justice: The Dangerous Intersection between Refugee Claims, Criminal Law and "Guilty" Asylum Seekers' (2012) 24 Int J Refugee L 1, 37.

103 *Chahal v UK* supra n64 para 79,80.

104 *Saadi v Italy*, App No 37201/06, 28 February 2008.

105 Ibid, para 147.

106 [1997] 24 EHRR 423.

found such arguments untenable.[107] Battjes argues that the ECtHR is adopting value judgements where competing interests are effectively balanced, notwithstanding the absolute nature of the provision.[108] In *N v UK* the applicant who suffered from advanced stages of HIV, sought protection from removal to Uganda where limited health care was available.[109] Her quality of life would certainly have been better in the UK and her life would have probably been prolonged if she had remained here. Nevertheless the Court's Grand Chamber adopted a pragmatic approach and ruled that expulsion would violate Article 3 only in the most exceptional of cases where the humanitarian grounds were compelling. Such circumstances arose in *Sufi and Elmi v UK*, a case involving two rejected asylum seekers of Somali nationality who feared return to Somalia.[110] The Court ruled unanimously that there were substantial grounds for believing that the applicants would experience a breach of Article 3 on return to Somalia or, via internal flight to a Kenyan refugee camp, due to the serious risk of indiscriminate violence.

In the recent decision of *SHH v UK*, the ECtHR applied the ruling in *N* to the case of an Afghan national who alleged that his Article 3 rights would be breached on return due to a serious disability suffered after a rocket attack.[111] By a narrow majority, the Court held that the case was not significantly exceptional so as to constitute a breach of Article 3.

The Court's reasoning reflects the pragmatic, proportionality arguments advanced by Walzer, but it seems at odds with the absolute language of the provision:

> Inherent in the whole convention is a search for a fair balance ... Article 3 does not place an obligation on the contracting State to [provide for] free and unlimited health care to all aliens with a right to stay within its jurisdiction.[112]

Battjes concludes that this balance does not significantly undermine the absolute nature of non-refoulement under Article 3. The case-law where a balance has been applied remains limited and it is evident that factors which may justify such a balancing assessment will be far fewer than those applied under alternative Convention articles, such as the right to family life. The norm, as Battjes concedes, is that no justification applies under Article 3.[113] This is demonstrated in *N v Finland* where the ECtHR found that removal of Zairean national to the

107 Veelke D, 'Expulsion of Illegal Residents (Aliens) with Medical Problems and Article 3 of the European Convention of Human Rights' (2006) 13 Eur J of Health Law 313.

108 Battjes, H 'In Search of a Fair Balance: The Absolute Character of the Prohibition of Refoulement under Article 3 ECHR Reassessed' (2009) 22 Leiden Journal of International Law 3, 583.

109 *N v UK* [2008] App No 26565/05 27 May 2008.

110 App 8319/07 and 11449/07, 28 June 2011.

111 App 60367/10 29 January 2013 by a majority of 4:3 judges.

112 Supra n109, para 44.

113 Battjes supra n108, 619.

Democratic Republic of Congo would constitute a violation of Article 3 despite doubts surrounding the applicant's credibility and his involvement in minor criminal activity in Finland.[114] It is now clear from the judgements in *TI v UK* and *MSS v Belgium and Greece*, that Article 3 will take precedence over transfers under the Dublin Regulation.[115] It can no longer be assumed that the latter is automatically consonant with Convention rights.

Removals Concerning Qualified Rights

The impact of the prohibition of refoulement where other Convention articles are engaged has had notably less effect. The ECtHR has endorsed the approach taken by the British judiciary in removal cases, requiring an exceptionally strong case suggesting a flagrant denial or gross violation of the right.[116] The question of proportionality arises under the qualified Convention articles, thus making it more difficult for an applicant to challenge removal based solely on family or private life arguments. In *Uner v The Netherlands*, the applicant argued that his removal would constitute a violation of his family life as he would be separated from his partner and two small children.[117] Furthermore, having lived in the Netherlands since he was 12 (lawfully for a period of 16 years) he no longer had any real ties with his country of origin. Having balanced his right to family life with the risk posed by his criminality, the ECtHR found that his removal to Turkey would not constitute a disproportionate interference. It may be deemed reasonable for the applicant's family to relocate rather than maintain family life in the host state.

A potential breach of Article 6, the right to a fair trial, was used to prevent removal in the controversial *Abu Qatada* judgement.[118] Here, the state wished to remove the applicant to Jordan where he had been convicted in absentia on terrorist charges. The Court ruled that, notwithstanding the public interest in removing him, such action would constitute a 'flagrant denial' of Qatada's right to a fair trial arising from the Jordanian authorities' reliance on evidence obtained by torture. The UK government's struggle to remove a clear national security risk became a matter of considerable embarrassment and frustration, prompting calls in the mainstream media for the UK to withdraw from the ECHR.[119]

---

114 *N v Finland* ECtHR 26 July 2005 App 38885/02.

115 *TI v UK* App 43844/98 7 March 2000 p16; *MSS* supra n67; See discussion of the Dublin Regulation in Chapter 4.

116 *R (Ullah) v Special Adjudicator* [2004] UKHL 26 and *R (Do) v Special Adjudicator* [2004] 2 AC 323; *Othman (Abu Qatada) v UK* App No 8139/09 17 January 2012.

117 App 46410/99 18 October 2006.

118 *Othman (Abu Qatada) v UK* App No 8139/09 17 January 2012.

119 Hartley-Parkinson, R 'How Can They Tell Us How to Run Our Country? Seven of Eleven Sitting at Europe's Human Rights Court Deciding Fate of Hate Preacher Qatada Have Never Been Judges' (Mail Online 19 April 2012). Available at: http://www.dailymail.co.uk/news/article-2131955/Abu-Qatada-deportation-case-ECHR-judges-making-judgment-appeal-little-experience.html#ixzz2MmgoKkwI. In March 2013, the Home

Indirect Refoulement

It has been argued that the non-refoulement obligation under Article 33 of the Refugee Convention and Article 3 ECHR will apply where a person is refused entry at the state's border. It also extends to cover indirect refoulement, i.e. removal of an applicant to an intermediate country where it is foreseeable that they will then be returned in breach of the obligation. This position was recognised by the UK House of Lords in *Bugdaycay v SSHD.*[120] In the subsequent case of *Adan and Aitseguer*,[121] concerning transfers under the Dublin Convention to European safe countries, the Court ruled that there was a danger of indirect refoulement. Neither Germany nor France recognised persecutory acts committed by non-state agents in the absence of state complicity (the so-called accountability theory) therefore they were unlikely to recognise the applicants' protection needs. Both the UK's senior courts referred to the good faith obligations in the Vienna Convention and rejected the approach of the EU Joint Position of 1996 which allowed a range of interpretations on this issue. When designating a country as safe, the Court's ruled that the Secretary of State had an obligation to ensure that the country applied the true rules of interpretation under the Refugee Convention. The approach was subsequently confirmed by the ECtHR in *TI v UK.*[122] The *Adan* judgement raised interesting questions about the true interpretation of the Refugee Convention, an issue which has now largely been resolved by the EU Qualification Directive.[123] It also confirms the danger of generalised assumptions about safety.[124] The recent decision in *Hirsi Jamaa* confirms that states will be responsible where they engage in removal or interception actions and fail to take into account the possibility of refoulement by a third country.[125]

Challenges to Non-Refoulement

Whilst the prohibition on refoulement is clearly enshrined as a core principle of international law, there are numerous challenges to the doctrine. Some of

Secretary announced that the Government planned to repeal the Human Rights Act 1998, which incorporated most of the ECHR into UK law, should they win the next general election. Mr Qatada was eventually removed after an 8-year battle, following assurances from the Jordanian authorities that no evidence obtained under torture would be used against him, in July 2013.

120 [1987] 1 AC 514.

121 *R v SSHD exp Adan and Aitseguer* [1999] 3 WLR 1274.

122 [2000] INLR 211.

123 Supra n42, Article 6c. This has recently been applied in the Administrative Court of Berlin, 7 July 2011, 33 K 79.10 A. Available at: http://www.asylumlawdatabase.eu/en/case-law/germany-administrative-court-berlin-7-July-2011-33-k-7910#content.

124 Stevens supra n8, 181.

125 *Hirsi Jamaa* supra n67.

the examples are blatant and attract international condemnation, such as the collective expulsions of Rwandan refugees in the Great Lakes region. However, the territorial focus of the obligation has resulted in states seeking more subtle ways to undermine the principle. These measures include the closure of borders, extraterritorial interception, refusal to admit applicants to the determination procedure and the implementation of policies which encourage premature departure, such as detention or restrictions on welfare.[126] Given the absence of a clear legal right to enter, the legality or otherwise of such measures is often difficult to pinpoint.

Pre-Entrée

Some of these measures take place before the applicant leaves their country of origin and thus before the obligations under the Refugee Convention apply. Article 1(A)(2) of the Refugee Convention defines a refugee as a person 'outside the country of his nationality'. Non-entrée mechanisms include the introduction of visa requirements, carriers' liability sanctions and the stationing of border staff at overseas airports or strategic points to prevent travel to the intended destination.[127] Despite the good faith obligations in the Vienna Convention, requiring states to conform to the purpose of the Convention by properly identifying those in need of protection,[128] European harmonisation has endorsed mechanisms which may undermine that objective.[129] The common visa list for example is informed by security and illegal immigration concerns and makes no specific exemption for asylum seekers.[130] Some states will allow an asylum seeker to request protection at overseas embassies but this position is far from the norm.[131] The common list clearly makes it more difficult for protection-seekers to access sanctuary. Indeed, research undertaken by Noll revealed that the original common visa list included three of the top refugee producing countries in the previous decade.[132]

The requirement to obtain a visa prior to travel to the EU is bolstered by sanctions imposed on carriers who have an obligation 'to take all necessary measures to ensure that an alien carried by air or sea is in possession of the travel documents

126 Goodwin-Gill and McAdam supra n12, 228.

127 Moreno Lax, V 'Must EU Borders have Doors for Refugees? On the Compatibility of Schengen Visas and Carriers' Sanctions with EU Member States' Obligations to Provide International Protection to Refugees' (2008) 10 Eur J Migration & L 323.

128 Marx, R 'Non-Refoulement, Access to Procedures and Responsibility for Determining Refugee Status' (1999) 7 Int J Refugee L 401.

129 Moreno Lax supra n127, 323.

130 Council Regulation No 574/99 OJ (1999) L 072 18 March 1999 now replaced by Regulation 539/2001 OJ (2001) L 81/1 21 March 2001; Goodwin-Gill, G and McAdam, J supra n12, 374.

131 Noll, G 'Seeking Asylum at Embassies: A Right to Entry under International Law' 2005 17 Int J Refugee L 3, 542.

132 Noll supra n35, 166.

required for entry into the territory of the Contracting parties'.[133] Initially rejected by the European Parliament, the French proposal had provided for an exemption from sanctions if the third country national is admitted to the territory for 'asylum purposes'. This was subsequently watered down so that the obligation to impose penalties is 'without prejudice to Member States' obligations in cases where a third country national seeks international protection'.[134] In order to avoid penalties, carriers will need to refuse transport to any inadequately documented passenger, refugee or otherwise.[135]

The stationing of Immigration Liaison Officers in third countries has also been formalised by an EU Regulation.[136] The emphasis in the Regulation is on identifying irregular migration routes and preventing irregular migration. In the *Prague Airport Case*, the discriminatory nature of these departure checks was highlighted by the UK House of Lords.[137] Airline liaison officers had singled out Roma passengers and prevented them from boarding flights to the UK on the basis that many were economic migrants who would attempt to claim asylum. However, the Court found that these pre-clearance actions by immigration officers did not violate the Refugee Convention as the asylum applicants had not yet left their country of origin. There is surprisingly no mention in the Regulation of international humanitarian obligations.

More recently Member States at the periphery of Europe have intercepted vessels on the high seas in an attempt to prevent them from accessing their territory. The spirit, and in some cases the letter, of the law on non-refoulement, is compromised by such initiatives. The dramatic fall by almost 50 per cent in asylum applications made in Italy in 2009 is almost certainly attributable to Italian interception efforts in the Adriatic which has pushed migrants back to North Africa.[138] In its investigation of seven such interceptions since 2009, the European Committee for the Prevention of Torture concluded that the obligation

133 *The Schengen Acquis – Convention implementing the Schengen Agreement of 14 June 1985 between the Governments of the States of the Benelux Economic Union, the Federal Republic of Germany and the French Republic on the gradual abolition of checks at their common borders* OJ L239, 22 September 2000 0019 – 0062 'Schengen Convention' Article 26(b) supplemented by Council Directive 2001/51/EC of 28 June 2001 Supplementing the provisions of Article 26 of the Convention implementing the Schengen Agreement of 14 June 1985 OJ L 187 (10 July 2001) 45–46.

134 Ibid, Article 4(2).

135 Moreno Lax supra n127, 326.

136 Council Regulation on the Creation of an Immigration Officers Liaison Network 377/2004 [2004] OJ L 64/1 19 February 2004; Peers, supra n85, 544.

137 *R v Immigration Officer at Prague Airport and another ex parte European Roma Rights Centre and others* [2004] UKHL 55.

138 ECRE 'Ill-Treatment of Refugees in Libya: The EU, A Silent Accomplice' Press Release (7 July 2010).

of non-refoulement had been violated, contrary to Article 3 of the ECHR.[139] Of particular concern is the evidence that protection from refoulement cannot be guaranteed in Libya which has not ratified the Refugee Convention. In 2010, the European Council on Refugee and Exiles called upon the Italian authorities to end the interdiction of Eritrean refugees to Libyan detention centres from which they were likely to be repatriated to Eritrea. Their report accused EU Member States of 'consenting silence'.[140]

There is international precedence for these evasive mechanisms. The United States authorities have argued in favour of a territorial basis for the non-refoulement obligation when interdicting Haitian migrants without any attempt to verify their status.[141] The Inter-American Commission on Human Rights subsequently found the US to be in breach of Article 33 Refugee Convention.[142] The Australian 'pacific solution', discussed in Chapter 1, demonstrates a similar strategy.

It is well-established that international human rights obligations will apply to a state where it assumes control of a rescue operation and this will include the subsequent treatment of the rescued, even when that treatment occurs in a different territory.[143] In the *Marine 1* case, Spain incurred ongoing responsibility under the CAT for the treatment of migrants in Mauritania following Spanish interception of a vessel carrying 369 migrants in Senegalese waters.[144] The first group of migrants were repatriated within one day of arrival, whereas a small group of 23 remained detained in an abandoned fish processing plant for several months. It is not clear whether the migrants were given the opportunity to apply for refugee status.

The ECtHR judgement in *Hirsi Jamaa*, discussed in Chapter 1, confirms this approach.[145] Whilst the need to establish a jurisdictional link remains crucial as a necessary condition to state liability,[146] states cannot avoid that responsibility by contracting with others to do their 'dirty work'. As Giuffre reasons, 'if States set in motion offshore mechanisms of either non-admission or removal after interdiction

139 Report to the Italian Government on the visit to Italy carried out by the European Committee for the Prevention of Torture and Inhuman or Degrading Treatment or Punishment (CPT) from 27 to 31 July 2009.

140 Vandvik, B ECRE's Secretary General quoted in ECRE Press release 'Ill-treatment of refugees in Libya: The EU a Silent Accomplice' ECRE 7 July 2010; See also Amnesty International *SOS Europe: Human Rights and Migration Control* (Amnesty International 2012).

141 *Sale, Acting Commissioner INS v Haitian Centres Council* 509 US (1993).

142 *Haitian Center for Human Rights v US* Case 10.675 Report No 51/96. Inter-Am CHR Doc OEA/Ser L/V/II 95 Doc 7 Red (1997).

143 *JHA v Spain* No 323/2007 CAT/C/41/D/323/2007 21 November 2008. The Committee ruled that the complainant, a member of a non-governmental organisation, did not have locus standi to proceed to a full hearing. Case comment by Wouters, K and Den Heijer, M 'The Marine 1 Case: A Comment' (2010) 22 Int J Refugee L 1, 1.

144 Ibid; Bruin supra n73, 31.

145 *Hirsi Jamaa* supra n67.

146 See also *Medvedyev and Others v France* [2010] 51 EHRR 39.

at sea – which limit the possibility of individuals to challenge State decisions – a violation of the right to an effective remedy under Article 13 of the ECHR would take place'.[147]

The application of the right to an effective remedy in *Hirsi* follows a consistent pattern of case-law under Article 13 which includes its application in cases of accelerated proceedings and summary removals.[148] Again, in this respect we can see that *lex generalis* principles of international human rights law may offer greater protection than the *lex specialis* of international refugee law. The Court's ruling effectively means that states must inform asylum seekers about their legal rights and ensure full access to a determination procedure which is in accordance with international obligations.[149]

The outsourcing of immigration control to countries beyond Europe's territorial borders should also be examined in this context. The right to 'seek' asylum depends on the right to exit a state that is not able to provide sanctuary to the particular applicant. Responsibility for exit control has been placed with the border staff of countries surrounding the EU under the Neighbourhood Policy yet in many cases the standard of asylum procedures in such countries is deficient.[150] There is no doubt that many migrants will be contained in these bordering countries and that this will inevitably include asylum seekers.[151] A 'closed-sack' situation results where applicants are trapped in a transit country that is not able or willing to provide the full range of rights guaranteed by international law.[152] The social, economic and political costs of this fate for the transit country may be significant and these concerns will undoubtedly influence their own refugee policy with the potential to further dilute protection.

The UNHCR has called on the new president of the EU to revisit the Common European Asylum System ('CEAS') with a view to ensuring greater convergence in standards and to 'make sure that Europe's borders do not become impenetrable for those who are seeking protection'.[153] Whilst the CEAS remains dominated by concerns about security and irregular migration, the risk of refoulement is significant.

---

147 Giuffre, M Watered-Down Rights on the High Seas: *Hirsi Jamaa and Others v Italy* (2012)' (2012)61 ICLQ 3, 742.

148 See for example *Jabari v Turkey* App 40035/98 1 July 2000; *Abdolkhani and Karimnia v Turkey* App 30471/08 22 September 2009.

149 Giuffre supra n147, 749.

150 Gammeltoft-Hansen, T *Outsourcing Migration Management: EU, Power and Immigration Policy* DIIS Working paper No 1 2006; see the discussion on neighbourhood policies in Chapter 6.

151 Gammeltoft-Hansen, ibid.

152 Byrne, R 'Future Perspectives: Accession and Asylum in an Expanded EU' in Byrne et al supra n156, 383.

153 Edward, A 'UNHCR recommendations for Belgian EU Presidency' Press briefing (25 June 2010).

On Arrival

The designation of certain countries as 'safe' leading to an expedited refugee determination process and the summary removal of applicants to 'safe' countries, raise serious concerns as both have the potential to constitute refoulement.

Notions of collective, generalised assumptions have come to underpin European asylum law in contrast to the individually determined assessments of refugee status and refoulement under the Refugee Convention. The concept of Safe Third Country ('STC') enables states to reject or expedite the examination of an application on the basis that the applicant should have availed themselves of protection elsewhere. A designation of a Safe Country of Origin ('SCO') allows an applicant to be returned to the state of origin on the basis that there is generally no risk of persecution in that country. In addition, the identification of a First Country of Asylum ('FCA') allows an asylum seeker to be returned to a country where they have been formally recognised as a requiring protection.[154] Whilst questions might remain over the parity of protection between states, the FCA is overall a less problematic concept. The presumption of safety inherent in the STC and SCO rules demands further analysis.

The STC principle underpins the Dublin Regulation and has been further extended by some states to cover listed states where it is believed that there is generally no risk of persecution.[155] The emphasis is less about protection and more about burden-sharing or 'deflection'.[156]

International refugee law does not specifically require that a refugee applies for asylum in the first safe country of arrival, but European Union law now establishes this as a key principle. Whilst it could perhaps be justified if procedures were truly uniform across the EU28, this is not borne out by the evidence which demonstrates wide variations in recognition rates of similar groups of applicants.[157] The situation in Greece which led to the ECtHR ruling in *MSS*, discussed in Chapter 4, illustrates the danger of generalised designations of safety. Prior to the suspension of transfers, Greece recognised only 0.04 per cent of asylum requests. When recognition rates for Iraqi applicants were 87.5 per cent in Cyprus and 85 per cent in Germany, the Greek recognition rate was 0 per cent.[158] The likelihood

154 Kjaerum, M 'The Concept of Country of First Asylum' (1992) 4 Intl J Refugee L 4, 514.

155 See discussion in Chapter 4.

156 Byrne, R and Vedsted-Hansen, J 'Western Asylum Policies for Export: The Transfer of Protection and Deflection Formulas to Central Europe and the Baltics' in Byrne, R; Noll, G and Vedsted-Hansen, J (eds) *New Asylum Countries? Migration Control and Refugee Protection in an Enlarged EU* (Kluwer 2002) 12.

157 Eurostat 2008 statistics have initial recognition rates at 65 per cent in Poland compared to 15.5 per cent in the Czech Republic and 0.2 per cent in Greece 'Asylum decisions in the EU27' 2008 Stat/09/175 Europa.

158 ECRE 'Background Information. Transfer of asylum seekers to Greece' 2007; statistics for the following year show the Greek refugee recognition rate was 0.2 per cent

of indirect refoulement in such cases is clear. The Council of Europe's Human Rights Commissioner, Thomas Hammarberg, apportions much of the blame on the burden-sharing ethos which inevitably results in most transferees being returned to countries on the Southern border of Europe.[159] The incongruity of protection regimes inevitably leads to 'asylum-shopping', paradoxically the very evil that states were attempting to prevent.[160] Costello predicts that any 'success' from the Dublin Regulation will only benefit the 'old' European states as the burden is pushed further eastwards to countries of first arrival.[161] Her prediction appears to have been borne out by reality. In the absence of uniform procedures, the possibility of refoulement would appear inevitable despite the safeguards employed.[162] The *MSS* judgement highlights the flaw in generalised presumptions of safety and questions the feasibility of common standards.[163]

In the EU, the Dublin Regulation designates state responsibility for a single determination of the applicant's case.[164] Yet there remain real concerns over the treatment of transferees following return.[165] In many cases applicants who are transferred do not have their case re-examined due to domestic rules prohibiting the re-examination of cases unless new evidence emerges. Applicants may thus be denied any substantive determination of their case. A study of 20 cases where individuals were subjected to the jurisdiction of the Regulation, painted a picture of disorganisation, poor communication and diverse systems, resulting in applicants being arbitrarily detained and expelled to countries of origin.[166]

---

of applicants (compared to the European average on initial decisions of slightly under 30 per cent) EUROSTAT Stat/09/175 'Asylum decisions in the EU27' (2008) Europa Press Release http://europa.eu/rapid/pressReleasesAction.do?reference=STAT/09/175&format=HTML&aged=0&language=EN&guiLanguage=en.

159 Hammarberg, T 'The Dublin Regulations Undermines Refugee Rights' 22 September 2010, Council of Europe Commissioner's Human Rights Comment.

160 Noll supra n35, 183.

161 Costello, C 'The Asylum Procedures Directive and the Proliferation of Safe Country Practices: Deterrence, Deflection and the Dismantling of International Protection?' (2005) 7 Eur J Migration & L 46.

162 Borchelt, G 'The Safe Third Country Practice in the EU: A Misguided Approach to Asylum Law and a Violation of International Human Rights Standards' [2002] Colum HR L Rev

163 Discussed in Chapter 3

164 Dublin III came into force on 16 July 2013. Regulation (EC) No 604/2013 26 June 2013 *Establishing The Criteria and Mechanisms for Determining the Member State Responsible for Examining an Asylum Application Lodged in One of the Member States by a Third Country National* (Recast) 29 June 2013 OJ L 180/31 'Dublin III Regulation'.

165 ECRE 'The Dublin Regulation: Ten Recommendations for Reform' AD1/3/2007/Ext/CN.

166 ECRE 'The Dublin Regulation: Twenty Voices: Twenty Reasons for Change' AD2/3/2007/ext/CN.

As originally conceived, the receiving country should signal their willingness to examine the applicant's refugee claim. However, the current position assumes that states that are signatories to the ECHR and the Refugee Convention will fully consider the applicant's asylum case.[167] According to the EU Procedures Directive, discussed in Chapter 4, the asylum claim will be inadmissible if: the applicant can be transferred to another Member State in accordance with the Dublin Regulation;[168] they have been granted refugee status in another state;[169] theyhave already obtained protection in another non-Member State;[170] or if the applicant has transited through or had access to a 'safe third country' in which they could have sought protection.[171]

Removals to STCs can occur outside the Dublin framework to countries where there is 'generally and consistently no persecution ... no torture or inhuman or degrading treatment or punishment and no threat by reason of indiscriminate violence in situations of international or internal armed conflict'.[172] If the applicant has come from a STC or a SCO their claims may be presumed 'manifestly unfounded'. They will then be subjected to an accelerated removal procedure which includes an opportunity to rebut the safety presumption.[173]Appeals may be non-suspensive in these cases and detention may be deployed on the basis that the claim can be determined quickly. International human rights agencies, including the UNHCR and the Human Rights Committee, have expressed concern over the move away from individualised assessments of protection needs in the STC designation.[174]

In addition to a common European list, the Procedures Directive authorises states to operate their own lists of STC and SCO's and expedite applicants to prioritised procedures.[175] Practice varies considerably across Europe but a list has been part of UK law for the past 20 years. The so-called 'white list' of safe countries includes Albania, Jamaica, Republic of Korea, Kosovo, Macedonia, Moldova, Serbia, Montenegro, Brazil, Ecuador, Bolivia, South Africa, Ukraine, India, and Bosnia Herzegovina, Mauritius, Peru. Additionally, Ghana, Nigeria,

167 EU Procedures Directive, Article 35A(2).

168 Dublin II Regulation Article 25(1).

169 Procedures Directive Article 25(2)a.

170 Procedures Directive Article 25(2)b.

171 Procedures Directive Article 25(2)c.

172 Annex II Procedures Directive.

173 Procedures Directive Art 23(4)(c)(i).

174 UNHCR 'Note on International Protection' UN Doc A/AC 96/914 7 July 1999; Report of the Human Rights Committee vol 1 (2002-03) UNGAOR 58 session Supp. No 40 (A/58/40) Estonia para 79 (13) CHECK.

175 Procedures Directive Art 30. The common list was declared ultra vires by the CJEU due to procedural irregularities, but the amended provisions still provide a platform on which such lists can be established, see discussion in Chapter 4.

Gambia, Kenya, Malawi, Liberia, Mali and Sierra Leone are also deemed safe in respect of male asylum claimants.[176]

The UK experience demonstrates the risk of generalised safety presumptions. In 2001, the inclusion of Pakistan was deemed 'irrational' by the Court of Appeal due to the prevalence of persecutory treatment towards women and members of the Ahmadi ethnic group.[177] Following the outbreak of civil war in Sri Lanka in 2003, the Home Office amended the list to remove Sri Lanka in 2005 (Bangladesh was similarly removed in 2006).[178]

Other cases can also be deemed 'manifestly unfounded' and subject to accelerated removal procedures. The European Council's 'Resolution on Manifestly Unfounded Applications for Asylum' (the 'London Resolution') marked a departure from the UNHCR position which had concluded that for an application to be deemed 'manifestly unfounded' it should be clearly fraudulent or unrelated to the Refugee Convention criteria.[179] The current European position includes applicants arriving from STCs and applications which raise issues that are irrelevant or of minimal relevance to the examination of refugee status.[180] Furthermore, it includes numerous situations where there are doubts as to the applicant's credibility, despite UNHCR concerns that such issues are too complex to be decided in an abridged procedure.[181]

The non-refoulement obligation is further compromised by reception conditions for arrivals. The routine use of detention in some states has been endorsed by the EU Reception Directive. Difficulties in accessing state welfare and housing support are compounded by the rules in the Reception Directive relating to the right to work.[182] At present applicants have to wait 12 months before they can request permission to work (although this is reduced to 9 months in the recast directive), this delay can consign applicants to poverty and further uncertainty following arrival. The UK's influence can also be seen by the inclusion of a provision allowing states to restrict benefits and support if the applicant does not make a claim as soon as practicable following arrival.[183]

---

176 s94 of the Nationality, Immigration and Asylum Act 2002.

177 *R v SSHD ex parte Javed, Ali and Ali* [2001] EWCA Civ 789. For the position of women in Pakistan *Islam v SSHD*; *R v IAT and Anor, ex parte Shah* (1999) 2 WLR 1015.

178 Asylum (Designated States) (Amendment) Order 2005 (S.I 2005/1016) and the Asylum (Designated States) (Amendment) (No 2) Order 2006 (S.I 2006/3275) respectively.

179 Council Resolution of 30 November 1992 *on Manifestly Unfounded Applications for Asylum* ('London Resolution'), 30 November 1992, available at: http://www.unhcr.org/refworld/docid/3f86bbcc4.htm; UN Ex COMM Conclusion 30 of 1988.

180 EU Procedures Directive Article 23.

181 Byrne supra n152, 404.

182 Council Directive 2003/9/EC of 27 January 2003 *Laying Down Minimum Standards for the Reception of Asylum Seekers* OJ L31/18 6 February 2003 'Reception Directive' Article 11(2), discussed in Chapter 5.

183 Reception Directive, Article 16. The implementation of this rule was successfully challenged in the UK HL in *R v SSHD exp Adam, Limbuela and Tesema* [2005] UKHL 66.

The UK's highest court has ruled that the denial of welfare support to asylum seekers who do not apply immediately on arrival, may lead to destitution contrary to Article 3 of the ECHR.[184] The conditions awaiting asylum seekers in Greece met this threshold in *MSS*.[185] However, in *EM (Eritrea)* the UK Court of Appeal found that the conditions awaiting applicants returned to Italy under the Dublin Regulation did not breach Article 3, notwithstanding evidence from the Council of Europe's Commissioner for Human Rights and various non-governmental organisations, presenting a picture of barely functioning procedures leaving many applicants destitute. As to whether the conditions in Italy constituted a systemic deficiency as required post *MSS*, Sir Stephen Sedley found that:

> The totality of the evidence about Italy, although it is extremely troubling and far from uncritical, does not in our judgment come up to this mark ... evidence does not demonstrate that Italy's system for the reception of asylum seekers and refugees, despite its many shortcomings and casualties, is itself dysfunctional or deficient.[186]

A great deal of weight was given to the evidence of the UNHCR in its *Recommendations on Important Aspects of Refugee Protection in Italy*[187] The report noted improvements since 2011 when the Italian system had been deemed insufficient, suggesting that the system is now functioning despite some shortcomings.

Penalties for Illegal Entry

Article 31 of the Refugee Convention provides:

> The contracting states shall not impose penalties, on account of their illegal entry or presence, on refugees who, coming directly from a territory where their life or freedom was threatened in the sense of article 1, enter or are present in their territory without authorisation, provided they present themselves without delay to the authorities ad show good cause for their illegal entry or presence.

Due to the various non-entrée mechanisms, many asylum applicants have no option but to travel irregularly. Irregular migration may arise from a variety of

The court found that where an applicant became destitute as a result of this position there would be a violation of Article 3 ECHR.

184 *R v SSHD ex parte Adam (FC); Limbuela (FC); ex parte Tesema (FC)* Conjoined Appeals UKHL [2005] 66.

185 *MSS v Belgium and Greece* supra n67.

186 Ibid, para 63.

187 UNHCR July 2012.

circumstances including the absence of official documentation, the use of forged documents, reliance on smugglers, or other clandestine entry. Article 31 operates to prevent such an applicant from incurring criminal penalties providing that they avail themselves to the authorities without undue delay. As such it marks a clear recognition that most refugees will be unable to secure official documentation prior to their flight; this was explicitly understood by Simon Brown LJ in the British case of *Adimi*:

> The need for Article 31 has not diminished. Quite the contrary … the combined effect of visa requirements and carrier's liability has made it well nigh impossible for refugees to travel to countries of refuge without false documents.[188]

Like Article 33, it applies to all persons claiming refugee status until and unless their claim is rejected. It can therefore mean that an applicant is actually charged with illegal entry but that any penalty is suspended until and unless a negative determination results. Article 31 has been the subject of much debate, particularly over the interpretation of 'penalty'. In many states, immigration detention is applied to all illegal entrants and in other states summary expulsion may be applied if applicants have not applied promptly.

Hathaway accepts that the original construction of Article 31 applies to criminal penalties in the strict sense.[189] However he argues in favour of a broader approach which would encompass civil penalties and the use of abbreviated procedures solely predicated on the fact of irregular entry. Indeed, this analysis is supported by the British decision in *Adimi* in which the potential denial of income support benefits was considered by Simon Brown LJ to constitute a penalty for this purpose.[190]

Subject to the absolute protection from refoulement, expulsion does not constitute a penalty. The increasingly common practice of detaining asylum seekers until their status is regularised also appears compatible with Article 31 and is specifically provided for in Art 31(2) Refugee Convention. In some cases this will legitimately result from concerns that the applicant will abscond or pursuant to a removal decision pending imminent expulsion. However, the routine application of administrative detention by some states marks a significant change such that the justification becomes one of administrative efficiency. The ECtHR has ruled that, providing such detention is not arbitrary and is for a short period of time, it will not breach the right to liberty contained in Article 5 of the ECHR.[191] Article 31(2) of the Refugee Convention provides:

---

188 *R v Uxbridge Magistrates Court exp Adimi* [1999] 4 All ER 520 per Simon Brown LJ at 523.

189 Hathaway supra n3, 411.

190 Ibid.

191 *Saadi v UK* App 13229/03 29 January 2008; discussed in Chapter 5.

> The Contracting States shall not apply to the movements of such refugees restrictions other than those which are necessary and such restrictions shall only be applied until their status in the country is regularized or they obtain admission into another country. The Contracting States shall allow such refugees a reasonable period and all the necessary facilities to obtain admission into another country.

The definition of regularised stay is discussed at length by Hathaway and he concludes that 'regularisation' of status occurs once an applicant has met the host states requirements to have their refugee claim assessed. Thus there is a right of free movement once an asylum claim is formally lodged. At this point the asylum seeker is only subject to restrictions which are strictly 'necessary'. Once the refugee determination process is commenced, Article 26 of the Refugee Convention, guaranteeing freedom of movement, becomes the appropriate article. Article 31(2) thus enables provisional detention in order to verify the applicant's identity and circumstances. According to Hathaway's analysis, this will be 'for a few days' at most and cannot be relied on to justify punitive detention used to deter the arrival of more refugees.[192]

Some light was shed on the definition of regularised stay in *Saadi v UK*.[193] The applicants had immediately applied for asylum and had complied with formal reporting instructions. They were subsequently detained at a designated reception centre whilst their claims were processed. The state argued that the clear restriction on the applicants' liberty fell within the exception in Article 5(1)f of the ECHR, as it was preventing 'unauthorised entry'. The applicants had fully complied with the authorities, their removal was not imminent and they showed no risk of absconding. Yet the Grand Chamber of the ECtHR ruled that unauthorised entry included any entry that had not been expressly authorised by the state.[194]

Thus it would seem that detention for short periods can be justified purely on the basis that a person is seeking entry as an asylum applicant. It is difficult to reconcile the ECtHR's position with the non-penalization provision in the Refugee Convention, especially given the standard of detention facilities in some Member States and the lack of safeguards for vulnerable groups. The use of accommodation centres is now endorsed by the EU Reception Directive which also allows for housing and education within such centres.[195] A similar policy had been proposed in the UK in 2001 but was specifically rejected by teachers, refugee groups and ultimately the House of Lords who described it as exclusionary, isolationist and stigmatising.[196]

Whilst the use of detention may not constitute a violation of the right to liberty providing the safeguards identified by the ECtHR are complied with,

192 Hathaway supra n3, 420–425.

193 Supra n191.

194 Supra n191, para 74.

195 Article 10 Reception Directive, see discussion in Chapter 5.

196 HL Debates 9 October 2002 Col 352.

it can be regarded as another piece in the puzzle of post entry measures which may deprive the applicant of the protection they need. The EU's endorsement of administrative detention suggests that protection needs are secondary to administrative efficiency. It also reinforces the public impression linking asylum with criminality. The asylum story is usually long, complicated and multifaceted. It is not easily reducible to abbreviated procedures in the name of administrative efficiency.

Concluding Observations

The current international legal framework is still governed by the 1951 Refugee Convention and accompanying protocol. Most states abide by the Convention definition of a refugee and the majority have accepted some form of supplementary humanitarian protection. The prohibition of refoulement is the cornerstone of the Refugee Convention but in order to promote an enhanced understanding of its obligations it needs to be read in line with international human rights standards and affirmations from human rights agencies. Human rights law, at least for interactions with states that are members of the Council of Europe, appears to offer greater scope for refugee protection but McAdam cautions against dependence on general human rights as the sole method of advancing refugee protection.[197] The Refugee Convention continues to offer important *lex specialis* principles.

The effectiveness of the non-refoulement obligation is hampered by the absence of a legal obligation to admit asylum seekers into the state's territory. Further, the right of non-discrimination cannot be effectively advanced to argue a case compelling entry. This creates an unfortunate discontinuity in the protection regime, as Goodwin-Gill and McAdam note:

> there is no *necessary* connection between *non-refoulement* and admission or asylum … in international law, as well as national practice, the discretion to grant asylum and the obligation to abide by *non-refoulement* remain divided.[198]

The Common European Asylum System ('CEAS') offers an opportunity to ensure the Refugee Convention's continuing relevance, as evidenced by the broader coverage of the Qualification Directive.[199] Yet this opportunity is threatened by the influence of Member States who appear more concerned with ways to escape their obligations in a desire to reduce the number of irregular migrants. A closer inspection of asylum procedures, in Chapter 4, and reception conditions, in Chapter 5, will reveal an institutional endorsement of worst practice,

197 McAdam, J *Forced Migration, Human Rights and Security* (Hart 2008) 268, 280.

198 Goodwin-Gill and McAdam supra n59, 415.

199 Supra n35.

including deflection policies, burden-sharing, routine detention and abbreviated procedures.[200] The individuals' right to seek and enjoy asylum, as enshrined in the 1948 Declaration, is often forgotten in a debate governed by particularist concerns over finite resources, national security and economic migration.

200 Byrne et al supra n156, 6.

Chapter 3
The Development of a Common Asylum System

Introduction

Competence over asylum policy seems at first glance to have little association with the original founding freedoms of the European Community. Whilst policies on migration became a Community concern as long ago as 1974, such initiatives typically centred on ensuring free movement for European labour.

The Single European Act 1986 aimed to develop and consolidate the internal European market, requiring states to cooperate on policies involving the entry, movement and residence of third country nationals.[1] A cooperative framework enabled state sovereignty to prevail in decisions involving inward migration from beyond the Community.[2] At the same time, the Schengen Agreement had come into operation between five signatory states.[3] The reasons for these 'two parallel universes' of internal migration control are explored by Guild who identifies concerns over the impact on state sovereignty and a particular hostility towards Schengen from the UK prime minister, Margaret Thatcher.[4]

The following year saw the creation of the Ad Hoc Group for Migration, which was tasked with examining how unauthorised migration could be prevented in the Schengen environment'.[5] A platform was thus established, albeit formally outside European law, linking common border policies to the objective of preventing irregular migration. When the Schengen Convention of 1990 came into force in 1995, it effectively established a single external border for the Schengen area where immigration checks could be carried out in accordance with common

---

1 OJ L169 29 June 1987.

2 Jacobson, D *Rights across Borders* (Johns Hopkins Press 1996) 90.

3 The initial states were Belgium, France, Netherlands, Luxembourg and West Germany, *The Schengen Acquis – Agreement between the Governments of the States of the Benelux Economic Union, the Federal Republic of Germany and the French Republic on the Gradual Abolition of Checks at Their Common Borders* OJ L239, 22 September 2000.

4 Guild, E *Security and Migration in the 21st Century* (Polity 2009) 180. The UK has still refused to become part of Schengen cooperation despite its expansion to cover 26 states.

5 Chou, M-H 'The European Security Agenda and the "External Dimension" of EU Asylum and Migration Cooperation' (2009) 10 Perspectives on European Politics and Society 4, 546. The Schengen Cooperation Agreements and the Acquis formally became part of EU Law following the Treaty of Amsterdam in 1997: Monar, J 'Justice and Home Affairs in the Treaty of Amsterdam: Reform at the Price of Fragmentation' (1998) 23 EL Rev 320.

procedures.[6] Uniform rules regarding visas and checks at external borders were adopted to allow the free movement of persons within the signatory states. The Schengen acquis formally became part of EU law following the Treaty of Amsterdam 1997. Today there are 26 states in the European Economic Area covered by Schengen.[7] The Schengen Border Code is complemented by the 'Visa Information System' which enables Schengen states to share visa data, including fingerprints of third country nationals.[8]

By 1998 the European Commission had decided to establish a communication and consultation procedure on migration policies vis-à-vis non-EC countries.[9] But concern over irregular migration really intensified following the dismantling of internal frontiers resulting from the fall of the Berlin Wall in 1989.[10] Many writers identify this period as the beginning of a new securitised analysis of migration.[11] The movement of migration and asylum to the Justice and Home Affairs pillar of Community law following the Maastricht Treaty of 1992 provided, as Chou demonstrates, a 'legal basis' for a 'securitarian approach'.[12] Levy concurs citing the need for consensus based decision-making as a 'drive to agree at the lowest common denominator'.[13]

Following the Amsterdam Treaty of 1997, asylum and migration became communitised with their move to the Community pillar.[14] Communitarisation allowed the Commission and the Council to draft proposals on asylum policy for a transitional period of five years before the right transferred to the Commission.[15]

6 European Council *The Schengen Acquis*. As Referred to in Article 1(2) of Council Decision 1999/435/EC of 20 May 1999 OJ L 176 10 July 1999.

7 Covering an estimated 400 million people, Schengen includes all EU states excluding UK, Ireland, Romania and Bulgaria whilst including Norway, Liechtenstein and Switzerland.

8 Reg 562/2006 of the European Parliament and of the Council of 15 March 2006 *Establishing a Community Code on the Rules Governing the Movement of Persons across Borders (Schengen Borders Code)* [2006] OJ 105/1; Reg 767/2008 of the European Parliament and of the Council of 9 July 2008 *Concerning the Visa Information System (VIS) and the Exchange of Data Between Member States on Short-Stay Visas (VIS Regulation)* OJ L218/60.

9 European Commission Decision of July 8 1985 *Setting up a Prior Communication and Consultation Procedure on Migration Policies in Relation to Non-Member Countries Brussels: Commission of the European Communities* 88/384/EEC, OJ L183, 14 July 1988 P0035–0036.

10 Byrne, R; Noll, G and Vedsted-Hansen, J *New Asylum Countries: Migration Control and Refugee Protection in an Enlarged European Union* (Kluwer 2002) ch 1; Guild supra n4, 8.

11 Guild supra n4, 7 and Huysmans, J *The Politics of Insecurity: Fear, Immigration and Asylum in the EU* (Routledge 2006) 16.

12 Chou supra n5.

13 Levy, C 'The European Union After 9/11: The Demise of a Liberal Democratic Asylum Regime?' (2005) 40 Government and Opposition 1, 26.

14 *Consolidated Treaty Establishing the European Community* 1997 OJ C 340 10 November 2007 'Amsterdam Treaty'.

15 Article 73o Amsterdam Treaty.

The Court of Justice of the EU ('CJEU') gained competence to rule on asylum provisions as regards their interpretation in the treaty and on the validity or interpretation of acts of the institutions of the Community, following references made from the final courts of appeal in each Member State.[16] Nevertheless, many states continued to regard migration control as primarily a matter of state sovereignty, thus European policies on immigration and asylum suffered from 'dual fragmentation'.[17] Referring to the veto and the variety of formal opt-outs which hampered harmonisation, along with the absence of legally binding commitments, Noll described the field as 'engulfed in a strait-jacket of intergovernmental decision-making'.[18]

The Treaty on the Functioning of the EU has simplified this position whilst increasing the opportunity for accountability.[19] Judicial oversight has been strengthened and the European Parliament is given a central role in asylum law-making as the ordinary legislative procedure now encompasses asylum matters.[20] Asylum is recognised as a subject of shared competencies under Article 4(2)j. Article 78 of the TFEU requires the adoption of a uniform status for individuals having been granted international protection, uniform standards on procedures and reception conditions as well as a common system of temporary protection. As *lex specialis*, Article 78 paved the way for the final stage of harmonisation, moving beyond minimum standards towards common procedures.

A further significant development arising from the TFEU is the legally binding status of the EU Charter of Fundamental Rights which contains both a right to asylum and the prohibition of refoulement.[21] Although the obligations of the Charter are applied only to EU institutions, the inclusion of these rights is very significant.

It has been widely predicted that the subtle transfer of power between the institutions following the TEFU will lead to greater advancements in refugee protection. The reduced legislative role for the Council should mean that the particularist interests of Member States, which dominated migration policy in the early stages, should now be balanced with the interests of the European Parliament.[22]

---

16 Article 73p Amsterdam Treaty.

17 Noll, G *Negotiating Asylum: The EU Acquis, Extraterritorial Protection and the Common Market of Deflection* (M Nijhoff 2000) 594.

18 Ibid.

19 *Consolidated Version of the Treaty on the Functioning of the EU* 30 March 2010 OJ C 83/47 'TFEU'.

20 For further discussion, see Peers, S 'Legislative Update: E Immigration and Asylum Competence and Decision-Making after the Treaty of Lisbon' (2008) 10 Eur J Migration & L 219.

21 Article 18 and Article 19 respectively, *EU Charter of Fundamental Rights* C 364/1 OJ 18 December 2000.

22 Kaunert, C and Léonard, S 'The Development of the EU Asylum Policy: Venue-Shopping in Perspective' (2012) 19 Journal of Eur Public Policy 9, 1406; Morano-Foadi, S and Andreadakis, S 'The Convergence of the European Legal System in the Treatment

Yet the sovereignty of Member States on fundamental territorial questions of entry and expulsion (at least in the case of non-EEA nationals) remains dominant.[23] So why has an organisation with a central emphasis on economic union become so immersed in developing common standards for asylum seekers? The answer to this question is central to understanding the priorities of European asylum policy and to an appreciation of that policy's limitations.

The Origins of the Common European Asylum System

In 1999 the European Council's Tampere milestones included a commitment to the Refugee Convention and international human rights standards by reaffirming the fundamental right to seek asylum:

> 4. The aim is an open and secure European Union, fully committed to the obligations of the Geneva Refugee Convention and other relevant human rights instruments, and able to respond to humanitarian needs on the basis of solidarity. A common approach must also be developed to ensure the integration into our societies of those third country nationals who are lawfully resident in the Union.[24]

Thus the desire for a common asylum system thus appears founded on justice, fairness and solidarity. The objective of providing a common standard and uniform system throughout Europe, including the pooling of resources and information, should enable fairness whilst simultaneously reducing inefficiency. The international humanitarian standards were considered by the Council to be central to the common approach delineated in Tampere.

Yet at the same time there is an acknowledgement of the need to control external borders in order to prevent illegal immigration and combat international crime.[25] It is regrettable but not unusual to see asylum and illegal immigration linked together in this way. Unfortunately, the illegal migration agenda has come to dominate the CEAS as asylum is viewed narrowly as a matter of immigration control and, perhaps more fundamentally, as a security concern. The need to combat terrorism became a central task of the common policy by the time it began

---

of Third Country Nationals in Europe: the ECJ and ECtHR Jurisprudence' (2011) 22 Eur J Intl L 4, 1971.

23 European Council *The Hague Programme, Strengthening Security and Justice in the European Union* 16054/04 (Council of the European Union 2004) para 3 January 4.

24 European Parliament *Presidency Conclusions Tampere European Council* 15 and 16 October 1999, para 4. Available at: http://www.europarl.europa.eu/summits/tam_en.htms-tc (accessed 11 November 2012).

25 Ibid, para 3.

its second phase with The Hague programme in 2004.[26] Consequently a range of surveillance and interception strategies have been introduced with the primary aim of controlling irregular migration.[27] For many, this development constitutes an 'inexorable move away from liberal values'.[28] At the same time, the external dimension of EU migration policy has developed since The Hague programme, so that third countries are co-opted into migration management.[29]

It is alleged that the promises of Tampere have not been realised as progress in the fight against illegal migration has been far greater than progress towards meeting protection needs. The European Council meeting in Seville in 2002 focused more on asylum abuse and the following Thessaloniki Council continued this theme by floating an accelerated procedure for certain applications.[30] A raft of Community legislation has since been introduced with a drive towards basic, minimum standards rather than enhanced protection. The former UN High Commissioner for Refugees, Ruud Lubbers, has argued that many of these measures actually increase the chance of refoulement, a view shared by the European Council for Refugees and Exiles.[31] The conflation of asylum and immigration enables increasingly restrictive asylum policies to form part of the fight against irregular migration, inevitably diluting protection. Stevens concludes that the focus of the European Member States and the Community as a whole is around deterrence, exclusion and security. Human rights commitments are then subsumed into bland statements of principle.[32]

---

26 Bendel, P 'Everything under Control? The EU's Policies and Politics of Immigration' in Faist, T and Ette, A (eds) *The Europeanisation of National Policies and Politics of Immigration* (Palgrave Macmillan 2007) 32; Hurwitz, A *The Collective Responsibility of States to Protect Refugees* (OUP 2009) 41. For the Commission's actions pursuant to The Hague Programme see Peers, S *EU Justice and Home Affairs Law* (OUP 2011) 304.

27 Mitsilegas, V 'Border Security in the EU' in Baldaccini, A; Guild, E and Toner, H (eds) *Whose Freedom, Security and Justice? EU Immigration and Asylum Law and Policy* (Hart 2007) 358.

28 Stevens, D 'Asylum Seekers in the New Europe: Time for a Re-Think?' in Shah, P (ed) *The Challenge of Asylum to Legal Systems* (Cavendish 2005) 30; See also Chou supra n5, 548.

29 Baldaccini, A 'The External Dimension of the EU's Asylum and Immigration policies: Old Concerns and New Approaches' in Baldaccini et al supra n27, 283. For further discussion see Chapter 6.

30 Seville European Council 21 and 22 June 2002; Presidency Conclusions, Brussels 24 October 2002 13463/02; Thessaloniki European Council 19 and 20 June 2003 Presidency Conclusions, Brussels 1 October 2003 11638/03.

31 Lubbers, R 'Lubbers Calls for EU Asylum Laws Not to Contravene International Law' (UNHCR Press Release 29.2004). Available at: http://www.unhcr.org/40645bd77.html; European Council for Refugees and Exiles *Broken Promises: Forgotten Principles* (ECRE 2004).

32 Stevens supra n28, 32.

The Development of a Control Industry

A range of initiatives have been introduced to control irregular migration which impact on the right to seek asylum and the non-refoulement obligation. The European security industry appears to be a self-generating industry with enormous resources and minimal accountability. A bewildering array of migration management measures now exist.[33] Their effectiveness is crudely measured in terms of numerical reductions in irregular migration. Not only does this present a false picture, which conveniently ignores the range of factors which contribute to migration flows, it also clumsily lumps protection seekers into the migration-security paradigm.

EURODAC

The EURODAC database enables fingerprints and data to be shared to enable the effective operation of the Dublin Regulation which involves the transfer of asylum seekers to the first country of arrival in the EU.[34] The rationale for Dublin, discussed further in Chapter 4, is based on the notion that asylum seekers should claim asylum in the first safe country of arrival. The EURODAC is thus intended to identify applicants who have engaged in secondary migration by crossing into another EU state.

The annual cost of EURODAC doubled between 2009 and 2010 to over €2 million whilst the number of successful transactions actually decreased by 15 per cent to just under 300,000 cases (only 11,156 of these cases involved irregular crossing of an external border).[35] The statistics clearly indicate that around half of the irregular border crossers who make a subsequent asylum claim, do so in the same Member State.[36] Interestingly, the limited success of EURODAC has been to demonstrate some of the misconceptions underpinning the Dublin Regulation.

In June 2012, the European Commission revisited earlier proposals to allow law enforcement officers to access the database for the purpose of combating

33 Mitsilegas supra n27.

34 Council Regulation No 2725/2000 of 11 December 2000 *Concerning the Establishment of 'EURODAC' for the Comparison of Fingerprints for the Effective Application of the Dublin Convention.* OJ L 316, 15 December 2000 P. 0001 – 0010. A new regulation has recently been enacted which will come into force on 20 July 2015 Reg No 603/2013 of *The European Parliament and of the Council of 26 June 2013 on the Establishment of 'EURODAC' for the Comparison of Fingerprints for the Effective Application of Regulation (EU) No 604/2013* L180/1 29 June 2013.

35 European Commission *Annual Report to the Parliament and the Council on the Activities of the EURODAC Central Unit in 2010* Brussels COM (2011) 549 final Brussels 12 September 2011.

36 Peers, supra n26, 365.

terrorism and other serious offences.[37] The new regulation which comes into force in 2015 makes specific provision for the exchange of EURODAC data with law enforcement officials from Member States and Europol.[38] There is a clear cost-cutting motivation behind the proposal but this is at the expense of further reinforcing a link between asylum and criminality. Concerns have also been raised that the sharing of data could compromise the safety of asylum seekers and effectively undermine the right to seek asylum, particularly if the data is shared with third countries.

Frontex

On the 26 October 2004 the European Agency for the Management of Operational Cooperation at the External Borders of the Member States of the EU (Frontex) was established by a Council regulation pursuant to Articles 62(2)a and 66 of the Treaty of the European Community.[39] The operations of Frontex are confined to the external borders of the Schengen area of 26 states. The purpose of the agency is to support the border control of Schengen states, particularly on the external border, so that they can control their borders more effectively in order to prevent illegal entry and cross-border crime.[40] The Agency's main tasks are to coordinate operational cooperation between Member States in the management of external borders; assist them in circumstances requiring increased technical and operational assistance at external borders; and provide them with the necessary support in organising joint return operations.[41] A rapid crisis response service is also available

---

37 European Commission *Amended Proposal for a Regulation of the European Parliament and of the Council on the Establishment of 'EURODAC' for the Comparison of Fingerprints for the Effective Application of Regulation (EU) No [… /…] (Establishing the Criteria and Mechanisms for Determining the Member State Responsible for Examining an Application for International Protection Lodged in One of the Member States by a Third-Country National or a Stateless Person) and to Request Comparisons with EURODAC Data by Member States' Law Enforcement Authorities and Europol for Law Enforcement Purposes and Amending Regulation (EU) No 1077/2011 Establishing a European Agency for the Operational Management OF Large-Scale IT Systems in the Area of Freedom, Security and Justice (Recast Version)* Brussels, 30 May 2012 COM(2012) 254 final 2008/0242 (COD).

38 Supra n34, Art 1(2).

39 Council Regulation (EC) No 2007/2004 of 26 October 2004 *Establishing a European Agency for the Management of Operational Cooperation at the External Borders of the Member States of the European Union* OJ L 349, 25 November 2004, p. 1; prior to this the Spanish government had invested heavily in SIVE = an Integrated System of External Vigilance along the coastline of the Canary Islands and Andalusia. Carling, J notes that it cost €1,800 for every migrant intercepted: 'Unauthorized Migration from Africa to Spain' (2007) 35 J Intl Migration 4, 3–37.

40 For further info see: http://frontex.europa.eu/about/origin.

41 Supra n39 at Article 2(1).

to Member States through RABIT (Rapid Border Intervention Teams). Frontex operations have been mounted at the behest of Spain, Malta and Italy to assist in operations off the African coast. The agency's budget for sea operations in 2009 was €34.4 million, representing well over half its allocated funding.[42]

Frontex operates in a grey area of migration control where there are no clearly demarcated national borders. Goodwin-Gill argues that the flexibility of these frontiers enables 'States to project a non-territorial conception of national interests into a common or even a contested space'.[43] Whilst a simple analysis suggests that Frontex operations have been successful in reducing illegal migration, their operations remain shrouded in secrecy and there have been repeated allegations that the principle of non-refoulement is not fully respected.[44] Estimates suggest that prior to the Italian coastguard's push-back operation, around 75 per cent of migrants arriving by sea applied for asylum of which approximately half were granted some form of protection.[45] These points were explored by the ECtHR in the *Hirsi* judgement which reveals worrying protection gaps between the various state actors and the agency.[46]

As a non-state actor and an EU agency, Frontex has previously argued that its operations were the primary responsibility of individual states. However, its extended remit now requires full compliance with the relevant Union law, including the Charter of Fundamental Rights, international law, including the Refugee Convention, and obligations related to international protection, in particular the principle of non-refoulement, and fundamental rights.[47] In terms of interception at sea by officers of the Agency, the principle of non-refoulement is key:

> 1b. In accordance with Union and international law, no person shall be disembarked in, or otherwise handed over to the authorities of, a country in contravention of the principle of non-refoulement, or from which there is a risk

---

42 Frontex Programme of Work 2010, Warsaw p11. Available at: http://frontex.europa.eu/gfx/frontex/files/justyna/pow2010.pdf.

43 Goodwin-Gill, G 'The Right to Seek Asylum: Interception at Sea and the Principle of Non-Refoulement' in Jesuit Refugee Service *Safe and Secure: How Do Refugees Experience Europe's Borders?* (JRS-Europe 2011) 8.

44 Goodwin-Gill ibid at 14; see Joint Operation Hera discussed by Marin, L 'Policing the EU's External Borders: A Challenge for the Rules of Law and Fundamental Rights in the Area of Freedom, Security and Justice? An Analysis of Frontex Joint Operations at the Southern Maritime Border' (2011) 7 J of Contemporary Eur Research 4, 468 and Moreno-Lax, V 'Seeking Asylum in the Mediterranean: Against a Fragmentary Reading of EU Member Sates' Obligations Accruing at Sea' (2011) 23 Int J Refugee Law 174; O'Dowd, J 'Mutual Recognition in European Immigration Policy' in Goudappel, F and Raulus, H *The Future of Asylum in the European Union* (TMC Asser 2011)73.

45 Jesuit Refugee Service Malta 'Do They Know? Asylum Seekers Testify to Life in Libya' (JRS December 2009) 19.

46 *Hirsi Jamaa and Others v Italy* App no. 27765/09.

47 Article 1 supra n39 as amended by Regulation 1168/2011.

> of expulsion or return to another country in contravention of that principle. The special needs of children, victims of trafficking, persons in need of medical assistance, persons in need of international protection and other vulnerable persons shall be addressed in accordance with Union and international law.[48]

Members of the European Border Guard are similarly required to respect fundamental human rights, including access to asylum procedures.[49] The Agency was tasked with developing a code of practice for the return of illegally present third country nationals, assuring that return will be undertaken in a humane manner and in full respect for fundamental rights; in particular the principles of human dignity, the prohibition of torture and inhuman or degrading treatment or punishment, the right to liberty and security, the right to the protection of personal data and non-discrimination. Yet these commitments appear to lack any genuine safeguards, such as independent monitoring. The Consultative Forum which was established following negotiations between Council and Parliament in 2011 is supposed to develop these safeguards but concerns have been expressed over the lack of independent oversight.[50] A Fundamental Rights Officer was appointed by the Management Board in September 2012 and will report to both the Management Board and the Consultative Forum, but there will be no reference to the European Parliament as initially proposed.[51] It remains to be seen what influence the Consultative Forum will have, given it will only have access to information the Management Board has agreed to transmit. Whilst the code of conduct makes explicit reference to the principle of non-refoulement,[52] the code's non-binding nature is a source of significant concern.[53] It is difficult to disagree with the conclusions of the independent monitoring group, Statewatch, who describe the fundamental rights strategy as mere 'window-dressing'.[54]

These concerns were borne out by the request for Frontex assistance from the Italian government following the arrival of several Tunisians on the Italian island of Lampedusa during the 2011 uprising.[55] The Government also sought to deploy

---

48 Article 2(1)b ibid.

49 Article 3b(4) ibid.

50 Office for the High Commissioner on Human Rights, UN 'Crossing Borders: For Millions of People on the Move, Borders Can Be a Dangerous Space' April 2012.

51 Statewatch News 'A Drop of Fundamental Rights in an Ocean of Unaccountability: Frontex in the Process of Implementing Article 26(a)' (15 May 2012). Available at: http://www.statewatch.org/news/2012/may/02-eu-frontex-article26a.html (accessed 3 July 2012).

52 Frontex (2011) Code of Conduct for All Persons Participating in Frontex Activities. Available at: http://frontex.europa.eu/assets/Publications/General/Frontex_Code_of_Conduct.pdf (accessed 20 March 2013).

53 Ibid.

54 Frontex Fundamental Rights Strategy 31 March 2011. Available at: http://www.statewatch.org/observatories_files/frontex_observatory/2011-03-31-frontex-fundamental-rights-strategy.pdf.

55 BBC News 'Tunisia Migrants Prompt Italy "Humanitarian Emergency"' (12 February 2011). Available at: http://www.bbc.co.uk/news/world-europe-12441613

Italian police in Tunisia to prevent departures, alleging that many were terrorists and criminals attempting to use the cover of the uprising to enter Europe.[56] Operation Hermes ran from February to August 2011 as a response to these requests for urgent action, the mandate being to assist in managing the arrivals and, where necessary, to identify claims for international protection.[57]

As it stands the European Parliament have continued to challenge and contest the extension of Frontex powers. The European Council's decision to amend the Schengen Border Code, prioritising disembarkation in the third country from which vessels had departed, drew particular criticism.[58] As a result of the amendment, Malta withdrew its support from Frontex on the basis that, should disembarkation in the third country prove problematic, the decision will require the host state to allow disembarkation.[59]

In April 2012, the CJEU's General Advocate, Paulo Mengozzi,[60] recommended annulment of the Council decision.[61] The CJEU agreed, ruling that the 'comitology' procedure which led to the adoption of the decision, was not suitable when significant and controversial changes were being enacted which would consequently extend Frontex and its powers of border control. Had the decision been enacted using the ordinary legislative procedure, the Parliament would have had greater opportunity to debate and amend the decision. Advocate Mengozzi acknowledged that the procedure had been adopted precisely because of disagreements between Member States as to the application of non-refoulement in extra-territorial operations.[62] As a result, Frontex is now left with non-binding

(accessed 20 March 2013).

56 BBC News 'Tunisia Rejects Italian Call to Send Immigration Police' (14 February 2011). Available at: http://www.bbc.co.uk/news/world-europe-12445008 (accessed 20 March 2013).

57 Martin, M 'The Arab Spring and the Death Toll in the Mediterranean: The True Face of Fortress Europe' (Statewatch Analysis, January 2012). Available at: http://www.statewatch.org/analyses/no-167-arab-spring-med.pdf (accessed 20 March 2013).

58 Council Decision 2010/252/EU of 26 April 2010 *Supplementing the Schengen Borders Code as Regards the Surveillance of the Sea External Borders in the Context of Operational Cooperation Coordinated by* [*FRONTEX*] OJ 2010 L 111, Part II, 2.1.

59 *The Sunday Times*, Malta 'No Frontex Mission around Malta' (15 May 2011). Available at: http://www.timesofmalta.com/articles/view/20110515/local/No-Frontex-mission-around-Malta.365397 (accessed 18 January 2012).

60 Opinion of Advocate General Mengozzi 17 April 2012 Case C-335/10 *European Parliament v Council of the European Union* Available at: http://curia.europa.eu/juris/document/document.jsf?text=&docid=121662&pageIndex=0&doclang=en&mode=lst&dir=&occ=first&part=1&cid=14821312 http://register.consilium.europa.eu/pdf (accessed 6 November 2012).

61 Supra n58; Reg 562/2006 of the European Parliament and of the Council of 15 March 2006 *Establishing a Community Code on the Rules Governing the Movement of Persons across Borders (Schengen Borders Code)* [2006]OJ 105/1.

62 Ibid, para 64.

texts and guidelines on the fundamental rights aspects of its border control and surveillance activities.[63] It seems likely that a new Council decision would need to be negotiated using the correct legislative procedure, enabling renewed debate over Frontex's sea operations and the Agency's responsibilities and accountability; questions left largely unaddressed by its original mandate.[64]

EUROSUR

Since 2008 the Commission has been examining mechanisms to improve European border surveillance.[65] The impetus to accelerate the plans came during the Arab Spring of 2011 when concerns about an exodus of migrants form North Africa prompted the Council to commence pilots of a new surveillance system.[66] EUROSUR establishes an information sharing and cooperation mechanism which will enable Member States to collaborate with Frontex at tactical, operational and strategic levels. Together with plans to introduce smart borders it has been described by the Heinrich Böll Foundation as the 'EU's cynical response to the Arab Spring'.[67] The emphasis again is on security and prevention through increasing use of extensive technology, including satellite drones.

Although the Commission has stressed one of the important EUROSUR objectives to be 'saving lives at sea' there does not appear to be any clear proposals on how this objective can be met. At present there is no strategy on how to intervene and assist in such situations, prompting allegations of cynicism from Green MEP, Ska Keller.[68] Keller identifies four problematic key trends in the proposals: the use of more joint European efforts, such as the strengthening of Frontex so that it becomes much more than a coordinating body; externalisation through the observation of territory outside the EU and cooperation with third countries, including readmission agreements; the increased use and reliance on technology, particularly through smart borders and; finally, the increasing use of

---

63 *European Parliament v Council of the European Union*. Case C-355/10 Judgment of the Court (Grand Chamber) of 5 September 2012 unpublished; COM (2012) 686 Final Report from the Commission to the European Parliament and the Council Second Biannual Report on the Functioning of the Schengen Area 1 May 2012 – 31 October 2012 Brussels, 23 November 2012.

64 Peers, S 'The Frontex Regulation – Consolidated Text After 2011 Amendments' (Statewatch). Available at: http://www.statewatch.org/analyses/no-140-frontex-reg-text.pdf.

65 Communication of 13 February 2008 from the Commission to the European Parliament, the Council, the European Economic and Social Committee and the Committee of the Regions: *Examining the Creation of a European Border Surveillance System* (EUROSUR) COM (2008) 68 final.

66 Current pilots operate in France, Spain, Italy, Poland, Slovakia and Finland.

67 Hayes, B and Vermeulen, M *Borderline: The EU's New Border Surveillance Initiatives* (Heinrich Böll Foundation June 2012).

68 EUROSUR Questioned in the European Parliament, ECRE Weekly Bulletin 29 June 2012.

databases which poses a risk to individual privacy (as discussed above).[69] Whilst the technology and the tools may be ready, the precise purpose of EUROSUR has still to be clearly defined. There are genuine concerns over the militarisation of a humanitarian need, as evidenced by the dominance of the technology and surveillance industries in the EUROSUR discussions.[70]

The predicted financial costs are unsurprisingly enormous, ranging from the Commission's conservative estimate of €388 million to the €837 million predicted by the Heinrich Böll study.[71] None of these costs relate to the identification and processing of asylum claims. The humanitarian dimension is dwarfed by the security objectives as the Commission's own press release makes very clear.[72] Cross-border crime is now given the same status as illegal immigration, further endorsing the self-reinforcing securitisation approach which emphasises the criminality of irregular migration.[73]

Lessons in Unintended Consequences

The Virtual Fence

Even leaving aside these humanitarian deficiencies, there remain significant flaws arising from the over-reliance on technology, coupled with the absence of accountability and transparency that such reliance typically engenders. This is another example of self-generating, crisis management which has not been fully thought out. Lessons could have been learnt from the American 'virtual fence' initiative which attempted to monitor both Northern and Southern borders at an estimated cost of $3.7 billion. It was abandoned in 2010, four years after it commenced, having failed to meet cost effectiveness and viability standards.[74] The initiative was beset by operational and organisational problems, including uncertainty as to how the technology would be delivered and utilised in a climate

69 European Parliament, Green group 26 June 2012. Discussion available at: http://greenmediabox.eu/archive/2012/06/26/migration/20120626_migration_en.mp4Lavenex.

70 Keller, S ibid; Hayes supra n67.

71 Supra n67, 8.

72 European Commission 'EUROSUR: Providing authorities with tools needed to reinforce management of external borders and fight cross-border crime' Memo 11/896 12 December 2011. Available at: http://europa.eu/rapid/pressReleasesAction.do?reference=MEMO/11/896&type=HTML (accessed 20 March 2013).

73 AEDH, Association Européenne pour la défense des Droits de l'Homme (Press Release, 20 June 2012).

74 Stana, R 'Testimony before the Subcommittee on Border and Maritime Security, Committee on Homeland Security, House of Representatives' (Border Security Preliminary Observations on the Status of Key Southwest Border Technology Programs, US Government Accountability Office GAO-11-448T). Available at: http://www.gao.gov/products/GAO-11-448T (accessed 7 November 2012).

of contradictory objectives. The US model also serves as a prescient reminder of the symbiotic relationship between policing and smuggling. As Andreas observes 'this is a story about how the state has helped make smuggling and how smuggling has helped to (re)make the policing apparatus of the state'.[75] The US Immigration and Naturalisation Service operates a 'prevention through deterrence' strategy which requires more physical barriers, surveillance equipment, legal sanctions and law enforcement agents to prevent illegal entry. Its financial costs are enormous yet its success has been negligible.[76] Far from causing a decrease in illegal entry, the policy has simply led smugglers to adopt more dangerous modes of travel in order to avoid detection.[77]

The unintended consequences and counter-productive effects of border strengthening in North Africa have included the diversification of migration routes as well as the professionalisation of smuggling.[78] In addition, there is a consequential negative effect on internal affairs, as evidenced by a rise in racism and xenophobia towards sub-Saharan migrants in many North African states.[79]

The management of European migration is being handed to agencies with limited accountability and enormous budgets. It is difficult to imagine a way back should these agencies fail in their objectives. Once the EUROSUR framework has been properly established, the system may be extended from the southern and eastern borders to all Schengen states with external land and maritime borders.[80]

Towards 'Smart' Borders

A common EUROSUR operation is expected to cover the Schengen region by the end of 2013. The introduction of the Visa Information System in 2012 allows for the sharing of visa data and fingerprints between the Schengen states.[81] Guild argues

75 Andreas, P 'The Transformation of Migrant Smuggling across the US-Mexican Border' in Kyle, D and Koslowoski, R (eds) *Global Human Smuggling: Comparative Perspectives* (Johns Hopkins UP 2001) 108.

76 The INS spent $877million on border enforcement in 1998 (double the amount spent five years earlier), Andreas ibid 113.

77 Andreas supra n75, 122; Koslowski, R 'The Mobility Money Can Buy: Human Smuggling and Border Control in the EU' in Andreas and Snyder (eds) *The Wall Around the West* (Rowman & Littlefield 2000) 205; Morehouse, C and Blomfield, M 'Irregular Migration in Europe' (Migration Policy Institute 2011).

78 De Haas, H 'The Myth of Invasion: The Inconvenient Realities of African Migration to Europe' 2008 29 3rd World Q, 1311; *Irregular Migration from West Africa to the Maghreb and the European Union* (International Organisation for Migration 2008).

79 Ibid.

80 European Commission Staff Working Paper *Determining the Technical and Operational Framework of the European Border Surveillance System (EUROSUR) and the Actions to Be Taken for Its Establishment* Brussels, 28 January 2011 SEC(2011) 145 final.

81 Reg (EC) No 767/2008 *Concerning the Visa Information System and the Exchange of Data Between Member States on Short-Stay Visas* L 218/74; European Commission

that the Schengen arrangements effectively divide the world's population into two groups; those inside the borders of the EU and those outside.[82] In the case of the latter, most will require a visa to enter the EU for a three-month stay.[83] In addition, the European Commission's Smart Borders plan aims to efficiently process all third country nationals, at an estimated cost of €1.1 billion. The Commission notes that the EU27 ordered 540,000 persons to leave the EU in 2010 but only 226,000 of these orders were actually carried out. Smart Borders will therefore supplement the VIS by including an entry-exit system (ESS) to identify over-stayers. This will necessitate a centralised European database containing biometric data of all third country nationals entering the Schengen countries. A registered traveller programme (RTP) is also proposed which will enable pre-vetting of travellers to enable faster entry.[84] The EU Agency for Large Scale IT systems, established in December 2012 is tasked with coordinating these systems.

These developments present a costly and complex system of border technology. There is inevitably a significant risk that important decisions on fundamental rights will be lost in this new technocratic order. Democratic accountability is certainly endangered by the allocation of considerable powers to the technology and security industries. The Commission's objective is to improve border efficiency as well as security, yet experience with similar technology elsewhere gives little cause for optimism in this respect.

Lessons could be learnt from the UK's own £1.2 billion e-borders programme which failed to generate cost effectiveness or operational efficiency, leading to long queues at borders, confusion amongst passengers and frustration amongst border staff.[85] In 2005 iris scanners were introduced to improve security only to be scrapped five years later at a cost to the taxpayer of £9 million. The Chair of the House of Commons' Parliamentary Select Committee, Keith Vaz MP, observed the dangers of introducing technology that has not been properly tested, noting that £750 million had been wasted over e-borders and £9.1 million on unreliable iris scanners.[86]

Communication from the Commission to the European Parliament and the Council *Smart Borders – Options and the Way Ahead* Brussels 25 October 2011 COM (2011) 680 final.

82 Guild supra n4 181.

83 The blacklist includes almost all of Africa, the Middle-East (excluding Israel), non-EU Europe and Asia (excluding Japan).

84 European Commission 'EU 'Smart Borders': Commission Wants Easier Access and Enhanced Security' Press Release Ip/11/1234, 25 October 2011.

85 In May 2012 a computer problem caused by the sheer volume of biometric residence permits needing to be processed led to further criticism of the UK Borders Agency. Travis, A 'UK Border Agency computer failure leaves thousands unable to travel' *The Guardian* (3 May 2012); Mitsilegas supra n27, 386.

86 Home Affairs Select Committee Adhoc Meeting 'The Work of the UK Border Agency and UK Border Force' (May 15 2012). Available at: http://www.parliamentlive.tv/Main/Player.aspx?meetingId=10786&st=12:36:20 (accessed on 16 July 2012).

It is to be hoped that the European Commission will await a full analysis of the cost effectiveness of the SIS (Schengen Information System) before investing heavily in further technology. SIS is effectively a computerised blacklist of undesirables within the European Union which enables the collation of information from law enforcement agencies and border guards on cross-border crime.[87] The SIS framework's combination of policing and immigration control poses some particular difficulties for the EU following the Treaty of Amsterdam when the Schengen acquis became formally part of EU law. Now in its second phase, SIS has been subject to considerable delays as national systems are aligned with the SIS architecture.[88] The Commission has reported that the total budgetary commitments for the Schengen II architecture amount to more than €135 million.[89] For those outside Schengen who seek access to the information, such as the UK, the initial cost is estimated to be well above £40 million in addition to recurrent running costs.[90]

It will be obvious to anyone reading that the range of overlapping, technological solutions to aspirations of human need is remarkable in its complexity and its costs. It is difficult to see how such measures can be justified in terms of the numbers of irregular migrants or the security threats posed by such migration. Yet it is these factors which continue to dominate the debate. Whether EU citizens become more secure in the presence of greater security initiatives is doubtful.[91]

The Legal Base for Enhanced Protection

Article 63 of the European Community Treaty, introduced in the Treaty of Amsterdam, conferred extensive powers on the Council to adopt measures on

87 Communication from the Commission to the European Parliament and the Council: Development of the Schengen Information System II COM(2001) 720 final; Regulation (EC) No 1987/2006 *of the European Parliament and of the Council of 20 December 2006 on the Establishment, Operation and Use of the Second-Generation Schengen Information System* (SIS II) 2006; Van Helden, WJ; Van Dorst, PC and Hendriksen, KE 'No Entry: Investigation of the Registration of Foreign Nationals in the Schengen Information System and the Provision of Information in this Connection' Report no. 2010/115 17 June 2010, National Ombudsman Netherlands.

88 For a full analysis of the SIS II see Peers, S 'Key Legislative Developments on Migration in the EU: SIS II' (2008) 10 EJML 77; House of Lords EU Select Committee 'Schengen Information System II' 9th Report 2006-07 HL Paper No 49 (HMSO 2007).

89 COM (2011) 907 final, 8.

90 House of Lords supra n88, para 33.

91 Huysmans, supra n11; Bigo, D 'When Two Become One: Internal and External Securitisations in Europe' in Kelstrup, MW and Williams, M (eds) *International Relations Theory and the Politics of European Integration: Power, Security and Community* (Routledge 2000) 171; Bigo, D and Guild, E (eds) *Controlling Frontiers: Free Movement into and within Europe* (Ashgate 2005).

asylum and refugee protection in accordance with international obligations. These were originally conceived as minimum standards. A series of legislative measures were introduced pursuant to the Treaty of Amsterdam, including a regulation for an EU fingerprint database,[92] a directive on temporary protection in cases of mass influx,[93] a reception conditions directive,[94] a regulation concerning the transfer of asylum seekers to safe European states[95] and the Refugee Qualification Directive.[96] Yet the number of exceptions and opportunities for flexible interpretation resulted in a 'legal framework of unprecedented complexity and opacity'.[97] A common European asylum policy was more aspiration than reality in the presence of differential protection systems and widely divergent recognition rates.

The original asylum directives attracted criticism from the UNHCR and have been described by the European Council on Refugees and Exiles as 'gravely flawed'.[98] The unanimity procedure under the Amsterdam Treaty, in a framework of minimum standards, combined to afford considerable influence to those states advocating greater restriction.[99] Significant differences in the number of asylum applications across Europe contributed to an atmosphere of competition between states.[100] A common perception that favourable welfare packages are particularly

92 Council Regulation (EC) No 2725/2000 of 11 December 2000 *Concerning the Establishment of 'EURODAC' for the Comparison of Fingerprints for the Effective Application of the Dublin Convention* OJ L316, 15/12/2000 P. 0001–0010.

93 Council Directive 2001/55/EC of 20 July 2001 *On Minimum Standards for Giving Temporary Protection in the Event of a Mass Influx of Displaced Persons and on Measures Promoting a Balance of Efforts between the Member States in Receiving Such Persons and Bearing the Consequences of Receiving* OJ L212, 07/08/2001 P. 0012–0023.

94 Council Directive 2003/9/EC of 27 January 2003 *Laying Down Minimum Standards for the Reception of Applicants for Asylum in Member States* OJ L 31, 6 February 2003, P. 18–25 'Reception Directive'.

95 Council Regulation 343/2003 of 18 February 2003 *Establishing the Criteria and Mechanisms for Determining the Member state Responsible for Examining an Asylum Application Lodged in One of the Member States by Third-Country Nationals* OJ L 50 25 February 2003 P1–10 'Dublin II Regulation'.

96 Council Directive 2004/83/EC of 29 April 2004 *On Minimum Standards for the Qualification and Status of Third Country Nationals or Stateless Persons as Refugees or as Persons Who Otherwise Need International Protection and the Content of the Protection Granted* OJ L304, 30/09/2004 P. 0012–0023 'Qualification Directive'.

97 Hurwitz supra n26, 39.

98 ECRE *Broken Promises – Forgotten Principles* (ECRE 2004); Stevens supra n28, 28.

99 Baldaccini, A and Toner, H 'From Amsterdam and Tampere to The Hague: An Overview of Five Years of EC Immigration and Asylum Law' in Baldaccini et al supra n27, 1.

100 European Commission '"Asylum Statistics" 2012 Eurostat Germany and France have the highest number of applicants in 2011 which constituted around one-third of the total for EU Member States. An additional 25 per cent of the EU total is made up by applications in Italy and Belgium. France and Germany have over twice the number that applied in the UK'. Available at: http://epp.eurostat.ec.europa.eu/statistics_explained/index.php?title=file:number_of_(non-eu-27)_asylum_applicants_in_the_eu_and_efta_

attractive to asylum applicants precipitated a reduction in generosity.[101] The minimum standard framework effectively enabled an overall reduction in the standard of protection.

The introduction of Article 78 of the TFEU paved the way for uniform procedures. The measures under Article 78 concern common criteria for identifying which member state is responsible for considering an application for asylum; common standards on the reception of asylum seekers in Member States, on the qualification of nationals of third countries as refugees, and on procedures for granting or withdrawing refugee status.[102] In addition, measures can be adopted aimed at common standards for the recognition of subsidiary protection and temporary protection of refugees and displaced persons. Pursuant to Article 78, recast instruments were proposed by the Commission in several areas, beginning with reception conditions in 2008.

The introduction of the qualified majority voting under the ordinary legislative procedure following the TFEU reduced the negative influence of particular states in the Council by increasing the role of the European Parliament to one of co-decision.[103] In theory this should enable a departurefrom the negative politics associated with asylum. The influence of the Green representatives in the European Parliament has been particularly welcome in this respect.[104] The enhanced role of the CJEU in asylum cases also promises greater accountability. The Parliament's legal challenge to common European lists of safe countries, discussed in Chapter 4, certainly suggests the potential for a more humanitarian outlook.[105]

Following its Green Paper on the 'Future of the Common European Asylum System' in 2007,[106] the Commission began work on a number of amendments to the existing secondary legislation with the goal of achieving a common standard of protection, greater equality in protection and a higher degree of solidarity between EU Member States'.[107] However, the success of the negotiations was anything but uniform. The recast Qualification Directive and Long-term Residents Directive

---

member_states_and_their_age_distribution,_2011.png&filetimestamp=20121012123334 (accessed 9 November 2012).

101 A process described by Guiraudon, V as 'venue-shopping', 'European Integration and Migration Policy: Vertical Policy-making as Venue Shopping' 2000 28 J of Common Market Studies 2, 251.

102 TFEU Article 78(2).

103 Mitsilegas, V 'A "Common" EU Immigration and Asylum Policy: National and Institutional Constraints' in Shah supra n28, 139.

104 The Green/European Free Alliance group of MEP's is the fourth largest group with 59 MEPs. Details of their work in this area can be found at http://www.greens-efa.eu/immigration-34.html (accessed 20 March 2013).

105 See for example, the Parliament's influence on the SIS II, as discussed by Peers, S 'Key Legislative Developments on Migration in the EU: SIS II' (2008) 10 Eur J Migration & L 77.

106 Brussels 6 June 2007 COM (2007) 301 Final.

107 Ibid, 1.

were successfully amended, extending rights to refugees and other beneficiaries of international protection.[108] However, the more contentious Dublin Regulation, Asylum Procedures Directive and Reception Conditions Directive were not agreed until June 2013.[109]

The third stage of the CEAS commenced in 2009 as the European Council announced the Stockholm programme which envisages 'a common area of protection and solidarity based on a common asylum procedure and a uniform status for those granted international protection.[110] The initial timetable for completion of the final stage was 2012, although most of the proposed amendments could not be agreed within this time-frame.[111] Stockholm offers a more pragmatic focus, including tools to assist Member States, such as the European Asylum Support Office and the European asylum curriculum which aims to provide common training in asylum determinations. There are concerns that this pragmatism has overtaken a real commitment to refugee protection due to the difficulty in establishing consensus on the latter.

The external dimension of the CEAS is now being pursued with rigour. Regional protection remains on the agenda and, pursuant to Stockholm, two new systems have been established in the Horn of Africa (including Kenya, Yemen and Djibouti) and Eastern North Africa (Egypt, Libya and Tunisia).[112] A Joint EU resettlement programme has been launched alongside negotiations on several readmission agreements.[113] In May 2012, the Council adopted *Conclusions on the Renewed Global Approach to Migration and Mobility*. These Conclusions define the objectives of the EU in its external action on migrationas well as on asylum; the subjects of cooperation with third partners, and the tools that need to be implemented and developed. Dialogues on migration, mobility and security with North African countries continued culminating in the fifth mobility partnership with Morocco in 2013.[114] The agreement offers the carrot of clearer European migration

108 Council of the EU *Long Term Residents' Directive Extended to Refugees and Other Beneficiaries of International Protection* Press release 11 April 2011.

109 For analysis see Chapters 4 and 5 respectively.

110 Council of the European Union 'The Stockholm Programme – An Open and Secure Europe Serving and Protecting the Citizens' 17024/09 2 December 2009, [2010] OJ C 115 'Stockholm Programme'; see discussion in Peers supra n26, 305–306. For an analysis of the relevance of the Stockholm Programme see Carrera, S and Guild, E 'Does the Stockholm Programme Matter? The Struggles over Ownership of AFSJ Multiannual Programming' (CEPS Paper Liberty and Security in Europe No 51 December 2012).

111 European Commission 'Common European Asylum System: Better Protection and Solidarity for People Seeking International Protection' Press Release IP/11/665 Event Date: 1 June 2011.

112 European Council *Stockholm Programme Mid-Term Review* 15921/12 13.11.2012.

113 For analysis see Chapter 6.

114 European Commission 'Migration and Mobility Partnership Signed between the EU and Morocco' Press Release IP/13/513 7 June 13. Other partnerships have been agreed with Moldova, Cape Verde, Georgia and Armenia.

opportunities for Moroccan nationals as a reward for ensuring readmission, capacity-building and assistance in preventing irregular migration.[115] Whilst the agreement is to be welcomed for its commitment to improving asylum capacity-building in line with international obligations, the push towards readmission in the absence of a fully functioning asylum system seems incongruous at best.

There is a clear danger that the strongly worded commitments of Tampere will continue to beside-lined.[116] The repeated reference to citizens' rights under Stockholm, although understandable in a Europe seeking to increase its democratic credentials, does not bode well for non-EU migrants. The Council considers that its priority 'will be to focus on the interests and needs of citizens. The challenge will be to ensure respect for fundamental freedoms and integrity whilst guaranteeing security in Europe'.[117] Whilst the need to provide 'legally safe and efficient asylum procedures' is recognised, it is immediately linked to the objective of preventing, controlling and combating 'illegal migration'.[118] There is an obvious inconsistency in these objectives as many asylum seekers will present as 'irregular' migrants and may consequently be deemed 'illegal' migrants. The latter is rarely defined but is certainly capable of being construed to include those in need of sanctuary.[119]

The UK Opt-Out

It is worth emphasising the unique (and arguably, unfortunate) position of the UK which has opted out of the recast provisions but will continue to be bound by the original directives to which it opted in. There is no doubt that some of the enhancements in the recast directives, notably in the area of detention, legal assistance and unfounded claims, have contributed to the UK's reluctance.[120] Ette and Geddes identify a specifically British 'way of doing things' which involves

---

115 Council of the European Union *Joint Declaration Establishing a Mobility Partnership between the Kingdom of Morocco and the European Union and Its Member States* 6139/13 Addl Rev 3 3 June 2013.

116 Collett, E 'The European Union's Stockholm Program: Less Ambition on Immigration and Asylum, but More Detailed Plans' (Migration Information Source, January 2010). Available at: http://www.migrationinformation.org/feature/display.cfm?id=768 (accessed 27 January 2012); Kaunert, C and Léonard, S 'The EU Asylum Policy: Towards a Common Area of Protection and Solidarity?' in Wolff, S (ed) *Freedom, Security and Justice after Lisbon and Stockholm* (TMC Asser Press 2011) 94.

117 Stockholm programme para 1.1.

118 Ibid.

119 Morehouse, C and Blomfield, M 'Irregular Migration in Europe' (Migration Policy Institute 2011). Their report suggests a shift in terminology from irregular towards illegal migration in the EU, notwithstanding a reduction in the number of unauthorised migrants since 2008.

120 Stefanelli, JN 'Whose Rule of Law? An Analysis of the UK's Decision not to Opt-in to the EU Asylum Procedures and Reception Conditions Directives' [2011] ICLQ 1059; Buckley supra n122.

selectively opting in to more coercive measures which do not require a significant change in domestic policy.[121] However, the UK may find that this position is compromised by the decision of the CJEU in *NS*, discussed in Chapter 4, which suggests that other legally binding principles, including the Charter of Fundamental Rights, will continue to be applied when assessing Member State's asylum laws, irrespective of whether the enhanced protection in the recast directives has been implemented.[122] The UK is thus likely to find itself in an unenviable position; having excluded itself from a position of significant influence on the recast provisions whilst being implicitly bound by their enhanced protection when interpreted in the light of the Charter of Rights.[123] Buckley asks whether these deficiencies in protection might be construed by the CJEU as systemic flaws.[124]

From Sharing to Shifting the Burden

The burden-sharing arrangements so fundamental to the operation of a common asylum system, are now predicated on a common and consistent approach to asylum determination. This should in turn produce greater uniformity and fairness in decision-making for applicants. As Noll contends:

> the logic of burden-sharing rests on the axiom that an equitable distribution of costs and responsibilities in protection will generate not only maximum of fairness among states, but also a maximum openness vis-à-vis protection seekers.[125]

If done correctly, both protection seekers and states stand to benefit. Consistency and predictability are absolutely fundamental to ensure a fair process which can identify protection needs and maximise cost effectiveness.[126] As Legomsky argues, 'the moral imperative of equal justice, the needs for certainty and predictability, the benefits of efficiency, and the objective of public acceptability all demand attention to consistency in any adjudicative framework'.[127] In the absence of

---

121 Ette, A and Geddes, J 'Against Exceptionalism: British Interests for Selectively Europeanizing Its Immigration Policy' in Faist, T and Ette, A (eds) supra n26, 97; see also Geddes, J *The Politics of Migration in Europe* (Sage 2003) 49.

122 *NS and ME V SSHD* C-4110/10, C493/10 CJEU Judgement 21 December 2011.

123 Buckley, J '*NS V SSHD* C-4110/10 ECJ, Case Comment' (2012) 2 EHRLR 210; Goodwin-Gill, G and Lambert, H *The Limits of Transnational Law* (CUP 2010) 209.

124 Goodwin-Gill ibid, 210.

125 Noll supra n17, 265.

126 Ibid, 266.

127 Legomsky, S 'Learning to Live with Unequal Justice: Asylum and the Limits to Consistency' (2007) 60 Stan L Rev 473; Price, M *Rethinking Asylum* (CUP 2009) 229.

consistency, the system breaks down as more informed asylum seekers are likely to forum-shop in order to maximise their chance of protection.

Yet, consistency in decision-making is difficult to achieve, even between adjudicators in the same country. In one US study of legally similar asylum applications, the variations in outcomes were striking, leading the authors to conclude that asylum outcomes are just as much down to luck as to the merits of the case.[128]

There are many different factors influencing adjudication in asylum cases.[129] Of particular relevance in the European context is the number of decisional units which are spread across all the Member States. The degree of discretion in asylum decision-making is considerable, making it difficult to establish a system of fairness between cases, let alone between decision-makers in different states. Reductions in free legal assistance can have considerable impact on the quality of legal argument and are likely to diminish an applicant's chance of success. Asylum and immigration law, whether European or domestic, is constantly evolving, further reducing the opportunity for consistent decision-making.[130] There are also subjective factors including the availability of training and guidance and the personal prejudices of the decision-maker which can be very influential in asylum determinations.[131]

To date there has not been a European study comparable to the US study but the raw data on refugee recognition rates presents serious cause for concern. During the first quarter of 2011 the initial recognition rate for refugee status was 31 per cent in Norway; 4.7 per cent in the Netherlands and 1.5 per cent in Greece.[132] Even for claimants with the same nationality, the variations between states are striking. Unfortunately, asylum seekers are most likely to arrive in the states with the lowest recognition rates and are therefore unfairly prejudiced by the operation of the Dublin Regulation, discussed in Chapter Four. The underpinning of 'mutual trust' that informs transfers under the Regulation fails to ensure that international law is fully respected; consequently asylum seekers face a protection lottery. The decisions of the ECtHR and the CJEU in *MSS v Belgium and Greece, NS v SSHD* and *M.E. and Others v Refugee Applications Commissioner* expose the common standards agenda as an illusion.[133] A proposal from the Commission to amend the Dublin Regulation to enable the temporary suspension of removals

128 Ramji-Nogales, J; Schoenholtz, A and Schrag, P 'Refugee Roulette: Disparities in Asylum Adjudication' (2007) 60 Stan L Rev 295.

129 Legomsky supra n127 lists 15 key factors influencing decision-making.

130 For example, in the UK there has been a new piece of legislation on immigration and/or asylum approximately every two years since 1999 (this is in addition to the UK regulations implementing EU asylum directives).

131 Supra n127, 379.

132 Eurostat Statistics in Focus No 48/2011 21 September 2011.

133 App 30696/09 21 January 2012, supra n121 and case comment in Buckley supra n122, 205.

to countries where there is no proper asylum system, proved unpopular with some Member States who feared that the burden-sharing process would be undermined.[134] Yet for states on the southern border of Europe, the Dublin mechanism appears more about deflection than burden-sharing.[135] Several states affected by a significant increase in irregular migration during the Arab Spring of 2011 issued a joint communication calling for the proposed Dublin amendments to include 'a mechanism to suspend transfers to Member States facing particular pressure on their national asylum systems'.[136] The urgent tone of the communication suggests a deep-seated frustration with the European institutions for failing to appreciate the demands placed on the economies and resources of the border-states. In addition to receiving the majority of arrivals fleeing the crisis in North Africa, the continuation of transfers under Dublin, has placed a disproportionate burden on the asylum systems of these states. Yet the amended Dublin III Regulation provides merely that in the case of systemic flaws in the receiving state's asylum system, such as would constitute a breach of Article 3 of the ECHR (or Article 4 of the EU Charter), the transferring state should identify another state responsible under Dublin or assume responsibility for the determination itself. Unlike the initial Commission proposal, no formal suspension of transfer is envisaged.

Assessing the Effects of European Cooperation

Notwithstanding the criticisms levelled at the harmonisation efforts by non-governmental organisations and academics, some scholars have argued by contrast, that cooperation has strengthened refugee protection. Boswell and Geddes argue against the prevailing view that cooperation has become an excuse for increasing restrictionism.[137] Indeed, the picture is not as simplistic as it may appear. Thielemann and El-Enany contend that the domestic laws of some states have been upgraded as a result of communitarisation; a movement they predict will continue towards better overall standards of refugee protection in the longer term.[138] One clear example is

134 COM (2008) 820 3 December 208; the proposals received support from the UNHCR 'Dublin Regulation'. Available at: www.unhcr.org/4a9d13d59.pdf (accessed 20 March 2013).

135 Byrne et al supra n10 ch 1.

136 The communication also included Cyprus, Malta, Spain: Joint Communiqué II, Nicosia, 19 April, 2011. Full text available at: http://migrantsatsea.wordpress.com/2011/04/21/cyprus-greece-italy-malta-spain-issue-joint-communique-regarding-response-to-north-african-migration (accessed 20 March 2013).

137 Boswell, C and Geddes, A *Migration and Mobility in the European Union* (Palgrave Macmillan 2011).

138 Thielemann, E and El-Enany, N 'Beyond Fortress Europe? How European Cooperation Strengthens Refugee Protection' Paper presented at the EU Studies Association's 11th Biennial International Conference, Marina Del Rey Los Angeles, April 23–25 2009.

provided by the implementation of the Qualification Directive into German law which has necessitated the inclusion of persecution by non-state agents in the absence of state complicity.[139] Cooperation does at least present an opportunity for national governments to deflect criticism from anti-immigration sections of their electorates by deferring to an overarching, common approach.[140] Kaunert and Leonard concur, arguing that the switch from the national to the European venue has made asylum policy more liberal.[141] The European Parliament's role in the ordinary legislative procedure may prove significant in this respect.

Boswell and Geddes are critical of the 'fortress Europe' analysis for its failure to fully engage with policy complexities.[142] Policies towards labour migration provide a good example of this complexity. The Long-term Residents Directive affords equal treatment to migrants with five years' lawful residence on the same basis as nationals in several areas, including access to paid and unpaid employment, conditions of employment and working conditions, education and vocational training, welfare benefits, social assistance including free health care, social benefits, and freedom of movement.[143] This status further enables migration and residence in other EU states for a period exceeding three months.[144]

It is certainly true that harmonisation offers the potential to improve the recognition and protection of refugees. Yet, it is equally true that some states have taken an opportunity to reduce the protection offered by their own legal system. In the UK the replacement of 'exceptional leave to remain' with 'humanitarian leave', in order to comply with EU rules on subsidiary protection, is accused of diminishing protection from conduct falling short of persecution.[145]

The Qualification Directive, discussed in Chapter 2, has extended the coverage of the Refugee Convention in a number of areas, including:the codification of subsidiary protection; the clarification of grounds for persecution and the inclusion of persecution by non-state agents. Yet there remains concern over its compatibility with fundamental human rights norms. The absolute protection against ill-treatment and torture established in Article 3 of the ECHR is not reflected in the

139 The Qualification Directive's definition of non-State actors of persecution (Article 6(b) and (c)) has been transposed literally into German law by Section 60(1) 4 Residence Act 2004 by virtue of the Immigration Act 2004; UNHCR *Asylum in the European Union: A Study of the Implementation of the Qualification Directive* (UNHCR 2007).

140 It should be pointed out that in the UK the anti-immigration lobby tends to express concern over European influence at the expense of state sovereignty, thus a reference to European common values is unlikely to be viewed as a satisfactory response!

141 Kaunert and Léonard supra n116.

142 Supra n137.

143 Council Directive 2003/109/EC of 25 November 2003 *Concerning the Status of Third-Country Nationals Who Are Long-Term Residents* OJ L 16, 23 January 2004, p. 44–53 'Long-term Residents Directive'; Groenendijk, K; Guild, E and Carrera, S *Integration of Third Country Nationals and Illiberal Practices in the EU* (Ashgate 2009).

144 Long-term Residents Directive Art 14(1).

145 Price, M *Rethinking Asylum* (CUP 2009) 178.

Qualification Directive which continues to include exceptions promulgated in the Refugee Convention. Article 21 of the recast Qualification Directive requires compliance with international obligations but the inclusion of exceptions to the non-refoulement principle inevitably undermines those obligations.[146] It seems unlikely that 'persecution' under the Qualification Directive can be defined in such a way for it to fall outside the scope of inhuman and degrading treatment or torture.[147] Despite the CJEU's attempt to draw a distinction between the Directive and Article 3 in the *Elgafaji* judgement by highlighting the broader definition of harm in the former, the ECtHR has expressed its view that Article 3 offers comparable protection to that afforded by the Directive.[148] Article 9 defines persecution, inter alia, as a serious violation of basic human rights, in particular the rights that are non-derogable (thus clearly including Article 3 of the ECHR and Article 4 of the Charter). Therefore the provisions in the Qualification Directive are inconsistent; the EU approach, which favours exceptions, is not compliant with this fundamental right.

There have been improvements to the under-developed asylum systems of many newer EU states but it remains difficult to see how the CEAS can be measured as a protection success when assessed as a package. It certainly does not seem legitimate to argue, as do Kaunert and Léonard, that the CJEU's annulment of the worst aspects of the CEAS means that we can have confidence in the system.[149] The recast Procedures Directive continues to include provision for a common list of safe countries of origin as well as allowing national governments to apply their own lists.[150] The allocation of resources to the European Refugee Fund[151] and the newly established European Asylum Support Office (EASO) is an important development but the resources of these agencies are dwarfed by the resources allocated to the migration control industry. Non-governmental organisations have expressed concern that their expertise is not being utilised when the EASO draws

146 Article 21(2) 2011/95/EU *On Standards for the Qualification of Third-Country Nationals or Stateless Persons as Beneficiaries of International Protection, for a Uniform Status for Refugees or for Persons Eligible for Subsidiary Protection, and for the Content of the Protection Granted.* L 337/6 OJ 20 December 2011.

147 Mink, J 'EU Asylum Law and Human Rights Protection: Revisiting the Principle of *Non-Refoulement* and the Prohibition of Torture and Other Forms of Ill-Treatment' (2012) 14 Eur J of Migration and L 147.

148 *Meki Elgafaji, Noor Elgafaji v Staatssecretaris van Justitie* C-465/07 [2009] para 221; *Sufi and Elmi v UK* App 8319/07 and 1149/07 28 June 2011 para 226; see also *QD (Iraq) v SSHD* [2009] EWCA Civ 620.

149 Kaunert and Léonard supra n22.

150 Directive 2013/32/EU *of the European Parliament and of the Council of 26 June 2013 on Common Procedures for Granting and Withdrawing International Protection (Recast)* OJ L180/60 29 June 13, Article 36(1), Art 37 and Art 38.

151 [2000] OJ 252/12; [2010] OJ 129/1; 628 million euros have been allocated for the 2008–2013 phase.

up Country of Origin information.[152] The acid test should be whether those with genuine claims for refugee status are identified promptly,processed equitably and directed towards appropriate durable solutions.

El-Enany has argued that the European refugee is treated better than ever before, through the guarantee of broader and more equitable protection in each Member State.[153] But the European refugee has, as El-Enany recognises, overcome numerous obstacles to reach that position. There are significant deficiencies in the system, preventing many people from ever getting to the point of claiming refugee status. European strategies aimed at intervention and prevention mean that those claiming refugee status in Europe are comparatively few in number. The EU continues to manage irregular migration from a control and security perspective which does not get close to addressing the needs of the most vulnerable. Geddes concedes that the openness of labour migration has been accompanied by an increased rigour in the fight against illegal migration, which runs a very real risk of demonising the asylum seeker.[154]

It is also evident that the paper commitments favouring a uniform, common asylum system are very far from becoming a reality in several states. Those states on southern border of Europe are the first port of safety for many asylum applicants. Rather than supporting the asylum system of these states with greater resources, training and support, the EU continues to endorse transfers under the Dublin Regulation, making matters much worse and placing the biggest burden on the states least able to cope.

A closer examination of the common standards on asylum procedures and reception conditions will serve to demonstrate the extent to which European cooperation has improved refugee protection whilst identifying areas where a protection gap continues to exist.

---

152 Amnesty International *Opinion on the EASO COI Report 'Afghanistan: Taliban Strategies – Recruitment'* July 2012. Available at: www.amnesty.eu/content/assets/EASO_COI_Report_.pdf (accessed 20 March 2013).

153 El-Enany, N 'Who is the New European Refugee' (2008) 33 EL Rev3. 313.

154 Geddes, A *Immigration and European Integration: Beyond Fortress Europe?* (Manchester UP 2008) 171. It also increases demand for people smugglers and trafficking, as argued by Morrison, J and Crossland, B 'The Trafficking and Smuggling of Refugees: The End Game in European Asylum Policy' (UNHCR 2000); Andreas supra n75; Koslowski supra n77.

Chapter 4
Burden-Sharing and Asylum Procedures[1]

Introduction

Of all the recent legislative developments pursuant to the Common European Asylum System it is the Asylum Procedures Directive that has attracted the most vociferous criticism, having been described as a 'catalogue of national practice which allows significant departures from accepted refugee and human rights law'[2] and a 'betrayal of the EU's promise to guarantee fundamental rights'.[3]

These criticisms predominately centre on two aspects: the use of accelerated procedures, and the designation of certain countries as generally safe. In respect of the latter we must also assess the effects of the Dublin Regulation with its inherent presumption of European safety.

Combining Fairness with Efficiency

It is axiomatic that protection under the Refugee Convention requires fair and accessible asylum procedures. The principle of non-refoulement requires individual determination of risk and the UN Handbook requires that the applicant is informed of the determination procedure and be given enough time to prepare for any appeal hearing.[4] This fair determination is particularly vital when, as in many asylum cases, there is a possibility of the applicant having experienced torture.[5] At the same time, it is in everyone's interest that the asylum system operates efficiently. Writing in 1993, Hailbronner found the European system, then it its infancy, to be

---

1 Council Directive *On Minimum Standards on Procedures in Member States for Granting and Withdrawing Refugee Status* 1 December 2005 OJ L 326/13 'Procedures Directive'. This will be replaced over the next two years by the recast Directive 2013/32/EU *Of the European Parliament and of the Council of 26 June 2013 on Common Procedures for Granting and Withdrawing International Protection (Recast)* OJ L 180/60 29 June 2013 'Recast Procedures Directive'.

2 Amnesty International *The EU – Now More Free, Secure and Justice? Amnesty International's Human Rights Assessment of the Tampere Agenda* (Brussels 2 June 2004).

3 Costello, C *Analysis and Critique of Council Directive on Minimum Standards on Procedures for Granting and Withdrawing Refugee Status* (ILPA 30 April 2004).

4 UN *Handbook On Procedures and Criteria for Determining Refugee Status under the 1951 Convention and the 1967 Protocol Relating to the Status of Refugees* HCR/IP/4/Eng/REV 1 Reedited, Geneva, January 1992, para 192 'The Handbook'.

5 *Jabari v Turkey* [2001] INLR 136; *TI v UK* [2000] INLR 211; *Hilal v UK* [2001] App 45276/99 6 June 2001.

'extremely inefficient in terms of wasted resources and of very doubtful value for the protection for those who need is greatest'.[6] He thus supported the concept of burden-sharing as a necessary means of preventing the collapse of the European asylum system.[7] An efficient and fair system with complimentary procedures should be the key objective when devising a common asylum system. If burden-sharing is able to secure these values then it has the potential to provide a workable solution to the difficulties experienced by individually over-burdened national asylum systems.

Yet there is an inevitable tension between efficiency and fairness. Critics argue that the European Council has been overly concerned with efficiency by limiting access to fair procedures. Craig and Fletcher suggest that state concerns based on broader public concerns, often whipped up by right-wing media coverage, have influenced the Council's cautious direction.[8] Furthermore, the inclusion of 10 new Member States, many of whom had underdeveloped asylum systems and were situated on the periphery of Europe, added to the pressure for a restrictive approach. Consequently, it is argued that the minimum standards established by the Procedures Directive:

> provide example after example of national worst practice reflecting the lowest common denominator approach to procedural protection. Worse still, the directive is littered with possibilities to enable Member States to derogate from these lowest and sometimes already qualified, procedural guarantees, rendering them at best illusive and at worse, illusory.[9]

As outlined in Chapter 3, the CEAS has now moved beyond minimum standards towards enhanced protection in the form of 'common procedures' as a result of the changing legal basis in Article 78 TFEU.[10] This has necessitated amendments to the main asylum directives and the Dublin Regulation but it is clear that harmonisation is far from complete with Member States continuing to take very different positions on important aspects of procedural protection.

---

6 Hailbronner, K 'The Concept of a "Safe Country" and Expeditious Asylum Procedures: A Western European Perspective' (1993) 5 Intl J Refugee L, 33.

7 Ibid, 31. It should be noted that 1993 saw a significant spike in asylum applications due to the conflict in the former Yugoslavia.

8 Craig, S and Fletcher, M 'Deflecting Refugees: A Critique of the EC Asylum Procedures Directive' in Shah P (ed) *The Challenge of Asylum to Legal Systems* (Cavendish, 2005) 60. See also Peers, S *EU Justice and Home Affairs Law* (OUP 2010).

9 Ibid, 355.

10 *Treaty on the Functioning of the European Union* 30 March 2011 OJ C 83/78 30 March 2011 ('TFEU').

The Dublin Regulation

The 1999 'Aznar Protocol'[11] and Dublin Convention introduced a presumption that all EU Member States are generally 'safe' and thus give rise to no individual risk of persecution. The rules are now contained in the Dublin III Regulation[12] which must be cross-referenced to the Procedures Directive which provides that all applications falling under the Regulation will be deemed inadmissible.[13]

Unlike the Schengen Convention, the main objective of the Dublin machinery is to prevent secondary movement of asylum seekers within Europe. All EU Member States[14] are considered to be safe and therefore the asylum applicant should have sought asylum in the first country of their arrival. It is thus predicated on mutual trust, described by Noll as a 'fictive equality of divergent domestic asylum systems'.[15] Applicants can be transferred back to the first state of arrival for determination of their claim in accordance with common rules and priorities. Concern over venue-shopping clearly informs the Dublin process with the Commission's working paper emphasising that choice of destination should not be an option.[16] This is a point which will be returned to in the context of durable solutions. However, it should be noted that the evidence of venue-shopping has been disputed by many researchers who identify the most common 'pull-factor' to be a perception of comparative tolerance in host states.[17]

The Dublin Convention received considerable criticism for operational failings which meant that in 1998 fewer than 2 per cent of persons who lodged a claim in a Member State were transferred under the rules.[18] In this respect the Convention's symbolic value as a burden-sharing instrument between states certainly outstrips

---

11 Protocol No 24 on Asylum for National of Member States of the EU, annexed to the Treaty of Amsterdam 1999.

12 Council Regulation (EU) No 604/2013 *Of the European Parliament and of the Council of 26 June 2013 Establishing the Criteria and Mechanisms for Determining the Member State Responsible for Examining an Application for International Protection Lodged in One of the Member States by A Third-Country National or a Stateless Person (Recast)*, 29 June 2013 OJ L180/31 'Dublin III'.

13 Article 25 Procedures Directive, Article 33 Recast Procedures Directive.

14 It also applies to Norway, Iceland, Lichtenstein and Switzerland.

15 Noll, G *Negotiating Asylum: The EU Acquis, Extraterritorial Protection and the Common Market of Deflection* (M Nijhoff 2000) 191.

16 European Commission Staff Working Paper 'Revisiting the Dublin Convention' March 2000 SEC (2000) 522.

17 See for example Collyer, M 'The Dublin Regulation and Algerians in the UK' (2004)17 J Refugee Studies 390; Castles, S: Crawley, H and Loughna, S *States of Conflict: Causes and Patterns of Forced Migration to the EU and Policy Responses* (Institute of Public Policy Research 2003).

18 Commission Staff Working Paper 'Revisiting the Dublin Convention: Developing Community legislation for determining which state is responsible for considering an application for asylum submitted in one of the member states' Sec (2000) 21

its effectiveness.[19] Today it continues to present over-burdened states with two practical solutions, neither of which offer promise for those in need of sanctuary; either block access to their territory altogether or curtail procedural rights.[20] As a result, the Dublin mechanism stands accused of eroding the safeguards envisaged by Hailbronner and the UNHCR, bringing limited operational efficiencies at the expense of claimants' rights.[21]

Originally conceived as a stand-alone instrument, Dublin has now been bought within the EU framework. Article 80 TFEU provides the current legal base and points to the need for solidarity and the fair sharing of responsibility in the context of the area of freedom, security and justice. The Procedures Directive exempts applicants from safe third countries from a full investigation of their case on the basis that their claim is unfounded. The designation of European safe country for the purposes of generating a common list under the Procedures Directive requires the ratification and observance of both the Refugee Convention and the rights contained in the ECHR in addition to an asylum procedure prescribed by law.[22] Significantly, it does not require proof that such rights are secured de facto. There is no opportunity for the applicant to rebut this presumption once the state is listed under Article 36.[23]

In secondary movement cases, the Member State responsible for deciding the claim is identified by means of a list of prioritised criteria which consider immediate family ties and residency rights or visa permits before considering illegal entry.[24] The message from the criteria is that those states with higher recognition rates, more liberal visa requirements or porous borders, will have greater responsibility. Thus the burden falls on two groups of states: the more generous state (where family reunion and residence permits could lead to an obligation) and the most inefficient state (where the criteria on illegal entry will result in obligation). The fifth criteria requires that the first Member State in which an application is lodged shall be deemed responsible if no other contracting state can be identified. The message to states who wish to reduce the burden of asylum determinations is

---

March 2000, 522, para 12,38; see also Peers, supra n8 who notes that only 3 per cent of total asylum applications were transferred in 2001, 359.

19 Hurwitz, A describes some of the system's absurdities and deficiencies, *The Collective Responsibility of States to Protect Refugees* (OUP 2009) 122–123.

20 Noll supra n15, 348.

21 Kneebone, S "'Safe Third Country' Concept" in McAdam, J (ed) *Forced Migration, Human Rights and Security* (Hart 2008) 137; Lenart, J "'Fortress Europe": Compliance of the Dublin II Regulation with the ECHR" (2012) Merkourios – Intl and Eur Migration L 4, 5.

22 Procedures Directive Article 36.

23 Goodwin-Gill, G and McAdam J *The Refugee in International Law* (OUP 2007) 400; Coleman, N *European Readmission Policy. Third Country Interests and Refugee Rights* (M Nijhoff 2009) 291; see discussion in Chapter 6.

24 Dublin III Regulation, Chapter III.

therefore very clear: improve your early detection and deflection strategies and/or avoid granting formal recognition.

The Principle of Mutual Trust

The 'mutual trust' presumption that regards all European states as safe for all applicants was and still is, fundamentally flawed. The 1990s saw a number of Spanish nationals from the Basque region and British nationals from Northern Ireland seeking asylum in other European countries.[25] In addition a significant number of Eastern European asylum seekers (predominately Roma) were granted protection in Canada following EU accession.[26] The presumption of trust was nevertheless supported by ECtHR case law. In *KRS v UK* the Court held that a challenge concerning the transfer of an Iranian national to Greece was inadmissible as 'In the absence of any proof to the contrary, it must be presumed that Greece will comply with [its] obligations in respect of returnees'.[27] This decision placed enormous faith in the mutual trust presumption despite a report by the European Council on Refugee and Exiles in 2006 which identified a common Greek practice of interrupting asylum claims where a transfer had taken place. The effect of interruption was to deny an applicant full access to the determination procedure on the basis that they had previously arbitrarily left their stated place of residence.[28] In 2008 the UNHCR advised Member States to cease removals to Greece as there was a significant risk of refoulement.[29] The European Commission initiated enforcement proceedings against Greece for failing to ensure an examination of the applications merits following transfers.[30] Yet two years later, Amnesty International reported that many states had subsequently resumed transfers arguing that discrepancies in the system of protection should be resolved through the Greek legal system.[31]

The presumption of safety can no longer be considered a tenable position following the ECtHR ruling in *MSS v Belgium and Greece*.[32] The ECtHR found that the Belgian authority's removal of an Afghan asylum seeker to Greece violated the prohibition against torture and inhuman treatment contrary to Article 3

25 Hatton, T *Seeking Asylum in the OECD: Trends and Policies* (Centre for Economic Policy Research 2011); Bigo, D; Carrera, S and Guild, E *Foreigners, Refugees and Minorities: Rethinking People in the Context of Border Controls and Visas* (Ashgate 2013).

26 O'Nions, H *Minority Rights Protection in International Law: The Roma of Europe* (Ashgate 2007).

27 App 32733/08 2 December 2008.

28 Article 2(8) Presidential Decree 61/99 as discussed in ECRE Supra n62 at 5.

29 UNHCR *Position on the Return of Asylum-Seekers to Greece under the Dublin Regulation* 15 April 2008 (UNHCR 2008).

30 *Commission of the EC v Hellenic Republic of Greece* C128/25 OJ 24 May 2008.

31 Amnesty International *The Dublin II Trap: Transfer of Asylum Seekers to Greece* (Amnesty International 2010).

32 App 30696/09 21 January 2011.

ECHR. The Belgian authorities could not hide behind burden-sharing rules when they ought to have known that the applicant was at risk of subsequent refoulement from Greece. The applicant had been transferred to Athens under Dublin II where he was immediately detained in dire conditions. Following his release he lived on the streets with no access to basic state support. These conditions were regarded as contravening, inter alia, the prohibition of inhuman and degrading treatment contrary to Article 3 of the ECHR with liability placed on both states. In the Court's opinion, the Belgian authorities should have recognised these deficiencies and activated the discretionary sovereignty clause under the former Dublin Regulation whereby states can process the asylum application themselves rather than initiate a transfer.[33] The decision led to the temporary suspension of some 531 Dublin transfers.[34]

The ECtHR approach was subsequently followed by the CJEU in a preliminary ruling on removals from the UK and Ireland to Greece under Dublin II.[35] The CJEU based their ruling on the serious risk of a breach of fundamental rights under the Charter of Fundamental Rights if the transfer was to take place.

It is evident that there can no longer be a 'conclusive presumption' that all EU states are safe.[36] Yet even a rebuttable presumption causes protection problems. Approximately 90 per cent of asylum seekers enter the EU via Greece; it is submitted that the significant failings in the Greek asylum system (including reception conditions and determinations) cannot be adequately addressed through a rebuttable presumption of safety without seriously compromising protection.

The facts of *NS* provide a good example of a system obsessed with bureaucratic procedures and burden-sharing at the expense of protection. The case concerned an Afghan asylum seeker who had travelled through various EU states including Greece where he had been arrested. He was then expelled to Turkey and detained for two months in conditions described by the court as 'appalling'. Once released, he travelled to the UK where he finally claimed asylum. The UK authorities then attempted to remove him to Greece as a Dublin transfer notwithstanding the evidence of systemic flaws in the Greek asylum procedure.

The general presumption of European safety was supported by the CJEU. However, in the Greek situation, the wealth of reports from the UNHCR and other organisations demonstrated sufficient evidence of a 'systemic deficiency' in the asylum procedure and reception conditions.[37] Effectively Member States are

33 Article 3(2) Dublin Regulation.

34 European Voice 'Greek Asylum System in disarray' 27 January 2011. Available at: http://www.europeanvoice.com/article/imported/greek-asylum-system-in-disarray/70044.aspx (accessed 1 November 2012).

35 *NS v SSHD* C-411/10 and *ME and Others v Refugee Application Commissioner, Minister for Justice, Equality and law Reform* C-493/10.

36 Buckley, J '*NS v SSHD* C-4110/10 ECJ Case Comment' (2012) EHRLR 2, 205.

37 Ibid, para 90; see also the pending preliminary reference from the Asylgerichtshof (Austria) lodged on 27 August 2012, *Shamso Abdullahi* Case C-394/12 concerning a Somali

now obliged to apply the discretionary 'sovereignty clause' in Article 3(2) when considering transfers to Greece for the foreseeable future.[38] The clause provides that each state 'may examine an application for asylum lodged with it by a third-country national, even if such examination is not its responsibility under the criteria laid down in the regulation'. In Germany the sovereignty clause was applied in 4,630 transfers to prevent removal to Greece in 2011.[39] Yet, the sovereignty clause is not always applied in practice and states differ in their assessment of systemic deficiencies.[40]

Whilst the Court of Justice's endorsement of the ECtHR's approach is to be welcomed, the imposition of an obligation to rely on a clause that is, by nature discretionary, is legally untenable. The European Commission proposed to elaborate on the rules for applying the sovereignty clause when recasting the Dublin Regulation but their proposal was rejected by the Council.[41]

A humanitarian clause also enables a state to assume responsibility where the asylum seeker is dependent on the assistance of a relative, or a relative is dependent on the asylum seeker, providing the family ties existed in the country of origin.[42] The CJEU has adopted a broad, teleological interpretation of the clause in a decision concerning a transfer from Austria to Poland.[43] The applicant originally claimed asylum in Poland but left prior to adetermination, travelling to Austria where she was caring for her disabled daughter-in-law (who had been granted refugee status) and grandchildren. The CJEU reasoned that the clause should be applied in cases involving other relatives who were caring for extended family members in the absence of exceptional circumstances. In such cases a Member State which is not technically responsible under the Dublin criteria becomes so responsible. This approach serves to ensure that states take the obligations of family unity seriously. However, the recast provision agreed between the European Parliament and the Council narrows the scope of this provision so that it only applies specifically

---

national who had transited through Greece and Hungary on her way to Austria.

38 Lenart supra n21, 17.

39 Dublin Project EU *The Dublin II Regulation: Lives On Hold* (ECRE 2013) 45. Available at: http://www.ecre.org/component/content/article/56-ecre-actions/317-dublin-ii-regulation-lives-on-hold.html (accessed 10 April 2013); UNHCR 'Information on National Practice in the Application of Article 3(2) of the Dublin II regulation in particular in the context of intended transfers to Greece' 31 January 2011 UNHCR para 22.

40 Dublin Project EU ibid.

41 Council *Position Proposal for a Regulation of the European Parliament and of the Council Establishing the Criteria and Mechanisms for Determining the Member State Responsible for Examining an Application for International Protection Lodged in One of the Member States by a Third-Country National or a Stateless Person and of the Council Laying Down Standards for the Reception of Asylum Seekers* (Recast) 2008/0243 (COD) 4 April 2012 ('Dublin III').

42 Dublin III Regulation Article 16(1).

43 C-245/11 *K v Bundesasylamt* 6 November 2012.

to children, siblings and parents.[44] Furthermore, the relevant child, sibling or parent must be legally resident, whereas no such requirement presently applies.[45] This demonstrates a significant weakening of protection standards as a result of Member State intervention. It is very apparent that the amending process bowed to concerns expressed by state representatives in the Council, effectively endorsing the symbolic value of burden-sharing over crucial aspects of protection.

Although the Regulation provides that the child's best interests are a primary concern, it allows the transfer of a separated child where they have made a previous claim for asylum.[46] Figures from the UK in 2010 indicated that 445 children had so far been removed under these provisions, of which two-thirds were unaccompanied.[47] Concerns have been expressed by child welfare and refugee groups which stress that removal may not be in the child's best interest and may conflict with the obligation to make the child's welfare a primary consideration under the UN Convention on the Rights of the Child.[48] Mindful of these concerns, the CJEU recently ruled that where an unaccompanied minor had lodged an application in more than one state and had no family legally present in the host state, the obligation to determine the claim fell on the host state.[49] The Court emphasised that the child's best interests should be a primary consideration and that accordingly a prompt determination was required.

The focus on Greece may obscure the fact that the case law pending before the ECtHR concerns transfers to a variety of countries. Many of the newer Member States were not considered safe by existing states prior to accession and widely diverging recognition rates continue to belie the image of uniform protection.[50] In 2005 a report from the Norwegian Refugee Council on Chechen asylum applicants found that they had far greater chance of being afforded refugee states in Austria, Belgium and France compared to Finland, the Czech Republic, Poland, Sweden, Germany and Slovakia.[51] Further, chain refoulement from Poland and Slovakia,

---

44 Dublin III Article 16(1).

45 Supra n41.

46 Dublin III Regulation Article 6; ECRE *The Dublin Regulation: Ten Recommendations for Reform* (ECRE 2007) AD1/3/2007/Ext/CN.

47 Puffett, N 'Anger as Hundreds of Children Deported Alone under EU Rules' (Children and Young People Now, National Children's Bureau 22 June 2010).

48 United Nations *Convention on the Rights of the Child* 1989 *Treaty Series* vol 1577, 3 Article 3(1); Dublin Project supra n39.

49 *MA, BT, DA v Secretary of State for the Home Department* C-648/11, CJEU Press Release No 71/13 Luxembourg, 6 June 2013.

50 UNHCR statistics 2010. Available at: www.unhcr.org/4dfa11499.html accessed 27 November 2012 reveals a number of disparities, eg Somali applicant had a 35 per cent of being recognised as a refugee in Sweden compared to 87 per cent in Austria. In 2011 the overall recognition rate was 66.7 per cent in Finland compared to 4.2 per cent in Ireland, UNHCR *Global Trends for 2011*(UNHCR 2012).

51 Based on data from 2003 in Norwegian Refugee Council *Report on the Protection of Internally Displaced Persons, Asylum Seekers and Refugees from Chechnya* (Norwegian

where refugee protection systems were in their infancy, was a real possibility. Yet the risk of refoulement did not prevent other states detaining Chechen applicants pending their transfer to both countries under the Dublin procedure.

In 2007, a Hungarian court reportedly prevented a transfer to Romania on the basis that it would infringe the prohibition of refoulement contrary to Article 3 ECHR.[52] Yet concerns have also been raised over the Hungarian asylum system.[53] The UNHCR has highlighted the routine use of detention and the absence of suspensive appeals pending deportation for Dublin returnees.[54] In June 2012, the transfer of an Afghan man to Hungary was suspended due to the concerns of the Lazio administrative court.[55] They found there to be a real risk that breach of fundamental rights contained in the EU Charter would occur following transfer, based on the CJEU ruling in *NS v UK*. The ECtHR similarly suspended the transfer of a Sudanese asylum seeker to Hungary pursuant to rule 39 of the rules of the Court.[56] Denmark and Finland have suspended some Dublin transfers to Italy due to concerns over its reception conditions and treatment of North African migrants.[57]

Refugee Council April 2005); see also ECRE *Report on the Application of the Dublin II Regulation* March 2006 AD3/3/2006/EXT/MH; similarly Tibetan asylum applicants are frequently treated as unfounded and sent back to China from Romania whereas in Switzerland most Tibetan applicants are regarded as having legitimate asylum claims: Federal Administrative Court Switzerland E-5265/2011 7 December 2011, cited by Dublin Project EU supra n39.

52 Metropolitan Court of Budapest 7 September 2007 *Abdelfatah Saadallah M'hammed v Office of Immigration and Nationality of the Republic of Hungary* 17.K.34.397/2007/8.

53 Hungarian Helsinki Committee *Access to Protection Jeopardised-Information Note on the Treatment of Dublin Returnees in Hungary* December 2011. Available at: http://www.unhcr.org/refworld/publisher,HHC,,,4f3e10ab2,0.html (accessed 1 November 2012).

54 UNHCR *Hungary as a Country of Asylum: Observations on the Situation of Asylum-Seekers and Refugees in Hungary* 24 April 2012 Available at: http//www.unhcr.org/refworld/docid/4f9167db2.html; see also ECRE Summary report on the Application of the Dublin II Regulation in Europe (ECRE 2006), 17; Dublin project EU supra n39, 61.

55 Statewatch News 'Court Annuls Afghan's Dublin II Return to Hungary' (28 June 2012). Available at: http://database.statewatch.org/article.asp?aid=31658 (accessed 1 November 2012).

56 ECtHR *Interim Measure Suspending the Expulsion of the Applicant to Hungary* App 2283/12 11 January 2012. Between 2007 and April 2012 there have been more than 910 interim measures granted under rule 39 suspending transfers under the Dublin Regulation due to a prime facie risk of ECHR violation, according to research by ECRE/ELENA *Research on ECHR Rule 39 Interim Measures* April 2012 Annex B[4] p100. Available at: http://www.ecre.org/component/content/article/56-ecre-actions/272-ecre-research-on-rule-39-interim-measures.html (accessed 15 April 2013).

57 'EU Lawmakers Reinforce Asylum Seekers' Rights' (EU Observer, 19 September 2012). Available at: http://euobserver.com/justice/117604 (accessed 26 March 2013).

Detention should not normally be used solely because the applicant is a protection seeker.[58] Yet detention is increasingly deployed in Dublin cases whilst the first country of arrival drags its heels over the transfer.[59] The Regulation expects transfer requests to be answered within two months.[60] However, in the experience of the Jesuit Refugee Service, transfer requests to Greece from Belgium and Germany often resulted in detention for months as the response was delayed with the increasing likelihood of the applicant absconding.[61] In 2006 the European Council on Refugees and Exiles documented procedural problems at both ends of the transfer which left many asylum applicants in a precarious position.[62] More recent research continues to demonstrate the same deficiencies with states adopting divergent procedural rules. The time frame to mount an appeal against a transfer varies from three days in Hungary to two months in France and Spain.[63] Further, appeals are non-suspensive in France and Austria which results in most applicants being transferred before any appeal is heard.[64] It seems inevitable that victims of torture and other vulnerable groups will be caught up in routine detention pursuant to transfer, ranging from 24 hours prior to travel to over 6 months where a transfer is delayed.[65]

Some states will close the application once the asylum seeker leaves their territory, resulting in a negative finding of refugee status in abstentia. A fresh application following transfer may subsequently be rejected in the absence of a material change in the facts. Even in cases where a second application is allowed applicants are typically fast-tracked on the basis of a presumption that their case is unfounded.[66]

This discussion illustrates how the focus of Dublin is on the mechanics of transfer rather than the fair determination of protection needs. Statistics suggest that certain states exchange similar numbers of asylum seekers between themselves, questioning the point of lengthy and expensive transfer procedures.[67] Despite a significant improvement from the 4.1 per cent of asylum applicants transferred in 2007, the figures remain low, with around one-quarter of requests resulting

58 Dublin III Regulation, Recital 20.

59 Dublin Project EU supra n39, 82. In 8 out of the 11 countries surveyed detention was applied in Dublin transfer cases. In three countries (Austria, Germany and Switzerland) this included unaccompanied child asylum seekers.

60 Article 21(1) Dublin III.

61 Jesuit Refugee Service 'Dublin II: A Summary of JRS Experiences in Europe' (JRS Belgium 2011).

62 ECRE *Summary Report on the Application of the Dublin II Regulation in Europe* (ECRE March 2006) 8.

63 Dublin Project EU supra n39.

64 Ibid.

65 Ibid, 86.

66 ECRE supra n62, 7.

67 The Dublin Project report notes that Germany sent 306 outgoing requests to Switzerland in 2010 and received 350 transfer requests from Switzerland in return. Similarly Norway sent 458 requests to Sweden and received 482 in return, supra n39, 21.

in transfer, notwithstanding the introduction of the costly EURODAC database.[68] The financial costs of the Dublin apparatus have yet to be publically reported but are officially recognised as 'substantial'.[69] In its Green Paper, the European Commission appeared to side-line the cost issue by emphasising the political objectives 'regardless of its financial implications'.[70] In the absence of such data, it is difficult not to concur with Peers who describes the system as 'an expensive waste of time'.[71]

The Asylum Procedures Directive[72]

The introduction of a directive on asylum procedures provided a welcome opportunity to ensure that a standard, fair system of refugee protection was implemented across the EU. Congruent procedures should result in comparable determinations thus providing a more secure platform for burden-sharing initiatives. Yet the wider focus on the prevention of irregular migration has generated a number of assumptions that have informed the directive as a component of the CEAS. These assumptions have emphasised speed at the expense of quality decision-making and, in so doing, they effectively militate against a fair, individualised procedure as required by international refugee and human rights standards.

---

68 The numbers of transfers in 2009–2010 amounts to around one-quarter of the requests made for transfer by states (and only one-third of the number of successful requests are actually transferred): Dublin Project EU *Dublin II Regulation: Lives on Hold: Comparative European Report* February 2013. Available at: http://www.ecre.org/component/content/article/56-ecre-actions/317-dublin-ii-regulation-lives-on-hold.html; European Commission 'Eurostat asylum statistics' 2011. Available at: http://appsso.eurostat.ec.europa.eu/nui/show.do?dataset=migr_dubin&lang=en.

69 European Commission *Staff Working Paper: Evaluation of the Dublin Convention* 2001 SEC [2001] 756, 13 June 2001, p18.

70 European Commission *Green Paper on the Future of the Common European Asylum System* COM [2007] 301 Final 6 June 2007, 13.

71 European Commission *Report from the Commission to the European Parliament and the Council on the Evaluation of the Dublin System* 6 June 2007 Com (2007) 299; Council Regulation (EC) No 2725/2000 of 11 December 2000 *Concerning the Establishment of 'EURODAC' for the Comparison of Fingerprints for the Effective Application of the Dublin Convention* OJ L 316, 15 December 2000, p. 1–10. Three categories of persons, who must be at least 14 years of age, can be fingerprinted and tracked: protection seekers; aliens apprehended in connection with irregular border crossing and aliens found illegally in a Member State. Peers supra n9 362; Raitio, J 'A Few Remarks To Evaluate the Dublin System' in Goudappel, F and Raulus, H (eds) *The Future of Asylum in the European Union: Problems, Proposals and Human Rights* (Springer 2011).

72 Supra n1; for a discussion on the negotiations behind the Directive see Ackers, D 'The Negotiations on the Asylum Procedures Directive' (2005) 7 Eur J Migration and L 1.

The amount of discretion given to Member States on important legal safeguards has attracted sustained criticism.[73] Given the minimum standards approach of the initial phase of European asylum law, such early criticism is to be expected and may be regarded as premature. However, now that the directive has had time to bed in, with the additional commitment towards common standards in Article 78 of the TFEU, we should expect to see notable improvements in the new provisions. The scale of the task is certainly ambitious given the range of asylum systems and experiences across the EU but harmonisation requires such differences as far as possible be eradicated and Member State discretion to be minimised.[74] This led to considerable disagreement between the different political actors, with many of the Commission's proactive proposals ultimately being rejected by the Council.

Accelerated Procedures

The use of expeditious procedures for cases that are 'clearly abusive' or 'manifestly unfounded' was endorsed by the UNHCR Executive Committee in 1983.[75] Certain guarantees must still be provided in these procedures, including a personal interview by a fully competent official and the right to appeal prior to rejection at the frontier or removal.[76] The UNHCR has been less willing to accept the proliferation of safe third country principles and has consistently emphasised the need for proper procedures so that the non-refoulement obligation can be secured.[77] Yet the agency has attracted criticism for failing to undertake a timely analysis of the effects of accelerated procedures, leaving too much initiative to states which has consequently allowed questionable practices to thrive.[78]

Article 47 of the Charter on Fundamental Rights guarantees the right to an effective remedy, echoing Article 13 of the ECHR. In 2010, the EU's Fundamental Rights Agency reported on interviews with almost 900 applicants who were challenging negative decisions.[79] They found numerous obstacles to an effective remedy including insufficient information, lack of access to legal advice and poor

---

73 Procedures Directive Article 27(3)b and Article 38(3)a; there is a large amount of state discretion on matters including state funded legal assistance; lists of safe third countries and the use of non-suspensive appeals: Mitsilegas, V 'A "Common" EU Immigration and Asylum Policy: National and Institutional Constraints' in Shah supra n9, 128; Costello supra n3, Chapter 2.

74 Harmonisation is also diminished by the position of the UK, Ireland and Denmark who are not bound by the recast directives.

75 UN EX Com No 30 XXXIV *The Problem of Manifestly Unfounded or Abusive Applications for Refugee Status or Asylum* (UNHCR 20 October 1983).

76 Ibid, para e.

77 UN Ex Com No 87*Conclusion On International Protection* (UNHCR 1999) para j.

78 Hurwitz, A *The Collective Responsibility of States to Protect Refugees* (OUP 2009) 260.

79 EU Fundamental Rights Agency *Access to Effective Remedies: The Asylum Seekers Perspective* Thematic Report (EU 2010).

communication which the applicant could not sufficiently understand. These problems are exacerbated in accelerated procedures as one applicant's statement aptly demonstrates: 'I went to a solicitor after my case was rejected, but he refused to take my case, and suggested I find another solicitor. But how was I going to find one to do everything for me in just five days?'[80]

Accelerated procedures are predominately related to formal or procedural grounds which can be determined quickly and efficiently without requiring a full determination of the merits.[81] By contrast more complex issues, such as those questioning credibility, demand a fuller procedure in order to ensure that the potential for refoulement is minimised.[82] State practice has varied enormously and in some cases, the Procedures Directive has resulted in a reduction in the use of expedited procedures.[83] At the same time, a broad category of manifestly unfounded claims allows accelerated proceedings in cases where the application could have substantial merit.[84]

Article 31(8) of the recast Procedures Directive provides a wide variety of situations which may result in an application being accelerated. This gives rise to concern that accelerated procedures may become viewed as the norm; a concern compounded by the fact that the accelerated procedure is not defined. In the past this omission has encouraged considerable divergence in state practice, as evidenced by the 12 states recently surveyed by the UNHCR.[85] In some countries acceleration has already become the norm, for example in Bulgaria 98.3 per cent of cases were accelerated in a statutory time frame of three days.[86] It is difficult to envisage how complex issues of refugee protection can be adequately and fairly determined in this time frame. In the UK, applicants, including their children, are detained during the accelerated procedure on the basis that such claims can

---

80 Ibid, 29.

81 Oakley, S 'Accelerated Procedures For Asylum In The EU. Fairness Versus Efficiency' Sussex Migration Working Paper No 43 University of Sussex 2007); Costello, C 'The Asylum Procedures Directive and the Proliferation of Safe Country Practices: Deterrence, Deflection and the Dismantling of International Protection' (2005) Eur J Migration and L 7, 35.

82 See for example, UNHCR '*Towards Common Standards on Asylum Procedures' Reflections on the Working Document Prepared by the European Commission* (UNHCR 1999).

83 Fullerton, M 'Inadmissible in Iberia: The Fate of Asylum Seekers in Spain and Portugal' (2005) 17 Intl J Refugee L 659; UNHCR *Improving Asylum Procedures: Comparative Analysis and Recommendations For Law and Practice* 2010; New Asylum Law 12/2009 for details see European Database of Asylum Law, available at: http://www.asylumlawdatabase.eu/en/content/edal-country-overview-spain (accessed 11 November 2012).

84 Oakley supra n81.

85 UNHCR supra n82, 226 and 258 which lists the different justifications used for acceleration under Article 23(4).

86 Ibid, 227.

be quickly determined.[87] In other states, such as the Czech Republic, Finland and Germany, applicants may not even realise that their applications have been accelerated as there is no formal channel directing the application to a prioritised procedure.[88] Appeals in the accelerated procedure are often non-suspensive despite the fact that around one-quarter of asylum decisions are overturned on appeal in France, Germany and the UK.[89]

The existing Procedures Directive provides for an accelerated procedure if the claim is delayed and there is no reasonable cause for the delay, thus sanctioning an 'approach which is sceptical of late applications'.[90] Yet Article 7(1) provides that asylum applications should neither be 'rejected nor excluded' on the sole ground that the applications have not been made as soon as possible.[91] This inconsistency is regrettable. Limitations on interviews and legal assistance along with non-suspensive appeals are unlikely to satisfy the standards outlined by ECtHR jurisprudence.[92] Lateness taken in isolation is not a reliable indicator of credibility as recognised by the ECtHR in *Jabari v Turkey* [2001].[93] The case concerned an Iranian woman who feared being stoned to death following allegations of adultery. Her asylum application was rejected by the Turkish authorities and deportation proceedings were initiated as she had not complied with a statutory time limit requiring her to claim within 5 days of arrival. The Court found that this automatic rejection, due to the strict time limit, was not consistent with Article 3 or the right to an effective remedy in Article 13 of the ECHR. Similarly, in *Hatami v Sweden* the Commission had found a violation of Article 3 where an application had been rejected due to inconsistencies in the applicant's story emerging from an interview which lasted less than 10 minutes.[94]

The recast directive deletes Article 23(4)(i), removing the acceleration of claims purely on the ground that they could have been made sooner.[95] However, Article 31(8)h provides for acceleration where an applicant entered or overstayed unlawfully and delayed making their application without good cause.

---

87 The UK's decision to reject the recast Procedures Directive is partly attributable to this practice which would need to be reviewed under the new, enhanced provisions: European Commission *Amended Proposal for a Directive of the EP and the Council on Common Procedures for Granting and Withdrawing International Protection Status* Brussels 1 June 2011 COM 2011/0319 final 'Recast Directive'.

88 Supra n85, 237.

89 Ibid, 254; Eurostat 2010 – the average for the three countries was 26.7 per cent.

90 Article 23(4)I discussed by Craig and Fletcher supra n8, 61.

91 Article 10, Recast Directive supra n87.

92 Peers, S *EU Justice and Home Affairs Law* (OUP 2010) 352.

93 App 40035/98, Council of Europe: European Court of Human Rights, 11 July 2000 .

94 32448/96 23 April 1988; see also *Said v Netherlands* App 2345/02 2005 where applicant's credibility had been damaged due to a failure to submit documentation.

95 European Commission supra n87 Article 9(1).

Inconsistent accounts may also attract accelerated procedures.[96] The UNHCR Handbook requires that determining authorities give the applicant the benefit of the doubt in the case of inconsistent testimonies; an acknowledgement that victims of torture often provide confused accounts due to the trauma that they have experienced.[97] The UN Committee Against Torture has reasoned that complete accuracy can seldom be expected in cases of sexual abuse and concludes that inconsistencies should not undermine credibility.[98] In *Tala v Sweden* the Committee found that inconsistencies could be attributed to Post Traumatic Stress Disorder arising from the applicant's experience of torture, thus removal would violate Article 3 of the Convention Against Torture.[99]

If the procedure is designed to achieve protection for the genuine applicant, the presumption that inconsistency indicates deception is highly problematic. The recast directive aims to address this by allowing adverse inferences only if an applicant makes clearly false or obviously improbable representations contradicting country of origin information.[100]

An additional reason for acceleration applies when an applicant cannot produce valid travel documents.[101] Yet it is widely acknowledged that a person fleeing persecution is extremely unlikely to be in possession of such a document.[102] Fortunately, the recast directive addresses this concern by only providing for acceleration 'if it is likely that the applicant acted in bad faith' in destroying or disposing of identity or travel documents.[103]

Suspensive appeals The Procedures Directive provides that the right to remain lasts only until the first instance decision is taken notwithstanding ample evidence that many refusals are successfully appealed.[104] The state is thus afforded broad discretion is determining whether appeals should be suspensive (ie, in–country).[105] This position is supported by the CJEU which has ruled that the right to an effective

96 Procedures Directive, Article 23(4)g.

97 *Hatami v Sweden* App 32448/96 ECtHR 23 January 1997.

98 *CT and KM v Sweden* 2007 CAT 279/2005.

99 *Tala v Sweden* CAT 43/1996.

100 Recast Procedures Directive, Article 31(8)e.

101 Procedures Directive, Article 23(4)f and Recast Directive 31(8)d.

102 UNHCR *Handbook* para 47; Craig and Fletcher supra n8, 73.

103 Recast Procedures Directive, Article 31(8)d.

104 Procedures Directive Article 7, Recast Directive Article 9(1). See for example Asylum Aid *Unsustainable: The Quality of Initial Decision Making in Women's Asylum Claims* (Asylum Aid 2011); Refugee Action 'National Asylum Charity Calls for Legal Aid Reform and Greater Access to Justice' (Press Release 6 August 2012). Available at: http://www.refugee-action.org.uk/news/2012/legalaidreform.aspx (accessed 26 March 2013); European Commission, Eurostat asylum statistics, 2012. Available at: http://epp.eurostat.ec.europa.eu/statistics_explained/index.php/Asylum_statistics.

105 Vedsted-Hansen, J 'Conditions and Criteria for Determining Asylum' in Goudappel and Raulus supra n71, 143.

remedy under the Procedures Directive does not demand a right of appeal against an accelerated designation.[106] However, the national courts must be able to review the reason behind the decision that determines the application to be unfounded. Further, there should not be an irrebuttable presumption as to the legality of those reasons.[107] The recast provisions provide that an applicant shall remain in order to exercise an effective remedy until the time period for that remedy has expired, however this does not necessarily apply for unfounded or inadmissible cases.[108] In these cases a national court or tribunal is empowered to rule on whether or not the applicant may remain on the territory of the state, either upon request of the concerned applicant or acting on its own motion.[109]

The time limit for appeals has also been a matter of considerable debate. The European Parliament has recommended a minimum time limit of 45 working days in the normal procedure and 30 working days in the accelerated procedure.[110] This is far more prescriptive that the Procedures Directive which allows states to determine a reasonable time limit which will not render the exercise of the appeal impossible or excessively difficult.[111] The CJEU have suggested that a 15-day time limit in accelerated cases might be reasonable and proportionate but this will depend on the circumstances of the case.[112]

Interviews and information A further concern arises from the requirement that the applicant has the right to be informed only in a language they may 'reasonably be supposed to understand'.[113] This phraseology is also found in the Dublin Regulation.[114] The right to an interpreter at an interview is provided if necessary but this does not clearly apply to other stages of the procedure.[115] The Commission's recast proposals sought to ensure that the applicant would be informed in a language that s/he understands and is able to communicate in. However, the amended directive endorses the existing approach and this remains a matter of significant concern[116] Research by the EU's Fundamental Rights Agency suggests that asylum seekers are often confused regarding information about their

106 Procedures Directive, Article 39.

107 CJEU C-69/10 *Brahim Samba Diouf v Ministre du Travail de l'emploi et de l'immigration* 28 July 2001 para 61.

108 Recast Procedures Directive Art 45(5) and (6).

109 Recast Procedures Directive, Art 46(6).

110 European Parliament *Asylum: Common Procedures for Granting and Withdrawing International Protection Status. Recast* 09/0165(COD) 6 April 2011 Amendment 93.

111 Recast Procedures Directive, Art 46(4).

112 Supra n107 para 61.

113 Procedures Directive, Article 10(1)a.

114 Dublin Regulation, Article 3(4).

115 Procedures Directive, Article 10(1)b.

116 Recast Procedures Directive, Art 12(1); ECRE *Comments from the ECRE on the Amended Commission Proposal to recast the Asylum procedures Directive* COM(2011)319 final. ECRE, 3.

case and this is particularly so when the information is imparted in a language which is not their own.[117] This is supported by findings from the UNHCR which demonstrate that applicants are not always given the information they require in order to understand the refusal.[118] Often the information in the applicant's language is brief and explains only that the application is unsuccessful whereas much of the pertinent information on the appeal process is in the national language.[119]

General concerns remain over the experience and knowledge of examining personnel. The revised provisions require the personnel to seek advice 'wherever necessary' from experts on particular issues; such as medical, cultural, religious, child-related or gender issues.[120] The personal interview is to be carried out by persons competent under national law.[121] However, again there is limited European direction on how this competence is to be measured. There is a requirement that interview personnel should not wear military uniforms[122] but there is no prescription as to specific training, with discretion left to the state on the rules for the identification and documentation of symptoms of torture and other forms of violence.[123] The reforms include an opportunity for applicants to present an explanation of any inconsistencies and to clarify mistranslations and misconceptions in the personal interview.[124] However, whilst the applicant's approval of the interview report is recognised as desirable, it is not mandatory.

There is considerable state variation in the provision of free legal advice and assistance to asylum seekers. Although the Procedures Directive makes reference to free assistance and/or representation, these terms have not been clearly defined and the state is therefore afforded considerable discretion in practice.[125] Further, Member States can specify that free legal advice and/or assistance can be restricted if the appeal or review is unlikely to succeed.[126] The recast provisions improve on the clarity of the current provisions by requiring free legal assistance and representation for those lacking sufficient resources in appeal procedures.[127] At a bare minimum this should include assistance with document preparation and representation in an initial hearing.[128] Yet the state retains the discretion to refuse

117 EU Fundamental Rights Agency *The Duty to Inform Applicants about Asylum Procedures: The Asylum-Seekers Perspective* (EU Fundamental Rights Agency 2010) and supra n79.

118 UNHCR supra n82, 50; lack of information provided to applicants is also a problem in Dublin transfer cases, Dublin project EU supra n39, 56.

119 Ibid.

120 Recast Procedures Directive, Article 10(3)d.

121 Ibid, Art 14(1).

122 Ibid, Art 15(3)d.

123 Recast Procedures Directive, Article 18(4).

124 Recast Procedures Directive, Article 17(3).

125 Procedures Directive, Article 15, Recast Directive Article 20(2).

126 Procedures Directive, Article 15(3)d.

127 Recast Procedures Directive, Articles 20, 21.

128 Recast Procedures Directive, Article 20(1).

free assistance and representation if the appeal is deemed to have 'no tangible prospect of success'.[129]

Given the sensitivity of asylum decision-making and the risks resulting from false-negatives, it is essential that interviews are confidential and that applicants' feel secure. In practice, the conduct of such interviews is open to wide divergence as demonstrated by the UNHCR study. Several interviews were conducted simultaneously in the same rooms in Greece and Italy despite the requirement for confidentiality.[130] The qualifications demanded of interviewers also varied with some states offeringadditional workplace training and mentoring to complement formal education.[131] By contrast, in Greece there is no specific training and interviews are conducted by police officers without any required knowledge of refugee law. In Spain (with the exception of Madrid) there is also no requirement of knowledge or specialist training.[132] It is vital that such interviews are carried out by suitably qualified and independent officials. The use of police officers is particularly problematic given the likelihood that victims of persecution will have previously suffered at the hands of state officials. The conduct of interpreters also gave rise to serious concern in the UNHCR report which found 'serious shortcomings in the ability of interviewers to work effectively with or manage the conduct of interpreters'.[133]

Country of origin information was not applied appropriately and was completely omitted in interviews in several countries, including the UK, Germany and France.[134] Again, of grave concern were the interviews in Greece which suffered from numerous shortcomings falling well short of the minimum standards of the directive. The overwhelming majority of the 49 interviews in Athens lasted under 10 minutes and interviewers failed to ask follow-up questions, focusing instead on the economic status of the applicant, their travel route and their choice of destination.[135]

Detention in accelerated procedures International and European law clearly establish that applicants should not be detained purely because they have made an application for international protection.[136] Yet this is not the practice in some states where short-term detention is used for no other purpose than administrative convenience. In the UK the Detained Fast Track (DFT) has been used since 2003 and its entire basis is that the application can be determined quickly. Following the Chief Inspector of the Border Agency's investigation in 2011 it became apparent

129 Recast Procedures Directive, Article 21(3).

130 Article 13(2); UNHCR supra n83, 101; Ascoli, A 'Conditions and Criteria for Determining Asylum' in Goudappel and Raulus supra n71, 125.

131 UNHCR supra n82, 105–106.

132 Ibid at 107.

133 Ibid at 122.

134 Ibid at 151.

135 Ibid at 151–152.

136 Asylum Procedures Directive, Article 18; Recast Procedures Directive, Article 26.

that 30 per cent of those detained were released early and almost half of the releases were attributed to health reasons, including experiences of trauma and torture.[137] In 2013 a successful judicial review found that the continued detention of five torture survivors was unlawful due to asystemic failure by the UK Border Agency to take their cases seriously.[138]

On average people waited for 13 days in the DFT rather than the advertised 3–4 days for an initial decision with most waiting 11 days for an initial interview. A presumption of illegitimacy permeates the DFT, as evidenced in the Government's original plan: '*... to deliver decisions quickly ensuring, amongst other things, that those whose claims can be quickly decided can be removed as quickly as possible in the event that the claim is unsuccessful*'.[139] Whilst short-term detention for administrative processing has been endorsed by the ECtHR such detention must not be arbitrary and is subject to certain safeguards.[140] The proliferation of detention centres, the use of private contractors and the absence of clear legal prescription in many states threaten to undermine these safeguards. Transfers under the Dublin Regulation often begin with detention, whilst external cooperation agreements have resulted in increased resort to detention in non-European states.[141] The 'last resort' principle that the UNHCR and Council of Europe regard as essential when deciding to detain, is evidently undermined by state practice.[142] Of great concern is the absence of a maximum time limit for detention which significantly increases the risk of arbitrary detention and adds to the trauma already experienced by many asylum seekers.

---

137 Independent Chief Inspector of the UK Border Agency *Asylum: A Thematic Inspection of the Detained Fast Track* 2011.

138 *R (on the application of EO, RA, CE, OE and RAN) v SSHD* [2013] EWHC 1236 Admin.

139 Ministerial Statement delivered by Minister for Immigration, Des Browne, House of Commons, 16 September 2004.

140 *Saadi v UK* App 13229/03 ECtHR 29 January 2008; Wilsher, D *Immigration Detention: Law, History, Politics* (CUP 2012).

141 See for example Global Detention Project *Ukraine: Detention Profile* (Global Detention Project December 2012); Amnesty International *Annual Report 2011: Ukraine* (Amnesty International POL/10/001/2011); Commissioner for Human Rights of the Council of Europe *Report by Thomas Hammarberg Commissioner for Human Rights of the Council of Europe Following His Visit to Turkey on 28 June – 3 July 2009: Human Rights of Asylum Seekers and Refugees* (Council of Europe 2009); Helsinki Citizens' Assembly *Unwelcome Guests: The Detention of Refugees in Turkey's 'Foreigners' Guesthouses* (Helsinki Citizens Assembly, Refugee Advocacy & Support Program 2007).

142 C/E Recommendation (2003) 5 *On Measures of Detention of Asylum Seekers* para 6; Parliamentary Assembly Resolution *Detention of Asylum Seekers and Irregular Migrants in Europe* 1707 (2010) para 3, available at: http://assembly.coe.int/Mainf.asp?link=/Documents/AdoptedText/ta10/ERES1707.htm (accessed 27 July 2013); UNHCR *Detention Guidelines* (UNHCR 2012). Available at: http://www.unhcr.org/505b10ee9.html (accessed 27 July 2013).

General Designations of Safety

First Country of Asylum (FCA)

The FCA designation applies when a country has previously recognised an asylum seeker as a refugee or provided sufficient protection to prevent refoulement and is willing to readmit the applicant. Its origins can be traced back to Article 31 of the Refugee Convention which prevents states from imposing penalties on account of illegal entry or presence on those refugees who have come *directly* from a territory where their life or freedom was threatened. It has a more secure legal basis than Safe Third Country principle but is not without its critics.[143]

The non-binding 'London Resolution on Host Third Countries' in 1992 paved the way for greater European recognition of the FCA concept along with safe countries of origin and manifestly unfounded applications.[144] Recognition that there was a FCA would prevent any further need to examine the merits of the applicant's claim.

Under the Procedures Directive an applicant who has been recognised as a refugee or otherwise enjoys sufficient protection in a third country and can reasonably be expected to avail themselves of the protection of that country, can have their application declared inadmissible provided they will be re-admitted to that country.[145] The question of effective protection is fundamental; demanding protection of human rights norms, due process of the law and measures to challenge the asylum decision.[146] The UNHCR regard the issue of family unity as central in this assessment:

> a person's fundamental right to family unity is an overwhelming consideration that countries of asylum should consider. It should thus take precedence over the availability of effective protection provided by the third country, in the assessment of whether the person shall be returned to that country.[147]

Yet again, state practice varies enormously with several states electing not to apply the rules. In the UK the question of effective protection is not addressed at all

---

143 Byrne, R and Shacknove, A 'The Safe Third Country Notion in European Asylum Law' (1996) 9 Harvard HR L.

144 European Council Conclusion of the meeting of the Ministers responsible for Immigration (London No3 – 1 December 1992) Doc 10579/92 IMMIG 2 'London Resolutions'.

145 Procedures Directive, Article 26, recast Procedures Directive, Art 35.

146 Goodwin-Gill and McAdam supra n23, 393.

147 UNHCR supra n83, 283; see also UNHCR Global Consultations Lisbon Expert Roundtable 'Summary Conclusions on the Concept of "Effective Protection" in the Context of Secondary Movements of Refugees and Asylum Seekers' UNHCR 9–10 December 2002.

in the applicable legislation.[148] In fact the requirement to ensure re-admittance is rarely found in national legislation with states focusing primarily on the de jure recognition of refugee status.[149]

Safe Third Countries (STC)

The initial practice of identifying safe third countries began to be sanctioned as part of a European strategy with the Dublin Convention in 1990.[150] It has since expanded to enable states to designate non-European STCs and safe countries of origin (SCO's). According to the respective provisions in the Procedures Directive any such designation is based on a substantiation of safety which must be objectively demonstrated through the recognition and implementation of human rights norms.[151] Yet these generalised presumptions of safety clearly challenge the fundamental building blocks of international refugee protection, particularly the need for individualised determinations and fair procedures.

The notion that an applicant should apply for asylum in the first safe country is the less controversial aspect which can be traced back to 1979 where the UNHCR Executive Committee reasoned that where an asylum seeker had close links with another state, it may be fair and reasonable for them to request asylum from that country.[152] Article 31 of the Refugee Convention forms the legal basis of the STC principle by protecting refugees from penalties incurred when they have come 'directly' from a territory where their lives or freedom was threatened.[153] Yet, others have argued against this literal interpretation, reasoning that Article 31 does not require a person to have come directly from the country where they experienced the specific threat.[154] The UNHCR confirm that Article 31 would include a person who had briefly transited through an intermediate country and emphasise that each case should be determined on its merits.[155] A correct interpretation would be unlikely

148 s33 and Schedule 3 Asylum Treatment of Claimants Act 2004.

149 UNHCR supra n83, 287–293.

150 *Convention Determining the State Responsible for Examining Asylum Lodged in One of the Member States of the EC* adopted 15 June 1990 entered into force 1 September 1997 [1997] OJ C254/1' Dublin Convention'.

151 Art 38 Recast procedures Directive; UNHCR 'The Concept of "Protection" Elsewhere' (1995) 7 Inl J Refugee L 123, 126.

152 UNCHR EX Committee Conclusion 15 *Refugees without an Asylum Country* (1979) para h (iv).

153 Byrne, R and Shacknove, A supra n143.

154 See for example Hathaway, JC *The Rights of Refugees under International Law* (CUP 2005) 399 and Goodwin-Gill, GS 'Article 31 of the 1951 Convention Relating the Status of Refugees: Non-Penalization, Detention and Protection' in Feller, E; Türk, V and Nicholson, F (eds) *Refugee Protection in International Law: UNHCR's Global Consultations on International Protection* (CUP 2003) 216.

155 UNHCR *Guidelines on Applicable Criteria and Standards Relating to the Detention of Asylum Seekers* (February 1999) para 4.

to reject applications made by refugees who had merely transited through a safe country, there being no 'close links' as required by UNHCR soft-law principles.[156]

Under Article 27 of the Procedures Directive an application will be considered inadmissible if, inter alia, a country which is not a Member State is considered to be a STC.[157] Whilst the applicant should have an opportunity to rebut this presumption there has been no requirement to hold a personal interview.[158] This position is undoubtedly improved by the recast provisions which include an obligation to hold an interview in such cases, enabling the applicant to challenge the application of the rules in their particular circumstances.[159] Data collected in the UNHCR survey reveals wide variations between European states over the right to such interviews and their conduct.[160] Given the presumption of safety and the consequence of finding an application inadmissible, the interview is an essential procedural safeguard and its inclusion in the recast proposals represents a significant upgrading from minimum standards. The agreed text of the recast Dublin III Regulation also includes an obligation to give applicants a personal interview with a qualified person under national law.[161]

From a protection perspective it is surprising that whilst Article 27(1) requires the receiving state to respect the principle of non-refoulement and the possibility of granting refugee status, it does not actually require the state to have ratified the Refugee Convention.[162] Given the widespread acceptance of the Refugee Convention there is concern that those states that have elected not to ratify its terms may be unable to guarantee protection from refoulement. This is illustrated in the case of Iraqi asylum seekers returned to Jordan and Syria which host a large number of refugees but are not parties to the Refugee Convention.[163]

The extent of the applicant's connection to the STC has become crucial in discussions over third country removals. The UNHCR has repeatedly stressed the

---

156 UN Ex Com 15 (XXX) *Refugees without an Asylum Country* 16 October 1979.

157 See also Recast Procedures Directive, Article 33.

158 Article 12(2)c in conjunction with Art 23(4) and Art27(2)c; *UNHCR Comments on the European Commission's Proposal for Directive of the European Parliament and of the Council on Minimum Standards on Procedures in MS for Granting and Withdrawing International Protection* COM(2009)554 (UNHCR 2010) 27.

159 Recast Procedures Directive, Article 34(1).

160 UNHCR supra n82, 86.

161 Article 5, European Commission *Proposal For a Regulation of the European Parliament and of the Council Establishing the Criteria and Mechanisms for Determining the Member State Responsible for Examining an Application for International Protection Lodged in One of the Member States by a Third Country National or Stateless Person* (Recast) COM (2008) 820 3 December 2008.

162 ECRE *Information on the Council Directive 2005/85/EC of 1 December 2005 on Minimum Standards on Procedures in Member States for Granting and Withdrawing Refugee Status* (ECRE 2006) 23 Available at: http://www.unhcr.org/refworld/docid/464317ab2.html (accessed 27 March 2013); Article 38(1) Recast Procedures Directive.

163 Hurwitz supra n19, 55.

importance of connections including family ties, language, cultural ties and prior residence.[164] However, the Procedures Directive refers merely to the 'possibility' of applying for protection, suggesting that a removal may take place without proof of any substantive link.[165] In the UK, transit is sufficient to establish a connection and earlier case law suggests that the applicant did not need to be aware that a possibility for claiming protection existed.[166] Furthermore, there has been no requirement placed on national authorities to ensure that the applicant will be admitted to a refugee determination procedure. Rather the authorities are required to 'provide him/her with a document informing the authorities of the third country, in the language of that country, that the application has not been examined in substance'.[167] This has resulted in applicants being 'bounced' between countries.[168] The question of genuine access to fair procedures is in danger of becoming an act of faith. The applicant can rebut the safety presumption by showing serious grounds for considering that the country 'is not safe in his or her circumstances' but this will be adversely affected by the application of accelerated procedures.[169]

International human rights law does not allow states to shift their responsibility so easily. From the rulings in *TI v UK*[170] and *MSS v Greece and Belgium*[171] we can see that the ECtHR requires the sending state to be satisfied that there is no risk of inhuman and degrading treatment or torture should the applicant be returned. Seen from this perspective, the Procedures Directive affords too much discretion to states on how they determine third country safety and how they establish a necessary connection.[172] The absence of individualised assessment in such cases is difficult to reconcile with the principle of non-refoulement or the recognition of refugee status which requires both an objective and subjective assessment of the risk of persecution.[173]

---

164 UNHCR *Observations on the European Commission's Proposal for a Council Regulation Establishing the Criteria and Mechanisms for Determining the Member State Responsible for Examining an Asylum Application Lodged in One of the Member States by a Third Country National* COM 2001 447 final (February 2002) para 7.

165 Procedures Directive, Article 27(2)d; Recast Directive Article 38(1)e; Hurwitz, supra n19, 56. It should be noted that the react directive does include provision for the applicant to challenge the link (Article 38(2)c).

166 *R v Special Adjudicator exp Linsam Kandasamy* [1994] Imm AR 333 (QB); Asylum, Immigration (Treatment of Claimants) Act 2004; Mitsilegas, supra n73.

167 Procedures Directive, Article 27 3(b); see also supra n162, Art 38(2)c.

168 Hurwitz supra n19, 57–58.

169 Craig and Fletcher supra n8, 71–72.

170 *TI v UK* App 43844/98 7 March 2000 re removal of Sri Lankan asylum seeker to Germany under Dublin Convention did not prevent UKs continuing obligation under Article 3 (satisfied here as German authorities had committed to re-examining his claim).

171 *M.S.S. v Belgium and Greece*, App 30696/09 21 January 2011.

172 Procedures Directive, Article 27(20b) and 27(20a) respectively.

173 UNHCR *Handbook* paras 37 and 38.

A number of assumptions underpin the safe country designation, including the availability of sufficient information to determine safety, the ability of countries to identify protection needs and the preference for protection in the immediate vicinity. Research by Byrne and Shacknove in the early 1990s demonstrated that these assumptions were difficult to substantiate:

> the evidence however, indicates that country of origin information is often insufficient to support general conclusions about safety; that cultural and political heterogeneity often means that asylum-seekers receive less protection form persecution in neighbouring states than in more distant ones; and that governments have not adequately substantiated their allegations of widespread abuse of asylum procedures.[174]

It is submitted that these concerns remain equally valid today where the emphasis on preventing irregular migration creates a culture of disbelief which permeates the decision-making process.

Common Lists: Safe Countries of Origin

In addition to rules on STC's, the Procedures Directive sought to establish a common European list of Safe Countries of Origin which would be applied when an applicant was either a national or was stateless with habitual residency in the SCO.[175] This designation would cover countries such as Albania, Russia, Turkey, Ukraine and Belarus, in effect extending the borders of Europe significantly. Annex II[176] requires four non-exhaustive criteria to be taken into account when determining safety, including: observance of fundamental rights, respect of non-refoulement and a system of effective remedies against violations of these rights. Once it is established that an applicant is from a country on the common list there is no requirement for states to assess individual safety; the application is deemed unfounded unless the applicant is able to rebut the presumption.

Negotiations on the safe countries to be included on the list unsurprisingly failed to generate consensus and exposed a number of tensions between the European institutions. In 2008 the negotiations were abruptly halted after a successful legal challenge by the European Parliament resulted in the annulment of the common list.[177] The CJEU ruled that the list required full participation by the European Parliament as part of the ordinary legislative procedure.

The decision represented a hollow victory for refugee advocates as states continued to operate their own lists for the purpose of accelerated decision-

174 Byrne and Shacknove supra n143, 194.

175 Procedures Directive, Article 31(1), Recast Procedures Directive Article 36(1).

176 Recast Directive Annex 1.

177 CJEU C-133/06 *European Parliament v European Union* [6 May 2008].

making.[178] These lists reveal the extent of the challenge when adopting a common position. Of the 12 countries surveyed by the UNHCR only France, the UK and Germany continue to have operational lists with only one country, Ghana, appearing as common to all three lists (in the UK Ghana is designated as safe for men only).[179] Eight countries appear as common to the lists of both France and the UK but that leaves a significant number of countries listed without any consensus as to their safety.

In the UK, inclusion on the list means that applicants will have their case certified, shifting the burden of proof to the applicant to show that there are serious grounds for considering the country not to be safe. Any appeal against the decision will be non-suspensive.[180] The UNHCR have expressed concerns that it is not always possible for applicants to effectively rebut the permission of safety as many are not informed that their country of origin is deemed 'safe' until they are notified of the refusal.[181] At this point the right to rebut the presumption could be rendered illusory if appeals are non-suspensive.[182]

The independent monitoring group, Statewatch, analysed the various national responses to the designation of seven African countries on the European Council's proposed common list.[183] Whereas the Czech Republic, France, Hungary, Portugal, Ireland and Slovakia regarded all seven countries as safe, the European Commission did not regard any as safe (a similar position to that advanced by Finland and Estonia).[184] The national responses reveal some troubling, convoluted reasoning. Perhaps most surprisingly, the data on the nationality of recognised refugees does not appear to have been afforded much weight.[185] Statewatch notes that there are some 11,000 Senegalese refugees (from an estimated population of 12.5 million) living outside the country of origin, hardly indicating that Senegal is generally free from persecution.[186] A number of countries on the proposed list already host a significant number of refugees from elsewhere (Senegal for example hosts around 20,000 Mauritanian refugees who fled ethnic violence in 1989), yet the designation of safety would also be applied to these non-nationals seeking protection. Although the UNHCR commenced repatriation of many Mauritanians in 2010 the operation has proceeded slowly. In 2012 Mauritanian refugees in Senegal began a hunger strike outside the UNHCR offices due to their unstable

178 Article 30 Procedures Directive. National lists are also authorised by the Recast Procedures Directive, Article 37(1).

179 UNHCR supra n82, 336.

180 Nationality, Immigration and Asylum Act s94(3) 2002.

181 UNHCR supra n82, 23.

182 Byrne and Shacknove, supra n143, 224.

183 Botswana, Benin, Cape Verde, Ghana, Mali, Mauritius and Senegal. Statewatch News 'EU Divided over List of "Safe Countries of Origin" – *Statewatch* calls for the list to be scrapped' (Statewatch, September 2004).

184 Ibid.

185 Costello supra n81, 67.

186 Statewatch supra n185.

position and uncertain status.[187] The inclusion of Senegal on a common safe country list is thus difficult to substantiate.

The advancement of a common safe list in the presence of such uncertainty is one of the clearest illustrations of the protectionist failure of the CEAS and the clumsy compromises of harmonisation. Given many states do not operate such lists, attempts to impose a common list constitutes a clear dilution of protection standards. The remaining discretion given to states to maintain a supplementary list contradicts common standards and raises issues of competence.[188] It should be noted that both provisions are included in the recast proposals. Thus there is a real risk of a race to the bottom as states try to match their neighbours by diluting protection standards and expediting procedures.[189]

Inadmissible and Manifestly Unfounded Applications

A state is not required to hear an application for refugee status if the case is deemed inadmissible. The situations when a state 'may' declare an application inadmissible include transfers under the Dublin Regulation in addition to cases within Article 25(1) Procedures Directive which includes non-European STC cases.[190] It is doubtful whether a non-suspensive remedy can be deemed truly effective in such cases.[191] ECtHR jurisprudence establishes that the right to an effective remedy under Article 13 ECHR could be breached if a procedure operates in such a way as to declare applications inadmissible without any access to the state so that the applicant could argue his case.[192] In *Abdolkhani v Turkey*[193] the ECtHR confirmed that Article 13 requires independent and rigorous scrutiny of a claim concerning serious allegations of a risk of refoulement. To be effective, a remedy must therefore have automatic suspensive effect in such situations. In the recent decision of *IM v France*[194] a breach of Articles 13 and 3 were found when the applicant's remedies had been limited by an accelerated unlawful entry

187 West Africa Democracy Radio 'Senegal Appeals to Mauritanian Refugees to End Hunger Strike' (9 July 2012). Available at: http://wadr.org/en/site/news_en/3933/Senegal-appeals-to-Mauritanian-refugees-to-end-hunger-strike.htm.

188 Craig and Fletcher supra n8, 73; Costello supra n3, 28.

189 For example: Craig and Fletcher n9, 76; Steiner, N observes that German politicians were typically more interested in keeping up with the asylum policies of their neighbours than they were about meeting international human rights norms; *Arguing about Asylum: The Complexity of Refugee Debates in Europe* (St. Martin's Press 2000) 79–80.

190 Recast Procedures Directive Article 33(1).

191 John-Hopkins, M 'The Emperor's New Safe Country Concepts: A UK Perspective on Sacrificing Fairness on the Altar of Efficiency' 2009 IJ Refugee L 21, 2, 250.

192 *Gebremedhin v France* App 24389/05 European Court of Human Rights, 26 July 2007.

193 Appl No 30471/08 European Court of Human Rights, 22 September 2009.

194 App 9152/09 European Court of Human Rights 2 February 2012.

procedure and the difficulties experienced in providing the required evidence whilst in detention.

By contrast, a manifestly unfounded application results in the decision being subjected to an expedited procedure. The difference between these two categories of case is one of degree but the inclusion of STC cases under both makes for a lack of clarity. The practice of the 12 states surveyed by the UNHCR indicates wide divergence on inadmissibility decisions. Whilst none of the states declare all the situations under Article 25 Procedures Directive to be inadmissible, only two states operate the rules in a broadly similar manner. A similar picture emerges regarding manifestly unfounded applications. Minimum standards have been interpreted and applied in very different ways such that the list of caveats and exceptions is too long to reiterate.[195]

Protecting Human Rights through Common Standards

Respect for human rights is listed as a core value for the EU.[196] The move towards common standards coincides with the elevated status of the EU Charter of Fundamental Rights which contains an explicit right to asylum as well as the prohibition of refoulement.[197] Yet the common asylum standards are accused of threatening the foundations in the Charter, in some cases requiring states to dilute the protection of their own asylum procedures to secure compliance with common standards.[198] The creation of a common SCO list remains a feature of the recast proposals and will undoubtedly result in a dilution of the procedural rights guaranteed in states that do not operate such a list at present.

Whilst the standards themselves can be criticised, a further unfortunate problem arises when states attempt to undercut these standards. Research by the European Council on Refugees and Exiles found that states administering border transfers often resorted to informal mechanisms rather than the lengthy Dublin process, thereby avoiding the limited protection that the latter provides.[199] Such practices have been observed at the borders between a number of Member States, including Germany and the Czech Republic, France and Switzerland, Austria and the Czech Republic and Italy and Greece. Additionally, Greece operates informal readmission arrangements with several other states outside the Dublin system.

195 UNHCR supra n83, 276.

196 *Treaty on the European Union* OJ C83/13, 30 March 2010 Article 6(3).

197 *EU Charter of Fundamental Rights* 2000/C 364/01 Article 18 and 19.

198 Costello supra n81, 65; Peers supra n92, 308.

199 ECRE supra n62, 19.

Towards Uniform Procedures: The Final Stage of Harmonisation

Whilst the creation of a common asylum system by 2012 may have been an ambitious objective of the Stockholm programme,[200] it will take until 2015 for the key directives to come into effect across the EU. In 2009 the European Commission proposed amendments to the Procedures Directive but the proposals failed to reach the trilogue dialogue discussions between the political institutions.[201] The original proposal was subsequently amended by the Commission in 2011pursuant to Article 78 TFEU to 'simplify and clarify rules' with the objective of ensuring procedures are efficient and fair. After four years, the new Procedures Directive was finally enacted with Commissioner Malmström describing the journey to common standards as 'a tough road'.[202]

It is clear that the latest provisions contain much to be welcomed and are generally an improvement on the existing directives. The term 'international protection' is preferred to refugee status, thus bringing subsidiary protection and refugee status under the same umbrella. The jurisdictional application is widened to specifically include applications made in territorial waters, in transit zones and at the border of the state.[203] Whilst a concentration on 'frontloading' aims to put 'adequate resources into the quality of decision making at first instance' with a view to providing a standard asylum procedure of no more than 6 months duration.[204]

This emphasis on initial decision-making is positive but it may obscure the effect of accelerated procedures on improved protection and fair determination. The six-month time limit is subject to a number of exceptions to take into account the particularities of Member States and may therefore quickly become redundant.[205] States are provided with an additional three months 'where necessary to ensure an adequate and complete examination of the application'. If one considers the relatively developed asylum system in the UK, it is notable that at present only 54 per cent of asylum cases are concluded within a 6 month period.[206] Thus states

200 Council of the European Union *The Stockholm Programme – An Open and Secure Europe Serving and Protecting the Citizens* 17024/09 2 December 2009, 69.

201 The European Parliament generally agreed with the Commission's original proposals but they were not supported by the Council: European Parliament Legislative Resolution 6 April 2011 *On the Proposal for a Directive of the EP and of the Council on Minimum Standards on Procedures in Member States for Granting and Withdrawing International Protection (Recast)* COM (2009) 0554 –C7-0248/2009-2009/0165(COD) Resolution P7_TA(2011)0136.

202 Europa Press Release 'Breakthrough for the Common Asylum System' (27 March 2013).

203 Recast Procedures Directive, Article 3(1).

204 Recast Procedures Directive, explanatory Memorandum para 3.1.3.

205 Recast Procedures Directive, Article 31(3).

206 'Asylum Performance Measures' 2010, UK Border Agency Management Information.

may be pushed to undercut standards by expediting procedures in a wider variety of cases to meet the 6 month target.

At present several states subject complex exclusion cases to accelerated procedures despite a Council of Europe recommendation to the contrary.[207] Some states also subject vulnerable people to accelerated procedures notwithstanding recommendations from the UNHCR and Council of Europe that these cases demand careful consideration.[208] In Germany for example, an accelerated procedure operates at airports irrespective of whether the applicant is a victim of torture or sexual violence.[209]

The new directive does make moderate improvements to some aspects of asylum procedures, reflecting the enhanced influence of the European Parliament. Yet it does not address the Parliament's recommendation for safe countries which included the abolition of national lists, thus 'ignoring their potentially devastating impact on access to protection for asylum seekers and on the objective of harmonisation of asylum procedures in the EU'.[210] States may continue to operate lists of SCO's despite the recognition that such a list 'can only take into account the general civil, legal and political circumstances in that country'.[211] This significant limitation is to be addressed by reversing the burden of proof and allowing the applicant to rebut the presumption in his or her case.

Ultimately, Member State concerns permeate the amendments, with efficiency winning out in the balance with fairness.[212] A large amount of discretion has been reintroduced threatening to undermine the goal of uniform protection notwithstanding the promise that 'similar cases should be treated alike and result in the same outcome'.[213]

It has been noted that the UK's piecemeal approach to the common asylum system, governed by an opt-out, has not been encouraging with minimal endorsement of positive initiatives.[214] Peers suggests that the EU's Short-term

---

207 Parliamentary Assembly Council of Europe Resolution 1471 (2005) *On Accelerated Procedures in Council of Europe Member States* paras 8.9 and 8.11 Council of Europe.

208 Ibid; UNHCR, supra n83, 265.

209 S18A Asylum Procedure Act, 7 July 1993 Federal Law Gazette I, 1361; UNHCR supra n83, 265; Fullerton, M 'Failing the Test: Germany Leads Europe in Dismantling Refugee Protection' (2001) 36 Texas Intl L Rev 231; UN Human Rights Committee Considers Report of Germany, 19 October 2012 Available at: http://www.ohchr.org/en/NewsEvents/Pages/DisplayNews.aspx?NewsID=12680&LangID=E (accessed 11 December 2012).

210 European Parliament supra n202; ECRE supra n117; Peers 'Revised EU Asylum Proposals: "Lipstick on a Pig"' (Statewatch Analysis, June 2011).

211 Recital 17 Recast Procedures Directive.

212 ECRE supra n117.

213 Recast Procedures Directive, Recital 4.

214 House of Lords 'A Common EU Policy on Illegal Immigration' 37th Report 2001–12 UK House of Lords, Paper 187. Of similar concern is the position of

Residents Directive was rejected by the UK largely due to a provision enabling permits for victims of human trafficking.[215] The UK's interaction with the preferential standards in the recast proposals has been limited, having also opted out of the amended Reception Conditions Directive, discussed in Chapter 5, on the basis that it does not wish to be bound by higher standards on detention and employment.[216]

Burden-Sharing post Stockholm

It has been noted that the term 'burden-sharing' is something of a misnomer, describing a process more accurately described as 'burden-shifting'. Further, that the foundation of its primary instrument, the Dublin Regulation, counteracts true solidarity in Europe.[217] It implies that refugees are a commodity that can be transferred between states and it amplifies a short-term bias that focuses on immediate costs and resource implications for host states.[218] The transfer system is constructed on the allocation of blame as asylum seekers will be removed to countries that fail to provide sufficient border scrutiny enabling irregular migration.[219]

Herein lies a catch-22 situation which the Dublin regime continues to neglect. The reason for migrants making secondary movements within Europe is reported to be the weakness in the asylum systems in the first country of arrival.[220] The systems in these countries become over-burdened due to their location and will thus operate less efficiently. As a direct consequence, migrants are encouraged to embark on secondary movement and in so doing they become increasingly desperate, resorting to dangerous and illegitimate means to avoid detection. Following reports that asylum seekers have burnt and mutilated their fingertips in order to avoid detection and inclusion on the EURODAC database, there seems little doubt that the system is failing in its protection mandate.[221]

Ireland and Denmark.

215 Mitsilegas supra n73, 134.

216 Stefanelli, J 'A Rule of Law Analysis of the Potential UK Opt-In to the Newly Tabled EU Asylum Procedures and Reception Conditions Directives' (Bingham Centre for the Rule of Law 2012). Available at: http://www.biicl.org/binghamcentre/eu_asylum (accessed 9 April 2013); Mitsilegas supra n73.

217 Dublin Project supra n39, 15.

218 Noll, G 'Risky Games? A Theoretical Approach to Burden-Sharing in the Asylum Field' (2003) 16 J Refugee Studies 3, 236; Lenart, J '"Fortress Europe": Compliance of the Dublin II Regulation with the European Convention for the Protection of Human Rights and Fundamental Freedoms' (2012) 28 Merkourios – Intl and Eur Migration L 109.

219 See also Noll supra n219.

220 Jesuit Refugee Service supra n61, 1.

221 Grant, H and Domokos, J 'Dublin Regulation Leaves Asylum Seekers with Their Fingers Burnt' *The Guardian* (7 October 2011). Available at: http://www.guardian.co.uk/world/2011/oct/07/dublin-regulation-european-asylum-seekers (accessed 28 March 2013).

The European Commission has acknowledged that the location of some countries will result in there being subject to additional burdens and migratory pressures.[222] This is demonstrated by a recent communication from five receiving states. In a joint communication, Cyprus, Malta, Spain, Italy and Greece called for urgent revision to Dublin to include a mechanism for suspending transfers to states facing particular pressure on their national asylum systems.[223]

The amended Dublin III Regulation will apply to the EU28 by the end of 2013.[224] States have been willing to accept the Commission's proposals regarding improved efficiency but less willing to improve legal safeguards such as family reunion. Crucially the Council rejected the proposed mechanism to suspend transfers to states which were unable (largely due to the Dublin rules themselves) to manage the influx of asylum seekers into their territory – despite the joint communication and recent rulings of the European courts'. Instead, Member States could only agree to an 'early warning mechanism' which would not affect the application of the Regulation as such.[225]

The European Parliament's intervention was significant in preventing further watering down of protection.[226] The Parliament convinced the Council to agree that asylum seekers should be provided with information on the right to request a suspension of transfer and the possibility that the responsibility criteria might be trumped by human rights concerns.[227] The rules on appeal rights were strengthened to specify that there must be a minimum degree of suspensive effect against a transfer. This should include a reasonable period to request an appeal, sufficient scrutiny of the application and the communication of reasons in a rejected request. On the other hand, the Parliament has accepted most of the Council's proposals weakening the legal aid provisions proposed by the Commission. As a result there is unlikely to be substantial change to the transfer system and the judiciary is likely to find itself again requiredto fill in the protection gaps.[228]

222 European Commission supra n70, 10.

223 Joint Communique II (developments in the southern Mediterranean region) Nicosia 19 April 2011. Full text available at: http://migrantsatsea.wordpress.com/2011/04/21/cyprus-greece-italy-malta-spain-issue-joint-communique-regarding-response-to-north-african-migration (accessed 1 November 2012).

224 Dublin III Regulation supra n12; Statewatch 'Council Text of Revised Dublin Rules' (April 2012). Available at: http://www.statewatch.org/analyses/no-173-dublin-III.pdf (accessed 28 March 2013).

225 Dublin III Regulation, Article 31.

226 Peers, S 'The Revised "Dublin" Rules on Responsibility for Asylum-Seekers: A Missed Opportunity' (Statewatch Analysis, June 2012). Available at: www.statewatch.org/analyses/no-173-dublin-III.pdf (accessed 28 March 2013).

227 Dublin III Regulation, Article 4(1).

228 Peers supra n226.

A Snapshot of State Divergence

The UNHCR has undertaken a detailed audit of current state practice which demonstrates the extent of state variation in the application of all aspects of the rules.[229] The findings offer little optimism when it comes to the implementation of the latest amendments.

In the 201 negative decisions examined from Greece, all contained standard phraseology (not exceeding three paragraphs)and there was no summary of the material facts or any legal reasoning pertaining to those facts. Strikingly, the only difference between the rejected applications was the name of the applicant, their country of origin and the time limit for lodging an appeal![230] In both France and Italy the rejection letters were brief with limited reference to the reasons for the decision. Many of the Italian rejections and all the Spanish ones failed to reference the specific facts of the application.[231] Similar problems surfaced in the majority of German rejection letters which comprised standard paragraphs referring to obsolete rules.[232] Few of the letters surveyed mentioned the possibility of the applicant receiving subsidiary protection which is defined in the Qualification Directive to include 'serious and individual threat ... by reason of indiscriminate violence'; even in cases where the country of origin was experiencing armed conflict.[233]

Many rejection letters were based on adverse credibility which was considered to undermine the applicant's case. In Germany, adverse credibility accounted for three-quarters of all refusals and several states, including France, Germany and the UK were inclined to prejudge the merits following an adverse credibility finding.[234]

The UNHCR report found systematic failures to consider country of origin information when refusing protection in Spain and Greece and minimal reliance on such data in France and Italy.[235] The European Asylum Support Office formed in 2010 is to publish its own country of origin information which should support harmonisation and consistency but concerns have already been expressed about the quality of this information.[236]

229 UNHCR supra n82.

230 UNHCR supra n82, 18.

231 UNHCR supra n82, 20.

232 UNHCR supra n82, 23–24.

233 Article 15(C) EU Qualification Directive; UNHCR supra n83, 24. These findings replicate earlier findings: UNHCR *Statement on Subsidiary Protection under the EC Qualification Directive for People Threatened by Indiscriminate Violence* (UNHCR January 2008); UNHCR *Asylum in the European Union: A Study of the Implementation of the Qualification Directive* (UNHCR November 2007) 82–90. Available at: http://www.unhcr.org/protect/PROTECTION/47302b6c2.pdf.

234 UNHCR supra n85, 26.

235 Ibid, at 29.

236 European Asylum Support Office 'The European Asylum Support Office Publishes Its First Country of Origin Information (COI) Report on Afghanistan' Press Release 10 July 2012.

Concluding Observations

European asylum policy can be accused of putting the cart before the horse by effectively basing a system of asylum transfers on uniform procedures which have yet to be fully realised. The assumptions underpinning the Common European Asylum System have been exposed by the ECtHR, the CJEU and the UNHCR as premature. It is not at all surprising that protection seekers undertake secondary movements in light of grossly divergent recognition rates and procedural practices which continue to undermine harmonisation.[237] Consequently the CEAS contributes to the very problem it is trying to address as protection seekers increasingly resort to smugglers in order to transit border countries with sub-standard procedures.[238]

The achievement of a common European standard of protection may be a laudable goal but it is evidently undermined by state practice and built in subsidiarity which continues to allow states a significant margin of discretion. A significant number of exceptions and derogations in procedural requirements can only mean that the opportunity for transparent, common standards is obscured.[239]

State practices are strongly influenced by other aspects of European migration policy with its focus on preventing irregular migration. These conflicting objectives continue to dictate the progress of the CEAS and will continue to threaten international refugee and human rights norms. The latest incarnation, the Stockholm programme, fails to detach refugee protection from immigration control and therefore contributes to this assimilation of objectives.[240]

Notwithstanding the rulings of the ECtHR and CJEU concerning Dublin transfers, the situation for all migrants in Greece remains particularly dire. Frontex estimates that some 90 per cent of illegal border crossings into the EU are via the Greek border and there are believed to be around 1 million undocumented migrants resident in Greece.[241] A disturbing rise in right-wing violence over the last 12 months has coincided with the rising popularity of the extreme-right 'Golden Dawn' who secured 18 seats in the Greek Parliamentary elections in 2012 and the far-right 'New Democracy' who have openly campaigned to 'reclaim the streets' from immigrants.[242] Refugees are caught up in a bureaucratic nightmare, with the UNHCR reporting queues of applicants sleeping on the steps of Athens

---

237 Dublin Project EU supra n39.

238 Jesuit Refugee Service documented this practice with respect to Iraqi nationals attempting to access the safety of Sweden in 2006–07.

239 Vedsted-Hansen supra n105, 153.

240 European Council *The Stockholm Programme – An Open and Secure Europe Serving and Protecting Citizens* 2010 OJ C 115/01 4 May 2010, Part 6.

241 Frontex Press Release 'Current Migratory Situation in Greece' 29 November 2010; noted by Ekathimerini.com 26 March 2012 cited in Sunderland, J *Hate on the Streets* (Human Rights Watch July 2012).

242 Athens News 'Samaras Claims Greeks Must 'take back' Cities from Immigrants' (19 April 2012); Sunderland ibid.

police station in order to file their asylum claims.[243] Perhaps the biggest failure of the CEAS to date has been its inability to decisively tackle this particular problem. Consequently other states with poorly functioning asylum systems may feel justified in ignoring inconvenient aspects of the common system.

On the road to common standards, the Commission's recast proposals attempted to reaffirm the central position of the protection seeker. However the adopted amendments reflect the Council's concern to ensure that the symbolic value of strong border controls prevail. The failure of the negotiations on the Dublin III Regulation to address the concerns of the European Parliament and over-burdened, border states, demonstrates the influence of the traditional big-players in such negotiations. It leaves applicants in the unenviable position of resorting to the European courts to prevent or postpone transfers which may breach their human rights. Whilst this may provide a judicial solution to a political problem, it is complicated by expedited asylum procedures which may well render such challenges illusory.

243 UNHCR Press Release 'Dozens Queue Every Week in Athens to Apply for Asylum' (12 March 2012).

Chapter 5
Reception Conditions

Introduction

The need to harmonise reception conditions and employment rights for asylum applicants was recognised by the EU's Justice and Home Affairs Council in 2000. Guidelines on general principles were soon devised, emphasising the need for asylum seekers to be received in dignity with comparable living standards across the Member States.[1] This position continues to be stressed in the preamble to the current EU Reception Directive.

The Reception Directive was adopted in January 2003[2] pursuant to the Tampere commitments. It covers a range of reception conditions including education, work, health, social benefits and movement. Although analysis has shown that states with preferential reception conditions have not in fact diluted those standards following the directive, it should be emphasised that the degree of discretion in key areas has afforded states the opportunity to avoid minimum standards where they are deemed to conflict with national interests. Anecdotally, the Commission has noted that transposition of the directive led to more favourable provisions at national level in several European states.[3] Yet, as Peers argues, there is very little evidence to demonstrate a significant upgrading of standards resulting from the directive.[4]

All EU Member States, with the exception of Ireland and Denmark who opted out, were required to transpose the Reception Directive by 6 February 2005. Many failed to meet the deadline resulting in enforcement proceedings in several cases.[5] The Commission's evaluation of 2007 noted that, despite the directive's application to all types of premises, seven states were not applying it to detention

1 European Council *Conclusion for the Reception of Asylum Seekers* Council Doc 13865/00 (Presse 457).

2 Directive 2003/9 [2003] OJ 31/18 'Reception Directive'.

3 Academic Network for Legal Studies on Immigration and Asylum in Europe *Comparative Overview of the Directive 2003/9 of 27 January 2003 Laying Down Minimum Standards for the Reception of Asylum seekers in All EU Member States* (European Commission 2006) 'Odysseus Network' 11.

4 Peers, S *EU Justice and Home Affairs Law* (OUP 2010).

5 Report from the Commission to the Council and to the European Parliament *On the Application of Directive 2003/9/EC of 27 January 2003 Laying Down Minimum Standards for the Reception of Asylum Seekers* Brussels, 26 November 2007 COM (2007) 745 Final; ECRE *The EC Directive on the Reception of Asylum Seekers: Are Asylum Seekers in Europe Receiving Material Support and Access to Employment in Accordance with European Legislation?* AD3/11/2005/EXT/SH (ECRE 2006).

centres.[6] Given the proliferation of detention facilities across the EU this is an area that demands particular scrutiny.

For the UNHCR the need for harmonisation in this field was fundamentally linked to the welfare and health of the refugee:

> Poor material reception conditions coupled with lack of employment opportunities during the asylum procedure can lead to a vicious circle of isolation, discrimination and poor integration prospects. This can have a negative impact on asylum seekers' physical and psychological health, leaving them demoralised after recognition as refugees, or unprepared to return if their applications are rejected.[7]

For the EU the motivation primarily centred on the prevention of secondary migration which supposed that asylum applicants moved between states seeking more favourable reception conditions ('venue-shopping').[8] As Hailbronner notes, the operation of the Dublin Regulation means that asylum applicants can only make one EU application and the conditions they face on arrival could significantly influence this choice.[9] According to the French delegation:

> The disparity between reception arrangements in Europe makes certain Member States more attractive than others for asylum applicants. Harmonisation in this respect would reduce these secondary movements and thus relieve pressure on the mechanism for determining the responsible State.[10]

The phenomenon of secondary movement is driven by a complex range of factors, including linguistic links, recognition rates and geography. The extent that reception conditions will influence the choice of destination is difficult to assess but it does seem probable that there is some impact, particularly in cases where the applicant is left waiting to access an asylum procedure in unfavourable circumstances. Perhaps more significantly, reception conditions are one of the few pull factors that the European institutions can exert any influence over.

As part of the final stage of the Common Asylum System a new Reception Directive ('recast Reception Directive') has now been agreed which should be

---

6 Ibid, 3.1.

7 UNHCR *Directive Laying Down Minimum Standards for the Reception of Asylum Seekers*. Available at: www.unhcr.org/4a9d129f6.html (accessed 28 July 2013).

8 Reception Directive, Preamble, para 8.

9 Hailbronner, K. 'Asylum Law in the Context of a European Migration Policy' in Walker, N (ed) *Europe's Area of Freedom, Security and Justice* (OUP 2004) 78.

10 French delegation to the Asylum Working Party *Conditions for the Reception of Asylum Seekers* Brussels 23 June 2000 Council Doc 9703/00 2 discussed by Peers, S and Rogers, N (eds) *EU Immigration and Asylum Law Text and Commentary* (M Nijhoff 2006) 300.

implemented across EU Member States by June 2015.[11] As with the Procedures Directive, the measures are intended to harmonise standards so that they function uniformly across the EU28.[12] Of particular note is the focus on detention which includes an exhaustive list of detention grounds, upgrading of legal guarantees and a commitment that detention should be a last resort option.

Scope of the Obligations

The current directive applies to applicants where a final decision has not been taken on their case and as long as they are permitted to remain on the territory as asylum seekers.[13] It does not apply to those seeking other forms of protection or when the Temporary Protection Directive is in force.[14] The CJEU has recently clarified that the provisions apply once the applicant applies for asylum even in cases where they will be transferred under the Dublin Regulation.[15]

Asylum applicants must be informed within 15 days of lodging their application of the rights and benefits to which they are entitled.[16] Within 3 days the applicant should be given a certificate of their status or legality of their presence in the state.[17] However, Member States may exclude application of this Article when the asylum seeker is in detention and during the examination of an application at the border or within the context of a procedure to decide on the right of the applicant legally to enter the state's territory.[18] In practice, many states are failing to comply with this deadline and the documentation given to non-detained applicants varies considerably in both form and content.[19]

---

11 *Position of the Council at First Reading with a View to the Adoption of a Directive of the European Parliament and of the Council Laying Down Standards for the Reception of Applicants for International Protection* (Recast) 6 June 2013 2008/0244 (COD) 'Recast Reception Directive'.

12 European Commission 'A Common European Asylum System' 2013. Available at: http://ec.europa.eu/dgs/home-affairs/what-we-do/policies/asylum/index_en.htm (accessed 1 August 2013).

13 Ibid, Art 2(c) and 3.1.

14 Council Directive 2001/55/EC of 20 July 2001 *On Minimum Standards for Giving Temporary Protection in the Event of a Mass Influx of Displaced Persons and on Measures Promoting a Balance of Efforts between Member States in Receiving Such Persons and Bearing the Consequences Thereof* OJ 7 August 2001 L212/12.

15 Case C-179/11 *Cimade and GISTI v Ministre de L'Intérieur, de l'Outre-mer, des Collectivités Territoriales et de l'immigration* 27 September 2012.

16 Reception Directive and Recast Reception Directive, Article 5.

17 Reception Directive and Recast Reception Directive, Article 6.

18 Reception Directive Article 6.

19 Commission supra n5, 3.2.2; Odysseus supra n44: Germany, Hungary, the Netherlands, Greece and Spain had not implemented the time-scale in their legal systems.

It has been noted that the obligations apply immediately an asylum application is made, yet several states are still to transpose the directive correctly. In the Netherlands for example, applicants are diverted to registration centres to officially lodge a claim. The process can take up to three weeks during which the applicant is not entitled to support as they have not officially entered the asylum procedure. In Spain a procedural obstacle which delays access to the formal procedure also has the effect of denying support contrary to the directive. To secure the 'pink card' required to access support in Greece has been known to take a year from the date of application.[20]

Access to Employment

Access to the labour market is essential for restoring self-esteem, promoting independence and reducing vulnerability. Employment is also vital in facilitating integration and reducing social exclusion.[21] Under the Refugee Convention, access to the labour market should be granted after three months of lawful presence as a refugee.[22] Whereas, the Reception Directive allows access to the labour market to be delayed for a period of one-year after which time, the state must, subject to conditions, grant access.[23] As the determination of refugee status is declaratory in nature, application of the directive may clash with that of the Refugee Convention; encouraging states to delay status determinations in order to restrict access to employment. There is considerable discretion in these provisions with states able to maintain more generous standards.[24] States may give priority to EU citizens, EEA nationals and legally resident third country nationals when determining employment access which will contribute to the practical obstacles facing asylum applicants.[25] It also runs against the grain of the Refugee Convention which provides that refugees should receive 'the most favourable treatment according to nationals of a foreign country in the same circumstances'.[26]

It is notable that at the time of enactment many EU states had preferential standards, whereas several states, including Germany, France and Ireland had attempted to restrict access to the labour market completely. One of the reasons

20 Odysseus supra n3, 35.

21 European Commission Staff Working Document *Impact Assessment* SEC (2008) 2944 3 December 2008, 17.

22 Article 17(1) Refugee Convention.

23 Reception Directive Article 11(2); Guild, E 'Seeking Asylum: Stormy Clouds between International Commitments and EU Legislative Measures' (2004) 29 EL Rev 2, 215. Kaunert, C. 'Liberty versus Security? EU Asylum Policy and the European Commission' (2009) 5 J of Contemporary Eur Research 2, 148.

24 Reception Directive Article 11(1).

25 Reception Directive Article 11(4); Battjes, H *European Asylum Law and International Law* (M Nijhoff 2006) 502.

26 Refugee Convention Article 17(1).

for state reluctance in facilitating access is the belief that easier access could encourage economic migration and therefore employment opportunities should be restricted to cases where the asylum decision is prolonged.[27] Given the unanimity requirement in the Council, the existing standards of Member States, and the traditional reluctance to provide economic rights for migrants, it is undeniably significant that any agreement was reached in this area.[28]

The Commission had initially proposed a maximum period of 6 months before access should be granted, receiving support from the Italian and Greek delegations.[29] However, the German delegation in particular resisted such pressure.[30] The Commission's evaluation study paints a picture of mixed success with evidence of some Member States improving access. All but one state, Lithuania, complied with the current provision. However, it is undeniable that the directive could have been more ambitious as nine Member States provided a shorter period.[31]

Material Reception Conditions

Article 13(2) establishes an obligation on states to make 'provisions on material reception conditions to ensure a standard of living adequate for the health of applicants and capable of ensuring their subsistence'. This includes housing, welfare benefits and health care. There is additional emphasis on the 'specific situation of persons who have special needs' as well as those in detention. This is, however, subject to the applicant having insufficient means to support himself.[32] In fact, the Odysseus Network's implementation evaluation found that the identification of persons with special needs was a common problem.[33] Several states had not defined what was meant by special needs which resulted in cases not be correctly identified and additional support being withheld.[34]

Member States are afforded some flexibility as to the nature of material conditions. They can require applicants who are working to contribute to their subsistence and may offer vouchers, financial payments or material support in kind. On the other hand, states are obliged to ensure that applicants receive the necessary health care which shall include, at least, emergency care and essential

27 French delegation Council Doc 10242/00: 4.

28 Kaunert supra n23.

29 The Commission continued to push for the six month delay in the amended directive but was unable to obtain the support of the Council, Recast reception directive, Article 15(1).

30 Mitsilegas, V 'A "Common" EU Immigration and Asylum Policy: National and Institutional Constraints' in Shah, P (ed) *The Challenge of Asylum to Legal Systems* (Cavendish 2005) 130.

31 Commission supra n5, 3.4.3; see also Odysseus Network supra n3, 69.

32 Reception Directive Article 13(3).

33 Odysseus Network supra n3 13.

34 See for example UK and Slovenia, ibid, 17.

treatment of illness.[35] Further, all necessary medical or other assistance shall be provided for those applicants identified as having a particular vulnerability.[36] Despite the mandatory nature of this provision early analysis found that it was routinely undermined by state practice. In many states the assistance is provided almost entirely by NGO's and in France and Cyprus there was no account taken of special needs.[37] Of notable concern was the lack of identification and support for the health needs of minors with special needs in 10 Member States.[38]

These basic welfare standards actually exceeded some of the existing standards in national asylum systems. In Italy where asylum reception in general is decentralised there is no national law laying down the amount of social assistance an asylum seeker is entitled to. Social assistance is provided by local communes and since the amount is often insufficient, non-governmental agencies provide additional support. In Greece material reception conditions tend to be provided by non-governmental organisations and there is no specific state support available.[39] This gives some insight into the reasons behind the preference for immediate access to the labour market in both countries.

Several years on, concerns are repeatedly raised over the amount and extent of financial support in some Member States which may fall short of enabling an adequate standard of living.[40] The Commission has found that the amounts are rarely commensurate with the minimum level of social support granted to nationals and in several states the amounts were too low to cover even basic subsistence.[41]

In the UK, asylum seekers are entitled to half the level of benefits normally paid to job-seekers and the operation of a compulsory dispersal scheme results in accommodation which may be sub-standard and prejudicial for the asylum seekers' health. The Odysseus Network's early evaluation found that financial payments were inadequate to cover the European obligations in almost half the Member States.[42] Additionally there were problems with asylum seekers receiving clothes and having to rely on inadequate hand-outs from charities in Slovenia, Slovakia,

35 Reception Directive Article 15(1).

36 Reception directive Article 15(2).

37 Odysseus Network supra n3, 75.

38 Odysseus Network supra n3, 82.

39 McDonough, P and Tsourdi, E 'Putting Solidarity to the test: Assessing Europe's Response to the Asylum Crisis in Greece' New Issues in Refugee Research, Research Paper no 231 (UNHCR 2012).

40 In 2012 the cash benefit payable to a lone, adult asylum applicant in the UK was £36.62 per week – this figure has fallen relative to inflation over the last five years. It amounts to approximately half the amount paid to unemployed people over 25 who receive job seekers allowance. France, Italy and Greece: ECRE supra n5, 6–7.

41 Commission supra n5, 3.3.2 – Cyprus, France, Estonia, Portugal, Slovenia and Austria failed to provide sufficient funds to enable basic levels of support.

42 Odysseus supra n3, 32 (Cyprus, France, Estonia, Austria, Portugal, UK, Slovenia, the Netherlands and Latvia).

Latvia and Cyprus. The provision of support in detention centres was variable with several states again falling well short of the standard in Article 13(2).[43]

Some states, including France and Italy, do not grant financial allowances after a certain period of time, undermining the minimum standards provided by the directive. Whereas in Greece almost all applicants with insufficient means rely entirely on charitable support.[44] Whilst these problems are more attributable to implementation than the standards per se, the operation of transfers under the Dublin Regulation will inevitably expose many applicants to standards breaching the Directive.

The Directive includes a provision allowing for reduction or withdrawal of support reception conditions.[45] This reflects the concerns of the UK which had implemented national legislation denying support to applicants that did not submit their claim 'as soon as practicable' (generally interpreted to mean within three days).[46] The UK House of Lords found the implementation of this policy to breach Article 3 of the ECHR in a case where applicants were forced to sleep rough in degrading conditions, their survival depending on occasional support from charity.[47]

One of the difficulties for harmonisation in this field comes down to competence. To rule on precise amounts for material support was not considered possible as it would necessitate harmonisation of state welfare systems, which is beyond the competencies of the EU. What is quite clear is that material reception conditions need to ensure living conditions which are not in breach of the prohibition on inhuman and degrading treatment in Article 3 ECHR. The Council documents do not suggest any major interventions by Member States opposing the idea of granting material reception conditions to ensure a decent standard of living at all times. Given that a number of Member States, especially in Southern Europe, face immense problems in implementing these standards it is interesting to note that they did not attempt to upload their existing policies. It seems probable that the lack of prescription in the Directive contributed to state acquiescence in this respect.

A significant deficiency in implementation relates to the enhanced rights of vulnerable persons. In almost half the Member States, the provisions were incorrectly and/or incompletely applied.[48] The test of adequacy is context dependant but where the reception standards are particularly poor, it could be argued that they constitute discriminatory treatment. In interpreting the non-

---

43 Odysseus supra n3, 32.

44 McDonough and Tsourdi supra n40.

45 Reception Directive Article 16(2).

46 S55 Nationality, Immigration and Asylum Act 2002.

47 *R v Secretary of State for the Home Department, ex parte Adam (FC); Limbuela (FC), Tesema (FC) (Conjoined Appeals)*, [2005] UKHL 66, 3 November 2005. Available at: http://www.refworld.org/docid/43fc2d1a0.html (accessed 23 April 2013); Handoll, J 'Directive 2003/9 on Reception Condition of Asylum Seekers: Ensuring "Mere Subsistence" or a Dignified Standard of Living? in Baldaccini, A; Guild, E and Toner, H (eds) *Whose Freedom, Security and Justice? EU Immigration and Asylum Law and Policy* (Hart 2007), 205.

48 Commission supra n5 3.5.1; European Commission supra n21, 11.

discrimination provision in Article 14 ECHR, the ECtHR has held that 'very weighty' reasons would be needed to justify differential treatment which is based solely on the applicant's nationality when emergency assistance benefits were denied to an unemployed third country national.[49] In *Koua Poirrez v France*, the Court ruled that the denial of a disability allowance to a non-national constituted discrimination on the grounds of nationality contrary to Article 14.[50] It will be difficult to objectively justify differential treatment particularly in cases involving acute vulnerability.[51] The Grand Chamber recently ruled that the segregation of vulnerable Roma school pupils was discriminatory despite the state's argument that specific educational provision was in the children's best interests.[52]

Freedom of Movement

Asylum applicants have a right to freedom of movement within the territory of the state or an area thereof.[53] The European Commission has found that the majority of Member States grant freedom of movement, with only Germany and Austria restricting it on a regular basis to one district.[54]

Additionally, Article 7 provides a legal platform for detention, stating that residence may be decided for 'reasons of public interest, public order or, when necessary, for the swift processing and effective monitoring of his or her

---

49 *Gaygusuz v Austria* App 17371/90 16 September 1996. The judgement can be contrasted with *Petrovic v Austria* App 20458/92 27 March 1998 in which the Court held that denial of parental child benefit to a father did not breach Article 14 as there was limited state consensus in the application of such an allowance. See also *Willis v UK* App 36042/97 11 June 2002 in which a breach of Article 14 arose from the denial of a widow's parent allowance to a surviving father.

50 *Koua Poirrez v France* App 40892/98 30 September 2003, 46; see also *Niedzwiecki v Germany* App 58453/00 15 February 2006; 5th.

51 This is acknowledged by the European Commission in their Impact Assessment supra n49, 19.

52 *Sampanis and Others v Greece* App 32526/05 11 December 2012; see also *DH v Czech Republic* App 57325/00 13 November 2007.

53 Reception Directive Article 7(1). The EU Returns Directive also allows for detention of third country nationals subject to return procedures, in particular where the person is at risk of absconding or if the person avoids or hampers the removal process, Directive on Commons Standards and Procedures in Member States for Returning Illegally Staying Third Country Nationals, COM (2005) 391.final, Art 15(1). For a critical analysis see Baldaccini, A 'The Return and Removal of Irregular Migrants under EU Law; An Analysis of the Returns Directive (2009) Eur J Migration & L 11, 1; there is an 18 months maximum tine limit for the detention pending deportation (Article 15(6); *Kadzoev* C-357/09 PPU Unreported 30 November 2009, ECJ.

54 European Commission supra n5 6–7.

application'.[55] The amount of discretion conferred upon states in Article 7 makes it very difficult to make meaningful comparisons.[56] But it has been alleged that detention for administrative processing marks a discernible goal-shift from the published reasons justifying detention to that of pure deterrence.[57]

There is surprisingly little EU guidance on detention conditions and in practice the type and length of detention vary enormously.[58] In Germany, detention is exceptional, whereas in Malta all asylum seekers who enter illegally will be detained with the exception of those with special needs.[59] The time period ranges from 7 days in Portugal to over one year in Hungary and Malta. It is undefined in the UK, Lithuania and Finland.[60] Whilst refugee organisations have rightly criticised the practice of restricting freedom of movement as being contrary to established human rights provisions, Hailbronner demonstrates that some state practices prior to the directive were even more restrictive.[61]

The absence of defined European detention standards has led the Council of Europe's Parliamentary Assembly to adopt 10 guiding principles on the legality of detention of asylum seekers and irregular migrants.[62] The principles note the increasing resort to detention and emphasise that it should be exceptional following a consideration of all other alternatives.[63] Further, it should only be ordered to prevent unauthorised entry or to deport or extradite. In order to comply with international human rights obligations, detention should not be arbitrary, must be prescribed by law, proportionate and 'only be used when necessary'.[64] It is the opinion of the Parliamentary Assembly that vulnerable people should not normally be detained and unaccompanied children should never be detained.

These principles are reflected in the UNHCR's latest detention guidelines which state, inter alia, that detention should only be used for one of three

---

55 Reception Directive Article 7(2); Mitsilegas, V "The Directive on the Reception of Asylum Seekers and Its Implementation in the UK' 1996 IANL 20, 1, 44.

56 European Commission supra n5, 7.

57 Weber, L and Gelsthorpe, L *Deciding to Detain: How Decisions to Detain Asylum-Seekers are Made at Points of Entry* Cambridge Institute of Criminology 2002; Wilsher, D *Immigration Detention: Law, History, Politics* (CUP 2012).

58 Odysseus Network supra n3, 87. There is no maximum limit on detention in the UK, Finland or Lithuania and detention is possible for up to 12 months in Hungary and Malta. Seven Member States deem that the directive does not apply to detention centres (UK, Belgium, Italy, Netherlands, Poland, Luxembourg and Cyprus). Problems existed in the provision of education to minors detained in over half the Member State Members.

59 Odysseus Network supra n3, 87.

60 Commission supra n5, 3.4.1.

61 Hailbronner supra n9, 80.

62 Parliamentary Assembly Recommendation 1900 (2010) *Detention of Asylum Seekers and Irregular Migrants in Europe* Council of Europe.

63 Ibid, para 21 and Appendix 1.

64 Ibid.

legitimate purposes: to protect public order, public health or national security.[65] Necessity and proportionality are essential to an assessment of whether detention is arbitrarily imposed. Detention must not be discriminatory and maximum limits must be clearly prescribed by law.[66] Thus, international standards on asylum detention are well established but it is only in the Recast Reception Directive that the European institutions have sought to reflect some of these standards in an enforceable capacity.

Whilst international soft law is reasonably clear, some states have tried to escape its application by re-defining detention. The use of airport detention is a case in point.[67] The authorities may argue that confinement at the port of entry does not constitute detention as individuals are free to return to their country of origin. Nevertheless, the ECtHR has ruled that this can constitute a deprivation of liberty contrary to Article 5 of the ECHR.[68] In *Amuur v France*, the Court rejected the French government's argument that Paris-Orly airport was an 'international zone' where the Article 5 obligations did not apply. The label a state places on the restriction of movement will be carefully scrutinised by the ECtHR to establish whether in fact there is a deprivation of liberty.

The Legal Basis of Detention

It is well-established that applicants should not be detained solely because they are asylum seekers.[69] Any lawful detention must conform to the standards of international law, i.e. it must not be arbitrary and should be proportionate. It will be recalled that Article 31(1) of the Refugee Convention prohibits penalties applied to refugees on account of their illegal entry or presence where they present themselves to the authorities without delay and show good cause for their illegal entry or presence. Hathaway notes that Article 31 'denies governments the right to subject refugees to any detriment for reason of their unauthorized entry or presence in the asylum country'.[70] A penalty could be interpreted to encompass detention.[71]

---

65 UNHCR *Detention Guidelines* (UNHCR 2012) Guideline 4.

66 Ibid, Guidelines 5 and 6.

67 See p155 above; Wilkinson, R 'Europe: The Debate over Detention' *Refugees* Magazine (UNHCR Issue 113).

68 *Amuur v France* (1996) 22 EHRR 533; see also *Riad and Idiab v Belgium* App 29787/03 and 29810/03 24 January 2008.

69 Recast Reception Directive Article 8(1); Asylum Procedures Directive, Article 18.

70 Hathaway, J *The Rights of Refugees under International Law* (CUP 2005) 410.

71 Goodwin-Gill, G 'Article 31 of the 1951 Convention Relating the Status of Refugees: Non-Penalization, Detention and Protection' in Feller, E; Türk, V and Nicholson, F (eds) *Refugee Protection in International Law: UNHCR's Global Consultations on International Protection* (CUP 2003) 195.

However, analysis suggests that a brief period of detention should not be construed as a 'penalty' in the strict sense but is merely an administrative measure.[72]

Hathaway argues that detention prior to the regularisation of stay does not constitute a penalty within Article 31(2).[73] Regularisation occurs when the asylum applicant has satisfied the formal requirements for verification of refugee status which would suggests that once the applicant complies with the initial procedural requirements any further detention would constitute a penalty unless defined as 'necessary'.[74] Other scholars specifically rule out the legitimacy of detention for administrative purposes, although it may be deemed necessary in order to ascertain identity or to otherwise assist the investigation.[75]

The UNHCR's guidelines and commentary suggest that restrictions on movement should only occur when strictly necessary and then should be afforded a narrow interpretation.[76] Any restrictions under Article 31(2) should be: prescribed by law; necessary; non-discriminatory and, applied only until status is regularised or until the person obtains admission elsewhere.[77] It is clear that international refugee law specifically requires necessity rather than simply a lack of arbitrariness or proportionality.[78] The Executive Committee have emphasised the need for necessity to be related to one of the legitimate aims stated.[79] These aims have now been updated by the most recent guidelines which emphasise necessity, reasonableness and proportionality in all cases.[80] The general principle remains that detention is an exceptional measure to be applied after a full consideration of alternatives.

The specific exceptions do allow for initial identity and security verification but only where identity is undetermined or in dispute, or if there are indications of a security risk.[81] Similarly detention is permissible for the purpose of an initial interview but only so far as this could not be achieved in the absence of such

72 Giakoumopoulos, C 'Detention of Asylum Seekers in the Light of Art 5 of the ECHR' in Hughes, J and Liebaut, F (eds) *Detention of Asylum Seekers in Europe: Analysis and Perspectives* (Kluwer 1998) 165.

73 Hathaway supra n71, 418.

74 Goodwin-Gill, G and McAdam, J *The Refugee in International Law* (OUP 2007) 462.

75 Grahl-Madsen, A *The Status of Refugees in International Law* (AW Sijthoff 1972) 148.

76 Landgren, K 'Comments on the UNHCR Position on Detention of Refugees and Asylum Seekers' in Hughes, J and Liebaut, F supra n73, 146.

77 Field, O and Edwards, E *Alternatives to Detention of Asylum Seekers and Refugees* UNHCR Legal and Protection Policy Research Series POLAS/2006/3 April 2006 para 74.

78 Cf Goodwin-Gill and McAdam, supra n75, 463.

79 Ex Com 44 (XXXVII) *Conclusion on Detention of Refugees and Asylum Seekers* 1986 A/AC.96/688.

80 UNHCR supra n65, 4.2.

81 UNHCR supra n65, para 24.

confinement.[82] Such detention must be for a minimal period and clearly prescribed by law. According to the Executive Committee, detention may be arbitrary if it is disproportionate or indefinite[83] and where it is used 'for insufficient reason, without adequate analysis of the individual circumstances'.[84] The individual basis of the decision to detain is also emphasised by the Human Rights Committee:

> the fact of illegal entry may indicate a need for investigation and there may be other factors *particular to the individual*, [my emphasis] such as likelihood of absconding and lack of cooperation, which may justify detention for a period. Without such factors detention may be considered arbitrary, even if entry was illegal.[85]

The conditions of detention are dealt with by the UNHCR's Conclusion *On Reception of Asylum-Seekers in the Context of Individual Asylum Systems*, which requires that states respect human dignity and applicable human rights law when choosing a suitable reception arrangement.[86] The Conclusion, however, could be criticised for failing to address the specific issues arising from detention in reception centres and it appears to allow states a degree of latitude when making such assessments.[87] The latest guidelines develop the conditions of detention by stressing that punitive facilities should not be used and that women and children should be separated unless within the same family unit.[88] Victims of torture and other serious violence should not generally be detained.[89]

Freedom from arbitrary detention is a 'fundamental human right'. Article 9 of the International Covenant on Civil and Political Rights provides inter alia, that no one shall be subject to arbitrary arrest or detention and the Human Rights Committee's General Comment *On the Right to Liberty and Security of Persons*, specifically includes immigration control.[90] This does not make all immigration detention per se unlawful but, as Edwards argues, it requires the decision-maker to

---

82 UNHCR supra n66, para 28.

83 Executive Committee of the High Commissioner's Programme Standing Committee *Detention of Asylum-Seekers and Refugees: The Framework, the Problem and Recommended Practice* EC/49/SC/CRP 13 4 June 1999, para 10.

84 Ibid, para 25.

85 1997 Comm 560/1993 3 April 1997 para 9.4, also discussed by Tootell, A-M; Hughes, J and Petrasek, D 'The Relevance of Key UN Instruments for Detained Asylum Seekers' in Hughes and Liebaut supra n73, 189.

86 UNHCR EX Com No 93 (LIII) 2002 O*n Reception of Asylum-Seekers in the Context of Individual Asylum Systems* para b, i and vi; Landgren supra n77, 150.

87 Ibid.

88 UNHCR supra n65, Guideline 8.

89 UNHCR supra n65, Guideline 9.

90 Human Rights Committee General Comment No 8 *Right to Liberty and Security of Persons* (Art 9) 30 June 1982 para 1.

consider alternatives such as sureties and reporting mechanisms prior to detention.[91] In *A v Australia*, the Human Rights Committee specifically linked necessity to the assessment of arbitrariness:

> ... remand in custody could be considered arbitrary if it is not necessary in all circumstances of the case, for example to prevent flight or interference with evidence: the element of proportionality becomes relevant in this context.[92]

This is particularly the case when the applicant has a specific vulnerability, such as a psychiatric illness, as confirmed by the Human Rights Committee in *C v Australia*.[93] However, an assessment of arbitrariness is more than simply an assessment of legality and will include decisions which are unreasonable, unjust, delayed and unpredictable.[94] Detention may thus be prime facie lawful but nevertheless arbitrary, resulting in a breach of Article 9.[95]

Article 12 ICCPR protects the freedom of movement of those deemed to be 'lawfully' within the state's territory. Asylum applicants are regarded as being 'lawfully resident' by the Human Rights Committee for the purpose of this provision.[96] Art 12(3) states that restrictions on movement must be provided by law and be necessary to protect national security, public order, health or morals, or the rights and freedoms of others. A restriction is therefore necessary when its severity and intensity are proportional to one of the purposes listed in this Article and when it is related to one of these purposes.[97]

The definition of arbitrary detention is informed by the UN Working Group on Arbitrary Detention established in 1991 by the Human Rights Commission. The Working Group has established criteria for determining whether custody is arbitrary and recommends that alternative, non-custodial measures should always be considered before resorting to detention and that: 'the detaining authorities must assess a compelling need to detain that is based on the personal history if each asylum seeker'.[98] The UNHCR and Council of Europe guidelines require that cases are dealt with on their individual merits and that consideration of non-

---

91 Edwards, A 'Human Rights, Refugees and the Right "to Enjoy" Asylum' (2005) 17 IJ Refugee L 319.

92 *A v Australia* Communication No 560/1993 CCPR/C/59/D/560/1993.

93 *C v Australia* Communication No 900/1999 CCPR/C/76/D/900/1999.

94 Commission on Human Rights *on Right to be Free from Arbitrary Arrest, Detention and Exile* UN Doc E/CN.4/826/Rev 1 paras 23–30.

95 *Van Alphen v Netherlands* No 305/1988 UN Doc CCPR/C/39/D/305/1988 (1990).

96 *Celepi v Sweden* Communication No 456/1991 CCPR/C/51/D/456/1991.

97 Nowak, M UN *Covenant on Civil and Political Rights – CCPR Commentary* (Engel Verlag, Kehl am Rhein 1993) 211; Goodwin-Gill supra n72, 223.

98 Report of the Working Group UN Doc E/CN.4/1999/63 18 December 1999. Recommendation 8, para 33; recommendation 9, para 34.

custodial alternatives is a 'pre-requisite for satisfying the principle of necessity in relation to lawful detention'.[99]

It is understood that the approach of the Human Rights Committee under the ICCPR should inform the Council of Europe institutions when interpreting the ECHR. Indeed Article 53 of the ECHR expressly recognises the importance of international human rights obligations. Furthermore, Articles 31–33 of the Vienna Convention on the Law of Treaties requires an interpretation which is consistent with other international law obligations, thus necessity, proportionality and lack of arbitrariness must be key aspects in the interpretation of the right to liberty in Article 5(1) of the ECHR.[100]

The Immigration Exception under the ECHR Proportionality is relevant when assessing the impact of detention on the right to private and family life under Article 8 ECHR. In the case of *Mayeka and Mitunga v Belgium*, a breach of Articles 3 and 5 and 8 of the ECHR were found in the case of a five-year-old unaccompanied child who had been detained for two months pending her removal:

> in the absence of any risk of the second applicant seeking to evade the supervision of the Belgian authorities, her detention in a closed centre for adults was unnecessary. Other measures could have been taken that would have been more conducive to the higher interest of the child ... [101]

Article 8 is a qualified right which provides the state with an opportunity to justify a restriction if it is pursuing a legitimate aim and its measures are necessary in a democratic society.

By contrast, the right to liberty in Article 5 can only be limited according to one of the specified exceptions which are narrowly construed by the Strasbourg authorities. The ECtHR has insisted that effective and regular judicial supervision is a key element of detention in the criminal justice process.[102] If a person of 'unsound mind' is to be detained under Article 5(1)e there must be a medical assessment of necessity to ascertain that the person is suffering from a mental illness. Further, the need to consider all the alternatives to detention was emphasised in *Litwa v Poland*[103] concerning the detention of alcoholics. The court made it clear that the purpose of Article 5 was the prevention of arbitrariness and emphasised that detention must 'be necessary in the circumstances' after a consideration of less severe measures.[104]

---

99 Field and Edwards supra n77, para 70.
100 23 May 1969 United Nations, *Treaty Series*, vol 1155, p. 331.
101 *Mayeka and Mitunga v Belgium* App 13178/03 12 October 2006 para 83.
102 *Brogan v UK* (1989) 11 EHRR 117.
103 *Litwa v Poland* App No 26629/95 4 April 2000.
104 Ibid, 73, 78.

The Article 5(1)f exception to the right to liberty allows detention in two situations: (i) to prevent unauthorised entry, and (ii) where an action of removal is to be affected. In the latter scenario, the decision in *Chahal v UK* established that detention did not need to be strictly 'necessary' although it could only be justified if the removal proceedings were in progress and were being processed with due diligence.[105]

The application of the first limb to routine, administrative detention was not explored until the decision in S*aadi v UK* concerning detention as part of an expedited procedure at a designated reception centre.[106] After a short period in the Detained Fast Track (initially up to 10 days) applicants would be granted temporary admission or moved to another place of detention.[107] Whilst such detention might be deemed appropriate where there is concern that an individual might abscond,[108] the applicants in *Saadi* had complied fully with reporting instructions before their detention. At first instance, Justice Collins ruled that if the applicant had done all that he reasonably could to report to the authorities he could in no way be regarded as affecting an unauthorised entry.[109]

The UK's House of Lords disagreed, ruling that detention did not have to be strictly 'necessary' and further, that all entry was unauthorised until it was expressly authorised by the state authorities.[110] The national appeal court emphasised the ability of a state to control its own borders within the limits conferred by statute and international obligations. The state is thus given power to detain until the entry is formally authorised.[111] The ECtHR agreed referring to the states 'undeniable right to control aliens' entry into and residence in their country'.[112] The Grand Chamber concluded that until a migrant has officially been granted leave to remain he has not affected a lawful entry.[113] He could thus be detained under Article 5(1)f as detention would be aimed at preventing unlawful entry.

105 *Chahal v UK* (1996) 23 EHRR 413, 464–466.

106 *Saadi v UK* App 13229/03 Judgement of 29 January 2008.

107 Barbara Roche MP, House of Commons Debates 16 March 2000 Col 263W; House of Commons Select Committee on European Union, Minutes of Evidence Memorandum by HM Inspectorate of Prisons 1 February 2006. The weekly cost of detention at Oakington in 2002 was calculated to be £1,620 per person, House of Commons Debates 25 October 2001 Col 333W.

108 Hughes, J and Liebaut, F (eds) *Detention of Asylum Seekers in Europe: Analysis and Perspectives* (Kluwer 1998) 21.

109 [2001] 4 All ER 961 para 29.

110 *R (on Application of Saadi) v SSHD* [2002] UKHL 41, [2002] 1 WLR 3131.

111 Ibid, 3142. For commentary on the case see Berkowitz, N 'Article 5, Detention of Asylum Seekers' (2006) 20 IANL, 3 223; 'Immigration and Asylum: Detention of Asylum Seeker for Speedy Processing of Application' (2006) 6 EHRLR 742; O'Nions, H 'No Right to Liberty: The Detention of Asylum Seekers for Administrative Convenience' (2008) 10 Eur J Migration & L 2, 149.

112 [2007] 44 EHRR 50 para 40.

113 Grand Chamber [2008] para 65.

On the issue of necessity, the Court emphasised the need to subject detention decisions to close scrutiny. However, they reasoned that decisions to detain persons with uncertain immigration status should confer a broader discretion on states than detention under other paragraphs of Article 5.[114] The reasons for this margin of appreciation have not been specifically elucidated, but it is a fair conclusion that it reflects the Court's assumptions about the relative importance of certain rights and interests in particular the emphasis on national sovereignty and territoriality.[115]

Whilst the Grand Chamber recognised that detention must not be arbitrary, this could be separated from a requirement of necessity:

> To avoid being branded as arbitrary ... such detention must be carried out in good faith; it must be closely connected to the purpose of preventing unauthorised entry of the person to the country; the place and conditions of detention should be appropriate ... and the length of the detention should not exceed that reasonably required for the purpose pursued.[116]

Yet the international right to seek and enjoy asylum is surely deprived of much of its meaning if its exercise results in an unnecessary deprivation of liberty.

It is of particular concern that the Court's decision blurs the distinction between migrants and asylum seekers.[117] According to the UNHCR:

> in order to detain asylum seekers ... there had to be something more that the mere absence of a decision on the claim; the detention had to be necessary, in the sense that less intrusive measures would not suffice, and proportionate to the aim pursued.[118]

The Grand Chamber's interpretation also seems at odds with the approach taken by the Human Rights Committee on the right to freedom of movement conferred by Article 12 ICCPR. The Committee held that an illegal entrant whose status has been regularised is lawfully within the state for the purpose of Article 12.[119] By extension this should apply equally to an asylum seeker who has been admitted to the asylum process.[120] Thus we see a paradox whereby a person's presence may be simultaneously lawful and yet, according to the ECtHR in *Saadi*, unauthorised.

---

114 [2007] 44 EHRR para 44.

115 Cornelisse, G 'Human Rights for Immigration Detainees in Strasbourg: Limited Sovereignty or a Limited Discourse?' (2004) Eur J Migration & L 6, 105, O'Nions supra n111.

116 Grand Chamber [2008] para 74; Boeles, P and Bruins, M 'Case Reports of the European Courts of Human Rights and the Human Rights Committee' (2007) Eur J Migration & L 9, 253.

117 Grand Chamber [2008] para 54.

118 Ibid.

119 *Celepli v Sweden* HRC Case 456/1991.

120 Field and Edwards supra n78, para 34.

In this respect international law, notably Articles 9 and 12 of the ICCPR and their interpretation by the Human Rights Committee, offers greater protection to that offered by the ECtHR. Consequently, the door is left open for states seeking to use administrative detention without an assessment of its appropriateness in the individual case.[121]

The consequence of the Grand Chamber's rejection of a proportionality assessment is twofold. Firstly, it results in insufficient consideration of non-custodial alternatives to detention and, secondly, it gives inadequate attention to the conditions of detention. Shortly before the first judgement of the ECtHR, the regime at the Oakington reception centre was subject to a BBC undercover documentary which identified incidents of racism, physical abuse and incompetence amongst the employees of the private company operating the centre.[122] An inquiry by the Prisons and Probation Ombudsman endorsed the BBC's findings resulting in a highly critical report.[123] The balancing act required in a proportionality assessment would have asked whether confinement in such a volatile situation could be justified solely by administrative efficiency. Most probably this would have resulted in a different outcome for the applicants.

Although Oakington closed in 2010, the detained fast track continues to operate in the UK and a recent judicial review challenge suggests that victims of torture are not receiving the psychological support needed during expedited procedures.[124] Human Rights Watch has identified the absence of significant procedural safeguards in the fast track which hamper detainees from effectively presenting their case.[125] Although Justice Slynn's reasoning authorises short-term detention in 'acceptable physical conditions', neither the House of Lords nor the

121 Costello, C 'Human Rights and the Elusive Universal Subject: Immigration Detention under International Human Rights and EU Law' (2012) 19 Indiana J of Global Legal Studies 1, 257; Edwards, A *Back To Basics: The Right to Liberty and Security of Person and 'Alternatives to Detention' of Refugee Asylum Seekers, Stateless Persons and Other Migrants* (UNHCR 2011); see also the dissenting opinions of Judges Rozakis, Tulkens, Kovler, Hajiyev, Spielmann and Hirvelä, *Saadi v UK*, 33.

122 BBC *Detention Undercover: The Real Story* 2005.

123 *Inquiry into Allegations of Racism and Mistreatment of Detainees at Oakington Immigration Reception Centre and While Under Escort* July 2005; see also HM Chief Inspector of Prisons *Report on a Short Follow-Up Inspection of Oakington Reception Centre* 5–7 June 2006.

124 *R (On Application of EO, RA, CO, OE) v SSHD* [2013] EWHC 1236 (Admin); Burnham, E *Challenging Immigration Detention: A Best Practice Guide* October (Immigration Law Practitioners Association 2003) BID, 18; Amnesty International *Seeking Asylum is not a Crime: Detention of People Who Have Sought Asylum* (Amnesty International UK 2005); Human Rights Watch *Fast-Tracked Unfairness Detention and Denial of Women Asylum Seekers in the UK* (HRW 2010).

125 Human Rights Watch ibid.

ECtHR defined what these conditions might be.[126] This omission is also found in the current Reception Directive.

The presumption in expedited procedures is that applicants grouped by their nationality can be fast-tracked with a view to speedy removal.[127] This is contrary to the latest UNCHR guidelines which confirm that racial discrimination may occur where applicants are detained on the basis solely of nationality.[128] Statistics indicate that over 95 per cent of detained fast track applicants in the UK have their initial applications refused.[129] Whilst this rate of initial refusal may be used to validate the decision to detain,[130] caution must be exercised as it could equally be indicative of poor- quality, hurried decision-making. In the *Saadi* case all applicants were rejected at first instance and subsequently found to have credible cases.

Allowing administrative convenience to justify any deprivation of liberty, albeit defined as 'short-term', seems to be a dangerous precedent. Much will depend on the interpretation of arbitrary detention; if construed to include inappropriateness, injustice, unpredictability and legal obscurity; proportionality and necessity may actually be intrinsic to the assessment.[131]

A further complication is added by the involvement of private security firms which now operate many European detention centres and assist in forced removals.[132] One of the dangers of private involvement is the dilution of accountability and there have been some disturbingly common allegations of mistreatment and abuse.[133] Typically the private companies involved also operate prisons and other

126 *Saadi* supra n110, 3139.

127 UK Select Committee on Home Affairs 2nd Report, part 6 *Detention and Removal* (HMSO 2004).

128 UNHCR supra n65, Guideline 5; UN GA Ex Comm of High Commissioners 53rd session 'Note on International Protection' A/AC 96/965 11 September 2002 para 44.

129 UK Home Office *Asylum Statistics* 1st quarter 2007 31 March 2007 Table 17, 18 indicate a 100 per cent rejection rate at Oakington; Human Rights Watch note the rejection rate at Yarls Wood was 96 per cent, supra n124.

130 This has been argued by the home office as justification for detention, Amnesty International *Seeking Asylum is not a Crime: Detention of People Who Have Sought Asylum* (Amnesty International UK 2005) 62.

131 Aire Intervention in *Saadi v UK* supra n110, para 6; Cornelisse supra n115, 96.

132 Bacon, C 'The Evolution of Immigration Detention in the UK: The Involvement of Private Prison Companies' (Refugee Studies Centre, University of Oxford, Working Paper Series. RSC Working Paper No. 27 2005); Flynn, M and Cannon, C 'The Privatisation of Immigration Detention: Towards a Global View' (Global Detention Project, the Graduate Institute September 2009).

133 Medical Justice *Outsourcing Abuse* (Medical Justice 14 July 2008). One particularly disturbing incident of excess force led to the death of an Angolan man, Jimmy Mubenga, who was asphyxiated during an attempted deportation in 2010. Three of the G4S security staff were arrested in connection with the death but a decision was subsequently taken not to prosecute.

custodial institution and thus perceive their involvement in immigration detention as 'firmly within the penal sphere'.[134]

The detention estate is also diversifying with states using prisons, dedicated removal centres, accommodation and reception centres.[135] These labels can mask wide variations in practice and make it difficult to draw valid comparisons between states.[136] Several countries continue to use prisons to accommodate foreign nationals, including asylum applicants.[137] In Poland, asylum seekers can be detained in a specific detention facility or a deportation prison for up to a year if they have made an application whilst illegally in Poland or awaiting deportation.[138] The Council of Europe's Committee for the Prevention of Torture has suggested that conditions in some designated centres may actually be worse than those found in prisons.[139] Detention facilities at the border of Greece and Turkey have been condemned by international human rights agencies including the UN Rapporteur on Torture and the European Committee for the Prevention of Torture.[140] The facilities are reportedly overcrowded with insufficient hygiene and sanitation, inadequate protection for women and children, lack of trained personnel and information on the applicants' rights. It has been suggested that Greece would have to quintuple its current reception capacity in order to satisfy accommodation needs.[141]

The absence of a specific time limit on asylum detention in the current Reception Directive is regrettable. Several states do not have maximum time limits in national legislation and there is no procedure by which alternatives to detention are first considered. In 2005, the Council of Europe's Commissioner for

---

134 Bacon, C 'The Evolution of Immigration Detention In The UK' (Refugee Studies Centre, University of Oxford, Working Paper Series. RSC Working Paper No 27 2005) 2.

135 Jesuit Refugee Service *Detention in Europe* October 2004 JRS listed 218 facilities for detaining migrants and asylum seekers in 23 European countries.

136 Mole, N and Harby, C *Immigration, Asylum and Detention* (ECRE, AIRE Centre June 2004).

137 European Committee for the Prevention of Torture, Inhuman or Degrading Treatment or Punishment. Visit report: Ireland (2006) CPT/Inf (2007) 40; CPT/Inf (2007) 18 Visit report: Germany, para 49 Hamburg remand prison is used to detain male and female foreign nationals with a view to expulsion alongside remand prisoners.

138 Visit: Poland (2004) CPT/Inf (2006) 11.

139 CPT/Inf (2006) 11 Poland para 59; CPT/Inf (2006) 41 Greece; see also European Parliament Resolution on the situation with refugee camps in Malta.

140 European Committee for the Prevention of Torture and Inhuman or Degrading Treatment or Punishment (CPT) *Public Statement Concerning Greece* 15 March 2011 Available at: http://www.cpt.coe.int/documents/grc/2011–10-inf-eng.htm (accessed 22 April 2013); Report of Special rapporteur on Torture and other cruel, inhuman or degrading treatment of punishment on his mission to Greece (10–20 October 2010) A/HRC/16/52/Add.4 21 April 2011; EU Fundamental Rights Agency *Coping with a Fundamental Rights Emergency: The Situation of Persons Crossing the Greek Land Border in an Irregular Manner* (FRA 2011).

141 McDonough and Tsourdi supra n35.

Human Rights expressed concern that detention for administrative reasons in the UK may become the norm.[142] Despite official commitments that alternatives will be used 'wherever possible' states appear unwilling to move beyond confinement.[143] Research by Field and Edwards suggests that asylum seekers are unlikely to abscond as they seek to be recognised as legitimate, lawful residents.[144] Further, they found that the provision of free legal advice and support would significantly reduce the potential for applicants to abscond.[145] A wide range of potential alternatives could be utilised by the state to maintain the objective of immigration control and security, the majority of which will be significantly more cost-effective.[146] Examples include the state-funded Toronto Bail programme, which supports those with no community ties to raise bail money, replacing confinement with a regular reporting mechanism.[147] Similarly, the Vera Institute's Appearance Assistance Programme in the US piloted a community based, supervised release scheme for those detained pending removal.[148] The UNHCR also suggest that much greater use could be made of residence at open reception centres, directed residence and sureties.[149]

Reception Conditions in Detention

It is important to examine both the length and conditions of detention in any assessment of arbitrariness. Yet the Reception Directive does not provide a clear standard and early analysis showed that many states failed to honour basic reception obligations when asylum applicants were detained.[150] Even short-term detention can have detrimental effects on detainees if the conditions of detention do not respect

142 Council of Europe Commissioner for Human Rights, Mr Gil Alvaro-Robles Report on visit to the UK 4–12 November 2004 Comm DH(2005)6 para 66.

143 UK Home Office *Operational Enforcement Manual* ch 38, 1; UNHCR supra n65, Annex A.

144 Ibid, para 90.

145 Edwards, A and Field, O *Alternatives to Detention of Asylum Seekers and Refugees* UNHCR Legal and Protection Policy Research Series POLAS/2006/03 April 2006, para 156.

146 Ibid, para 166–172 produces evidence from projects in countries including UK, Lithuania, Australia and the US which supports this conclusion.

147 Ibid, Appendix 1.

148 Sullivan, E et al *Testing Community Supervision for the INS: An Evaluation of the Appearance Assistance Program Vera Institute of Justice* 2000 8. Available at: http://www.vera.org/pubs/testing-community-supervision-ins-evaluation-appearance-assistance-program (accessed 22 April 2013).

149 UNHCR supra n65, Appendix A.

150 European Commission supra n5.

the applicants' dignity.[151] Detention contributes to severe psychological problems and is undoubtedly harmful to the mental health of detainees, compounding the stress that many have endured in their home countries.[152]

As detention becomes commonplace in accelerated proceedings and Dublin removals, there is a real risk that victims of torture and other ill-treatment are unable to communicate the full extent of their experiences to the authorities.[153] A successful judicial review bought by five torture survivors detained in the UK for an average of 226 days is sadly not atypical.[154] The applicable immigration rules[155] require persons to be released following medical evidence of torture, but research suggests that this rarely happens in practice due to procedural difficulties and a culture of disbelief amongst detention centre staff.[156]

The UNHCR consider that detention can and has been shown to aggravate illnesses and symptoms and therefore the necessity of detaining such individuals will be difficult to demonstrate.[157] Along with specified time limits, appropriate medical services and mechanisms for ensuring the detainee is fully informed are essential safeguards which are not clearly addressed by the current the directive.[158]

---

151 BBC supra n122; Her Majesty's Inspector of Prisons 'Report on the Unannounced Inspections of Five Non-Residential Short-Term Holding Facilities: Queen's Building and Terminals 1–4 Heathrow Airport' 10–13 October 2005, 5. HM Chief Inspector of Prisons Report on Unannounced inspection of Harmondsworth Immigration Removal Centre 17–21 July 2006 revealed that over 60 per cent of detainees felt unsafe and 44 per cent said they had been victimised by staff. The regime at Lindholme has been criticised for its 'prison culture' and lack of respect for the detainees: BBC News 'Prison Culture at Asylum Centre' 16 June 2004. June 2007, up to 100 detainees at Dungavel removal centre in Scotland were refusing food following the suicide of Kurdish asylum seeker. Specific issues included lack of legal representation and the indefinite time limit of the detention with a view to deportation (in some cases more than 18 months) BBC News 'Food Protest by Asylum Detainees' 11 June 2007.

152 Pourgourides, C 'The Mental Health Implications of the Detention of Asylum Seekers' in Hughes and Liebaut supra n73, 208.

153 UK Parliamentary Joint Committee on Human Rights 'Government Response to the Committee's Tenth Report of This Session: The Treatment of Asylum Seekers' 17th Report of Session 2006–07 HL Paper 134, HC 790 5 July, para 226; Human Rights Watch supra n124.

154 *R (On Application of EO, RA, CO, OE) v SSHD* [2013] EWHC 1236 (Admin); Travis, A 'Torture Victims Held in UK Immigration Detention Centres Launch Legal Action' Guardian Online (22 May 2012). Available at: http://www.guardian.co.uk/uk/2012/may/22/torture-victims-immigration-detention-centres (accessed 6 November 2012).

155 Immigration Rules HC 395, rule 35 1 October 1994.

156 Ibid, Medical Justice *The Second Torture* (Medical Justice 2012); see also detention of children in the UK which continues despite the deputy prime minister's 2010 commitment to ending it, Taylor, D 'Britain's Still Locking Up Children' *The Guardian* (23 October 2012).

157 UNHCR supra n65, Guideline 9.1.

158 UK Joint Committee supra n153, paras 305, 310, 274.

Amnesty International has conducted interviews with several detainees, including families, detained in the UK despite having complied with all Home Office instructions.[159] Many reported a lack of information regarding the reasons and length of detention. These complaints are equally applicable to short periods of detention; in one case a torture-survivor and her daughter had been placed in the DFT, in clear contravention of international standards, for 10 days.[160]

Inappropriate detention conditions have been held to constitute inhuman and degrading treatment in *Mayeka v Belgium* when a five-year-old child was detained alone in an adult facility pending her removal to the Democratic Republic of Congo.[161] The denial or delay of adequate medical treatment during detention can also constitute inhuman and degrading treatment.[162] The Committee for the Prevention of Torture regularly reviews detention practices across Europe and has expressed criticism of the detention standards in several European countries.[163]

It is hard to disagree with the UNHCR's conclusion that the necessary public support for the reception of asylum seekers has been hampered by both media and politicians who regularly conflate illegal migration with refugee movements.[164] In many countries the decision to detain appears to be subject to wide discretion and it is impossible to determine the limits of its use. Apart from an increased vulnerability to detention experienced by certain nationalities, the process all too often appears arbitrary.[165]

Towards Common Standards: The Recast Directive

The Commission's 2007 evaluation report noted wide variations in all aspects of reception conditions.[166] Many of the problems rest with the implementation of the Directive but they have been enabled by the amount of discretion and flexibility afforded in its key provisions. The Commission were therefore committed to upgrading and harmonising the standards of reception pursuant to

159 Amnesty International supra n124.

160 Ibid, 17–18.

161 13178/03 12 October 2006 unreported; See also *The Greek Case* 1969 Yearbook Book 12; *Peers v Greece* App 28524/95 19 April 2001 and *Dougoz v Greece* App 40907/98 6 March 2001.

162 *Hurtado v Switzerland* App 17549/90 (1994) Series A No 280-A.

163 CPT/Inf (2007) 18 of 18 April 2007 reports on detention conditions in Germany; CPT/Inf (2006) 1 of 20 December 2006 criticises two centres in Greece; CPT/Inf (2005) 13 21 July 2005 criticises detention prior to deportation in Austria; CPT/Inf (2006) 9 23 February 2006 describes conditions in Lithuania as 'unacceptable'.

164 Ibid, para 45.

165 Hayter, T *Open Borders: The Case against Immigration Controls* (Pluto 2000) 119.

166 European Commission supra n5.

the Hague Programme.[167] Shortly after its damning evaluation report, the European Commission proposed the first recast Directive on reception conditions.[168]

These proposals, which included measures limiting detention, improving access to work and support for vulnerable asylum seekers, were broadly welcomed by refugee organisations.[169] Indeed, the Commission has been praised for upholding the rights of asylum seekers and ensuring the centrality of the Refugee Convention in negotiations over the CEAS.[170] The European Parliament subsequently made mostly minor amendments to the proposals but regrettably, the required support from the Council was not forthcoming.[171] The Commission's amended proposals were tabled in 2011 and constituted a significant watering down of the earlier commitments.[172] Whilst the use of clearer, consistent concepts (such as international protection) and simplified rules were welcomed, the proposals were undoubtedly influenced by state concerns over potential abuse of national asylum systems.[173] After two years of negotiations which involved some further down-grading of standards, the recast Directive was enacted in 2013. Refugee organisations reacted with disappointment, with the European Council for Refugee and Exiles noting that 'the initial ambition to aim for high standards of reception conditions whilst ensuring a sufficiently high level of harmonisation has been seriously lowered'.[174]

Material Reception Conditions

On material reception conditions, the Commission proposed to ensure a standard of living adequate for the health of asylum seekers and capable of ensuring their

167 European Commission supra n21, 24; UNHCR *Comments on the European Commission's Proposal for a Recast of the Directive Laying Down Minimum Standards for the Reception of Asylum-Seekers* COM(2008)815 final 3 December 2008.

168 Commission *Proposal for a Directive of the European Parliament and of the Council Laying Down Minimum Standards for the Reception of Asylum Seekers (Recast)* COM (2008) 815 final – 2008/0244 (COD) '2008 Commission Recast proposal'.

169 For example, ECRE *Comments from the European Council on Refugees and Exiles on the Amended Commission Proposal to Recast the Reception Directive* (COM (2011) 320 final) September 2011.

170 Kaunert supra n23.

171 European Parliament *European Parliament Legislative Resolution 7 May 2009 on the Proposal for a Directive of the European Parliament and the Council Laying Down Minimum Standards for the Reception of Asylum Seekers (Recast)* COM(2008)8015-C6-0477/2008 – 2008/0244(COD).

172 European Commission *Amended Proposal for a Directive of the European Parliament and the Council Laying Down Minimum Standards for the Reception of Asylum Seekers (recast)* COM (2011)320 final Brussels 1 June 2011 'Commission 2011 Recast'.

173 Ibid, 3.

174 ECRE *Comments from the European Council on Refugees and Exiles on the Amended Commission Proposal to Recast the Reception Directive* (COM (2011) 320 final) September 2011.

subsistence. Member States were obliged to take into consideration the level of social assistance provided for nationals when determining levels of financial support. The European Parliament rejected these proposals and unsurprisingly, there were significant reservations amongst national representatives. Article 17(5) now proposes a system based on reference points established by each Member State in order to ensure an adequate standard of living comparable with nationals but there is no obligation to provide for equality of treatment. More worryingly is the inclusion of a caveat allowing states to grant less favourable reception treatment 'where it is duly justified' in situations where there is a housing shortage or where necessary to determine a vulnerable applicant's particular needs.[175] There is no elaboration of the basis for such justification. Further, a requirement that health care be provided on the same basis as that available to nationals for applicants with special reception needs, has been replaced with an obligation to provide necessary medical or other assistance for those with special reception needs.[176]

The provisions restricting support for asylum seekers had been narrowed to ensure minimal material reception conditions are provided to all asylum applicants. The revised Article 20 now provides that states can reduce or, in 'exceptional and duly justified cases', withdraw material reception conditions where an asylum seekers abandons a place or residence (without informing the authorities or without permission), does not comply with reporting duties or has lodged a subsequent asylum application. Further, under Article 20(2) the reception conditions can be reduced if the applicant, for no justifiable reason, has not lodged an application as soon as reasonably practicable after arrival in the state.[177]

It is regrettable that this position does not adequately reflect established case-law under Article 3 of the ECHR. In the UK, the implementation of a similar provision, was held to constitute a breach of Article 3 when the applicant had become homeless and destitute as a direct result of being denied state support.[178] This approach found favour with the ECtHR in the seminal *MSS v Belgium and Greece* and it is now established principle that Article 3 will be violated where destitution results from the state's failure to provide basic support.[179] Given the obligation to provide basic assistance and 'decent material reception conditions' has 'now entered into positive law' it is unfortunate that the new Directive does not reflect that position.[180]

It is of course somewhat ironic to see the UK's influence in the recast reception provisions. The UK has opted out of the new Directive, yet its recommendation will continue to offer the opportunity for states to offer lower standards for applicants that delay their application for asylum. Applicants may have legitimate reasons for

175 Recast Reception Directive, Article 18(9).

176 Recast Reception Directive, Article 19(2).

177 Recast Reception Directive, Article 20(2).

178 S55 Nationality Immigration and Asylum Act 2002 – the provision is still in force but must be implemented with regard to the obligations in Article 3 ECHR supra n48

179 *MSS v Belgium and Greece* App 30696/09 26 January 2011, para 263.

180 Ibid, para 250.

delaying their application on arrival and there is no objective evidence to support the contention that a late application is less likely to be genuine.

The Council have improved access to health care so that states are now obliged to ensure that applicants receive necessary health care, which shall include 'at least, emergency care and essential treatment of illness and serious mental disorders'.[181] However, it is submitted that the obligation to provide essential health care does not go far enough in addressing the aforementioned judicial pronouncements. It is difficult to envisage how a 'dignified standard of living for all asylum seekers' required by Article 20(5) can be interpreted consistently with Article 20(2).

Access to Employment

It has been noted that current provisions on the right to work vary across the EU. The Commission has maintained its position of seeking to reduce the period of delay to six months, having observed that almost half the Member States already apply the lower threshold.[182] Their impact assessment based on asylum statistics from 2006 showed that if all asylum applicants gained access to the labour market this would represent an increase of just 0.11 per cent in the employed population of EU states.[183] Consequently, the impact on the national labour market would be minimal whilst the economic and social benefit for those concerned would be significant. Whilst the latest proposals remove a proposed exception in the case of large scale arrivals where access to the labour market could be delayed for 12 months, the Council's compromise position is to extend the permissible period of delay from 6 to 9 months.[184] This constitutes a marginal improvement on the current Directive but it falls well short of the standards in the Commission's proposal and those of several Member States. On a more positive note, states will now have a positive obligation to ensure 'effective' access to the labour market thus making it difficult for them to legitimately restrict access once the delay period ends.[185] However, a caveat is again inserted which offers states an opportunity to avoid this obligation by prioritising EU nationals and legally resident third-country nationals 'for reasons of labour market policies'.[186]

Detention

In the original recast proposals detention was only to be provided according to the exceptional grounds specified in the Directive, including the provision that it

181 Recast Reception Directive, Article 19(1).
182 European Commission supra n21, 37.
183 European Commission supra n21, 41.
184 Recast Reception Directive, Article 15(1).
185 Recast Reception Directive, Article 15(2).
186 Ibid.

should only be used as a matter of last resort. It was specifically prohibited in the case of unaccompanied minors.[187]

The new provisions do contain an exhaustive list of grounds for detention but there are concerns that Article 8(3)a, which allows detention to verify identity or nationality, may be open to wide interpretations and possible abuse. Although the UNHCR guidelines include detention for the purposes of verifying identity this is limited to cases where identity is either undetermined or in dispute.[188] Article 8(3)b 'in order to determine … the elements on which the application is based' had been limited to a preliminary interview by the Commission and Parliament but this limitation was removed by the Council. Although the latter added a rather weak compromise such that it is used 'in particular when there is a risk of absconding'. Similarly, recast Article 8(3)c allows detention 'in the context of a procedure, to decide on the right to enter the territory'. This provision is also open to conflicting interpretations, lacks clear legal safeguards (notably a maximum time limit) and may breach Article 31 of the Refugee Convention. It will be recalled that Article 31(2) only allows restrictions on movement that are 'necessary' and until the stay is 'regularised' or the applicant obtains admission into another country. Furthermore, detention justified when 'national security or public order so requires' under Article 8(3)d, fails to reflect internationally accepted standards of proportionality.[189] The Council added a new ground for detention in the context of return proceedings where there are reasonable grounds for believing that the application is made in order to delay or frustrate the return and when the state can substantiate that the applicant has made their claim after being apprehended during an illegal stay.[190] Detention is also explicitly authorised in the context of the Dublin Regulation.[191]

The recast Directive stops short of including a maximum time limit for detention, requiring that administrative procedures related to Article 8(3) are carried out with 'due diligence' and are for 'as short a period as possible'.[192] It is difficult to see how common standards can be developed in the light of such subjective terminology. The European Council have interpreted due diligence to require, de minimis, 'concrete and meaningful steps to ensure that the time needed to verify the grounds for detention is as short as possible, and that a real prospect exists that such verification can be carried out successfully in the shortest possible time'.[193] They emphasise the international position that detention should be a last

---

187 2008 Commission Recast proposal, Article 11(1).

188 UNHCR supra n65.

189 See for example the requirement for expulsion decisions to be based on proportionality in Directive 2004/38 *On the Right of Citizens of the Union and Their Family Members to Move and Reside Freely within the Territory of the Member States* 30 April 2004 L158/77, Article 27. NB Article 8(3)d becomes 8(3)e in the final directive.

190 Recast Reception Directive, Article 8(3)d.

191 Recast Reception Directive, Article 8(3)f.

192 Recast Reception Directive Article 9(1).

193 Recast Reception Directive, Recital 9, para 15(a).

resort which may be applied after a consideration of all alternative measures.[194] The requirement in the initial proposal that administrative bodies could only authorise detention in urgent cases has also been abandoned, although the Council have added a vital safeguard, requiring a timely judicial review to challenge its lawfulness in such cases.[195]

The Commission's initial proposal that the applicant should be informed of the procedure and reasons for detention in a language which they can actually understand has also been rejected. In line with the Procedures Directive, the language in which key information on detention is imparted needs only to be one that the asylum applicant 'understands or is reasonably supposed to understand'.[196] Information on the process of applying for asylum is of essential to the success of the applicant's claim. In several EU states the number of languages in which information is made available does not suggest that this duty is being complied with. In Finland, Portugal, Italy and Greece, information is published in five languages (compared to 34 in Austria and only 3 in Malta).[197] The Council have added an exemption clause allowing the state to derogate from this obligation in duly justified cases for a reasonable period when the asylum seeker is detained at a border or in a transit zone.[198]

Detention in prisons was expressly prohibited in the Commission proposal, reflecting the concerns of the Council of Europe and UNHCR.[199] Article 10 now provides that prisons can be used when specialised detention facilities are not available, effectively giving an option to over-burdened states which is open to abuse. It may therefore conflict with the judgement of the ECtHR in *MSS*.[200] Applying Article 3 ECHR, the Court reasoned that detention conditions must be compatible with respect for human dignity and emphasised the positive obligation on the state to provide decent reception conditions.[201]

As the numbers of people detained on immigration grounds is increasing across Europe, its use has become less targeted. The absence of a maximum time limit challenges the notion that detention should not be arbitrary and may result in more people being locked up for longer periods.[202] Whilst detention will be traumatic for many, adding to the experience of persecution, it is also damaging

194 Recast Reception Directive, Recital 10, para 17(a) and Article 8(2).

195 Recast Reception Directive, Article 9(3).

196 Recast Reception Directive, Article 9(4).

197 Odysseus supra n3 40.

198 Recast Reception Directive, Article 10(5).

199 European Committee for the Prevention of Torture and Inhuman or Degrading Treatment or Punishment CPT Standards CPT/Inf/E(2002)1 – Rev 2010 par 28; *Mayeka and Mitunga v Belgium* supra n101, 102; UNHCR Guidelines supra n66.

200 ECRE supra n174, 14.

201 *MSS v Belgium and Greece* App 30696/09 26 January 2011 para 221.

202 Bacon supra n134, 3 observes that private companies operating immigration centres in the UK see this as an extension of the prison regime and as a highly profitable growth area.

to future integration should the detainee be awarded refugee status. On a societal level, it furthers the public perception of asylum seekers as a problem group, potentially fuelling intolerance and racism.[203] For Landgren, detention 'enhances the perception that there is something amiss with that group of people' and 'contributes to animosity towards asylum seekers as a whole'.[204]

A brief period of detention may be viewed as a practical solution to the demands of immigration control.[205] Yet its generalised application to particular nationalities, often coupled with accelerated procedures, without the safeguard of proportionality, is discriminatory and undermines the right to seek and enjoy asylum. Generalised assessments of proportionality have come to denude persons of their individual right to liberty.[206] If one accepts the contention that there is a humanitarian obligation owed to those fleeing persecution, it is surely inappropriate to subject those people to detention where it is not strictly necessary. The rule of law requires that deprivations of liberty are predicated on narrowly prescribed, accessible criteria. The degree of discretion under which most detention regimes operate, directly challenges this assumption.

Identifying and Protecting Vulnerable Persons

Given the criticism of the current standards and their implementation, the Commission proposed enhanced standards for identifying vulnerable persons and their specific needs. The non-exhaustive list of vulnerable persons now includes victims of trafficking, victims of sexual violence (including female genital mutilation) and persons with mental disorders.[207] Initially, the proposal introduced a welcome safeguard so that those with special needs would not generally be detained but this has been omitted from the recast Directive.[208] Further, the European Parliament's amendment recommended that detention would only be allowed in these cases following an individual examination by a qualified independent professional who concluded there would be no significant deterioration of the applicant's mental health and well-being. This safeguard has been removed and replaced with a weak statement of general principle, stating

203 Tuitt, P *False Images: The Law's Construction of the Refugee* (Pluto 1996) passim; Schuster, L 'A Comparative Analysis of the Asylum Policy of Seven European Governments' 2000 J of Refugee Studies 13, 1, 128; O'Nions supra n111.

204 Landgren supra n76, 159.

205 Hathaway, J *The Rights of Refugees under International Law* (CUP 2005) 413; see also Cornelisse, G *Immigration Detention and Human Rights: Rethinking Territorial Sovereignty* (M Nijhoff 2010).

206 Wilsher supra n57, 170.

207 Recast Reception Directive, Article 21.

208 Recast Reception Directive, Article 11(1).

that the health of vulnerable applicants in detention 'shall be of primary concern to national authorities'.[209]

The detention of unaccompanied minors, similarly prohibited in the initial proposals, is now back on the agenda albeit confined to cases as a last resort, requiring a full consideration of whether less coercive means are available.[210] This will not satisfy the criticism of children's rights agencies who have noted the extreme vulnerability of child asylum seekers.[211] It is also unlikely to address the concerns of the Council of Europe, the ECtHR in the *Mayeka* judgement, or the UN Working Group on Arbitrary Detention.[212] The EU Economic and Social Committee called for the Commission to systematically emphasise the principle that the 'best interest of the child shall be a primary consideration' as stated in the UN Convention on the Rights of the Child.[213] They condemned the detention of minors and persons with special needs, advocating an appropriate hospital environment for the care of persons suffering physical or mental health problems.[214] Although the Council has stressed that unaccompanied minors shall not be kept in prisons and will only be detained following a consideration of less coercive measures, it is difficult to accept that detention can ever be in the child's best interest.[215]

States are obliged to 'ensure a standard of living adequate for the minor's physical, mental, spiritual, moral and social development'[216] but it is also doubtful that this reflects established ECtHR case-law.[217] Article 11(2) requires that minors shall *as far as possible* be provided with age appropriate accommodation, falling short of an absolute guarantee and failing to adequately protect the child's best interests. Education for minors can be delayed for up to three months following an application for international protection. A recommendation from the Parliament

---

209 Ibid.

210 Recast Reception Directive, Article 11(2) – NB, this requirement is not included when considering the detention of vulnerable people under Article 11(1).

211 Hamilton, C et al for UNICEF and the Children's Legal Centre *Administrative Detention of Children: A Global Report* Discussion Paper (UNICEF 2011); Medical Justice 'State Sponsored Cruelty: Children in Immigration Detention' (Medical Justice 2010) Available at: http://www.medicaljustice.org.uk/content/view/1420/89 (accessed 23 April 2013).

212 UN Human Rights Council *Report of the Working Group on Arbitrary Detention* 18 January 2010 A/HRC/13/30 par 60.

213 Article 3(1) UN Convention on the Rights of the Child; European Economic and Social Committee on the *Proposal for a Directive of the European Parliament and the Council laying Down Minimum Stands for the Reception of Asylum Seekers* COM(2008) 815 Final C317/110 23 December 2009, 1.2.

214 Ibid, 4.7.2.

215 Recast Reception Directive, Article 11(2).

216 Recast Reception Directive, Article 23.

217 *Mayeka* supra n101.

that it should be 'ensured as soon as possible', was rejected by the Council.[218] The Commission had also proposed that minor's would be guaranteed representation and assistance by a legal guardian as soon as possible.[219] The Council's amendment is less prescriptive, preferring a representative who will act in the best interests of the child and shall have the necessary expertise to that end.[220]

Appeals

The right to free legal assistance and representation, as in the Procedures Directive, is restricted to appeal or review procedures.[221] Free legal assistance and representation is also available to challenge a detention order but may be restricted to those who lack sufficient resources and limited to the services provided by designated legal advisers.[222] Further, States may impose monetary and/or time limits on the assistance and representation, provided that the limits do not arbitrarily restrict access.[223] The applicant may subsequently been asked to reimburse the cost should their financial situation improve. These caveats also apply to representation and assistance in appeals more generally.[224]

Given the number of problems associated with correctly identifying protection needs, it is essential that asylum applicants have access to legal advice at all stages of the procedure. Yet, the provisions continue to fall short by only requiring states to inform applicants of organisations that are able to provide legal assistance and advice.[225]

The new directive provides that free legal assistance and representation can be withdrawn if the appeal or review is considered by a competent authority 'to have no tangible prospect of success'.[226] The fact that such support is limited to the appeal or review may challenge the emphasis on procedural front-loading in the recast Procedures Directive. If procedures are accelerated or appeals non-suspensive this support might come too late for some applicants and may deny the possibility of an effective remedy contrary to established principles in Article 13 ECHR and Article 47 Charter of Fundamental Rights.[227]

218 Recast Reception Directive, Article 14(2).

219 Commission Recast 2011, Article 24(1) in conjunction with Article 2(j).

220 Recast Reception Directive, Article 24(1).

221 Recast Reception Directive, Article 26(2).

222 Recast Reception Directive, Article 9(7). The provision also allows state to reclaim the cost of this assistance if and when the applicant's financial situation has improved (Article 9(8).

223 Recast Reception Directive, Article 9(8)a.

224 Recast Reception Directive, Article 26(4).

225 Recast Reception Directive, Article 5(1).

226 Recast Reception Directive, Article 26(3).

227 See for example *Jabari v Turkey* ECtHR 11 July 2000, App 40035/98; EU Fundamental Rights Agency *Access to Effective Remedies: The Asylum-Seeker Perspective*

Conclusion

This chapter has demonstrated how the reception standards pursuant to the final stage of the Common Asylum System continue to be imprecisely worded, conferring a great deal of interpretative discretion on states.[228] Whilst the Commission's initial recast proposals would have led to an upgrading of standards, the cautious approach of the Council has not resulted in a significant upgrade from minimum standards. The intervention of the Parliament had some positive effect on the Council proposals but they continue to fall well short of significant improvement and are unlikely to provide the basis of harmonised conditions.[229]

The compromise position on employment, which allows for a period of nine months during which access to the labour market can be delayed, constitutes a longer period of delay than already applied in the national legislation of many states.[230] Although access to employment must be 'effective', priority can be given to EU citizens, nationals of the EEA and lawfully resident third country nationals.[231]

The provisions on material reception conditions continue to be open to wide interpretation, the Parliament's attempt to provide clearer direction being rejected by the Council. Further, 'Member States may grant less favourable treatment to asylum seekers compared to nationals' where some of the support is provided in kind or where national standards of living are higher than what is prescribed for asylum seekers under the Directive.[232]

The position of vulnerable applicants also remains a cause for great concern. The Council refused to discuss a proposal from the European Parliament to introduce a new clause ensuring that torture victims are directed to a care centre appropriate to their situation.[233] As a result, victims of torture and other trauma will continue to find themselves detained as will unaccompanied minors, in direct contravention of UNHCR guidelines.

Detention for no other purpose than administrative convenience is at odds with the UNHCR's established position that detention should in principle be

---

Thematic Report (FRA 2010). Available at: http://fra.europa.eu/en/publication/2010/access-effective-remedies-asylum-seeker-perspective (accessed 24 April 2013).

228 Peers supra n4, 372.

229 Statewatch Analysis 'The EU Directive on Reception Conditions: A Weak Compromise' (Statewatch July 2012); see also their commentary on the Council's proposals 'The Revised Directive on Asylum-Seekers' Reception Conditions: The Member States Hit Rock-Bottom' (Statewatch March 201).

230 Recast Reception Directive, Article 15(1) – the Council had originally wanted the delay to remain at 12 months whereas the Council and Parliament had lobbied for six months.

231 Recast Reception Directive, Article 15(2).

232 Council recast 2012 Article 17(5).

233 European Parliament supra n171, Article 20.

avoided.[234] The decision of the Grand Chamber in *Saadi* to rule out a specific requirement of necessity may effectively deprive applicants of full protection from arbitrary detention contrary to both international human rights and refugee law. Asylum seekers now have less of a right to liberty than those suspected of criminal offences.[235]

The recast proposals began with commitments to end the detention of children and vulnerable people but the position has gradually shifted so that there is little substantive difference from the current position. Most significantly, there is no maximum time limit for detention. Implementation reports consistently reveal how detention is used to deny applicants basic reception rights, a position which is not justified by the terms of the Directive. The inability of the recast Directive to guarantee common requirements for detention conditions will inevitably leave this issue unaddressed. The right to seek and enjoy asylum is certainly compromised by the routine use of detention.

A further problem of application arises from the evolution of external cooperation agreements towards policies of readmission and resettlement. The European Union has actively maintained its external frontiers by funding initiatives on the periphery of Europe to enable the detention and removal of irregular migrants. An estimated 40,000 people per annum travel illegally through Ukraine to the EU and those identified by the authorities are likely to be detained. The conditions in these centres are miserable and do not attract the same degree of scrutiny as those in EU states.[236] The externalisation of migration control which inevitably impacts on asylum seekers means that many of the basic standards in the European directives can be pushed aside. In the past, the UNHCR and the EU have appeared at loggerheads over the fundamentals of such initiatives, with the former High Commissioner for Refugees, Ruud Lubbers, arguing that 'the tendency is to shift the burden to other EU states, or countries outside the EU that are ill-equipped to handle asylum claims'.[237] In the next chapter I will explore some of these challenges and consider whether it is desirable or even possible to move the locus of asylum determination without damaging international protection and undermining state responsibility.[238]

---

234 General Assembly EX Com of the High Commissioners Programme 52nd Session 'Note on International Protection' A/AC.96/951 13 September 2001 para 46; EXCOM Conclusion 44 (XXXVII) 1986; 85 (XLIX) 1998, paras cc–ee.

235 The dissenting judges in *Saadi v UK* ask 'Is it a crime to be a foreigner?' supra n113.

236 BBC News 'Ukrainian Detention Centre' 13 December 2002; Make Borders History Campaign 'No Border Camp: Ukraine' (August 2007); UN Special Rapporteur on the Human Rights of Migrants, Annual Report 2002 E/CN.4/2003/85 para55 and Annual Report 2005 27 December 2004 E/CN 4/2005/85.

237 *The Guardian* 'Make Asylum Claims Fair Not Fast' (3 November 2004).

238 Wilsher supra n58, 203.

Chapter 6
Externalisation and Burden-Shifting

Introduction

Burden-sharing and solidarity arrangements belong to soft law principles of international law. Whilst they may lack the 'characteristics of international normativity', they are nevertheless capable of producing legal effects.[1] With the development of the Dublin transfer mechanism, burden-sharing has become a key driver in European asylum policy but the last decade has also seen increasing efforts, largely at the initiative of individual Member States, to export burdens beyond the EU. Arrangements such as readmission, external processing and resettlement have the potential to jeopardise the international protection regime and dilute state accountability. Notwithstanding the fall in asylum applications, states appear keener than ever to look to external solutions for refugee management.

As part of a toolbox of protection-oriented measures, the Commission has developed EU Regional Protection Programmes to support third countries in offering durable solutions to some of the 6.5 million refugees estimated to live in developing countries.[2] Asylum has also been integrated into development cooperation strategies which, along with an EU resettlement initiative, could provide a solution based on international solidarity.[3] Since 2005 the EU's Global Approach to Migration has been grounded on three pillars: facilitation of labour migration, prevention or irregular migration and fostering links between migration and the development of countries of origin. It now encompasses numerous strategies, action plans and partnerships on aspects of migration management covering most of the developing world.[4]

Whilst it is apparent that Member States retain legal responsibility for actions which are under their control, many of these mechanisms effectively remove the

---

1 Hurwitz, A *The Collective Responsibility of States to Protect Refugees* (OUP 2009) 163.

2 UNHCR Statistical Yearbook UNHCR 2005).

3 European Commission *Green Paper on the Future of the Common European Asylum System* Brussels 6 June 2007 COM(2007)301 final.

4 Council of the EU *Outcome of Proceedings of High Level Working Group on Asylum and Migration on 21 January 2013* 5663/13 22 February 2013. In terms of the geographical approach, priority is given to the Southern Mediterranean, Africa and Eastern Europe but attention is now also given to other regions in addition to general thematic strategies. See for example the Cotonou Partnership Agreement between African, Caribbean and Pacific states and the EU, OJ L317 15 December 2000 10–11; 79 states have agreed on the implementation of the agreement which contains a general readmission clause for nationals.

element of Member State control. The responsibility for processing and refugee determination is transferred to the third country raising significant problems for accountability.[5] The conflation of asylum and migration control continues to pose a risk of refoulement as refugee detection is difficult to prioritise in a system aimed at reducing the headline figure of irregular migrants.[6] This is particularly the case with readmission agreements where third countries appear to be weaker partners in negotiations.

Readmission

The main purpose of readmission agreements is to cooperate over the return of irregular migrants and thus combat illegal immigration but they inevitably impact on asylum seekers who find themselves liable for removal due to safe third country or country of origin designations.[7] Given this reservation, it is perhaps surprising to note that the UNHCR initially supported such agreements as a way of ending asylum procedures and discouraging their misuse.[8]

Return of migrants with no right to remain has become a key feature in the fight against irregular migration. The Laeken Council meeting in 2001 identified EC readmission agreements as the best strategy for securing returns.[9] A designated Returns Directive now enables the detention and compulsory return of migrants following a period allocated for voluntary departure.[10] The provisions must be implemented with regard to the best interests of the child, family life, health needs and the principle of non-refoulement.[11] In addition, a number of readmission agreements pave the way for return of irregular migrants, including return of asylum applicants to safe third countries or safe countries of origin as defined in the Procedures Directive.

---

5 Giuffre, M 'The European Union Readmission Policy after Lisbon' (2011) 1 Interdisciplinary Political Studies 0, 17.

6 Lindstrøm, C *European Union Policy on Asylum and Immigration: Addressing the Root Causes of Forced Migration: A Justice and Home Affairs Policy of Freedom, Security and Justice?* (2005) 39 Social Policy and Administration 6, 592.

7 Phuong, C 'Building a Community Return Policy' in Baldaccini, A; Guild, E and Toner, H (eds) *Whose Freedom, Security and Justice? EU Immigration and Asylum Law and Policy* (Hart 2007) 337.

8 UNHCR *Position on Readmission Agreements 'Protection Elsewhere' and Asylum Policy* UNHCR August 1994.

9 Laeken European Council *Presidency Conclusions* 14–15 December 2001 SN 300/1/01 REV 1.

10 Directive 2008/115/EC of the European Parliament and of the Council of 16 December 2008 on Common Standards and Procedures in Member States for Returning Illegally Staying Third-Country Nationals L348/98 24 December 2008.

11 Returns Directive Article 5.

Since the 1990s European states have attempted to negotiate bilateral readmission agreements with third countries.[12] Many of these agreements implicitly recognise the need to provide financial assistance in order to improve immigration control, particularly at the border.[13] The UNHCR has lobbied for higher protection standards in these agreements but Lavenex presents a more cynical picture, suggesting that these early agreements were 'an attempt by major Western refugee receiving countries to relieve their domestic asylum procedures by transferring their legal and humanitarian responsibilities to other, usually less wealthy states'.[14]

Most states continue to negotiate their own agreements but the Treaty of Amsterdam provided competence to the EC to sign and ratify readmission treaties.[15] The High Level Working Group on Immigration and Asylum commenced work in 1998 with the task of identifying a list of states suitable for action plans linking aspects of migration policy with economic development, humanitarian aid and improvements in irregular migration control.[16] The Tampere Council meeting then provided the platform on which to begin negotiations on the readmission of irregular migrants (including unsuccessful asylum applicants) with Afghanistan, Somalia, Iraq, Sri Lanka, Morocco and Albania. The EU now has operational readmission agreements with Hong Kong, Macao, Sri Lanka, Albania, Russian Federation, Ukraine, Macedonia, Serbia, Bosnia and Herzegovina, Montenegro, Moldova, Pakistan, Georgia and Turkey.[17]

---

12 There are now hundreds of these agreements in operation. For example, in 2010 Spain had 24 readmission agreements, Serbia was a party to 17 according to questionnaires received by the special rapporteur Tineke Strik: Parliamentary Assembly *Readmission Agreements: A Mechanism for Returning Irregular Migrants* Council of Europe Doc 21268 17 March 2010, 26. This is notwithstanding UNHCR recommendations that Roma should not be returned to Serbia.

13 Lavenex, S *Safe Third Countries: Extending the EU Asylum and Immigration Policies to Central and Eastern Europe* (Central European UP 1999) 82.

14 Lavenex, S 'Passing the Buck: EU Refugee Policies towards Central and Eastern Europe' (1998) 11 J of Refugee Studies 2, 144; UNHCR supra n8 and UNHCR *NGO Background Paper on the Refugee and Migration Interface* UNHCR Geneva 28–29 June 2001; Coleman, N *European Readmission Policy: Third Country Interests and Refugee Rights* (M Nijhoff 2009) 223.

15 Treaty of the European Communities Article 63(3)b.

16 EU High Level Working Group on Asylum and Migration *Report to the European Council in Nice* 2001. Available at: http://www.consilium.europa.eu/uedocs/cms_data/docs/pressdata/en/misc/13993.en0%20ann.doc.html (accessed 8 May 2013). The group's work was extended in 2002 to include China and Central Asia in addition to North and Sub-Saharan Africa: Council of the EU *Modification of the Terms of Reference of the HLWG* 30 May Doc 9433/02.

17 EU Council Thematic Programme 'Cooperation with Third Countries in the areas of Migration and Asylum' 2011–2013 Multi-Annual Strategy Paper; *EU Readmission Agreements: State of Play* (June 2011). On the details of negotiations see Billet, C 'EC Readmission Agreements: A Prime Instrument of the External Dimension of the EU's fights

Several of these states are themselves refugee producing countries with asylum seekers from Russia and Pakistan constituting 13 per cent of asylum arrivals in the EU.[18] Thus great care has to be taken to ensure that individuals are not returned in breach of non-refoulement.[19] Most recently, successful negotiations were concluded with Armenia and Cape Verde.[20] However, the Commission continues to struggle in some of its negotiations. This is particularly notable in its negotiations with Morocco and Algeria; states that are effectively been used as gate-keepers to Europe.[21] The EU has been accused of bullying its neighbours to accept the terms of negotiations, resulting in the Moroccan Foreign Minister, Saâdeddine El Othmani reportedly refusing the Commission's demand to act as the 'gendarme of the European Union'.[22]

Despite these difficulties, particularly over the return of non-nationals, the European Pact on Migration and Asylum adopted in 2008 endorses readmission agreements with the European Union and this is further supported by the Stockholm Programme which continues to view readmission agreements as pivotal in migration management.[23] The EU Global Approach is identified as the strategic framework for this external policy.

The agreements essentially require the non-EU party to take back its own nationals who have entered or stayed illegally in addition to the nationals of non-contracting states who have stayed in or entered their state illegally. Peers notes that each of the agreements is without prejudice to international law including human rights and refugee law, yet is alarmed to observe that there is no specific mention of human rights or refugee law in readmission treaties with Hong Kong, Macao, Sri Lanka, Ukraine and Pakistan.[24] Because the Action

---

Against Irregular Immigration. An Assessment after Ten Years of Practice' (2010) 12 Eur J Migration and L 45.

18 EU 'Asylum Applications Continue to Increase in EU' EU Spotlight 28 March 2013 (Applicants from Afghanistan were the largest group at 8 per cent whereas applicants from Syria and Russian constituted 7 per cent and Pakistan 6 per cent).

19 Coleman supra n14, 228.

20 Council of the EU 'EU-Armenia Readmission Agreement' Brussels, 19 April 2013 8630/13 PRESSE 160.

21 Statewatch 'Political Agreement on Mobility Partnership: Towards the First Readmission Agreement with an African Country?' (Statewatch, News 7 March 2013); Billet supra n17, 55.

22 Quoted in Statewatch ibid; Phuong, C 'Building a Community Return Policy with Third Countries: An Equal Parternship?' in Baldaccini, A; Guild, E and Toner, H *Whose Freedom, Security and Justice? EU Immigration and Asylum Law and Policy* (Hart 2007) 356.

23 European Council *European Pact on Immigration and Asylum* 13444/08 Brussels, 24 September 2008; European Council *The Stockholm Programme – An Open and Secure Europe Serving and Protecting Citizens* C 115/01, 4 May 2010.

24 Peers, S *EU Justice and Home Affairs Law* (OUP 2011) 588–589; Hurwitz also observes the absence of UNHCR involvement in the early bilateral agreements, Hurwitz

Plans are concerned with migration in general, economic concerns are prioritised over political considerations and human rights.[25] Commentators also accuse the plans of ignoring structural stability in order to push ahead with the agenda of migration control.[26] This can be seen clearly in the action plan with Sri Lanka, a state that has neither signed nor ratified the Refugee Convention and where there have been serious allegations of widespread human rights abuses during and after the recent civil war. Serious questions must be asked over Sri Lanka's ability to offer protection from refoulement.[27] More generally, the Council of Europe's Parliamentary Assembly notes a real risk of refoulement may arise in the case of irregular migrants returned to a country that is not their own.[28] For this reason it recommends that states attempt to return migrants to countries of their nationality where at all possible.[29]

Until recently the 'non-affection clause' was the only reference to international commitments in the agreements as it was argued that human rights concerns only materialise at the time that the specific return decision is taken.[30] For this reason, Coleman argues that there is no basis in international refugee law to incorporate additional protection standards into Community readmission agreements.[31] Since 2005, following pressure from the European Parliament, readmission agreements have referred to specific instruments, including the Refugee Convention, but this is unlikely to be sufficient.[32] The EU action plan for Afghanistan is accused of enabling a platform for forced returns by some Member States despite evident instability and insecurity.[33]

---

supra n1, 70.

25 See for example Morgades S 'The Externalisation of the Asylum Function in the European Union' (2002) 4 GRITIM Working Paper Series 18 and Lindstrøm supra n6.

26 Lindstrøm supra n6, 595; Van Selm, J 'The High Level Working Group: Can Foreign Policy, Development Policy and Asylum and Immigration Policy Really Be Mixed?' Conference Paper WIDER, UN University Conference Tampere, 2002, 16.

27 Bouteillet-Paquet, D 'Passing the Buck: A Critical Analysis of the Readmission Policy Implemented by the European Union and Its Member States' (2003) 5 Eur J Migration & L 371.

28 Parliamentary Assembly supra n12, para 4; see also ECRE *Safe Third Countries: Myths and Realities* 1995 ECRE; Kumin, J *Asylum in Europe: Sharing or Shifting the Burden?* UNHCR World Refugee Survey 1995; Byrne, R and Shacknove, A 'The Safe Third Country Notion in European Asylum Law' (1996) 9 Harvard HR J 185; Lavenex supra n13; Legomsky, S 'Secondary Refugee Movements and the Return of Asylum Seekers to Third Countries: The Meaning of Effective Protection' (2003) 15 Intl J Refugee L 4, 567.

29 Ibid para 6.8.

30 Giuffre, supra n5, 34; Parliamentary Assembly supra n12, para 2; Lavenex supra n13; Legomsky supra28.

31 Coleman supra n14, 316.

32 Billet supra n17, 72.

33 Bouteillet-Paquet supra n27, 374.

Readmission clauses are also inserted into other EC external agreements.[34] This is in addition to the standard migration cooperation clause which includes a commitment to examine root causes and the joint examination of illegal immigration issues.[35]

The Commission has been keen to explore ways of linking development aid with better immigration control.[36] The Thessalonkiki Council and subsequent Commission initiatives have continued on this path, although there has been resistance from partner states who found themselves treated like a poor relation.[37] Consequently a more balanced policy has emerged which links financial assistance and visa agreements to readmission and support in the form of non-legally binding mobility partnerships.[38] Since 2009 the agreements have centred on three dimensions: controlling illegal migration (including readmission and support for voluntary return and reintegration, promotion of mobility and legal immigration, and support for development.[39]

The European Neighbourhood Policy launched in 2003 contains an objective of joint border management where border control can be moved beyond European Union borders to adjacent states.[40] Partnership over border control is one of a number of goals advanced in the partnerships, which include a reduction in poverty, increased economic cooperation and improved political and cultural relations. Yet it is border control that has become the priority in action plans, particularly through readmission agreements.[41] As Baldaccini observes, these countries were not necessarily signatories to the Refugee Convention and in several cases, did

34 Coleman supra n14.

35 Since the Seville meeting of the European Council in 2002 this clause has included a provision for compulsory readmission in the event of illegal immigration: *Presidency Conclusions* 21–22 June 2002 Doc 13463/02 POLGEN 52, 33; discussed by Morgades supra n25, 17.

36 European Commission COM (2002) 703, 3 December 2002.

37 Presidency Conclusions, Thessaloniki European Council 19–20 June 2003, Hurwitz supra n1, 77; Phuong supra n7, 356.

38 Peers supra n24, 594; Hurwitz supra n1, 77; yet Reslow provides evidence that partner States are not been fully consulted in these Mobility Partnerships either – this failure to fully appreciate the particular perspective of the third-country has resulted in limited success, Reslow, N 'The Role of Third Countries in EU Migration Policy: The Mobility Partnerships' (2012) 14 Eur J Migration and Law 4.

39 Commission of the European Communities 'Communication from the Commission to the European Parliament and the Council: An Area of Freedom, Security and Justice Serving the Citizen' COM (2009) 262/4 Brussels.

40 European Commission *Communication on Wider Europe* March 2003 COM (2003) 104 final 11 March 2003. Available at: http://ec.europa.eu/world/enp/pdf/com03_104_en.pdf (accessed 10 June 2013).

41 Baldaccini, A 'The External Dimension of the EU's Asylum and Immigration Policies: Old Concerns and New Approaches' in Baldaccini, A; Guild, E and Toner, H (eds) *Whose Freedom, Security and Justice?* (Hart 2007) 294.

not have functioning asylum systems.[42] None of the agreements addressed asylum capacity with the onus placed on the third country to deal with readmissions and prevent further access to the EU. These second generation buffer states in turn negotiate their own readmission arrangements with third countries, making it ever more difficult for undocumented migrants to reach the EU. As the EU has integrated the first generation of buffer states through enlargement, it is now accused of rebuilding its buffer by expanding even father into Central Asia, North Africa, and the Middle-East.[43] There is a real risk to the integrity of the refugee system as many of these states would not be recognised as safe countries for the purpose of EU common designations under the Procedures Directive.[44]

Most of the problems generated by readmission agreements fall on the shoulders of the migrant and on the receiving state. This can create a conflict which has the potential to provoke a climate of xenophobia and instability in the receiving state.[45] Several EU states have negotiated readmission agreements with Kosovo despite evident security problems and discrimination against minorities, particularly Roma. Forcible returns have been negotiated and facilitated by these agreements without full consideration of international obligations. Similarly, returns from Greece to Turkey are accused of causing the refoulement of Iranian and Iraqi asylum applicants who were not given an opportunity to make a claim for protection.[46] Billet argues that the EU has no real control over what could happen to non-national migrants following their expulsion.[47] In many states irregular migration is a crime and returnees may find themselves imprisoned on arrival.[48] The potential conflict with the non-refoulement obligation is very real.

Financial support is available via the AENEAS programme which was established in 2004 to offer technical assistance and support to non-EU states, particularly in the area of readmission. The programme's 2007–13 budget increased dramatically to €4,020 million for the 'solidarity and management of migration flows'.[49] Yet the external dimension remains difficult to sell to neighbouring states many of whom are experiencing their own challenging economic and political

42 Ibid, 294. She gives the example of Morocco which received a €50 million grant to assist in controlling migration flows. One of the ways this control has been implemented is through the construction of fences around the Spanish enclaves of Ceuta and Melilla. Similar observations can be made in respect of Ukraine, discussed below.

43 Hurwitz supra n1, 75; Statewatch 'EU Buffer States and the UNHCR "Processing" Centres and "Safe Havens" (2003) 3 Statewatch Bulletin 2; Lindstrøm supra n6, 590.

44 Guild, E 'The European Geography of Refugee Protection – Exclusions, Limitations and Exceptions from the 1967 Protocol to the Present' (2012) 4 EHRLR 422.

45 De Haas 'The Myth of Invasion: The Inconvenient Realities of African Migration to Europe' (2008) 29 3rd World Q 7, 1319.

46 Parliamentary Assembly supra n12, 53.

47 Billet supra n17, 74.

48 Billet supra n17, 64.

49 Geddes, A *Immigration and European Integration: Beyond Fortress Europe?* (Manchester UP 2008)182.

circumstances.[50] A European Return Fund became operational in January 2088 with a five year budget of €676 million.[51]

These problems are illustrated by the readmission agreements with Ukraine, a secondary buffer state which would be considered a European safe country under the Procedures Directive.[52] From the mid 1990s neighbouring EU countries (Poland, Slovakia and Hungary) negotiated bilateral agreements with Ukraine to summarily return migrants.[53] Since 1998 a Cooperation and Partnership agreement has governed relations between the EU and Ukraine and migration has become a central issue.[54] The Ukraine has been Europe's biggest donor state but it has exhibited notable reluctance to take on responsibility for third country returns.[55] In 2010, after four years of negotiations and despite the concern of many human rights agencies, a formal readmission agreement came into force for third country nationals.[56] European resources have been primarily directed towards capacity building in Ukraine with some €35 million allocated to the state border guard and Ministry of Interior to deal with irregular migrants, including through the construction and upgrading of the detention estate.[57] This dwarves the €1.5 million provided to NGOs to develop legal and social protection programmes for asylum seeking children and child trafficking and the €4.9 million allocated to the Regional Protection Support Project and the Local Integration of Refugees Project, which covers Ukraine, Belarus and Moldova.[58] Here again we see a similar pattern where mechanisms to secure protection are side-lined.

---

50 Lavenex, S 'The External Face of Europeanization: Third Countries and International Organizations' in Faist, T and Ette, A (eds) *Mechanisms of Immigration Control, A Comparative Analysis of European Regulation Policies* (Berg 1999), 248; Billet supra n17, 75.

51 Dec No 575/2007/EC of the *European Parliament and the Council establishing the European Return Fund for the Period of 2008–2013 as Part of the General Programme 'Solidarity and Management of Migration Flows'* OJ L144 6 June 2007, 45.

52 See discussion in Chapter 4.

53 Human Rights Watch *Buffeted in the Borderland* (Human Rights Watch 2010) 3.

54 Council and Commission Decision of 26 January 1998 *On the Conclusion of the Partnership and Cooperation Agreement between the European Communities and Their Member States, of the One Part, and Ukraine, of the Other Part* 98/149/EC, OJ L 049 19 February 1998 pp0001–0002.

55 Rettman, A 'EU-Ukraine Relations Hit Visa Bump' (EU Observer, 2 October 2006).

56 Council Decision *On the Signing of the Agreement between the European Community and Ukraine on Readmission of Persons* 9312/07 Council of the EU, Brussels 5 June 2007. The agreement came into force for Ukrainian nationals on 1 January 2009; Human Rights Watch 'Managing Migration Means Potential EU Complicity in Neighbouring States' Abuse of Migrants and Refugees' Number 2 (HRW, October 2006); Jesuit Refugee Service Europe *No Other Option* (JRS June 2011).

57 European Neighbourhood and Partnership Instrument Indicative multi-annual allocations for the period of 2007–10 Available at: http://ec.europa.eu/world/enp/pdf/country/0703_enpi_figures_en.pdf (accessed 7 November 2012).

58 Human Rights Watch supra n53, 27–28.

There are consistent testimonies documented by human rights agencies indicating that the human rights of returnees is not adequately protected in Ukraine with common allegations of torture, mistreatment and corruption.[59] In August 2010 the asylum system was restructured for the eighth time in 10 years (including a 12-month period from August 2009 when there was no functioning system at all). There are very few grants of refugee status with most cases rejected as inadmissible or manifestly unfounded without a substantive examination.[60] The number of applications for asylum has also dropped dramatically and it is widely reported that asylum claims are being lost in the system, particularly when transferred from border guards to the regional migration service.[61] Resettlement of recognised refugees from the Ukraine has been lamentable, with less than 30 per cent (116 individuals) of those identified by the UNHCR being resettled in 2009.[62] A systemic culture of disbelief is apparent in the testimonies featured in the reports. Amnesty International has recently reported allegations of racism and police brutality towards residents of the Zhuravich detention centre in western Ukraine.[63] Residents, including some 20 children, predominately of Eritrean and Somali nationality had been sentenced to detention for one year pending deportation but there was little prospect of removal due to the likelihood of refoulement.[64] This uncertain status of restricted mobility, described as 'warehousing' by several writers, is unlikely to satisfy international standards.[65] More troubling are revelations in a recent Human Rights Watch report suggesting that around 80 residents attempted

---

59 Human Rights Watch supra n53, 45.

60 Ibid, 6. UNHCR statistics indicate that between 1993 and 2008 there were only 5,459 grants of refugee status and almost half that number remained in the country. Bucking the international trend the number of people granted refugee status in Ukraine has decreased dramatically year on year since 2002 to 890 applications in 2011 (a decrease of 41 per cent between 2010 and 2011) UNHCR 'Asylum levels and trends in Industrialised countries' (UNHCR 2012) 21. At the same time 370 Ukrainians sought asylum in the US and Canada. Ukrainians made up the highest group of nationals seeking asylum in the Czech Republic. NB 4,452 Hungarians did the same in 2011!! Available at: http://www.unhcr.org/4e9beaa19.html (accessed 12 July 2012).

61 There were only 88 applications for asylum in the first eight months of 2010: Human Rights Watch supra n53, 36.

62 The EU took 67 out of the 116 individuals who were resettled with Sweden taken 43. Human Rights Watch supra n53, 29.

63 Amnesty International 'Ukraine Must Protect Detained Asylum Seekers Attacked by Security Forces' (Amnesty International News, 21 January 2012). Available at: http://www.amnesty.org/en/news/ukraine-must-protect-detained-asylum-seekers-attacked-security-forces-2012-01-31 (accessed 23 May 2013).

64 Any return would also breach Article 3 ECHR following the decision of the ECTHR in *Sufi and Elmi v the United Kingdom* App 8319/07 and 11449/07 28 June 2011.

65 Smith, M 'Warehousing Refugees: A Denial of Rights, A Waste of Humanity' and Chen, G 'A Global Campaign to End Refugee Warehousing' in US Committee for Refugees *World Refugee Survey* 2004. See the standards on detention discussed in Chapter 5.

to claim asylum but were refused permission to do so by the authorities.[66] This confirms that ratification of the ECHR and Refugee Convention are not sufficient to guarantee observance of such rights and highlights the need for an independent monitoring mechanism in the case of safe third countries.[67] Allegations of bribery and corruption are common and there are significant legal gaps, most notably concerning an absence of subsidiary protection mechanisms and protection for unaccompanied minors. Summary returns, including the high-profile removals of 10 Uzbeck asylum seekers, have been reported in clear violation of international obligations.[68] There is a significant threat to the underlying humanitarian spirit of the international refugee protection regime, in addition to broader principles of international solidarity and responsibility-sharing.[69]

The failures of refugee protection in Ukraine are not unique. The Council of Europe has reported on the disparity in refugee recognition rates across the wider region.[70] Their resolution observed how up to half of all applications are overturned on appeal in some states and that this is compromised by the absence of suspensory appeal rights.[71] The EU was thereby invited to revise the Dublin Regulation and the safe country mechanism to prioritise, through the European Asylum Support Office, improved quality and consistency in asylum determinations.[72] Detention conditions are further criticised by the Council of Europe who highlight overcrowding, inappropriate accommodation and appalling conditions which have a 'negative impact on the mental and physical well-being of persons detained both during and after detention'.[73] It is perhaps unreasonable to expect states experiencing their own economic and political difficulties to act

66 Human Rights Watch 'Ukraine: Open Letter regarding the Arbitrary Detention of Somali Asylum Seekers' (31 January 2012). Available at: http://www.hrw.org/news/2012/01/31/ukraine-open-letter-regarding-arbitrary-detention-somali-asylum-seekers (accessed 23 May 2013).

67 This is all that is required for the Procedures Directive to designate the European state as safe for the purposes of the Asylum Procedures Directive, Article 36. Compared to non-European safe countries, it is much more difficult to rebut this presumption of safety; Coleman supra n14, 291.

68 US Dept of State 'Ukraine: Country Report on Human Rights Practices' US 6 March 2007 and Human Rights Watch Interview with UNHCR, Kyiv 25 June 2010; ECtHR interim ruling *Khamroyev and Others v Ukraine* Communication 26 July 2010.

69 Edwards, A 'The Optional Protocol to the Convention Against Torture and the Detention of Refugees '(2008) 57 ICLQ 816.

70 For example, in the case of Iraqi asylum applicants, the refugee recognition rates varied across the Council of Europe between 0 per cent and 81 per cent: Resolution 1695 (2009) *Improving the Quality and Consistency of Asylum Decisions in the Council of Europe Member States* C/E 20 November 2009.

71 Ibid.

72 Ibid, para 9.2, 0.3.

73 Council of Europe Parliamentary Assembly Resolution 1707 (2010) *Detention of Asylum Seekers and Irregular Migrants in Europe* 28 January 2010 para 4.

as Europe's gate-keepers without significant resources and support.[74] There is enough evidence available to demonstrate that the European institutions are aware of the humanitarian risks of removals as well as the dire situation facing migrants who are effectively trapped in Ukraine and other states bordering the EU.

It will be recalled that the EU Charter of Fundamental Rights prohibits refoulement and guarantees the right to asylum. The rights in the Charter should be interpreted in line with comparable rights in the ECHR.[75] These rights of course should apply to Ukraine as a signatory state.[76] The TFEU makes provision for the EU to accede to the ECHR which would make the EU institutionally bound by the absolute prohibition on torture and inhuman or degrading treatment as well as the right to an effective remedy.[77] In the meantime, the application of the Charter is limited as it only applies to the actions of the EU and Member States when implementing EU law.[78] It is therefore argued that this will prevent its application to the implementation of directly applicable provisions including the Dublin Regulation. However, the testimonies collected suggest that these human rights provisions are in danger of being violated as a direct consequence of the EU readmission policy.[79] The ECtHR has ruled that a state will be responsible for human rights violations which occur when transferring applicants to countries where there is evidence to demonstrate a significant risk of refoulement.[80] It seems likely that, should the EU accede to the ECHR, its readmission policies could similarly attract responsibility, either solely or jointly with the state transferring. An arguable case for European responsibility can also be based on Article 53 of the Charter which recognises the relevance of international agreements in enabling an expansive interpretation of human rights as enshrined in the Charter. Giuffre argues that the rights and obligations of the Charter are clearly relevant in the enforcement of readmission agreements with third countries where those countries do not offer the same legal safeguards as those offered by Member States.[81]

---

74 Vachudová, M A 'Eastern Europe as Gatekeeper: The Immigration and Asylum Policies of an Enlarging EU' in Andreas, T and Snyder, P *The Wall around the West* (Rowman & Littlefield, 2000); Gonzáles-Enriques, C and Triandafyllidou, A 'Comparing the New Hosts of Southern Europe' (2009) 11 Eur J Migration and L 109.

75 Article 52(4) Charter of Fundamental Rights and Explanatory notes.

76 Ukraine ratified the ECHR on 11 September 1997 but there have been disturbing signs that the rule of law is under threat. In particular see the recent decision of the ECtHR in *Tymoshenko v Ukraine* App 24987/11 30 April 2013.

77 TEU Article 6(2) and TFEU Article 218.

78 Article 51(1) CFR applies 'only to the institutions, bodies, offices and agencies of the Union with due regard to the principle of subsidiarity and to the Member States only when they are implementing EU law'.

79 Lenart, J '"Fortress Europe": Compliance of the Dublin II Regulation with the European Convention for the Protection of Human Rights and Fundamental Freedoms' (2012) 28 Merkourios – Intl and Eur Migration 75, 11.

80 *MSS v Belgium and Greece* 2011 ECtHR Grand Chamber App 30696/09.

81 Giuffre supra n5, 15.

The one-sided nature of many readmission negotiations and the burden they place on receiving states inevitably dilutes their effectiveness and erodes refugee protection. Many successful negotiations exist outside the enlargement process, depending instead on bilateral relations.[82] The EU has applied pressure to third countries so that they assume responsibility for non-nationals. Whilst the Commission proposal omitted this clause from readmission agreements it remains part of the Mobility Partnerships.[83]

External Processing

As well as readmission of irregular migrants, there has been frequent discussion on ways of reducing the burden of processing and distributing irregular migrants. The 'outsourcing' of border controls, such as the Australian 'Pacific Solution', enables the processing of asylum applicants away from the destination state.[84] This keeps asylum seekers geographically distant from the potential host state whilst distancing states from their legal obligations.[85] This is an aspect of Zolberg's 'remote control' migration, a term that he also applies to include safe third country designations and the stationing of border staff at overseas embarkation points.[86] For Samers this externalising approach has become necessary due to the rise in smuggling and trafficking, although this requires us to acknowledge the epiphenomenal nature of illegal immigration, which suggests that national and European policies have themselves created this growth.[87]

External processing could enable successful applicants to be resettled whereas unsuccessful applicants can be more easily returned having been accommodated and processed in a designated detention centre. Proponents argue that external processing confers a number of benefits; deterring irregular migrants and improving

82 Bouteillet-Paquet, supra n27, 370 gives the example of Hong Kong in which negotiations were only successful after the EU lifted visa restrictions for permanent residents; Weinar, A 'EU Cooperation Challenges in External Migration' Research Report EU-US Immigration Systems 2011/12 (European University Institute 2011).

83 Reslow supra38, 415.

84 Discussed in Chapter 3.

85 Goodwin-Gill, G and McAdam, J *The Refugee in International Law* (OUP 2007)408.

86 Zolberg, A and Benda, P (eds) *Global Migrants, Global Refugees: Problems and Solutions* (Berghahn Books 2001); Fahrmeir, A; Faron, O and Weil, P (eds) A *Migration Control in the North Atlantic World the Evolution of State Practices in Europe and the US: From the French Revolution to the Inter-War Period* (Berghahn Books 2003). Michael Samers goes a step further in describing such strategies as 'very remote control': Samers, E 'An Emerging Geopolitics of "Illegal" Immigration in the European Union' (2004) 6 Eur J Migration and L 27.

87 Samers ibid, 29.

the integrity of the asylum system whilst improving credibility decisions by making it easier to substantiate claims in regions of origin and reducing costs.[88]

In 1993, the Dutch Secretary for Justice, Aad Kosto, advocated a new asylum system where arrivals would be returned to reception centres in the region of origin for their claims to be determined.[89] State responses did not indicate significant support for the proposal of exclusive processing centres but the notion of extraterritorial centres as a way of managing irregular migration remained in the background of subsequent discussions.

Following the Tampere Conclusions, the UK Government attempted to influence European discussions on burden-shifting by proposing the externalisation of refugee management through external processing camps.[90] The former British foreign secretary, Jack Straw, envisaged replacing the Refugee Convention with an international quota system under which European states would share asylum seekers.[91] Straw's suggestion encompassed assisting countries in the region of origin, improving access to asylum procedures for genuine refugees and dissuading illegitimate claimants from using the Refugee Convention. As such the proposal evidences the political desire to reduce numbers and the uncertain costs associated with the territorial approach. The Commission replied by floating a complementary external processing scheme and resettlement package as part of their Common Asylum Procedure Communication.[92] The UNHCR responded cautiously by suggesting that the Commission also consider means of implementing a humanitarian visa system to ensure that individuals at risk can adequately seek protection.[93] Both agencies are thus acknowledging a value in external mechanisms but their central objective differs: whilst the UNHCR sought to offer better access to protection, the European Commission focused on reducing the burden for Member States:

> Member States should, therefore, explore possibilities of offering rapid access to protection so that refugees do not need to resort to illegal immigration of people smugglers … Such approaches could ensure sufficient refugee protection within

88 De Vries, K 'An Assessment of "Protection in Regions of Origin" in Relation to European Asylum Law' (2007) 9 Eur J of Migration and L 84.

89 Speech by Aad Kosto at the 5 Conference of European Ministers Responsible for Migration Affairs, Athens 18–19 November 1993, reprinted in Inter-governmental Consultations *Working Paper on Reception in the Region of Origin* IGC, Geneva 1994, 52.

90 Boswell, C 'The "External Dimension" of the EU Immigration and Asylum Policy' (2003) 79 Intl Affairs 619.

91 Straw, J 'Towards a Common Asylum Procedure' European Conference on Asylum, Lisbon 16 June 2000.

92 European Commission Communication 22 November 2000 *Towards a Common Asylum Procedure and a Uniform Status, Valid throughout the Union, for Persons Granted Asylum* COM (2000) 755, ch 2.3.2.

93 UNHCR *Towards a Common Asylum Procedure and Uniform Status Valid throughout the EU, for Persons Granted Asylum* Geneva, UNHCR November 2001, para10.

and compatible with a system of efficient countermeasures against irregular migratory flows.[94]

The Blair Vision

In 2003 former prime minister Tony Blair tabled his 'vision' entitled 'New International Approaches to Asylum Protection' in which he advocated an entirely new extraterritorial regime which would allow managed migration to Europe. The proposal encompassed both Regional Protection Areas and Transit Processing Centres to which those asylum seekers arriving spontaneously in the EU would be removed for their claims to be processed.[95] The plan was promoted as 'pro-refugee but anti-asylum'.[96]

In Blair's plan the Regional Protection Zone would be located near to the source of the refugee movement, necessitating capacity building in the region of origin, whereas Transit Processing Centres were to be situated adjacent to theEU border. Managed resettlement from the Protection Zone would depend on burden-sharing agreements, although it was acknowledged that 'not all refugees would be accepted for resettlement'. Blair's proposal was certainly radical in its departure from the universalism of the Refugee Convention and unsurprisingly it elicited overwhelming criticism from human rights agencies with Amnesty International calling the plans 'inherently unlawful'.[97] For Noll it was 'no exaggeration to state that it could very well mean the end of the 1951 Refugee Convention'.[98]

Blair was attempting to exert control over irregular movement through deterrence and cost-reduction at a time when European asylum applications peaked. From a protection perspective the proposals are poorly thought-out. It is difficult to see how state accountability could be maintained when there is a complex interaction between processing and resettlement states facilitated by international agencies. The standard of reception conditions, including the use of

94 European Commission Communication 15 November 2001 *On a Common Policy on Illegal Immigration* COM (2001) 672 Final, p8.

95 Letter from Tony Blair to Costas Simitis 10 March 2003. Full text available at: http://www.statewatch.org/news/2003/apr/10safe.htm; Tony Blair *New Vision for Refugees* 2003; Commission COM (2003) 315 Final *Towards More Accessible, Equitable and Managed Asylum Systems*; COM (2004) 410 Final *Improving Access to Durable Solutions*; see discussion in Goodwin-Gill and McAdam supra n85, 409. The plan had particular support from Denmark and Netherlands; Levy, C 'The European Union After 9/11: The Demise of a Liberal Democratic Asylum Regime?' (2005) 40 Government and Opposition 1, 31.

96 Blair ibid, 1.

97 Amnesty International *Unlawful and Unworkable: Amnesty International's View on Proposals for Extraterritorial Processing of Asylum Claims* 2003 Available at: http://www.amnesty.org/en/library/info/IOR61/004/2003 (accessed 8 May 2013).

98 Noll, G 'Visions of the Exceptional: Legal and Theoretical Issues Raised by Transit Processing Centres and Protection Zones' (2003) 5 Eur J Migration and L 310.

closed detention camps, raises serious questions in terms of human rights norms. The assumed cost saving to destination states is also described by one commentator as nothing more than 'science fiction'.[99] The Australian external processing model suggests that there is unlikely to be significant savings for European states. Here again we see the symbolic value of tough immigration control dominating the refugee debate in the face of serious humanitarian shortcomings.

Notwithstanding support from the Danish and Dutch representatives, the UK proposals were condemned by other Member States as a cynical attempt to avoid the humanitarian obligations of the Refugee Convention. Some comfort should result from this response as it suggests widespread governmental support for the fundamental, universal basis of the Refugee Convention.[100] The Commission responded with alternative proposals, including resettlement and Protected Entry Procedures but maintained the position that determination and protection within Member States would remain at the forefront of international refugee processing.[101]

This rejection did not deter individual states from developing unilateral 'migration partnerships' with third countries. For the UK these included Tanzania, Kenya and (perhaps most surprisingly) Somalia. Germany also put forward plans to set up transit camps in North Africa where EU officials would receive and examine asylum applications with a view to resettling refugees in Europe (albeit with a lesser status to that afforded by European law).[102] Such initiatives risk undermining universal protection, allowing states to cherry-pick refugees, leaving the most vulnerable with an uncertain future.[103] Implicit in external processing arrangements is the need for some form of compulsory detention, and questions will inevitably arise over the transfer of responsibilities in such situations.[104] Can for example a state party to the UN Convention Against Torture effectively transfer its obligations to a state that is not a state party?[105] Further, even if a third country is a signatory of the international conventions, its observance would be difficult to guarantee without institutional monitoring and enforcement.

The question of external processing has remained on the European agenda despite the negative reception for Blair's vision. The European Commission

---

99 Noll ibid, 327.

100 Levy supra n95, 48.

101 European Commission *Communication to the Council and the European Parliament: Towards More Accessible, Equitable and Managed Asylum Systems* 3 June 2003 COM (2003) 315 final.

102 Dietrich, H 'The Desert Front-EU Refugee Camps in North Africa?' (Statewatch News Online, March 2005); Crawley, H 'Europe Looks to Africa to Solve the "Asylum Problem"' (2005) Forced Migration Rev, 23–26 May; Hurwitz supra n1, 79.

103 Hayes, B '"Killing Me Softly?" Improving Access to Durable Solutions' Doublespeak and the Dismantling of Refugee Protection in the EU' (Statewatch July 2004) 4–5; Garlick, M 'The EU Discussions on Extraterritorial Processing: Solution or Conundrum?' (2006) 18 Intl J Refugee L 601.

104 Edwards supra n69, 818.

105 Ibid, 820.

responded by tabling alternatives, including a resettlement scheme and additional funding for capacity building in countries of origin and transit.[106] The Hague Programme provided the platform for two Commission enquiries, one on joint processing within the EU; the other on processing outside the EU, with Mauritania and Libya earmarked for feasibility studies.[107] The risk of these regions becoming viewed as safe havens was considerable. In the event the Commission decided to focus on containing migration in regions of origin, through the implementation of two Regional Protection Programmes: one in the western newly independent states (Ukraine, Moldova, Belarus) and the other in sub-Saharan Africa, predominately Tanzania.[108] The choice of these locations in predominately transit countries rather than countries of origin is perhaps surprising. Of greater concern is the absence of any resettlement element in the programmes, suggesting that this initiative is less about ensuring durable protection and more about managing migration before it impacts on the EU.[109]

Protection from refoulement would need to be provided in such arrangements in order to ensure compatibility with the international and regional law.[110] Yet the prohibition of refoulement alone would obviously fall short of guaranteeing access to material reception conditions which has the potential to breach obligations under the ECHR and the Reception Directive.[111] Recent ECtHR decisions have imposed obligations on European states to fully consider such factors when returning asylum seekers under the Dublin Regulation.[112] The *Hirsi* judgement

---

106 Dombey, D 'UK Asylum Proposals Draw Mixed Response' *Financial Times* (29 March 2003) 12; European Commission *Communication from the Commission to the Council and the Parliament on the Managed Entry in the EU of Persons in Need of International Protection and Enhancement of the Protection Capacity of the Regions of Origin: Improving Access to Durable Solutions* COM (2004) final, 4 June 2004.

107 European Commission Communication from the Commission to the Council and the Parliament *The Hague Programme: Ten Priorities for the Next Five Years, the Partnership for European Renewal in the Field of Freedom, Security and Justice* COM (2005) 184 final, 10 May 2005; Ref 491/2004 of the European Parliament and the Council of 10 March 2004 *Establishing a Programme for Financial and Technical Assistance to Third Countries in the Areas of Migration and Asylum* AENEAS [2004] OJ L80/1.

108 European Commission Communication to the Council and the European Parliament of 1 September 2005 *On Regional Protection Programmes* COM (2005) 388 final.

109 Oxfam GB *Comment on the Communication from Commission to Council and the European Parliament on the Regional Protection Programmes* (Oxfam 16 October 2005); Baldaccini supra n41, 292.

110 Including the EU Qualification Directive: Council Directive 2004/83/EC of 29 April 2004 *On Minimum Standards for the Qualification and Status of Third Country Nationals or Stateless Persons as Refugees or as Persons Who Otherwise Need International Protection and the Content of the Protection Granted* O J L 304, 30/09/2004 P. 0012 – 0023, Art 21(1).

111 De Vries supra n88, 93.

112 *MSS* supra n80.

places responsibility on Member States who intercept and return migrants beyond the EU in breach of their ECHR rights.[113] The difficulty here is in ensuring these norms are met prior to the return action which will surely necessitates a degree of independent monitoring which could prove both expensive and divisive.

Despite these reservations, detention centres have been constructed in several states outside the EU in order to assist in the management of returns and to prevent onwards travel. The Spanish government have supported the construction of detention centres in the Canary Islands and Mauritania in order to redirect and return irregular migrants. The conditions in these centres, like those in Ukraine, fall well short of those demanded by European human rights standards.[114] Most recently, Israel constructed a new detention centre at the Ktzi'ot prison complex intended for all categories of irregular migrant. Despite some 13,683 migrants entering Israel unlawfully in 2010, the state has only ever recognised 170 people as satisfying the definition of refugee under the Refugee Convention (with one family granted refugee status in 2011).[115] A new law allows detention for up to three years for anyone entering illegally with a longer period for those entering from hostile states.[116] Most will eventually be returned to Egypt or given an uncertain legal status of 'group protection' which does not attract any state support.

Convention Plus[117]

The UNHCR initially rejected proposals for external processing as premature, noting the problems of harmonisation in the EU over minimum standards, significant cost and procedural implications.[118] Following a series of global consultations and the designation of an Agenda for Protection, the UNHCR's

113 *Hirsi Jamaa and Others v Italy* App 27765/09 23 February 2012.

114 Morgades supra n25, 30.

115 Israel signed the Refugee Convention in 1949. 95 per cent of those arriving were from Eritrea or Sudan, both states where persecution occurs regularly: *The Guardian* 'Huge Detention Centre to Be Israel's Latest Weapon in Migration Battle' (17 April 2012). Available at: http://www.guardian.co.uk/world/2012/apr/17/detention-centre-israel-migration (accessed 12 May 2013).

116 Prevention of Infiltration Law 1954 as amended on 10 January 2012. Available at: http://www.knesset.gov.il/Laws/Data/BillGoverment/381/381.pdf (accessed 15 May 2013); Lis, J 'Knesset Passes Bill That Could Put Asylum Seekers in Jail without Trial' (Haaretz, 10 January 2012); Human Rights Watch 'Israel: Amend Anti-Infiltration Law'. Available at: http://www.hrw.org/news/2012/06/10/israel-amend-anti-infiltration-law (accessed 13 May 2013).

117 Convention Plus was launched by Ruud Lubbers on 13 September 2002 at the European Union Justice and Home Affairs meeting, UNHCR 'Lubbers Calls for "Convention Plus" Approach to New Challenges' 2002.

118 HL EU Committee 'Handling EU Asylum Claims: New Approaches Examined' 11 report 2003–04 (HL paper 74 Stationary Office 2004).

Convention Plus initiative ran for three years from October 2002 with the aim of supplementing refugee protection with a normative burden-sharing framework.[119] Three areas were singled out for special arrangements: the strategies use of resettlement, development assistance and irregular secondary movements. The aim was to provide generic agreements which could be applied in specific situations in order to enhance protection and enable durable solutions.[120]

The starting point of the UNHCR initiative is clearly different to that of the European Council in that Convention Plus observes a gap in protection where the vast majority of the world's refugees remain in the South, placing a disproportionate burden on these states. Thus, for the UNHCR the objective is to find a durable solution through the re-balancing of state responsibilities; an approach which implies that European states will need to do much more. This would certainly encompass financial support for host states and assistance with resettlement of refugees. This ambitious, global burden-sharing approach may well have contributed to the acknowledged failure of the initiative as debates became increasingly polarised.[121]

The EU Prong of Convention Plus attempted to distinguish migrants that were likely to be illegitimate with a view to sending them to a designated reception centre in the EU where their claims would be rapidly examined by joint EU teams. The system would require registration and pre-screening of applicants in order to enable a uniform decision-making process with settlement of refugees across the EU and return of unsuccessful applicants to countries of origin.[122] The registration would channel applicants into the national system or into the EU reception centre whilst identifying family members who can be reunited and victims of trafficking. Those cases generally viewed as ill-founded, such as Dublin transfers and safe countries of origin cases, would be filtered into the EU reception centre. A European Union Asylum Agency and a European Asylum Review board would improve consistency and fairness in the decision-making and resettlement process.[123] On the surface this certainly offered a practical solution to the twin problems of irregular migration management and burden-sharing. The difficulty

119 For a critical analysis see Betts, A 'Convention Plus: Continuity or Change in North-South Responsibility-Sharing?' Paper presented at *New Asylum Paradigm*? Workshop COMPAS, University of Oxford, 14 June 2005.

120 Betts, A and Durieux, JF 'Convention Plus as a Norm-Setting Exercise' (2007) 20 J Refugee Studies 509.

121 Ibid, 514.

122 UNHCR Working Paper 'A Revised 'EU Prong' Proposal'' (UNHCR December 2003). Available at: http://www.unhcr.org/refworld/docid/400e85b84.htm (accessed 21 January 2013).

123 The plans were strongly criticised in the UK by the Immigration Law Practitioners' Association 'Submission in response to the Commission Green Paper on the Future Common European Asylum System COM(2007) 301 Final and the House of Lords supra n118, para 83.

from a protection perspective is that EU states have generally been unwilling to embrace resettlement initiatives.[124]

Resettlement

The UNHCR and the European Commission have been keen to promote resettlement as a durable solution to refugee protection. The Multilateral Framework of Understanding on Resettlement was possibly the most tangible output from the Convention Plus initiative.[125] The criteria for identifying states for resettlement would include: effective links, including family, educational, or cultural ties; the absorption capacity of Member States; and the contribution to burden-sharing made, for instance, by Member States with EU Reception Centres on their territory.[126]

At the same time, the European Commission's Green Paper *on the Future of the Common European Asylum System*, included resettlement as an essential part of the external dimension of the European system.[127] The following year, the Commission floated the idea of an EU-wide resettlement programme.[128] For Member States this could be viewed as an attractive option, offering a degree of predictability and therefore enabling a more managed approach to migration.[129] Similarly, there are potential benefits for applicants who may find that their case is determined more equitably and that, once selected for resettlement, it is easier for them to integrate into the host state. In a policy field typically marked by stalemate, resettlement offers a durable solution that may provide a way forward for all stake-holders.

Yet it seems clear that only a small minority of refugees will really benefit from resettlement.[130] UNHCR figures for 2010 indicate that only 73,000 refugees of the 108,000 refugees identified for resettlement were actually resettled, a decrease of 20,000 from 2007.[131]The UNHCR's most recent report indicates that there has

124 Betts notes that the only tangible success from the Convention Plus discussion on resettlement was the UK's offer to annually resettle 500 refugees from Ghana, supra n119.

125 Hurwitz supra n1, 152.

126 UNHCR supra n122, para 10.

127 European Commission *Green Paper on the Future of the Common European Asylum System* Brussels 6 June 2007 COM (2007) 301 final.

128 European Commission supra n106.

129 Although El-Enany cautions against such a conclusion as it is unclear how it would actually be applied to unsolicited arrivals: 'Who is the New Refugee?' (2008) 33 EL Rev 3, 332.

130 Milner, J 'Recent Developments in International Resettlement Policy: Implications for the UK Programme' in Gelthorpe, V and Herlitz, L (eds) *Listening to the Evidence: The Future of UK Resettlement* (UK Home Office 2003).

131 UNHCR EX Com Standing Committee 'Progress Report on Resettlement' June 2008; UNHCR 'UNHCR Calls for More Resettlement Places and Better Support for

been a marginal increase but that resettlement is not reaslitic option for the vast majority of those needing protection.[132] The USA and Canada admit nearly 90 per cent of those resettled with Sweden being the only EU state to offer a significant number of places.[133] Plans to identify suitable locations for the processing centres have also been beset by organisational problems. Dutch plans to pilot five North African processing centres and further attempts by Germany and Italy in 2004 to establish transit processing centres in Libya and Tunisia received a lukewarm response from other Member States.[134] The UNHCR model clearly envisages processing within the EU but it is difficult to imagine how this would receive the necessary support from Member States.

The UNHCR figures suggest that resettlement is unlikely to prove a solution in Europe any time in the near future. In his quest to provide a way forward for refugee protection, Hathaway rejects resettlement as a solution to refugee protection on the basis that the worlds' developed governments have provided only 'numerically insignificant opportunities'.[135] Morgades agrees arguing that one of the main objectives of the external dimension of EU asylum policy has been to prevent the need to resettle people.[136] Even if agreement could be reached on the location and mechanics of processing applications, it would be vital to ensure a fair and equitable system of resettlement that prevented states from cherry-picking the most desirable refugees. At the present time, resettlement efforts have demonstrated the tendency of states to offer protection to those with the best chance of integration.[137] This may be understandable from a Walzerian perspective but it does little to address the protection needs of the most vulnerable. The UNHCR's role in managing processing and resettlement would have to be central. Otherwise it is quite conceivable that the most vulnerable refugees would continue to lose out in a system that allowed too much state interference.

Despite the UNHCR's preference for European processing, the agency has been criticised for aligning itself to the EU position, adding legitimacy to some of the latter's more retrograde proposals.[138] Noll captured the mood of many academics and refugee advocates when he described Convention Plus as 'three prongs of compromise and evasion'.[139] Stevens suggests that the agency's support of resettlement in the EU and regions of origin is a 'dangerous path' which could result in the very outcome the agency wishes to avoid, namely the

---

Resettled Refugees' UNHCR 4 July 2011.

132 UNHCR *Global Trends* (UNHCR 2012) 18

133 Ibid

134 EURACTIV 'EU Divided over African Asylum Camps' 5 October 2004.

135 Hathaway, J 'Why Refugee Law Still Matters' (2007) 8 Melb J Intl L 94.

136 Morgades supra n25, 32.

137 Hathaway supra n135, 95.

138 See for example, Betts supra n119.

139 Noll supra n98, 308.

regionalisation of asylum policy beyond EU borders.[140] This is an unfortunate position given the UNHCR's role as guardian of the rules, principles and norms of refugee protection.[141] The agency's protection remit is much wider than the EU's irregular migration focus and as such it should be a vital counterweight.[142] Yet it is constrained by a non-political, humanitarian mandate which requires, and generally enables, it to get permission to work in host countries and to secure funding from donor governments. As such it has remained largely outside the UN human rights programme and this has regrettably contributed to the marginalisation of refugee issues.[143] The UNHCR's response to large-scale refugee problems such as the Rwandan genocide, the Bosnian war and the current Syrian conflict often looks disjointed and inadequate. Loescher recognises a 'serious disjuncture between expectations of UNHCR and human rights agencies to work on this new international environment and the institutional capacity of these organisations to respond to massive human rights abuses'.[144] Whilst governments everywhere have a responsibility towards asylum seekers and refugees, it is obvious that any attempt to improve protection needs to be properly supervised and supported. The UNCHR's experience and expertise makes it the perfect candidate but effective monitoring would demand greater independence and a more secure financial footing.[145]

Protected Entry Procedures

Given the influence of Member States in shaping the direction of the CEAS coupled with the limited effectiveness of the UNHCR, it is perhaps naïve to expect an improved protection system allowing easy access to refugee determination within the EU. One solution proposed by the Danish Centre for Human Rights under the direction of the eminent academic and advocate, Gregor Noll, was to enable

---

140 Stevens, D 'Asylum Seekers in the New Europe: Time for a Rethink' in Shah, P (ed) *The Challenge of Asylum to Legal Systems* (Cavendish 2005) 25.

141 Lavenex, S 'The External Face of Europeanization: Third Countries and International Organizations' in Faist, T and Ette, A (eds) *Mechanisms of Immigration Control, A Comparative Analysis of European Regulation Policies* (Berg 1999), 253.

142 Lavenex ibid, comments that it has shifted from counterweight to sub-contractor in recent years, 261.

143 Loescher, G 'The UNHCR and World Politics: State Interests Versus Institutional Autonomy' (2001) 35 Intl Migration Rev 33.

144 Loescher, G 'Protection and Humanitarian Action in the Post-Cold War Era' in Zolberg, A and Benda, P *Global Migrants, Global Refugees: Problems and Solutions* (Berghahn Bools 2001).

145 Anker, D; Fitzpatrick, J and Shacknove, A 'Reply to Hathaway/Neve' (1998) 11 Harvard HR J 310. The European Asylum Support Office may seem suitable for this role but its current mandate does not extend towards an active monitoring role.

asylum seekers to seek protection from a Member State outside its territory.[146] The Protected Entry Procedure (or 'PEP') would allow a residence permit to be provided by an embassy in the event of a successful protection request. The European Commission envisaged two ways of operating the PEP scheme: either by an EU Regional Task force which could disseminate information and assist with determination and resettlement; or by a harmonised Member State system such as an entry visa.[147]

At first glance the PEP has a great deal to recommend it as one part of a durable solution, at least in cases where it is relatively easy to access the appropriate embassy or task force. It could reduce the need for applicants to rely on clandestine methods of travel whilst decreasing the number of unpredictable arrivals. The authors also point to the unquestionable value in establishing a 'dialogue with would-be migrants at the earliest conceivable stage of the migration continuum'.[148]

Whilst several states already operated unilateral PEP variants, their use was generally exceptional and migrants were seldom made aware of the option where it existed.[149] Thus the study advocated a uniform, harmonised approach which would enable a pooling of resources and recognition of best practice. PEPs enable the differentiation of migrants before they reach EU borders, 'offering legal alternatives to illegal migration channels'.[150] For states anxious to control irregular migration, they permit a more manageable response by acting as an early warning system on forced migration and allowing states to screen applicants before they access the state's territory.[151]

Significantly, the autonomy of the protection seeker is fundamental to the proposals. They can help to address the protection imbalance that leaves that many of the most vulnerable refugees unable to reach the EU because they lack the resources needed for clandestine methods of travel.[152]

From a cost perspective, the PEP will certainly be cheaper than the proposed external processing centres which demand a sizeable infrastructure. They are also likely to be cheaper than ordinary territorial procedures which tend to be bogged down in questions of credibility and where removals are typically protracted resulting in ongoing costs. Thus, as one element of a durable solution, the PEP scheme seemingly has much to recommend it to all stake-holders.

---

146 Noll, G; Fagerlund, J and Liebaut, F *Study on the Feasibility of Processing Asylum Claims outside the EU Against the Background of the Common European Asylum System and the Goal of a Common Asylum Procedure* (European Commission 2002).

147 European Commission *Towards More Accessible, Equitable and Managed Asylum Systems* COM [2003] 315 3 June 2003 s6 1.2.3.

148 Supra n146, 3.

149 The most advanced model of PEP could be seen in Switzerland, whereas the UK and France had far less developed examples which were rarely used.

150 Noll supra n146, 22.

151 Noll et al supra n146, 79.

152 El-Enany supra n129.

Similar schemes have been proposed by other migration organisations.[153] In a holistic attempt to manage irregular migration, the think-tank Demos proposed creating EU mobility service points overseas which would enable potential migrants to register in one of four categories: visitor, worker, refugee or sponsored resident.[154] International transit centres would provide security and support for displaced persons, a key element being the creation of an individualised personal development plan to assist the migrant in determining a migration plan which allows for a managed and durable solution. Resettlement of refugees would be based on a quota system and refugees would be expected to pay for appeals and accommodation in the transit centre. The plans thus ensure a deterrent element for vexatious claimants whilst reducing operational costs. Whilst the scale of the Demos plan is ambitious in its attempts to organise and manage all types of migration, it is submitted that it does not adequately address the protection needs of refugees. Viewing asylum as simply one part of irregular migration fails to address the application of international refugee and human rights norms. It has been noted that the asylum route is occasionally abused by those unable to take regular migratory paths and that this results in an inevitable overlap between voluntary and forced migration. However, for those most in need, a system requiring payments for accommodation and processing which is then dependent on resettlement quotas is likely to fall short. Unsolicited arrivals are unlikely to diminish unless the transit centres are coupled with even tougher migration controls. Yet it is accepted that tougher controls may actually encourage rather than reduce irregular migration.[155] Whilst managing voluntary migration externally might appear attractive, the management of refugee movement presents wholly different problems.

Initially the European Commission's Communication of 2003 advocated the development of a PEP system linked to a resettlement scheme which could be developed alongside better burden-sharing between the EU and third countries.[156] However, Member States expressed their anxieties over the suggestion of a right of entry for refugees and were keener to endorse resettlement, albeit only as far as a general principle. Thus the Commission abandoned the proposal and directed its attention towards regional processing centres and resettlement.[157]

Yet even resettlement has its detractors. As a matter of policy rather than law, Noll argues that it invites individuals in need of protection but it does not entitle

153 For a list of similar initiatives see Pécoud, A and de Guchteneire, P 'International Migration, Border Controls and Human Rights: Assessing the Relevance of a Right to Mobility' (2006) 21 Journal of Borderlands Studies 1, 69.

154 Veenkamp, T; Bentley, T and Buofino, A 'People Flow: Managing Migration in a New European Commonwealth' (Demos 2003).

155 Samers supra n86; Andreas, P and Snyder, T *The Wall around the West* (Rowman & Littlefield, 2000).

156 European Commission *Towards More Accessible, Equitable and Managed Asylum Systems* COM (2003) 315 3 June 2003.

157 Peers supra n24, 379–380: European Commission supra n101 para 35.

them to access protection. Its minimal use as a tool for refugee management to date suggests that it cannot match the demand for protection. Thus, Noll concludes 'if we study the behaviour of would-be refugees, illegal migration seems to remain the better choice for those who can afford its costs'.[158] Given the limited options on the table however, resettlement and PEPs offer a more positive approach for refugee protection within a framework of managed migration, solidarity and burden-sharing.

Concluding Observations

The development of an external dimension to migration management is clearly important but this must be done through sharing rather than shifting responsibility for refugee protection with full acknowledgement of international human rights and refugee law obligations. As it is, the EU has become a platform to recruit neighbouring and developing countries into schemes of migration management which push protection away from Europe. These initiatives often lack the full commitment of the third country.

Given that many partner states generate a significant number of asylum applicants themselves it seems perverse to expect that they receive and process other applicants. The treatment of sub-Saharan refugees in many countries, including Libya and Israel, remains exceptionally precarious. Such factors appear to be side-lined as states rely on empty assurances of compliance with human rights norms. The question of how best to manage economic migration has dictated the terms for policies restricting and deflecting access to asylum procedures.[159]

Dialogue with third countries has tended to concentrate on the implementation of the EU's plans rather than on the drafting of the plans itself.[160] As such the plans will have limited success and may be viewed with suspicion and cynicism by the third country. For Pirjola, 'the EU seems to be more and more willing to come up with innovations to distribute legal obligations to third countries and to relieve itself of them'.[161] Such initiatives must be carefully situated within a fundamental rights paradigm rather than detached from humanitarian concerns.[162]

In this respect the EU is again failing to respect the sentiment behind the Refugee Convention. De Haas argues that pressure from the EU-led Morocco

158 Noll, G 'From "Protective Passports" to Protected Entry Procedures? The Legacy of Raoul Wallenberg in the Contemporary Asylum Debate' New Issues in Refugee Research (UNHCR Working Paper 99, December 2003).

159 Stevens supra n140, 31.

160 Reslow supra n38, 414.

161 Pirjola, J 'European Asylum Policy – Inclusions and Exclusions under the Surface of Universal Human Rights Language' (2009) 11 Eur J Migration L 361.

162 Benhabib, S *The Claims of Culture: Equality and Diversity in the Global Era* (Princeton UP 2002) 152; Hurwitz supran1, 82.

and Tunisia to introduce tough new immigration laws in 2003–04 with severe punishments for irregular migration and smuggling. In order to reduce the burden of sub-Saharan migration, both countries regularly transport migrants to their external borders where they're left to their fate.[163] Similar questions arise from the Spanish government's efforts to seal off sea borders using early warning radars at Gibraltar and the Canary Islands in addition to their construction of heavily securitised fences around the autonomous cities of Cueta and Melilla in Morocco.[164] Meanwhile, significant time and energy is expended on costly burden-shifting initiatives.[165] The decision of the Australian government to abandon its extraterritorial processing was in large part attributable to the scheme's considerable expense.[166]

De Haas provides an alternative analysis of migration partnerships, referring to powerful interest groups in Europe and Africa that have little genuine interest in stopping migration. He notes how receiving economies benefit from irregular migration whilst remittances sent home can be an incentive to turn a blind eye.[167] Thus, he argues, many African states pay lip service to the fight against illegal migration in order to benefit from aid negotiations. It is well known that Colonel Gadaffi's cooperation with Italy led the EU to lift its arms embargo, allowing the import of semi-military equipment to Libya in order to improve border controls.[168] Similarly, Morocco benefits from migration cooperation, positioning itself as a leading partner, but the focus on sub-Saharan migration diverts attention from the fact that Morocco is an important source country.[169]

The considerable resources that have been made available in external cooperation would be more appropriately directed towards two priorities. Firstly, initiatives to genuine address the causes of migration in countries of origin. This must be grounded in normative discourse that seeks to improve conditions in the country of origin, rather than lessening migration pressure on the EU.[170] As Lindstrøm argues, making readmission and repatriation the priority of the EU High Level Working Group and action plans is hardly the way to build peace and

---

163 De Haas supra n45.

164 European Commission 'Visit to Ceuta and Melilla – Mission Report. Technical mission to Morocco on illegal immigration' 7 October– 11 October 2005 EMO/05/380 Brussels, 19 October 2005.

165 Goodwin-Gill, G *The Refugee in International Law* (OUP 1998) 30.

166 Noll, G 'Visions of the Exceptional: Legal and Theoretical Issues Raised by Transit Processing Centres and Protection Zones' (2003) 5 Eur J Migration L 303, 327.

167 De Haas supra n45, 1315.

168 Ibid, 1310.

169 Ibid, 1316. De Haas also notes that the overwhelming majority of African migrants to Europe (approximately 4.5 million) come from Morocco, Algeria and Tunisia – the majority of which remain as over-stayers: De Haas 'Morocco's Migration Experience: A Transnational Perspective' (2007) 45 Intl Migration Rev 4, 39.

170 Lindstrøm supra n6, 600.

prevent future conflict.[171] The second priority, which features in the latest version of the EU Procedures Directive, is to establish a uniform procedure of refugee determination with high-quality, efficient decision-making at first instance.[172] A properly funded, front-loaded decision-making process where resources can be concentrated should reduce the need for protracted legal challenges which can undermine the institution of asylum whilst serving to encourage those seeking to remain without a legitimate claim.[173] From this position a system based on solidarity and global burden-sharing, inevitably including financial aid and resettlement, can be devised without undermining the spirit of the Refugee Convention. Contrary to the current requirements of the Procedures Directive, any transfer to a safe third country should only take place after an assessment that the returnee will receive effective protection. This will require not only a formal compliance with the Refugee Convention but also, respect for the dignity of the applicant and a determination procedure which is based on due process of the law.[174] Temporary solutions are unlikely to be durable from the perspective of the protection seeker. As Price recognises, asylum is a distinctive remedy for a very distinctive situation in which the existing political community has failed to provide membership.[175] To be effective the remedy needs to address this deficiency rather than providing an uncertain half-status. That is not to imply that permanent settlement is the only option for protection-seekers but rather to emphasise the special acknowledgement that a grant of asylum represents. Without resettlement there is too much emphasis on control over protection in the external dimension of EU policy; a matter that demands to be 'faced squarely and addressed urgently'.[176]

In the event that such decision-making is to be contracted to third countries it will necessitate compliance with the preferential standards in the ECHR and European law and it will demand full, independent monitoring to that end. The European Asylum Support Office can provide some support by compiling and updating independent country of origin information, whereas the UNHCR's mandate could be extended to include greater scrutiny, ensuring full compliance with international law.

171 Ibid.
172 Stevens supra n140, 26; Bouteillet-Paquet supra n27, 376.
173 Price, M *Rethinking Asylum* (CUP 2009) 222.
174 Baldaccini supra n41, 277.
175 Price supra n173, 167.
176 Baldaccini supra n41, 298.

Conclusion

The need to ensure a functioning refugee protection system remains just as important today as it did in 1951. The general trend towards falling numbers of asylum applications in Europe does not suggest that the demand for sanctuary has diminished; rather it demonstrates the limited success of surveillance and deflection policies which serve to make flight increasingly difficult and dangerous. The spike in applications following the Arab Spring of 2011 illustrates a clear, discernible link between instability in countries of origin and asylum migration. Syrian refugees now constitute the second biggest group of asylum applicants arriving in Europe but, as this example sadly demonstrates, most of the most vulnerable remain confined to regions of origin in situations of extreme insecurity.[1]

The creation of a common asylum system presented an opportunity to upgrade and harmonise standards of protection, procedures and reception conditions. The pooling of national resources and expertise should have enabled significant efficiencies which could free funds for improved refugee detection counterbalanced by a more robust return strategy. Harmonisation further provided a significant opportunity for the EU to collectively lobby for political and economic change in countries of origin, thereby reducing the demand for irregular migration.

Yet the direction of the Common Asylum System has been unduly influenced by narrow national interests which have concentrated on preventing irregular migration, regardless of the human costs. These interests are driven principally by two concerns: the unpredictable economic cost of such migration and the damage irregular migration might produce to stability in the host country. These concerns may appear legitimate but it is unlikely that they can be substantially addressed when the demand for irregular migration remains significant. The cost of prevention mechanisms have spiralled despite falling asylum numbers whilst the security discourse continues to dominate political rhetoric. The only clear

1 The latest statistics show that 7 per cent of the 332,000 asylum applicants are from Syria: Eurostat 'Asylum in the EU27' 48/2013 22 March 2013; the number of refugees from Syria rose considerably in 2011 and has continued to rise as the conflict intensifies: European Asylum Support Office 2011 *Annual Report on the Situation of Asylum in the European Union and on the Activities of the European Asylum Support Offic*e European Union Asylum Support Office 2012; UN High Commissioner for Refugees, *As Syria Crisis Continues, UNHCR Urges EU States to Uphold Common Asylum System Principles*, 16 October 2012, available at: http://www.refworld.org/docid/5087d5cc2.html (accessed 20 May 2013). The experience of Rwandan refugees in neighbouring countries also demonstrates how this insecurity can be prolonged for many years.

beneficiaries to date have been the technology and surveillance industries whose success has been crudely measured by reductions in irregular arrivals. Meanwhile, the international obligation of non-refoulement is seriously compromised by policies which aim to deflect and deter all irregular migration.

Paradoxically, the security problematic has left the European citizen more insecure.[2] The visibility of refugees as a problem group has increased due to the expansion of the European detention estate and reductions in welfare support, whilst positive interaction between settled and refugee communities has been frustrated by rules limiting access to the labour market. The number of people seeking asylum in the EU currently averages less than 12,500 applicants per Member State.[3] But this number is typically overestimated in the public consciousness, contributing to a range of national anxieties. A recent British survey found that 40 per cent of the public believed the refugee population to be 10 per cent (rather than 1 per cent) of the total population.[4] This finding is unsurprising given the media attention given to asylum and the resources allocated to the management of irregular migration, but it is difficult to justify this focus and expense through numbers alone.[5] The focus on deterrence and deflection rather than root causes means that there will be a marginal impact on irregular migration. Instead, the resources are deployed to maintain an image of control and security which has become essential to the construction of European identity.[6]

---

2 Beutin, R; Canoy, M; Horvath, A, Hubert A; Lerais, F; Smith, P and Sochacki, M *Migration and Public Perception* (European Commission 2006).

3 It should be noted that 70 per cent of total European applications are received by Germany (77,500), France (60,600), Sweden (43,900), UK (28,200) and Belgium (28,100), Eurostat supra n1. Compared with the population of each Member State, the highest rates of applicants registered were recorded in Malta (5,000 applicants per million inhabitants), Sweden (4,600), Luxembourg (3,900), Belgium (2,500) and Austria (2,100).

4 Jolley, R and Ketwala, S *Hopes and Fears* (British Future January 2012). Available at: http://www.britishfuture.org/articles/news/british-future-launches-hopes-and-fears-report/. The Refugee Council found that 44 per cent of those surveyed believed there to be over 100,000 applicants receiving refugee status in 2009 (compared to the actual figure of 4,175 'Helping Others is part of the British DNA' Press Release (Refugee Council 18 April 2011); Home Office Control of Immigration. Quarterly statistical Summary Quarter 1, January–March 2011 UKBA; Arimatsu, L and Samson, G *The UN Refugee Convention at 60: The Challenge for Europe* Briefing Paper (Chatham House 2011) report that 80 per cent of the world's refugees are in developing regions, with over 1.7 million in Pakistan alone.

5 See Chapter 3 and in particular the costs allocated to the EURODAC database designed to detect secondary movement pursuant to the Dublin Regulation.

6 Brochmann, G 'Controlling Immigration in Europe' in Brochmann, G and Hammar, T (eds) *Mechanisms of Immigration Control: A Comparative Analysis of European Regulation Policies* (Berg 1999); Andreas, P and Snyder, T *The Wall around the West* (Rowman & Littlefield, 2000; Zolberg, A 'Introduction: Beyond the Crisis' in Zolberg, A and Benda, P (eds) *Global Migrants, Global Refugees: Problems and Solutions* (Berghahn Books 2001).

At the same time, public support for the institution of asylum in Europe remains fairly constant – with around 80 per cent of European citizens supporting the grant of asylum to those who satisfy the Refugee Convention (the figure ranges from 65 per cent in Hungary to 95 per cent in Sweden).[7] The status of residents *sans papiers* attracted widespread public support on the streets of Paris and it was public outcry that persuaded the German government to accept 350,000 Bosnian refugees in the summer of 1993.[8] This offers room for encouragement, suggesting that the asylum debate may have been hijacked by particularly vocal minority interests.[9] The majority of European citizens accept an international obligation of hospitality towards refugees and this offers a building-block for a common European policy based on tolerance and protection.

Ultimately refugee movement is an expression of human need, the demand for sanctuary will not be eradicated in an unequal and unstable world. The question should not be whether the developed world can afford to offer sanctuary but rather, whether they can afford not to. To acknowledge that a demand for sanctuary will remain requires the developed world to do more in meeting its obligations of hospitality to those in greatest need. The original governing principles of the Common Asylum System, as evidenced by the Tampere commitments, have gradually given way to a general migration objective, resulting in the side-lining of international human rights obligations. There are a number of principles that can help re-orientate the common asylum system to a better, protection-focused end.

Decoupling Immigration and Asylum

The international refugee regime is certainly confronted by many challenges but it is clear that the way the regime is characterised 'can be very significant to how it is managed'.[10] The mischaracterisation of asylum as simply an aspect of irregular migration has contributed to a failure to identify and protect those in greatest need.

---

7 Those states where support is lowest tend to be the newer member states. There is also widespread support for sharing the burden equally between Member States: Special Eurobarometer 380 'Awareness of Home Affairs' European Commission 2012 Available at: http://www.aedh.eu/Third-Annual-Report-of-the.html (accessed 20 May 2013).

8 Thränhardt, D 'Germany's Immigration Policies and Politics' in Brochmann and Hammar supra n6; Price, M *Rethinking Asylum* (CUP 2009) 189. There have also been regular large public demonstrations in support of sans papiers migrants in Paris and other French cities, see for example http://koletink.wordpress.com/2010/03/01/24h-sans-nous-protest-in-paris-shows-impact-of-immigrants (accessed 1 June 2013).

9 Dean, M *Democracy under Attack: How the Media Distort Policy and Politics* (Policy Press 2013); concern over the vocalisation of minority interests in the immigrate debate was expressed by Anker, D; Fitzpatrick, J and Shacknove, A 'Crisis and Cure: A Reply to Hathaway/Neve and Schuck' (1998) 11 Harvard Human Rights J 306l.

10 Feller, E 'A Comparative Analysis of the Response of the UNHCR and Industrialised States to Rapidly Fluctuating Refugee Status and Asylum Applications:

The conflation of asylum seekers and other migrants into one homogeneous, problematised mass must be avoided in a search for durable solutions. There is of course a relationship between irregular migration and asylum but the nexus should not be overstated to the extent that asylum becomes simply an aspect of immigration control.[11] Certainly the preferential free movement rules for European citizens have restricted legal migration channels for non-European migrants, resulting in an increase in irregular migration and the intermediaries who plug the gap to facilitate it.[12] Yet there is no evidence to support the view that the overwhelming majority of asylum seekers are economic migrants.[13] Nevertheless, the presumption of illegitimacy pervades the policy approach in many states, influencing the legal position to the extent that asylum-seeking becomes a 'social menace', to be dealt with sceptically and severely.[14] The Common European Asylum System fails to systematically differentiate refugees from other migrants at all stage of irregular movement.[15] Detection initiatives such as EURODAC, the visa information system, SIS II and Frontex are directed at tracking and preventing all irregular migration rather than identifying protection needs.[16] The absence of

---

Lessons and Best Practise for RDS Systems Design and Administration' (2010) 22 Intl J Refugee L 1, 72.

11 Phuong, C 'Protecting Refugees in the Context of Immigration Controls' in Shah, P (ed) *The Challenge of Asylum To Legal Systems* (Cavendish 2005) 36; Faist describes the relationship as more of a continuum between voluntary and forced migration Faist, T *The Volume and Dynamics of International Migration and Transnational Social Spaces* (OUP 2000) 23.

12 Van Liempt, I *Navigating Borders – Inside Perspectives on the Process of Human Smuggling into the Netherlands* (Amsterdam UP 2007); De Haas, H 'The Myth of Invasion: The Inconvenient Realities of African Migration to Europe' (2008) 29 3rd World Q 7, 1319.

13 The latest statistics (October–December 2012) show that 36 per cent of initial decisions resulted in either: refugee status, humanitarian leave or leave based on the right to family life. Typically around 30 per cent of appeals will also be successful. Home Office *Immigration Statistics. Oct–Dec 2012* (Home Office 2012) Available at: https://www.gov.uk/government/publications/immigration-statistics-october-to-december-2012/immigration-statistics-october-to-december-2012 (accessed 20 May 2013); The Migration Observatory 'Migration to the UK: Asylum' (Briefing, 13 February 2013). Available at: http://migrationobservatory.ox.ac.uk/briefings/migration-uk-asylum (accessed 18 February 2013).

14 Craig, S and Fletcher, M 'Deflecting Refugees: A Critique of the EC Asylum Procedures Directive' in Shah supra n11, 76.

15 Moreno Lax, V 'Must EU Borders have Doors for Refugees? On the Compatibility of Schengen Visas and Carriers' Sanctions with EU Member States' Obligations to Provide International Protection to Refugees' (2008) 10 Eur J Migration & L 332; Guild, E 'The Europeanisation of Europe's Asylum Policy' (2006) 18 IJ Refugee L 3–4, 630.

16 The effects of many of these initiatives are dealt with in the collection of essays edited by Baldaccini, A; Guild, E and Toner, H (eds) *Whose Freedom, Security and Justice? EU Immigration and Asylum Law and Policy* (Hart 2007).

a nuanced approach inevitably fails to identify and protect, as evidenced by the *Hirsi Jamaa* judgement.[17]

Yet there must be a response to those fearing that a more generous asylum policy could be abused by economic and other migrants. The integrity of asylum policy depends on a robust system of returns which follow promptly once all appeal rights are exhausted. Although much criticised, the EU Returns Directive marks an attempt to address this issue.[18] The Directive allows for a period of between 7 and 30 days for voluntary departure after which more coercive methods, including detention may be applied.[19]

Efforts to reduce refugee flows are likely to frustrate those who aim to combat smuggling, serving merely to encourage more dangerous methods of travel.[20] This has been the experience in the US where illegal border crossings increased as a direct consequence of tightened border control elsewhere, effectively redirecting rather than preventing irregular flows.[21] For De Haas *symbolic* policy instruments have created an *appearance* of control.[22] In the EU, human trafficking and document fraud have increased despite greater vigilance and resources.[23] Meanwhile, the European border has been stretched outwards into neighbouring states and inwards, such that European citizens are increasingly called upon to assist in monitoring and policing irregular migration.[24]

---

17 *Hirsi Jamaa and Others v Italy* ECHR App 27765/09 23 February 2012.

18 *Directive of the European Parliament and of the Council on Common Standards and Procedures in Member States for Returning Illegally Staying Third-Country Nationals* 2008/115/EC final; Askola, H 'Illegal Migrant's Gender and Vulnerability: The Case of the EU Returns Directive' (2010) 18 Fem Leg Stud, 159; Acosta, D 'The Good, the Bad and the Ugly in EU Migration Law: Is the European Parliament Becoming Bad and Ugly? (The Adoption of Directive 2008/15: The Returns Directive)' (2009) 11 Eur J Migration & L 1, 19.

19 Ibid, Article 7. In some cases voluntary departure may not be offered, for example if there is a risk of the applicant absconding or if the application has been deemed manifestly unfounded or fraudulent.

20 Pécoud, A and Guchteneire,P 'International Migration, Border Controls and Human Rights: Assessing THe Relevance of a Right to Mobility' (2006) 21 J of Borderlands Studies 1, 74.

21 Andreas, P and Snyder, T *The Wall around the West* (Rowman & Littlefield, 2000); Lahav, G and Guiraudon, V 'Comparative Perspectives on Border Control: Away from The Border and outside the State' in Andreas and Snyder ibid, 55.

22 De Haas supra n12, 1316.

23 Supra n57, 133; Doomernik, J 'Migration and Security: The Wrong End of the Stick?' in Van den Anker, C (ed) *The Political Economy of New Slavery* (Palgrave Macmillan 2004) 37. The cost of crossing the Greek border at Evros is reported to have doubled to 5,000 euros as a result of tighter border control; ECRE Bulletin 7 September 2012.

24 Examples include the introduction of ID cards and penalties on employers, Lahav and Guiraudon supra n21, 3. A further example can be seen with the introduction of the duty on marriage registrars to report suspected sham marriages in the UK. (Asylum and

Reasserting the Primacy of the Refugee Convention

For some scholars, the Refugee Convention has become part of the problem and there have been suggestions that it should be abandoned as it is no longer fit for purpose.[25] In my view this would be a retrograde step. Without a specific Refugee Convention, the rights of refugees become simply a matter of ordinary human rights law. This is not by itself problematic as international human rights law already offers greater protection than the Refugee Convention in some cases, particularly in its conception of non-refoulement.[26] The danger, however, is that the absence of *lex specialis* provision will only add to the dominance of the irregular migration discourse. The right of states to restrict entry is certainly limited by a legal obligation to avoid refoulement which is equally provided under human rights law, but it is also curtailed by a moral duty of hospitality towards those seeking asylum. The latter is underpinned by the 1951 Refugee Convention. Without the Refugee Convention it is not at all clear that states would respect an ongoing obligation to admit and integrate refugees. The refugee would instead be viewed narrowly as one category of irregular migrant.

Whilst the standards in the Refugee Convention should be the starting point for refugee determination, they do not need to be the end point. In this respect the European move towards a unified status of 'protection seeker', which includes forms of subsidiary protection, is to be welcomed as is the more expansive approach of persecutory treatment to cover serious harm as a ground for protection.[27] But there remains an urgent need for open discussion over the structural contradictions and tensions that devalue commitments to protection.[28] This debate demands that states acknowledge the unequal distribution of refugees across the globe.[29] It also requires that the voice of the refugee be given prominence.[30] A common system based on mutual trust necessitates that states are called to account politically and judicially for mechanisms which undermine their international obligations. To date there has been some accountability resulting from judgements of the ECtHR and CJEU but this should not be a substitute for political accountability.[31]

Immigration (Treatment of Claimants Act) 2004) and the proposed new health levy for non-EU migrants which will be monitored by NHS medical personnel.

25 I am grateful to Professor Patricia Tuitt for her view on this point.

26 See for example Article 3 ECHR which, unlike Article 33 Refugee Convention, admits no exceptions to the principle of non-refoulement.

27 EU Qualification Directive, Article 15.

28 Pirjola, J 'European Asylum Policy – Inclusions and Exclusions under the Surface of Universal Human Rights Language' (2009) 11 Eur J Migration & L 349.

29 Phuong, supra n11, 35.

30 Soguk, N *States and Strangers: Refugees and Displacements of Statecraft* (University of Minnesota 1999).

31 *MSS v Belgium and Greece* App 30696/09 21 January 2011; *NS v SSHD* C411/10 and *ME v Refugee Applications Commissioner* C493/10 21 December 2011. Available

Asylum cooperation should be informed by the Refugee Convention, the ECHR and the EU Charter of Fundamental Rights.[32] Article 21 of the Treaty of the European Union extends fundamental principles such as democracy, the rule of law and the universality and indivisibility of human rights and fundamental freedoms to the EU's external relationships[33] and the European Commission has asserted that the 'Union's action must be above reproach when it comes to fundamental rights'.[34] Whilst the CJEU has made reference to ECtHR jurisprudence, the EU's planned accession to the ECHR will enable the Strasbourg court to assess the EU's institutional compliance with the Convention rights, providing a further, much-needed layer of accountability.

One of the weaknesses of international refugee law is the absence of a legal obligation on states to admit asylum seekers, inevitably leading to a 'clash between sovereign rights and human rights'.[35] The problem here is not so much one of space but of political organisation.[36] Pirjola recommends more practical cooperation between Member States and solidarity as a way of dealing with the 'open concepts' of the Refugee Convention.[37] The common asylum system provides an invaluable opportunity to enable a higher degree of political organisation and supervision by avoiding the competitive urges of national governments to drive down standards.[38] Although the outcome so far has been labelled 'disappointing',[39] the current focus on uniform procedures does provide a platform for higher common standards. The approach of the EU Qualification Directive suggests that harmonisation has the

---

at: http://eurlex.europa.eu/LexUriServ/LexUriServ.do?uri=CELEX:62010CJ0411:EN:HTML (accessed 11 July 2013).

32 Article 51(1) EU Charter of Fundamental Rights Official Journal C364/21 18 December 2000; for detailed discussion see Di Frederico, G (ed) *The EU Charter of Fundamental Rights: From Declaration to Binding Instrument* (Springer 2011).

33 Treaty of the European Union OJ C 326 26 October 2012.

34 Communication from the Commission 'Strategy for the Effective Implementation of the Charter of Fundamental Rights by the EU' COM (2010) 573, para 1. Available at: http://europa.eu/legislation_summaries/human_rights/fundamental_rights_within_european_union/dh0004_en.htm (accessed 11 June 2013).

35 Haddad, E 'The Refugee: Forging National Identities' (2002) 2 Studies in Ethnicity and Nationalism 2, 326; Field, JRC 'Bridging the Gap Between Refugee Rights and Reality' (2010) 22 Int J Refugee L 4, 514.

36 Arendt, H *The Origins of Totalitarianism* (Harcourt, Brace & World 1966) 294.

37 Pirjola supra n28, 362.

38 The desire of Governments to avoid venue-shopping is well-documented, leading states to compete with neighbouring states to reduce the attraction of favourable asylum policies. See for example Vink, M who makes this observation in relation to Dutch asylum policy before the CEAS: *Limits of European Citizenship: European Integration and Domestic Immigration Policies* (Palgrave Macmillan 2005) 94.

39 Peers, S *EU Justice and Home Affairs Law* (OUP 2010) 380.

potential to expand the protection offered by the Refugee Convention.[40] And whilst it is easy to be pessimistic over the direction and pace of European harmonisation, Vink reminds us to consider the counterfactual position.[41] It is undisputable that, in the absence of a common policy, some European governments would have adopted less generous reception regimes whilst resorting to ever more ingenious means of burden-shifting in an attempt to eradicate 'venue-shopping'.[42] The dire situation of the Greek asylum system may have come to typify the asylum provision in many neighbouring states.

Asserting the primacy of the Refugee Convention requires us to move away from collective determinations and generalised assessments of safety. The variety of procedures permitted under the CEAS suggests that it is possible to determine the cogency of refugee claims on the basis of generalisations or cursory examinations.[43] This collective determination is not supported by the Refugee Convention. Transfers to 'safe' states increase the likelihood of violations of state obligations towards refugees and have a negative effect on inter-state relations.[44] Whilst, the EU's external migration policy has encouraged greater cooperation on migration control without giving sufficient attention to the protection dimension by supporting the asylum systems of partner countries.[45]

Reinvigorating the Supervisory Role of the UNHCR

The quest for greater political accountability requires an effective system of monitoring to ensure that European states are complying with their international obligations. The European Parliament has on occasion stepped into this role but it lacks expertise and is compromised by its role in the legislative process. The newly established, European Asylum Support Office would seem the logical agency to

40 Council Directive 2004/83/EC of 29 April 2004 *On Minimum Standards for the Qualification and Status of Third Country Nationals or Stateless Persons as Refugees or as Persons Who Otherwise Need International Protection and the Content of the Protection Granted OJ L 304 30/09/2004 P. 0012 – 0023. Particularly positive developments include* the addition of serious harm as a ground for subsidiary protection and the specific inclusion of non-state agents as potential perpetrators of persecutory treatment.

41 Vink supra n38, 115.

42 The term 'venue-shopping' was first introduced by Guiraudon,V 'European Integration and Migration Policy: Vertical Policy-making as Venue Shopping' (2000) 38 Journal of Common Market Studies 2, 251.

43 Baldaccini, A and Toner, H 'From Amsterdam to Tampere and The Hague: An overview of Five years of EC Immigration and Asylum Law' in Baldaccini, A; Guild, E and Toner, H (eds) *Whose Freedom, Security and Justice* (Hart 2007) 192.

44 Hurwitz, A *The Collective Responsibility of States to Protect Refugees* (OUP 2009) 5; *MSS v Belgium and Greece* supra n31.

45 Baldaccini, A 'The External Dimension of the EU's Asylum and Immigration Policies: Old Concerns and New approaches' in Baldaccini et al supra n43, 277.

undertake this task but its current mandate does not extend beyond supporting states towards a more active monitoring and compliance role.[46] Therefore the UNHCR remains the best placed to provide the significant expertise and experience necessary for an effective supervisory role.

The UNHCR has been less willing to accept the proliferation of safe third country principles and has consistently emphasised the need for proper procedures to secure the non-refoulement obligation.[47] However, it has been the subject of considerable criticism from refugee advocates who argue that pragmatism often wins out over a more principled, protectionist stance.[48] It is unfortunate that the agency's current supervisory role is relatively weak due in large part to its dependence on voluntary contributions from donor states.[49] The credibility of an international approach to refugee protection depends on its position being reaffirmed with a strengthened monitoring capacity. The global consultations culminating in the 'Agenda for Protection'[50] and the 'Convention Plus' initiative, suggest that the agency is capable of assuming greater responsibility and influence. It has not shied away from criticising the direction of the CEAS and has identified significant protection gaps in the developed world.[51] In 2007, the UNHCR announced a 10-point plan on refugee protection and mixed migration which called for protection sensitive entry procedures, additional training for immigration officials and as part of a comprehensive approach to protection involving a mix of solutions.[52] But the effects of these initiatives remains limited and the absence of a defined monitoring strategy makes it impossible to effectively challenge national interests. The Executive Committee offers the potential to improve supervision as it has a particular specialised mandate as an advisory body which is formally

---

46 The organisation was established pursuant to Regulation (EU) 439/2010 *Establishing a European Asylum Support Office* 29 May 2010 OJ L132/11. For the mandate of the EASO see http://easo.europa.eu/about-us/tasks-of-easo (accessed 11 June 2013).

47 UNHCR Ex Com No 87 *Conclusion on International Protection* (UNHCR 1999) para j.

48 Hurwitz supra n44, 260; Harrell-Bond, B 'Comments on "New Directions to Avoid Hard Problems"' (1995) 8 J Refugee Studies 3 299. See also Waters, T Assessing the Impact of the Rwandan Refugee Crisis on Development Planning in Rural Tanzania, 19941-996' (1999) 58 Human Organisation 2, 142; Bigo, D 'Protection: Concept and Technique' in Huysmans, J; Dobson, A and Prokhovnik, R (eds) *The Politics of Protection* (Routledge 2006) 95.

49 Hurwitz supra n44, 262.

50 UNHCR *Agenda for Protection* UN DOC A/AC.96/965/Add 1 26 June 2002.

51 Betts, A and Durieux, JF 'Convention Plus as a Norm-Setting Exercise' (2007) 20 J Refugee Studies 509, 531.

52 UNHCR *Refugee Protection and Mixed Migration: A 10-Point Plan of Action* (UNHCR 2007). Available at: http://www.refworld.org/docid/45b0c09b2.html (accessed 11 June 2013).

independent of the UNHCR.[53] Enabling regular monitoring and sanctions for non-compliance is essential to counterbalance state interests and to ensure the principle of mutual trust is fully respected.

Identifying and Committing to Durable Solutions

The search for durable, international solutions to the challenge of refugee management has been at the centre of UNHCR activity for the past decade.[54] Yet what seems striking about the agency's annual appeal for solutions is the absence of the EU as a significant player.[55] It is axiomatic that durable solutions be applied fairly and efficiently, but they must also command the confidence of those who seek to benefit from them. When he initially supported burden-sharing as a way of saving the Refugee Convention, Hailbronner argued against freedom of choice in destination on the basis of a politically homogeneous Europe where there would be no significant difference in the protection afforded.[56] It is doubtful whether this approach can be part of a durable solution, at least until genuine harmonisation is realised.[57] At the very least, for solutions to be durable they must consider factors such as family ties and other substantive links such as linguistic and educational ties.[58] The CJEU has effectively recognised this in its recent judgement on unaccompanied minors arriving in the UK via a safe European country.[59]A failure to base durable solutions on substantive links will ensure that the solutions are temporary at best and consequently secondary movement will remain a significant problem.

53 Hurwitz supra n44, 276; see also Kälin, W 'Supervising the 1951 Refugee Convention and Beyond' in Feller, E; Türk, F and Nicholson, N (eds) *Refugee Protection in International Law: UNHCR Global Consultations on International Protection* (CUP 2003).

54 See for example, UNHCR Agenda for Protection supra n50.

55 For example see UNHCR 'Finding Durable Solutions' UNHCR Global Report 2012. Available at: http://www.unhcr.org/51b1d61d0.html and Global Appeal 2013. Available at: http://www.unhcr.org/50a9f81116.html (accessed 14 July 2013). The 2013 appeal records a protection gap of 100,000 resettlement places.

56 Hailbronner, K 'The Concept of a "Safe Country" and Expeditious Asylum Procedures: A Western European Perspective (1993) 5 Intl J Refugee L 58 and Hathaway, J 'A Reconsideration of the Underlying Premise of Refugee Law' (1990) 31 Harv Intl L J 129, 182.

57 Kneebone points out that a search for durable solutions may require a strategy to embrace asylum seekers choices of destinations in 'Safe' Third Country Concept' in McAdam, J *Forced Migration, Human Rights and Security* (Hart 2008) 153; ECRE *The Way Forward: Europe's Role in the Global Refugee Protection System towards Fair and Efficient Asylum Systems in Europe* (ECRE September 2005) 343–7, 3.3.

58 UN EXCom No. 15 (XXX) *Refugees without an Asylum Country* (UNHCR 1979).

59 *MA, BT and DA v SSHD*, case C-648/11 Judgement of June 2013.

Trying to bridge the gap between the seemingly irreconcilable positions of refugee advocates and governments, Hathaway offered an alternative scheme for protection which retains the Refugee Convention as the normative starting point. He argues that the obligation to protect should not be conceived as a permanent obligation. In this model space could be made available for new arrivals as mandated repatriation would follow for refugees when the crisis in their home country abated.[60] The trade-off would require the West to contribute significantly more of its resources to those states in the South who shoulder the bulk of the refugee burden at present. Fiscal burden-sharing would not be a substitute for burden-sharing more generally but would help to improve protection in regions of origin. States could then allocate responsibility between themselves when determining solutions.[61] The proposal may also have a deterrent effect as economic migrants would not see an advantage in using the asylum channel to circumvent ordinary migration control.

Hathaway accepts that his proposal is 'structuring a compromise' and his ability to situate the proposal within the parameters of the Refugee Convention is to be welcomed. How far this position can be situated within a human rights paradigm is perhaps more questionable. Noll argues that the individual autonomy of the protection seeker is considerably reduced in an attempt to provide a solution for the protection of refugees as a group. The refugee will have limited choice as to where to seek protection and will be unable to take root in a new state.[62] Thus the refugee's story will continue to remain one of precarious uncertainty. This uncertainty could last for many years as most refugee crises are enduring rather than temporary and this would almost certainly present new problems. At present European law gives additional rights to third country nationals after five years of lawful residence; excluding refugees from these rights would be difficult to justify.[63]

To some extent Hathaway's proposals are predicated on the illusion of comparable rights protection in the global North and South. The notion that refugees should predominately remain in developing regions means that many will be consigned to live in poverty and insecurity. Even if richer states were prepared to contribute significant resources for capacity building in the region of origin, the human rights of refugees would hardly be comparable to those available in the West. In this respect Noll regards Hathaway's challenge to wealthy states to pool their protection resources for the benefit of southern states as fantastical:

60 Many writers contest the view that temporary protection will free up space in the system for new applicants, Zieck, M 'Vanishing Points of the Refugee Law Regime' (2005) 1 Ohio J on Dispute Resolution 217; Anker et al supra n9.

61 Hathaway, J 'Why Refugee Law Still Matters' (2007) 8 Melb J Intl L 89.

62 Noll, G 'Why Refugees Still Matter: A Response to James Hathaway' (2007) 8 Melb J Intl L 536.

63 Anker et al supra n9, 300.

> migration movement would need to be subjected to complete control. Where this is not possible, governments would find themselves engaged in a new and ambitious protection scheme, while remaining stuck with the costs associated with spontaneous movements and arrivals. Surely, no government will accept this.[64]

It is difficult not to concur with Noll's criticism and it is something that Hathaway has acknowledged. Current state practice does not give cause for optimism when it comes to enhancing refugee protection. It is more likely that states will rely on notions of fiscal burden-sharing to fully abdicate responsibility, further undermining protection and exacerbating North–South tensions.[65] It might also be suggested that these proposals are a 'tactical error' as they effectively reward states for breaching their current international obligations.[66]

It should not be impossible to construct a refugee status determination procedure which is efficient, rights-sensitive and capable of providing a deterrent to illegal immigration.[67] A variety of complementary approaches may be the only way to organise refugee solutions so that they attract the confidence of the applicant and the respect of national governments and their electorates. The deterrent element can be provided by improving and front-loading decision-making (as seen in the recast Procedures Directive) so that subsequent legal challenges are reduced and the removal of unsuccessful applicants can be secured in a timely manner.

Regional protection may be one component of a refugee management solution but is not likely to provide the whole solution. Often there will be intense group and military conflict within regions of origin and protection in such an environment will then be inconceivable.[68] This raises the spectre of increased instability in neighbouring states should refugees be expected to remain in these regions. General assumptions about cultural and social affinities in regions of origin are often unsustainable and are not supported by evidence on the ground.[69] Any search for durable solutions also needs to consider that asylum seekers may have stronger ties to countries outside the region that have become destinations for other similar émigré communities.

Schuck's proposal for a refugee quota system similarly hinges on the transfer of resources to developing states in exchange for the physical protection of refugees. As such it introduces the market to a space where human need is greatest and potentially undermines global hospitality whilst entrenching the divide between

64 Noll supra n62, 538.

65 Anker et al supra n9, 300.

66 Ibid, 308.

67 Byrne, R and Shacknove, A 'The Safe Country Notion in European Asylum Law' (1996) 9 Harvard HR J 227.

68 See Harrell-Bond's observations regarding Rwandan repatriations from Tanzania supra n48.

69 Byrne and Shacknove supra n67, 198.

North and South. If citizens of the developed world are isolated from the refugee experience they are unlikely to develop sympathy or understanding. This is borne out by opinion polls which suggest that those who come into contact with refugees exhibit greater tolerance and understanding of their plight.[70] To date the CEAS has completely neglected those who lack the capabilities to penetrate the EU's wall of restrictive measures.[71] Therefore a multifaceted solution which develops resettlement along with humanitarian visas and Protected Entry Procedures may offer the best hope.

Reconceptualising the Asylum Crisis

Much of the political criticism of international refugee law stems from the oft-cited accusation that the international system is in crisis. Indeed, the existence of a crisis is rarely contested with some commentators describing it as irreparable.[72] Over a decade has passed since these accusations originally surfaced and the indicators of a crisis are less obvious today. Refugee numbers in Europe have fallen significantly since the time of Hathaway's original proposal. Although a considerable amount of money is spent on preventing irregular movement this does not by itself suggest that refugee movement is out of control, rather it could be argued that the response of European governments is misguided and disproportionate.[73]

Certainly some asylum applicants disappear from the radar once afforded temporary admission and this may be deemed evidence of asylum abuse. Yet in many ways we can see that the current emphasis on deterrence encourages such conduct.[74] An asylum seeker arriving in Greece may put their faith in a system that rejects 99.8 per cent of asylum applicants and provides little reception support or they may decide that the system is dysfunctional and will undertake secondary movement. In order to avoid detection and transfer under Dublin, the applicant may decide to destroy travel documents or may seek assistance from a smuggler in order to secure entry. To argue that this makes the applicant bogus is a non sequitur. The European asylum system creates the perception of illegitimacy and perpetuates the crisis myth. The role of the mainstream European media in fuelling this imaginary crisis, coupled with an

---

70 Mori Attitudes towards Refugee and Asylum Seekers: A Survey of Public Opinion (Mori 2002).

71 El-Enany, N 'Who is the New European Refugee?' (2008) 33 EL Rev 3, 327.

72 Schuck, P 'Refugee Burden-Sharing: A Modest Proposal' (1997) 22 Yale J Intl L 243.

73 Laczko, F *Recent Trends in Irregular Migration in Europe* (International Organization for Migration 2012) – the report notes a significant decrease in both irregular migration and asylum seeking in the EU since 2008.

74 Noll, G 'Protection in a Spirit of Solidarity?' in Byrne, R; Noll, G and Vedsted-Hansen, J (eds) *New Asylum Countries? Migration Control and Refugee Protection in an Enlarged European Union* (2002) 323.

absence of political will to challenge the closed anti-immigration lobby, has allowed the debate on refugee protection to be hijacked through the language of inflated numbers, security threats and cultural fragmentation.

Once we acknowledge the real number of asylum seekers who arrive in the EU the sense of crisis dissipates, giving way to a demand for better organisation. Resources can then be spent on helping to address the causes of refugee movement. European governments may be understandably daunted by Castles' observation that 'reducing North-South inequality is the real key to effective migration management'[75] but there is much more that could be done in this direction. The EU's success in pushing forward with migration partnerships suggests that it commands a powerful lobbying position which could be deployed to support non-governmental organisations and refugee determination systems in the developed world whilst reducing economic support for illegitimate regimes whose policies increase the likelihood of irregular migration.

The need to address root causes of undocumented migration is paramount as it is the only way to make long-term changes to the number of irregular migrants seeking to enter Europe.[76] To date such discussions have been subsumed into questions of border control and surveillance; consequently policies have been narrow and contradictory, sometimes resulting in unintended, counterproductive consequences. It is of course extremely difficult to establish a way of successfully addressing causative factors but this does not mean it is a goal that should not be pursued with rigour. The consequences of failing to get to grips with the causes of the problem are already evident. One can highlight the increasing reliance on smugglers, the extensive resources spent on fighting irregular migration and the perception of insecurity that this fight leaves in its wake. Meanwhile less-developed countries lose their best workers through aggressive recruitment drives in developed countries (the so-called 'brain drain') and their economies become dependent on remittances sent home to relatives.

The CEAS provides an invaluable opportunity to pool national resources in a collective effort to tackle root causes.[77] It is deeply worrying that the concerns of national governments in the Council have dominated the latest phase of negotiations, often steering the recast asylum directives away from enhanced protection proposed by the Commission back towards a fortress mentality. Too often EU external migration policy has linked migration management initiatives to development aid and has failed to fully engage with root causes.[78] There is little doubt that the Commission could have done more to support non-governmental

75 Castles, S 'Why Migration Policies Fail' (2004) 27 Ethic and Racial Studies 221.

76 Castles, S; Crawley, H and Loughna, S *States of Conflict: Causes and Patterns of Forced Migration to the EU and Policy Responses* (Institute of Public Policy Research 2003).

77 De Haas is sceptical about root cause solutions, predicting that development in regions of origins will increase aspirations and that this will be likely to increase emigration at least in the short to medium term, supra n12, 1314.

78 Supra n75.

organisations in regions of instability and make diplomatic representations to countries where human rights are routinely abused.[79]

Addressing root causes requires an understanding of the 'push-and-pull' factors in migratory movements. Although such research exists it has not significantly influenced migration policy and this may in part be attributed to the lack of support such findings provide for the prevailing security discourse. Research findings suggest that indicators of conflict are far more relevant than indicators of development. The most common push factors in one study were repression and discrimination against minorities, ethnic conflict and human rights abuse.[80] Most migrants (including refugees) will remain in the immediate geographical region[81] but European pull factors centre on its relative peace, security and stability as well as a functioning health and welfare system. The factors which pull people towards specific countries are less about favourable welfare than they are down to past colonial ties, family links, language and diaspora communities. In 2002, the UK Home Office undertook interviews with 65 asylum applicants to determine the factors motivating their movement.[82] The findings challenged the prevailing media representation of asylum seekers as predominately economic migrants. The overwhelming majority were concerned primarily with escaping their country of origin and were often directed to particular destinations by agents, including smugglers and traffickers. For those with a choice in their destination, the most commonly cited factors of influence were links to family or friends, a belief in the safety and tolerance of the UK and a previous relationship with the UK (such as colonial ties or linguistic knowledge). Economic motivations were minimal as only four had been unemployed prior to their departure and none suggested that the welfare system was a significant pull factor. Unfortunately findings such as this rarely make it into mainstream media and their influence on policy tends to be marginal.[83]

Deconstructing the European Citizen

The European Commission considers that Union citizenship confers a sense of legitimisation on the integration process, offering citizens a sense of belonging

79 Castles et al supra n76, 50.

80 Ibid, 17; see also Koser, K and Pinkerton, C *The Social Networks of Asylum Seekers and the Dissemination of Information About Countries of Asylum* (Migration Research Unit, University College London 2002).

81 Schmeidl, S 'Conflict and Forced Migration: The Role of Economic Policies' in Zolberg, A and Benda, P (eds) *Global Migrants, Global Refugees: Problems and Solutions* (Berghahn Books 2001), 62.

82 Robinson, V and Segrott, J 'Understanding the Decision Making of Asylum Seekers' (Home Office Research Study 243 2002); similar findings were seen in the Netherlands: Doorheim, L and Dijkhoff, N 'Toevlucht Zoeken in Nederland' cited by Robinson and Segrott.

83 Boswell, C *The Political Uses of Expert Knowledge* (CUP 2009).

through the cultivation of a European identity.[84] In a Union informed by common liberal values of democracy, human rights and the rule of law, we must be careful not to predicate the construction of the European citizen on her relationship with the Outsider. This is particularly so when there is genuine unease over the future of the euro and a rise in extremist politics.[85] There has been a notable departure from the active endorsement of multiculturalism in the domestic politics of many states which may be related to an isolationist construction of European citizenship.[86] It appears impossible to disengage the influence of hostile immigration and asylum policies from this overall trend.

Guiraudon contends that politicisation of refugee issues is a high-risk strategy which tends towards right-wing extremism and xenophobia with the security agenda directed towards maintaining a particular political identity.[87] Kymlicka agrees, suggesting that if immigrants feel that they are presented as undeserving burdens they will feel uncomfortable with mainstream institutions, creating a 'racialized underclass' in permanent opposition to the larger society.[88]

---

84 European Commission *Report from the Commission – Third Report from the Commission on Citizenship of the Union* 7 September 2001 COM/2001/0506 final para 5(2).

85 The rise of the Dansfolkeparti ('Danish Peoples Party') established in 1995 is one example where Euro-scepticism and anti-immigrant rhetoric are frequently aligned in campaigning activities.

86 Vink supra n38, 166. The acquittal of Dutch Freedom Party politician, Geert Wilders, for inciting racial hatred was widely seen as symptomatic of Dutch society's declining belief in multiculturalism: Comiteau, L 'Is This the Death of Dutch Multiculturalism' *Time* Magazine (29 June 2011); Kern, S 'The Netherlands to Abandon Multiculturalism' (Gatestone Institute, 23 June 2011). Available at: http://www.gatestoneinstitute.org/2219/netherlands-abandons-multiculturalism; 'Multiculturalism Has Failed: Verhagen' (Dutch News.nl, 5 February 2011); Koopmans, R 'Trade-offs between Equality and Difference: Immigrant Integration, Multiculturalism and the Welfare State in Cross-National Perspective' (2010) 36 J of Ethnic and Migration Studies 1, 1. The Dutch move away from multiculturalism culminated in the Integration Bill of 2013 which requires, inter alia, immigrants to learn Dutch and reduces the state's role in seeking to integrate immigrant communities. In 2010 Angela Merkel announced that multiculturalism in Germany had failed: Clark, M 'Germany's Angela Merkel: Multiculturalism Has "Utterly Failed" *The Christian Science Monitor* (17 October 2010). Kymlicka argues that much of the backlash stems from a failure to fully conceptualise multiculturalism and that, contrary to some of the populist rhetoric, many states have moved towards inclusive policies of democratic citizenship which involve multicultural strategies. He also suggests that Germany had not adopted an overtly multicultural stance before Merkel's statement: Kymlicka, W *Multiculturalism: Success, Failure and the Future* (Migration Policy Institute February 2012).

87 Guiraudon, V 'Citizenship Rights for Non-citizens: France, Germany and Netherlands' in Joppke C (ed) *Challenges to the Nation-State* (OUP 1998) 290; Hayter, T *Open Borders: The Case Against Immigration Controls* (Pluto 2000) 150.

88 Kymlicka, W *Multiculturalism: Success, Failure and the Future* Migration Policy Institute February 2012, 24.

It could be argued that the fabrication of insecurity operates as a strategy of political legitimisation which is used to sustain political unity between people with a diversity of opinion.[89] Situating the EU within an existentially hostile environment has helped to maintain the illusion that the only conflict stems from external forces which are brought to us by migration. An external enemy can thus usefully 'unite the functionally fragmented society of the liberal state'.[90] This constitutive dialectic protects the identity of the community within a plural world by demanding its separation and isolation from external disruptive forces.[91] Walzer's national community is largely constructed by maintaining strong entry barriers, protecting those within from those without.[92] The Stockholm Programme 'An open and secure Europe serving and protecting its citizens'[93] envisages a privileged position of security for European citizens. This is confirmed by readmission negotiations with third countries which reveal that liberal values are conceived as territorially defined. Pécoud and Guchteneire argue that:

> the values that guide societies cannot stop at their borders; they must also inspire attitudes towards outsiders ... the evolution of migration controls towards greater harshness may eventually backfire and threaten the principles and freedoms that lie at the core of democratic societies.[94]

If Huysmans is correct in his diagnosis of a security paradox, the growth of the European surveillance and detection industry is likely to undermine and destabilise the liberal state and its democratic values. There is certainly a contradiction between demands to deepen the elements of freedom and security in European policy and the drive to securitise asylum and immigration policy.[95]

Border control and surveillance mechanisms serve to separate the wanted from the unwanted.[96] Those wanted are typically young, independent and economically productive but the security agenda has also come to dominate this legal migration route. In 2000, the European Commission called on the Council and Parliament to

89 Huysmans, J *The Politics of Insecurity: Fear, Immigration and Asylum in the EU* (Routledge 2006) 128.

90 Schmitt, C *The Concept of the Political* (University of Chicago Press 1932; reprinted 1996); Huysmans ibid 129.

91 Huysmans supra n89, 50.

92 See discussion in Chapter 1; Huysmans supra n89, 64.

93 Council of the EU *The Stockholm Programme: An Open and Secure Europe Serving and Protecting Citizens* 5713/10 Brussels, 3 March 2010.

94 Pécoud, A and Guchteneire,P 'International Migration, Border Controls and Human Rights: Assessing the Relevance of a Right to Mobility' (2006) 21 J of Borderlands Studies 1, 52.

95 Pirjola supra n28, 353; Levy, C 'The European Union after 9/11: The Demise of a Liberal Democratic Asylum System' (2005) 40 Government and Opposition 265–269.

96 Van Liempt, I *Navigating Borders – Inside Perspectives on the Process of Human Smuggling into the Netherlands* (Amsterdam UP 2007).

rethink Europe's zero immigration policy owing to predicted shortages of skilled and unskilled labour.[97] Meanwhile, rulings from the CJEU transformed national discretion and allowed resident third country nationals and family members to benefit from European citizenship rights in unexpected ways.[98] The Long Term Residents Directive further ensured that third country nationals did not remain permanent outsiders as a result of prescriptive national citizenship rules.[99] However, the adverse impact of the 2001 terrorist attacks on future European migration policy was considerable.[100] An association of asylum with terrorism enabled governments to legitimise arguments of restriction, in some cases even closing borders in order to protect their citizens from the externally conceived threat.[101] Border control subsequently became a matter of protecting the political and cultural hegemony of European citizenship and a dangerous division began to appear between Europe and the rest of the world, demanding ever-increasing fortification. Given the economic instability in many parts of the less-developed world and the predicted impact of climate change on the environment and its inhabitants, each extra security provision is simply another layer insulating European citizens from the developing world.

On the other hand, it has been contended that the grand narrative of security attributes too much rationality and uniformity to the policy process.[102] Koser cautions against such simplistic narratives, highlighting the example of people smuggling where beneficiaries not only include the smuggler but also families back home, employers and migrants.[103] Nevertheless, this is an area of policy where

97 European Commission COM (2000) 757 final *Communication from the Commission to the Council and the European Parliament on a Community Immigration Policy* Brussels 22 November 2000.

98 Carrera, S and Wiesbrock, A 'Whose European Citizenship in the Stockholm Programme? The Enactment of Citizenship by Third Country Nationals in the EU' (2010) 12 Eur J Migration & L 337, 357; see for example C-127/08 *Metock and Others* [2008] ECR I 6241.

99 Council Directive 2003/109/EC of 25 November 2003 *Concerning the Status of Third-Country Nationals Who Are Long-Term Residents* OJ L 16, 23 January 2004, p. 44–53.

100 Levy, C 'The European Union after 9/11: The demise of a liberal democratic regime?' (2005) 40 Government and Opposition 1, 34.

101 Penelope, M 'Resolution 1373: A Call to Pre-Empt Asylum Seekers? (Or 'Osama' the Asylum Seeker) in McAdam, J (ed) *Forced Migration, Human Rights and Security* (Hart 2008) 52. For example, China and Iran shut their borders after 11 September 2001 even though both are parties to the Refugee Convention.

102 Boswell, C and Geddes, A *Migration and Mobility in the European Union* (Palgrave Macmillan 2011) 225; Brunnson, N *The Organisation of Hypocrisy: Talk, Decision and Action in Organizations* (Copenhagen Business School Press 2003); Boswell and Geddes give the example of welfare payments which are often available to migrants in a similar way to those payable to citizens, ibid, 173.

103 Koser, K 'Why Migrant Smuggling Pays (2008) 46 Intl Migration 2, 3.

tough talk really does matter. European governments find themselves engaged in a fire-fighting exercise as they struggle to respond to unrealistic demands from sections of the public and media.[104] Tough anti-immigration rhetoric, even when not followed by similar actions, encourages xenophobia and undermines tolerance and democratic values.[105] A common European approach offers a way for national governments to avoid reactionary fire-fighting and to deflect criticism from more conservative sections of their electorate.[106]

Better detection and protection for refugees certainly requires desecuritisation and a departure from politics based on expectations of hostility.[107] However, as securitisation is a uniting factor across the EU 28 it is difficult to envisage the significant political will to challenge the status quo. The complex integration project has created a governmental identity which is rather precarious; navigating numerous challenges presented by various political actors. It has shored up this identity by centralising liberal values within a territorial dimension which needs to be defended from outside influence. Thus unease with open borders, human trafficking, terrorism, labour migration, asylum and cross-border criminality have been integrated into an internal security field.[108]

Samers applies the work of Power and Miller to explain how policies of governments and the media depiction of migration has not just contributed but created the 'problem' of asylum.[109] Legitimacy has come to depend on the symbolism of tough immigration control rather on the operation of a fair and efficient system of international protection. This makes states and their migration industries less transparent and more opaque, frustrating the opportunity to reduce bureaucracy and improve accountability.[110]

It is axiomatic that public attitudes will be influenced by political rhetoric and the prevailing political discourse.[111] When empowered with information the

104 Supra n,103 44.

105 One example is the hostile reaction to the academic Mary Beard on BBC's Question Time in 2013. Beard's suggestion that immigration could contribute to the local economy made her the subject of a vitriolic, hate campaign in certain sections of the media. BBC News 'Question Time panellist Mary Beard on sexist online abuse' 23 January 2013 BBC.

106 Supra n103, 155.

107 Huysmans supra n89, 130.

108 Ibid, 148.

109 Samers, M 'An Emerging Geopolitics of Illegal Immigration in the European Union' (2004) 6 Eur J Migration & L 1, 27; Power, M *The Audit Explosion* (Demos 1994) and Miller, D 'Conclusion: A Theory of Virtualism' in Carrier, J and Miller, D (eds) *Virtualism: A New Political Economy* (Berg 1998) 202.

110 Miller ibid, 201.

111 Opinion polls reveal public confusion over asylum and negative responses often follow from negative suggestions in the questioning; Power, P 'Australian Attitudes to the Acceptance of Refugees' at 'Racism Revisited' Anti-Racism Leadership and Practice Conference, Murdoch University, Perth, 20 March 2010.

public exhibit hospitality and sympathy toward refugees.[112] Conversely, hostile immigration rhetoric associating asylum with criminality encourages feelings of insecurity, fanning the flames of intolerance.[113] The popularity of extremist political parties in several countries, including Austria, Greece, France and Denmark, can be demonstrably linked to anti-immigration and security rhetoric.[114]

European citizenship should not be allowed to evolve into an entitlement based on exclusionary politics. For Habermas a political culture based on liberal values should be isolated from any privileged form of cultural life, as:

> only within the constitutional framework of a democratic legal system can different ways of life coexist equally. These must however overlap within a common political culture which again implies an impulse to open these ways of life to others.[115]

A common political, liberal culture cannot be based solely on exclusionary policies. Whilst it is not possible to offer a right of entry for ever migrant, the claim of the asylum seeker must be afforded special significance in a European Union founded on 'human dignity, liberty, democracy, equality, the rule of law and respect for human rights, including the rights of persons belonging to minorities'.[116]

Final Observations

The protection of refugees is a measure of a tolerant and fair national community and helps to ensure a stable and just global community which prioritises the equal worth of all human beings. A common European approach offers an opportunity to develop best practice in ensuring an asylum system that is both fair and efficient. For the sake of credibility, it must also be possible to identify and reduce fraudulent claims (although this is unlikely to have a significant impact on the number of claims overall), providing assiduous removal of unsuccessful claimants.[117]

Exclusionary policies begin at the border and continue after entry, with the potential to undermine the democratic legal system. Refugees must, as Walzer

---

112 Supra n7.

113 Crawley, H *Evidence on Attitudes to Asylum and Immigration: What We Know, Don't Know and Need to Know* Centre on Migration, Policy and Society 'COMPAS' Working Paper No 23 University of Oxford; Finney, N *Key Issues: Public Opinion on Asylum and Refugee Issues* (ICAR October 2005). Available at: http://www.icar.org.uk/ng_attitudes%2020051-01-9.pdf (accessed 16 July 2013).

114 Holllifield, J 'Ideas, Institutions and Civil Society: On the Limits of Immigration in France' in Brochmann and Hammar supra n6, 80.

115 Habermas, J 'Citizenship and National Identity: Some Reflections on the Future of Europe' (1992) 12 Praxis Intl 1, 1.

116 *Treaty of the European Union* OJ C83/13 30 March 2010, Article 2.

117 Price supra n8, 234.

concedes, be afforded rights to participate in the community so that they are not alienated from that same community. However, the right to 'seek' and 'enjoy' asylum cannot be secured in an environment dominated by the prevailing security discourse where generalisations replace individual determinations.[118] As Noll argues, control should not be allowed to enjoy a 'first mover's advantage over protection'.[119]

It is imperative that inaccurate representations which exaggerate numbers and fuel a perception of crisis are debunked. This necessitates the shoring-up rather than dismantling or reallocating of international norms. A range of durable solutions, including resettlement must be more equitably applied with a shift of emphasis from 'burden-sharing' to 'protection sharing'.

Failure to do this allows the security paradox to dictate the future direction of European relations, both internally and externally. Exclusionary policies begin at the border and continue after entry, with the potential to undermine the democratic legal system. As security and technology industries prosper, European citizens become less secure, governments become less tolerant and the rule of law, predicated on equality before the law, will be substantially eroded. In 2006, the European Parliament labelled European immigration policy a failure, highlighting the number of irregular migrants dying in the Mediterranean and the human rights abuses resulting from increased administrative detention.[120] The recent revision of the main asylum directives to reflect the common standards programme does little to address this indictment. As Dowty argues:

> justice is not the special privilege of those who are privileged already; the arbitrary rules of birthplace and parentage work for justice when they create safeguards, not when they make victims ... [121]

Efforts to manage the mythical 'crisis' of irregular migration have generated a very real crisis of protection which undermines the fundamental right to seek and enjoy asylum and which depends on a rhetoric of criminality and security, allowing states to justify the allocation of endless resources.[122] The indiscriminate manner in which non-entrée policies operate coupled with the impact of non-arrival measures, serves only to confine refugees to their region of origin, cementing global inequality and insecurity.

---

118 Guild, E *Challenges and Prospects for the EU's Area of Freedoms, Security and Justice: Recommendations to the EC for the Stockholm Programme* CEPS Working Document No 313 April 2009.

119 Noll supra n74, 261.

120 European Parliament *Resolution on the Common Immigration Policy* B60-508/2006 26 September 2006, para L.

121 Dowty, A *Closed Borders* (Yale UP 1987) 281.

122 ECRE *Broken Promises-Forgotten Principles: An ECRE Evaluation of the Developments of EU Minimum Standards for Refugee Protection Tampere 1999 – Brussels 2004* (ECRE 2004).

Bibliography

ABC News 'Immigration Minister Tony Burke Admits Malaysia Asylum Seeker Swap Deal No Longer Viable' (ABC News Australia, 6 July 2013). Available at: http://www.abc.net.au/news/2013-07-06/government-admits-malaysia-asylum-seeker-deal-no-longer-viable/4803756 (accessed 4 September 2013)

Academic Network for Legal Studies on Immigration and Asylum in Europe *Comparative Overview of the Directive 2003/9 of 27 January 2003 Laying Down Minimum Standards for the Reception of Asylum seekers in All EU Member States* (European Commission 2006) 'Odysseus Network'

Ackers, D 'The Negotiations on the Asylum Procedures Directive' (2005) 7 Eur J Migration & L 1–34

Acosta, D 'The Good, the Bad and the Ugly in EU Migration Law: Is the European Parliament Becoming Bad and Ugly? (The Adoption of Directive 2008/15: The Returns Directive)' (2009) 11 Eur J Migration & L 1, 19–39

Ager, A and Strang, A 'Indicators of Integration: Final Report' Home Office Development and Practice Report 28 (Home Office 2004)

Ager, A and Strang, A 'The Experience of Integration: A Qualitative Study of Refugee Integration in Local Communities of Pollokshaws and Islington' (Home Office Online Report 55, 2004)

Albertinelli, A 'Population and Social Conditions' (2010) Eurostat Statistics in Focus 27/2010

Aleinikoff, A 'Citizens, Aliens, Membership and the Constitution' (1990) 7 Const Commentary 9, 28

Amnesty International *Unlawful and Unworkable: Amnesty International's View on Proposals for Extraterritorial Processing of Asylum Claims* 2003. Available at: http://www.amnesty.org/en/library/info/IOR61/004/2003 (accessed 8 May 2013)

Amnesty International *The EU – Now More Free, Secure and Justice? Amnesty International's Human Rights Assessment of the Tampere Agenda* (Amnesty International June 2004)

Amnesty International *Seeking Asylum is not a Crime: Detention of People Who Have Sought Asylum* (Amnesty International UK 2005)

Amnesty International *The Dublin II Trap: Transfer of Asylum Seekers to Greece* (Amnesty International 2010)

Amnesty International *Annual Report 2011: Ukraine* (Amnesty International POL/10/001/2011)

Amnesty International 'Ukraine Must Protect Detained Asylum Seekers Attacked by Security Forces' (Amnesty International News, 21 January 2012). Available at: http://www.amnesty.org/en/news/ukraine-must-protect-detained-asylum-seekers-attacked-security-forces-2012-01-31 (accessed 23 May 2013)

Amnesty International *SOS Europe: Human Rights and Migration Control* (Amnesty International 2012)

Amnesty International *Opinion on the EASO COI Report 'Afghanistan: Taliban Strategies – Recruitment'* (July 2012). Available at: www.amnesty.eu/content/assets/EASO_COI_Report_.pdf (accessed 20 March 2013)

Anderson, B *Imagined Communities: Reflections on the Origin and Spread of Nationalism* (Verso 1983)

Andreas, P and Snyder, T (eds) *The Wall around the West* (Rowman & Littlefield, 2000)

Andreas, P 'The Transformation of Migrant Smuggling across the US-Mexican Border' in Kyle, D and Koslowski, R (eds) *Global Human Smuggling: Comparative Perspectives* (Johns Hopkins UP 2001) 107–128

Andrysek, O 'Gaps in International Protection and the Potential for Redress through Individual Complaints Procedures' (1997) 9 Intl J Refugee L 392–414

Anker, D; Fitzpatrick, J and Shacknove, A 'Crisis and Cure: A Reply to Hathaway/Neve and Schuck' (1998) 11 Harvard Human Rights J 295

Arendt, H *On Violence* (Harcourt, Brace & World 1970)

Arendt, H *Origins of Totalitarianism* (Harcourt, Brace & World 1966)

Arimatsu, L and Samson, G *The UN Refugee Convention at 60: The Challenge for Europe* Briefing Paper (Chatham House 2011)

Ascoli, A 'Conditions and Criteria for Determining Asylum' in Goudappel, F and Raulus, H (eds) *The Future of Asylum in the European Union* (TMC Asser 2011) 125–133

Askola, H 'Illegal Migrant's Gender and Vulnerability: The Case of the EU Returns Directive' (2010) 18 Fem Leg Stud, 159

Asylum Aid *Unsustainable: The Quality of Initial Decision Making in Women's Asylum Claims* (Asylum Aid 2011)

Athens News 'Samaras Claims Greeks Must 'take back' Cities from Immigrants' (19 April 2012)

AEDH, Association Européenne pour la défense des Droits de l'Homme (Press Release, 20 June 2012)

Back, L; Keith, M; Khan, A; Shukra, K and Solomos, J 'The Return of Assimilationism: Race, Multiculturalism and New Labour' (2002) (7 Sociological Research Online 2). Available at: http://www.socresonline.org.uk/7/2/back.html (accessed 5 November 2012)

Bacon, C 'The Evolution of Immigration Detention in the UK: The Involvement of Private Prison Companies' (Refugee Studies Centre, University of Oxford, Working Paper Series. RSC Working Paper No 27 2005)

Baldaccini, A 'The External Dimension of the EU's Asylum and Immigration Policies: Old Concerns and New Approaches' in Baldaccini, A; Guild, E and Toner, H (eds) *Whose Freedom, Security and Justice: EU Immigration and Asylum Law and Policy* (Hart 2007) 277–298

Baldaccini, A 'The Return and Removal of Irregular Migrants under EU Law: An Analysis of the Returns Directive (2009) Eur J Migration & L 11, 1–17

Baldaccini, A and Toner, H 'From Amsterdam and Tampere to The Hague: An overview of Five Years of EC Immigration and Asylum Law' Baldaccini, A; Guild, E and Toner, H (eds) *Whose Freedom, Security and Justice: EU Immigration and Asylum Law and Policy* (Hart 2007) 1–22

Baldaccini, A; Guild, E and Toner, H (eds) *Whose Freedom, Security and Justice: EU Immigration and Asylum Law and Policy* (Hart 2007)

Balibar, E 'The Nation Form: History and Ideology' in Balibar, E and Wallerstein, I (eds) *Race, Nation, Class: Ambiguous Identities Politics* (Verso 1991)

Battjes, H *European Asylum Law and International Law* (M Nijhoff 2006)

Battjes, H 'In Search of A Fair Balance: The Absolute Character of the Prohibition of Refoulement under Article 3 ECHR Reassessed' (2009) 22 Leiden J of Intl L 3, 583–621

BBC News 'Ukrainian Detention Centre' 13 December 2002

BBC News 'Prison Culture at Asylum Centre' 16 June 2004

BBC *Detention Undercover: The Real Story* 2005

BBC News 'Food Protest by Asylum Detainees' 11 June 2007

BBC News 'What Does "British Jobs" Pledge Mean?' 16 November 2007

BBC News 'Tunisia Migrants Prompt Italy "Humanitarian Emergency"' (12 February 2011). Available at: http://www.bbc.co.uk/news/world-europe-12441613 (accessed 20 March 2013)

BBC News 'Tunisia Rejects Italian Call to Send Immigration Police' (14 February 2011). Available at: http://www.bbc.co.uk/news/world-europe-12445008 (accessed 20 March 2013)

BBC News 'Question Time panellist Mary Beard on Sexist Online Abuse' 23 January 2013

BBC News 'Italian Police Arrest Somali over Lampedusa Boat Tragedy'8th Nov. 2013. Available at: http://www.bbc.co.uk/news/world-europe-24865115 (accessed 20 November 2013)

Beating Borders '3 Dead and 15 Wounded at Melilla Border Fence' (2013). Available at: http://beatingborders.wordpress.com/2013/03/26/3-dead-and-15-wounded-at-melilla-border-fence (accessed 10May 2013)

Bendel, P 'Everything under Control? The EU's Policies and Politics of Immigration' in Faist, T and Ette, A (eds) *The Europeanisation of National Policies and Politics of Immigration* (Palgrave Macmillan 2007) 32–48

Benhabib, S *The Claims of Culture: Equality and Diversity in the Global Era* (Princeton UP 2002)

Berkowitz, N 'Article 5, Detention of Asylum Seekers' (2006) 20 IANL 3, 223

Berkowitz, N 'Immigration and Asylum: Detention of Asylum Seeker for Speedy Processing of Application' (2006) 6 EHRLR 742

Betts, A 'Convention Plus: Continuity or Change in North-South Responsibility-Sharing?' Paper presented at *New Asylum Paradigm*? Workshop COMPAS, University of Oxford, 14 June 2005

Betts, A and Durieux, JF 'Convention Plus as a Norm-Setting Exercise' (2007) 20 J Refugee Studies 509–535

Beutin, R; Canoy, M; Horvath, A, Hubert A; Lerais, F; Smith, P and Sochacki, M *Migration and Public Perception* (European Commission 2006)

Beutin, R; Canoy, M; Horvath, A; Hubert ; Lerais, F; and Sochacki, M 'Reassessing the Link between Public Perception and Migration Policy' (2007) 9 Eur J Migration & L 389–418

Bigo, D 'When Two Become One: Internal and External Securitisations in Europe' in Kelstrup, MW and Williams, M (eds) *International Relations Theory and the Politics of European Integration: Power, Security and Community* (Routledge 2000) 171–204

Bigo, D 'Protection: Concept and Technique' in Huysmans, J; Dobson, A and Prokhovnik, R (eds) *The Politics of Protection* (Routledge 2006) 84–100

Bigo, D and Guild, E (eds) *Controlling Frontiers: Free Movement Into and Within Europe* (Ashgate 2005)

Bigo, D; Carrera, S and Guild, *E Foreigners, Refugees and Minorities: Rethinking People in the Context of Border Controls and Visas* (Ashgate 2013)

Billet, C 'EC Readmission Agreements: A Prime Instrument of the External Dimension of the EU's Fights Against Irregular Immigration. An Assessment after Ten Years of Practice' (2010) 12 Eur J Migration & L 1, 45–79

Birrell, I 'The Immigration Debate: Evidence-Free and More Rancid Than Ever' (Guardian Online, 25 March 2013). Available at: http://www.guardian.co.uk/commentisfree/2013/mar/25/immigration-debate-evidence-free-rancid (accessed 25 March 2013)

Tony Blair Letter to Costas Simitis 10 March 2003 and *New Vision for Refugees.* Full text available at: http://www.statewatch.org/news/2003/apr/10safe.htm

Bohman, A 'Articulated Antipathies: Political Influence on Anti-Immigrant Attitudes' (2011) 52 IJCS 6 457–477

Boeles, P and Bruins, M 'Case Reports of the European Courts of Human Rights and the Human Rights Committee' (2007) 9 Eur J Migration and L 2, 253–276

Bond, J 'Excluding Justice: The Dangerous Intersection between Refugee Claims, Criminal Law and "Guilty" Asylum Seekers' (2012) 24 Intl J Refugee L 1, 37–59

Borchelt, G 'The Safe Third Country Practice in The EU: A Misguided Approach to Asylum Law and A Violation of International Human Rights Standards' (2002) 33 Columbia HR L Rev 473

Bosniak, L *The Citizen and the Alien: Dilemmas of Contemporary Membership* (Princeton UP 2006)

Boswell, C 'The External Dimension' of the EU Immigration and Asylum Policy' (2003) 79 Intl Affairs 619–638

Boswell, C *The Political Uses of Expert Knowledge* (CUP 2009)

Boswell, C and Geddes, A *Migration and Mobility in the European Union* (Palgrave Macmillan 2011)

Bouteillet-Paquet, D 'Passing the Buck: A Critical Analysis of the Readmission Policy Implemented by the European Union and Its Member States' (2003) 5 Eur J Migration & L 359–377

Bright, M 'Asylum Crisis Hyped in Europe, says UN' *The Observer* (2 June 2002) 5

Brochmann, G and Hammar, T (eds) *Mechanisms of Immigration Control: A Comparative Analysis of European Regulation Policies* (Berg 1999)

Brochmann, G 'Controlling Immigration in Europe' in Brochmann, G and Hammar, T (eds) *Mechanisms of Immigration Control: A Comparative Analysis of European Regulation Policies* (Berg 1999) 297–334

British Institute of International and Comparative Law 'The EU Asylum Directives: Is Opting in Necessary?' (Bingham Centre for the Rule of Law, 2012). Available at: http://www.biicl.org/binghamcentre/eu_asylum (accessed 9 April 2013)

Bruin, R 'Border Control: Not a Transparent Reality' in Goudappel, F and Raulus, H (eds) *The Future of Asylum in the European Union* (TMC Asser 2011) 21–42

Brunnson, N *The Organization of Hypocrisy: Talk, Decision and Action in Organizations* (Copenhagen Business School Press 2003)

Buckley, J '*NS V SSHD* C-4110/10 ECJ, Case Comment' (2012) 2 EHRLR 210

Burnham, E *Challenging Immigration Detention: A Best Practice Guide* October (Immigration Law Practitioners Association 2003)

Byrne, R 'Future Perspectives: Accession and Asylum in An Expanded EU' in Byrne, R; Noll, G and Vedsted-Hansen, J (eds) *New Asylum Countries? Migration Control and Refugee Protection in an Enlarged EU* (Kluwer 2002) 373–422

Byrne, R and Shacknove, A 'The Safe Third Country Notion in European Asylum Law' (1996) 9 Harvard HR J 185–226

Byrne, R; Noll, G and Vedsted-Hansen, J (eds) *New Asylum Countries? Migration Control and Refugee Protection in an Enlarged EU* (Kluwer 2002)

Byrne, R and Vedsted-Hansen, J 'Western Asylum Policies for Export: The Transfer of Protection and Deflection formulas to Central Europe and the Baltics' in Byrne, R; Noll, G and Vedsted-Hansen, J (eds) *New Asylum Countries? Migration Control and Refugee Protection in an Enlarged EU* (Kluwer 2002) 5–28

Carens, J 'Aliens and Citizens: The Case for Open Borders' (1987) 49 The Rev of Politics 2, 251–273

Carens, J 'Who Should Get In? The Ethics of Immigration Admissions' (2003) 17 Ethics and Internal Affairs 1, 95–110

Carling, J 'Unauthorized Migration from Africa to Spain' (2007) 35 J Intl Migration 4, 3–37

Carrera, S and Guild, E 'Does the Stockholm Programme Matter? The Struggles over Ownership of AFSJ Multiannual Programming' (CEPS Paper Liberty and Security in Europe No 51 December 2012)

Carrera, S and Wiesbrock, A 'Whose European Citizenship in the Stockholm Programme? The Enactment of Citizenship by Third Country Nationals in the EU' (2010) 12 Eur J Migration &L 3, 337–359

Carrier, J and Miller, D (eds) *Virtualism: A New Political Economy* (Berg Press 1998)

Castles, S 'Why Migration Policies Fail' (2004) 27 Ethic and Racial Studies 205–227

Castles, S and Davidson, A *Citizenship and Migration: Globalisation and the Politics of Belonging* (Psychology Press 2000)

Castles, S; Crawley, H and Loughna, S *States of Conflict: Causes and Patterns of Forced Migration to the EU and Policy Responses* (Institute of Public Policy Research 2003)

Chen, G 'A Global Campaign to End Refugee Warehousing' in US Committee for Refugees *World Refugee Survey* 2004

Cholewinski, R *EU Policy on Irregular Migration: Human Rights Lost* Paper presented to Conference on Irregular Migration and Human Rights, University of Leicester 28–29 June 2003

Cholewinski, R 'The Criminalisation of Migrants' in Baldaccini, A et al (eds) *Whose Freedom, Security and Justice: EU Immigration and Asylum Law and Policy* (Hart 2007) 310–336

Chou, M-H 'The European Security Agenda and the "External Dimension" of EU Asylum and Migration Cooperation' (2009) 10 Perspectives on European Politics and Society 4, 541–559

Clark, M 'Germany's Angela Merkel: Multiculturalism Has "Utterly Failed" *The Christian Science Monitor* (17 October 2010)

Cohen, R 'The Free Movement of Money and People: Debates before and after 9/11' CSGR Working Paper No 160/05 (University of Warwick 2005)

Cohen, R 'Response to Hathaway' (2007) 20 J Refugee Studies 370–376

Coleman, N 'Non-Refoulement Revised: Renewed Review of Non-Refoulement as Customary International law' (2003) 5 Eur J Migration & L 23–68

Coleman, N *European Readmission Policy: Third Country Interests and Refugee Rights* (M Nijhoff 2009)

Collett, E 'The European Union's Stockholm Program: Less Ambition on Immigration and Asylum, but More Detailed Plans' (Migration Information Source, January 2010). Available at: http://www.migrationinformation.org/feature/display.cfm?id=768 (accessed 27 January 2012)

Collyer, M 'The Dublin Regulation and Algerians in the UK' (2004)17 J Refugee Studies 4, 375–400

Comiteau, L 'Is This the Death of Dutch Multiculturalism' *Time* Magazine (29 June 2011)

Cornelisse, G 'Human Rights for Immigration Detainees in Strasbourg: Limited Sovereignty or a Limited Discourse?' (2004) 6 Eur J Migration & L 2, 93–110

Cornelisse, G *Immigration Detention and Human Rights: Rethinking Territorial Sovereignty* (M Nijhoff 2010)

Cossé, E 'Greece's Epidemic of Racist Attacks' Human Rights Watch News. 26 January 2012. Available at: http://www.hrw.org/news/2012/01/26/greeces-epidemic-racist-attacks

Costello, C *Analysis and Critique of Council Directive on Minimum Standards on Procedures for Granting and Withdrawing Refugee Status* (ILPA 30 April 2004)

Costello, C 'The Asylum Procedures Directive and the Proliferation of Safe Country Practices: Deterrence, Deflection and the Dismantling of International Protection?' (2005) 7 Eur J Migration & L 1, 35–70

Costello, C 'Human Rights and the Elusive Universal Subject: Immigration Detention under International Human Rights and EU Law' (2012) 19 Indiana J of Global Legal Studies 1, 257–303

Craig, S and Fletcher, M 'Deflecting Refugees: A Critique of the EC Asylum Procedures Directive' in Shah, P (ed) *The Challenge of Asylum to Legal Systems* (Cavendish, 2005) 52–81

Crawley, H 'Europe Looks to Africa to Solve the "Asylum Problem"' (2005) Forced Migration Rev, 23–26 May

Crawley, H *Evidence on Attitudes to Asylum and Immigration: What We Know, Don't Know and Need to Know* Centre on Migration, Policy and Society 'COMPAS' Working Paper No 23 University of Oxford, 2005

Da Costa, R *Rights of Refugees in the Context of Integration: Legal Standards and Recommendations* POLAS/2006/02 (UNHCR 2006)

Dauvergne, C *Making People Illegal: What Globalization Means for Migration and Law* (CUP 2008)

Davy, U *Asyl und Internationales Flüchtingrecht, Band I: Völkerrechtlichter Rahmen* (Verlag Österreich 1996)

Dean, M *Democracy under Attack: How the Media Distort Policy and Politics* (Policy Press 2013)

De Haas, H 'Morocco's Migration Experience: A Transnational Perspective' (2007) 45 Intl Migration Rev 4, 39–70

De Haas, H 'The Myth of Invasion: The Inconvenient Realities of African Migration to Europe' 2008 29 3rd World Q, 1305–1322

De Haas, H *Irregular Migration from West Africa to the Maghreb and the European Union* (International Organisation for Migration 2008)

De Vries, K 'An Assessment of "Protection in Regions of Origin" in Relation to European Asylum Law' (2007) 9 Eur J Migration & L 1, 83–103

Dietrich, H 'The Desert Front-EU Refugee Camps in North Africa?' (Statewatch News Online, March 2005)

Di Frederico, G (ed), *The EU Charter of Fundamental Rights: From Declaration to Binding Instrument* (Springer 2011)

Dombey, D 'UK Asylum Proposals Draw Mixed Response' *Financial Times* (29 March 2003) 12

Doomernik, J 'Migration and Security: The Wrong End of the Stick?' in Van den Anker, C (ed) *The Political Economy of New Slavery* (Palgrave Macmillan 2004) 37–52

Doorheim, L and Dijkhoff, N 'Toevlucht Zoeken in Nederland' cited by Robinson and Segrott 'Understanding the Decision- Making of Asylum Seekers' (Home Office Research Study 243, 2002)

Dowty, A *Closed Borders* (Yale UP 1987)

Dummett, A 'The Transnational Migration of People Seen from within a Natural Law Tradition' in Barry and Goodin (eds) *Free Movement: Ethical Issues in the Transnational Migration of People and of Money* (Wheatsheaf 1992) 162–180

Dummett, A and Nicol, A *Subjects, Citizens, Aliens and Others* (Weidenfeld & Nicolson 1990)

Dummett, M *On Immigration and Refugees* (Routledge 2001) 133

Dutch News 'Multiculturalism Has Failed: Verhagen' (Dutch News.nl, 5 February 2011)

ECRE (European Council for Refugees and Exiles) *Broken Promises- Forgotten Principles* (ECRE 2004)

ECRE *Safe Third Countries: Myths and Realities* (ECRE 2005)

ECRE *The Way Forward: Europe's Role in the Global Refugee Protection System towards Fair and Efficient Asylum Systems in Europe* (ECRE September 2005)

ECRE *Summary Report on the Application of the Dublin II Regulation in Europe* AD3/3/2006/EXT/MH (ECRE March 2006)

ECRE *Report on the Application of the Dublin II Regulation* March 2006 ECRE *Information on the Council Directive 2005/85/EC of 1 December 2005 on Minimum Standards on Procedures in Member States for Granting and Withdrawing Refugee Status* (ECRE 2006) 23. Available at: http://www.unhcr.org/refworld/docid/464317ab2.html (accessed 27 March 2013)

ECRE 'Background Information: Transfer of Asylum Seekers to Greece' (ECRE 2007)

ECRE 'The Dublin Regulation: Ten Recommendations for Reform' AD1/3/2007/Ext/CN (ECRE 2007)

ECRE 'The Dublin Regulation: Twenty Voices: Twenty Reasons for Change' AD2/3/2007/ext/CN (ECRE 2007)

ECRE *Comments From the European Council on Refugees and Exiles on the European Commission Proposal to recast the Qualification Directive* (ECRE March 2010)

ECRE 'Ill-Treatment of Refugees in Libya: The EU A Silent Accomplice' Press Release (7 July 2010)

ECRE *Comments from the European Council on Refugees and Exiles on the Amended Commission Proposal to Recast the Reception Directive* (COM(2011) 320 final) September 2011 (ECRE 2011)

ECRE/ELENA *Research on ECHR Rule 39 Interim Measures* April 2012 Annex B [4] p100. Available at: http://www.ecre.org/component/content/article/56-ecre-actions/272-ecre-research-on-rule-39-interim-measureshtml (accessed 15 April 2013)

ECRE Dublin Project EU *The Dublin II Regulation: Lives on Hold* (ECRE 2013)

The Economist 'Refugees Keep Out' (19 September 1992) 4

Edwards, A 'Human Rights, Refugees and the Right "to Enjoy" Asylum' (2005) 17 IJ Refugee L 2, 293–330

Edwards, A and Field, O *Alternatives to Detention of Asylum Seekers and Refugees* UNHCR Legal and Protection Policy Research Series POLAS/2006/03 April 2006

Edwards, A 'The Optional Protocol to the Convention Against Torture and the Detention of Refugees' (2008) 57 ICLQ 789–825

Edwards, A 'UNHCR Recommendations for Belgian EU Presidency' Press briefing (25 June 2010)

Edwards, A *Back to Basics: The Right to Liberty and Security of Person and 'Alternatives to Detention' of Refugee Asylum Seekers, Stateless Persons and Other Migrants* (UNHCR 2011)

El-Enany, N 'Who is the New European Refugee?' (2008) 33 EL Rev 3, 313–335

Ette, A and Geddes, J 'Against Exceptionalism: British Interests for Selectively Europeanizing Its Immigration Policy' in Faist, T and Ette, A (eds) *The Europeanisation of National Policies and Politics of Immigration* (Palgrave Macmillan 2007) 93–115

Europa Press Release 'Breakthrough for the Common Asylum System' (27 March 2013)

European Migration Network *Impact of Immigration on Europe's Societies* (European Commission, March 2006)

European Asylum Support Office 'The European Asylum Support Office Publishes Its First Country of Origin Information (COI) Report on Afghanistan' Press Release 10 July 2012

EU Observer 'EU Lawmakers Reinforce Asylum Seekers' Rights' (EU Observer, 19 September 2012). Available at: http://www.euobserver.com/justice/117604 (accessed 26 March 2013)

European Voice 'Greek Asylum System in disarray' (27 January 2011). Available at: http://www.europeanvoice.com/article/imported/greek-asylum-system-in-disarray/70044.aspx (accessed 1 November 2012)

Fahrmeir, A; Faron, O and Weil, P *Migration Control in the North Atlantic World: The Evolution of State Practices in Europe and the US: From the French Revolution to the Inter-War Period* (Berghahn Books *2003*)

Faist, T *The Volume and Dynamics of International Migration and Transnational Social Spaces* (OUP 2000)

Faist, T and Ette, A (eds) *The Europeanisation of National Policies and Politics of Immigration* (Palgrave Macmillan 2007)

Feller, E 'Asylum, Migration and Refugee Protection: Realities, Myths and the Promise of Things to Come' (2006) 18 Intl J Refugee L 509–536

Feller, E 'The Responsibility to Protect' in McAdam, J (ed) *Forced Migration, Human Rights and Security* (Hart 2008) 283–394

Field, JRC 'Bridging the Gap between Refugee Rights and Reality' (2010) 22 Intl J Refugee L 4, 512–557

Finney, N *Key Issues: Public Opinion on Asylum and Refugee Issues* (ICAR October 2005). Available at: http://www.icar.org.uk/ng_attitudes%202005-10-19.pdf (accessed 16 July 2013)

Fitzpatrick, J 'Flight from Asylum: Trends towards Temporary "Refuge" and Local Responses Towards Forced Migrations (1994–5) 35 Va J Intl L 13

Flynn, M and Cannon, C 'The Privatisation of Immigration Detention: Towards a Global View' (Global Detention Project, the Graduate Institute September 2009)

Fullerton, M 'Failing the Test: Germany Leads Europe in Dismantling Refugee Protection' (2001) 36 Texas Intl L Rev 231–250

Fullerton, M 'Inadmissible in Iberia: The Fate of Asylum Seekers in Spain and Portugal' (2005) 17 Intl J Refugee L 659–687

Gammeltoft-Hansen, T *Outsourcing Migration Management: EU, Power and Immigration Policy* DIIS Working paper No 1 2006

Gammeltoft-Hansen, T and Gammeltoft-Hansen, H 'The Right to Seek-Revisited: On the UN Human Rights Declaration Article 14 and Access to Asylum Procedures in the EU' (2008) 10 Eur J Migration & L 4, 439–459

Garlick, M 'The EU Discussions on Extraterritorial Processing: Solution or Conundrum?' (2006) 18 IJ Refugee L 3–4, 601–629

Geddes, A *The Politics of Migration and Immigration in Europe* (Sage 2003)

Geddes, A *Immigration and European Integration: Beyond fortress Europe?* (Manchester UP 2008)

Gent, S *The Root Causes of Migration: Criticising the Approach and Finding a Way Forward* Sussex Migration Working Paper No 11 2002, University of Sussex

Giakoumopoulos, C 'Detention of Asylum Seekers in the Light of Art 5 of the ECHR' in Hughes, J and Liebaut, F (eds) *Detention of Asylum Seekers in Europe: Analysis and Perspectives* (Kluwer 1998) 161–182

Gibney, M *Strangers or Friends: Principles for a New Alien Admission Policy* (Greenwood Press 1986)

Gil-Bazo, M 'Refugee Status and Subsidiary Protection under EC Law: The Qualification Directive and the Right to be Granted Asylum' in Baldaccini, A et al (eds), *Whose Freedom, Security and Justice? EU Immigration and Asylum Law and Policy* (Hart 2007) 229–264

Giuffre, M 'The European Union Readmission Policy after Lisbon' (2011) 1 Interdisciplinary Political Studies 0, 7–19

Giuffre, M 'Watered-Down Rights on the High Seas: *Hirsi Jamaa and Others v Italy* (2012)' (2012)61 ICLQ 3, 728–750

Global Detention Project *Ukraine: Detention Profile* (Global Detention Project December 2012)

Goldston, J 'Fighting Terrorism While Fighting Discrimination: Can Protocol No 12 Help?' in *Non-Discrimination as a Human Right* Seminar to mark the entry into force on Protocol 12 (Council of Europe, 2006)

Gonzáles-Enriques, C and Triandafyllidou, A 'Comparing the New Hosts of Southern Europe' (2009) 11 Eur J Migration and L 109–118

Goodwin-Gill, G *The Refugee in International Law* (OUP 1998)

Goodwin-Gill, G 'Article 31 of the 1951 Convention Relating the Status of Refugees: Non-Penalization, Detention and Protection' in Feller, E; Türk, V and Nicholson, F (eds) *Refugee Protection in International Law: UNHCR's Global Consultations on International Protection* (CUP 2003) 185–252

Goodwin-Gill, G 'Convention Relating to the Status of Refugees, Geneva, July 1951' (UN Audiovisual Library of Intl law). Available at: http://www.untreaty.un.org/cod/avl/ha/prsr/prsr.html (accessed 5 November 2012)

Goodwin-Gill, G 'The Right to Seek Asylum: Interception at Sea and the Principle of Non-Refoulement' in Jesuit Refugee Service *Safe and Secure: How Do Refugees Experience Europe's Borders?* (JRS-Europe 2011) 6

Goodwin-Gill, G and McAdam, J *The Refugee in International Law* (OUP 2007)

Goodwin-Gill, G and Lambert, H *The Limits of Transnational Law* (CUP 2010)

Goudappel, F and Raulus, H (eds) *The Future of Asylum in the European Union* (TMC Asser 2011)

Grahl-Madsen, A *The Status of Refugees in International Law* (AW Sitjhoff 1972)

Grahl-Madsen, A *Commentary on the Refugee Convention 1951: Article 2–11, 13–37* (1963, published by UNHCR, 1997)

Grant, H and Domokos, J 'Dublin Regulation Leaves Asylum Seekers with Their Fingers Burnt' *The Guardian* (7 October 2011). Available at: http://www.guardian.co.uk/world/2011/oct/07/dublin-regulation-european-asylum-seekers (accessed 28 March 2013)

Groenendijk, K; Guild, E and Carrera, S *Integration of Third Country Nationals and Illiberal Practices in the EU* (Ashgate 2009)

The Guardian 'Make Asylum Claims Fair Not Fast' (3 November 2004)

The Guardian 'Huge Detention Centre to Be Israel's Latest Weapon in Migration Battle' (17 April 2012)

Guild, E 'Seeking Asylum: Stormy Clouds between International Commitments and EU Legislative Measures' (2004) 29 EL Rev 2, 198–218

Guild, E 'The Europeanisation of Europe's Asylum Policy' (2006) 18 IJ Refugee L 3–4, 630

Guild, E *Security and Migration in the 21 Century* (Polity 2009)

Guild, E *Challenges and Prospects for the EU's Area of Freedoms, Security and Justice: Recommendations to the EC for the Stockholm Programme* CEPS Working Document No 313 April 2009

Guild, E 'The European Geography of Refugee Protection – Exclusions, Limitations and Exceptions from the 1967 Protocol to the Present' (2012) 4 EHRLR 413–426

Guiraudon, V 'Citizenship Rights for Non-citizens: France, Germany and Netherlands' in Joppke C (ed), *Challenges to the Nation-State* (OUP 1998) 272–318

Guiraudon, V 'European Integration and Migration Policy: Vertical Policy-Making as Venue Shopping' 2000 28 J of Common Market Studies 2, 251–271

Habermas, J 'Citizenship and National Identity: Some Reflections on the Future of Europe' (1992) 12 Praxis Intl 1, 1–19

Haddad, E 'The Refugee: forging National Identities' (2002) 2 Studies in Ethnicity and Nationalism 2, 23–38

Hailbronner, K 'The Concept of a "Safe Country" and Expeditious Asylum Procedures: A Western European Perspective (1993) 5 Intl J Refugee L, 31–65

Hailbronner, K. 'Asylum Law in the Context of a European Migration Policy' in Walker, N (ed), *Europe's Area of Freedom, Security and Justice* (OUP 2004) 41–88

Hamilton, C et al for UNICEF and the Children's Legal Centre *Administrative Detention of Children: A Global Report* Discussion Paper (UNICEF 2011)

Hammarberg, T 'The Dublin Regulations undermines Refugee Rights' 22 September 2010, Council of Europe Commissioner's Human Rights Comment

Hamood, S 'EU–Libya Cooperation on Migration: A Raw Deal for Refugees and Migrants?' (2008) 21 J Refugee Studies 1, 19–42

Handoll, J 'Directive 2003/9 on Reception Condition of Asylum Seekers: Ensuring "Mere Subsistence" or a Dignified Standard of Living?' in Baldaccini, A et al (eds) *Whose Freedom, Security and Justice? EU Immigration and Asylum Law and Policy* (Hart 2007) 195–228

Harrell-Bond, B 'Comments on "New Directions to Avoid Hard Problems"' (1995) 8 J Refugee Studies 3, 299–300

Harris, N 'Migration without Borders: Economic Perspectives' (UNESCO). Available at: www.unesco.org/most/migration/paper_n_harris.pdf

Harris, N *The New Untouchables* (Penguin 1996)

Harris, N *Thinking the Unthinkable: The Immigration Myth Exposed* (I.B. Tauris 2001)

Hartley-Parkinson, R 'How Can They Tell Us How to Run Our Country? Seven of Eleven Sitting at Europe's Human Rights Court Deciding Fate of Hate Preacher Qatada Have Never Been Judges' (Mail Online, 19 April 2012). Available at: http://www.dailymail.co.uk/news/article-2131955/Abu-Qatada-deportation-case-ECHR-judges-making-judgment-appeal-little-experience.html#ixzz2MmgoKkwI

Harvey, C 'The Right to Seek Asylum in the European Union' [2004] EHRLR 17–36

Hathaway, J 'A Reconsideration of the underlying Premise of Refugee Law' (1990) 31 Harvard Intl L J 129–183

Hathaway, J *The Law of Refugee Status* (Butterworths 1996)

Hathaway, J *Reconceiving International Refugee Law* (M Nijhoff 1997)

Hathaway, J 'What's in a Label' (2003) 5 Eur J Migration & L 1, 1–22

Hathaway, J *The Rights of Refugees under International Law* (CUP 2005)

Hathaway, J 'Why Refugee Law Still Matters' (2007) 8 Melb J Intl L 89–103

Hatton, T *Seeking Asylum in the OECD: Trends and Policies* (Centre for Economic Policy Research 2011)

Hayes, B and Vermeulen, M *Borderline: The EU's New Border Surveillance Initiatives* (Heinrich Böll Foundation June 2012)

Hayes, B '"Killing Me Softly?" Improving Access to Durable Solutions' Doublespeak and the Dismantling of Refugee Protection in the EU' (Statewatch July 2004) 4–5

Hayter, T *Open Borders: The Case against Immigration Controls* (Pluto 2000)

Helsinki Citizens' Assembly *Unwelcome Guests: The Detention of Refugees in Turkey's 'Foreigners' Guesthouses* (Helsinki Citizens Assembly, Refugee Advocacy & Support Program 2007)

Heisler, M and Layton-Henry, Z 'Migration and the Links between Social and Societal Security' in Weaver, O; Buznan, B; Kelstrup, M and Lemaitre, P *Identity, Migration and the New Security Agenda in Europe* (Pinter 2003) 148–166

Her Majesty's Inspector of Prisons *Inquiry into Allegations of Racism and Mistreatment of Detainees at Oakington Immigration Reception Centre and While under Escort* July 2005 (HMSO 2005)

Her Majesty's Inspector of Prisons *Report on the Unannounced Inspections of Five Non-Residential Short-Term Holding Facilities: Queen's Building and Terminals 1–4 Heathrow Airport* 10–13 October 2005 (HMSO 2005)

Her Majesty's Chief Inspector of Prisons *Report on A Short Follow-Up Inspection of Oakington Reception Centre* 5–7 June 2006 (HMSO 2006)

Her Majesty's Chief Inspector of *Prisons Report on Unannounced inspection of Harmondsworth Immigration Removal Centre* 17–21 July 2006 (HMSO 2006)

Hollifield, J 'Ideas, Institutions and Civil Society: On the Limits of Immigration in France' in Brochmann, G and Hammar, T (eds) *Mechanisms of Immigration Control, A Comparative Analysis of European Regulation Policies* (Berg 1999) 59–96

Home Affairs Select Committee Adhoc Meeting *The Work of the UK Border Agency and UK Border force* (15 May 2012). Available at: http://www.parliamentlive.tv/Main/Player.aspx?meetingId=10786&st=12:36:20 (accessed 16 July 2012)

Home Office *Control of Immigration: Quarterly Statistical Summary* Quarter 1, January–March 2011 (Home Office 2011)

Home Office *Immigration Statistics October– December 2012* (Home Office 2012). Available at: https://www.gov.uk/government/publications/immigration-statistics-october-to-december-2012/immigration-statistics-october-to-december-2012 (accessed 20 May 2013)

House of Commons Select Committee on European Union, *Minutes of Evidence Memorandum by HM Inspectorate of Prisons* 1 February 2006 (House of Commons 2006)

House of Commons Barbara Roche MP, House of Commons Debates 16 March 2000 Col 263W

House of Commons Debates 25 October 2001 Col 333W

House of Lords 'A Common EU Policy on Illegal Immigration' 37th Report 2001–2 UK House of Lords, Paper 187 (HMSO 2002)

House of Lords EU Committee 'Handling EU Asylum Claims. New Approaches Examined' 11th Report 2003–4 (HL paper 74 HMSO 2004)

House of Lords EU Select Committee 'Schengen Information System II' 9th Report 2006–7 HL Paper No 49 (HMSO 2007)

Hughes, J and Liebaut, F (eds) *Detention of Asylum Seekers in Europe: Analysis and Perspectives* (Kluwer 1998)

Human Rights Watch 'Managing Migration Means Potential EU Complicity in Neighbouring States' Abuse of Migrants and Refugees' Number 2 (Human Rights Watch October 2006)

Human Rights Watch *Pushed Back, Pushed Around: Italy's Forced Return of Boat Migrants and Asylum Seekers, Libya's Mistreatment of Migrants and Asylum Seekers* (Human Rights Watch 2009)

Human Rights Watch Interview with UNHCR, Kyiv 25 June 2010

Human Rights Watch *Buffeted in the Borderland* (Human Rights Watch 2010)

Human Rights Watch *Fast-Tracked Unfairness Detention and Denial of Women Asylum Seekers in the UK* (Human Rights Watch 2010)

Human Rights Watch 'Ukraine: Open Letter Regarding the Arbitrary Detention of Somali Asylum Seekers' (31 January 2012). Available at: http://www.hrw.org/news/2012/01/31/ukraine-open-letter-regarding-arbitrary-detention-somali-asylum-seekers (accessed 23 May 2013)

Human Rights Watch 'Israel: Amend Anti-Infiltration Law'. Available at: http://www.hrw.org/news/2012/06/10/israel-amend-anti-infiltration-law (accessed 13 May 2013)

Hungarian Helsinki Committee *Access to Protection Jeopardised-Information Note on the Treatment of Dublin Returnees in Hungary* (December 2011). Available at: http://www.unhcr.org/refworld/publisher,HHC,,,4f3e10ab2,0.html (accessed 1 November 2012)

Hurwitz, A *The Collective Responsibility of States to Protect Refugees* (OUP 2009)

Huysmans, J *The Politics of Insecurity: Fear, Immigration and Asylum in the EU* (Routledge 2006)

Independent Chief Inspector of the UK Border Agency *Asylum: A Thematic Inspection of the Detained Fast Track* (Home Office 2011)

ICAR (Information Centre about Asylum Seekers and Refugees) *Detention of Asylum Seekers in the UK* (ICAR 2007)

Inter-governmental Consultations *Working Paper on Reception in the Region of Origin* (IGC Geneva 1994)

Jacobson, D *Rights across Borders* (Johns Hopkins UP 1996)

Jesuit Refugee Service *Detention in Europe* (JRS October 2004)

Jesuit Refugee Service, Europe 'Dublin II: A Summary of JRS Experiences in Europe' (JRS 2008)

Jesuit Refugee Service Malta 'Do They Know? Asylum Seekers Testify to Life in Libya' (JRS December 2009)

Jesuit Refugee Service *Safe and Secure: How Do Refugees Experience Europe's Borders?* (JRS-Europe 2011)

Jesuit Refugee Service Europe *No Other Option* (JRS June 2011)

John-Hopkins, M 'The Emperor's New Safe Country Concepts: A UK Perspective on Sacrificing Fairness on the Altar of Efficiency' 2009 21 IJ Refugee L 2, 218–255

Joint Communique II (Developments in the Southern Mediterranean Region) Nicosia 19 April 2011. Full text available at: http://www.migrantsatsea.

wordpress.com/2011/04/21/cyprus-greece-italy-malta-spain-issue-joint-communique-regarding-response-to-north-african-migration (accessed 1 November 2012)

Jolley, R and Ketwala, S *Hopes and Fears* (British Future January 2012). Available at: http://www.britishfuture.org/articles/news/british-future-launches-hopes-and-fears-report (accessed 31 July 2013)

Joppke, C 'Asylum and State Sovereignty. A Comparison of the United States, Germany and Britain' in Joppke (ed) *Challenges to the Nation-State* (OUP 1998) 109–152

Joppke C (ed), *Challenges to the Nation-State* (OUP 1998)

Joseph, S; Mitchell, K and Gyorki, L *Seeking Remedies for Torture Victims: A Handbook on the Individual Complaints Procedures of the UN Treaty Bodies* (OMCT Series Handbook, UN 2006)

Kälin, W *Das Prinzip des Non-Refoulement: Das Verbot der Zuruckweisung, Asuweisung under Auslieferung von Flüchtingen, den Verfolgerstaat im Völkerrecht und im scweizerischen Landesrecht* (Peter Lang 1982)

Kälin, W 'Supervising the 1951 Refugee Convention and Beyond' in Feller, E; Türk, F and Nicholson, N (eds) *Refugee Protection in International Law: UNHCR Global Consultations on International Protection* (CUP 2003) 613–666

Kaye, R 'Defining the Agenda: British Refugee Policy and the Role of Parties' (1994) 7 J Refugee Studies 2/3, 144 –159

Kaye, R 'Redefining the Refugee: The Media Portrayal of Asylum Seekers' in Koser, K and Lutz, H *The New Migration in Europe: Social Constructions and Social Realities* (Palgrave 1998) 163–182

Kaunert, C. 'Liberty versus Security? EU Asylum Policy and the European Commission' (2009) 5 J of Contemporary Eur Research 2, 148–170

Kaunert, C and Léonard, S 'The EU Asylum Policy: Towards a Common Area of Protection and Solidarity?' in Wolff, S (ed) *Freedom, Security and Justice After Lisbon and Stockholm* (TMC Asser Press 2011) 79–95

Kaunert, C and Léonard, S 'The Development of the EU Asylum Policy: Venue-Shopping in Perspective' (2012) 19 J of Eur Public Policy 9, 1396–1413

Kern, S 'The Netherlands to Abandon Multiculturalism' (Gatestone Institute, 23 June 20011). Available at: http://www.gatestoneinstitute.org/2219/netherlands-abandons-multiculturalism

Kesby, A *The Right to Have Rights* (OUP 2012)

Kjaerum, M 'The Concept of Country of First Asylum' (1992) 4 Intl J Ref L 4, 514–530

Kneebone, S 'Outing Off-Shore Processing: The High Court of Australia Defines the Role of the Refugee Convention' (2012) 26 J IANL 2, 156–174

Kneebone, S '"Safe Third Country" Concept' in McAdam, J (ed) *Forced Migration, Human Rights and Security* (Hart 2008) 129–154

Kneebone, S *Refugees, Asylum-Seekers and the Rule of Law* (CUP 2009)

Koopmans, R 'Trade-offs between Equality and Difference: Immigrant Integration, Multiculturalism and the Welfare State in Cross-National Perspective' (2010) 36 J of Ethnic and Migration Studies 1, 1–41

Koser, K 'Why Migrant Smuggling Pays (2008) 46 Intl Migration 2, 3–26

Koser, K and Lutz, H *The New Migration in Europe: Social Constructions and Social Realities* (Palgrave 1998)

Koser, K and Pinkerton, C *The Social Networks of Asylum Seekers and the Dissemination of Information About Countries of Asylum* (Migration Research Unit, University College London 2002)

Koslowski, R 'The Mobility Money Can Buy: Human Smuggling and Border Control in the EU' in Andreas, P and Snyder, T (eds) *The Wall Around the West* (Rowman & Littlefield 2000) 203–218

Kritz, M 'Population Growth and International Migration: Is There a Link' in Zolberg, A and Benda, P (eds) *Global Migrants, Global Refugees: Problems and Solutions* (Berghahn Books 2001) 19–41

Kumin, J 'Asylum in Europe: Sharing or Shifting the Burden?' in UNHCR *World Refugee Survey* (1995)

Kymlicka, W *Multiculturalism: Success, Failure and the Future* (Migration Policy Institute February 2012)

Laczko, F *Recent Trends in Irregular Migration in Europe* (International Organization for Migration 2012)

Lahav, G 'Migration and Security: The Role of Non-State Actors and Civil Liberties in Liberal Democracies' (United Nations, Population Division, New York: UN/Pop/Mig/2003). Available at: http://www.un.org/esa/population/publications/secoord2003/secoord.htm

Lahav, G and Guiraudon, V 'Comparative Perspectives on Border Control: Away from the Border and outside the State' in Andreas, P and Snyder, T (eds) *The Wall around the West* (Rowman & Littlefield, 2000) 55–80

Lambert, H 'Protection Against Refoulement from Europe: Human Rights Law Comes to the Rescue' (1999) 48 Int & Comp L Q 3 515–544

Lambert, H 'The European Convention on Human Rights and the Protection of Refugees: Limits and Opportunities' (2005) 4 J Refugee Studies Q 2, 39–55

Landgren, K 'Comments on the UNHCR Position on Detention of Refugees and Asylum Seekers' in Hughes, J and Liebaut, F (eds) *Detention of Asylum Seekers in Europe: Analysis and Perspectives* (Kluwer 1998) 141–160

Lauterpacht, H *International Law and Human Rights* (Stevens & Sons 1950)

Lauterpacht, E and Bethlehem, D 'The Scope and Content of the Principle of Non-Refoulement: Opinion' in Feller, E; Türk, V and Nicholson, F (eds) *Refugee Protection in International Law: UNHCR's Global Consultations on International Protection* (CUP, 2003) 87–177

Lavenex, S 'Passing the Buck: EU Refugee Policies towards Central and Eastern Europe' (1998) 11 J of Refugee Studies 2, 126–145

Lavenex, S 'The External Face of Europeanization: Third Countries and International Organizations' in Faist, T and Ette, A (eds) *The Europeanization of National Policies and Politics of Immigration: Between Autonomy and the European Union* (Palgrave Macmillan 2007) 246–264

Lavenex, S *Safe Third Countries: Extending the EU Asylum and Immigration Policies to Central and Eastern Europe* (Central European UP 1999)

Lazarus, L 'Securing Rights of Securitising Rights?' in Dickinson, R; Katselli, E; Murray, C and Pedersen, O *Examining Critical Perspectives on Human Rights* (CUP 2012) 87–106

Legomsky, S 'Immigration, Equality and Diversity' (1993) 31 Columbia J Transnational L 319–335

Legomsky, S 'Immigration, Minorities and Pluralism: What Kind of Society Do We Really Want?' (1998) 6 Willamette J of Intl and Dispute Resolution 153–161

Legomsky, S 'Secondary Refugee Movements and the Return of Asylum Seekers to Third Countries: The Meaning of Effective Protection' (2003) 15 Intl J Refugee L 4, 567–677

Legomsky, S 'Learning to Live with Unequal Justice: Asylum and the Limits to Consistency' (2007) 60 Stan L Rev 413–474

Leitner, H 'Reconfiguring the Spatiality of Power: The Construction of a Supranational Migration Framework for the European Union' (1997) 16 Political Geography 2, 123

Lenart, J '"Fortress Europe": Compliance of the Dublin II Regulation with the European Convention for the Protection of Human Rights and Fundamental Freedoms' (2012) 28 Merkourios – Intl and Eur Migration L 75, 4–19

Levy, C 'The European Union after 9/11: The Demise of a Liberal Democratic Asylum Regime?' (2005) 40 Government and Opposition 1, 26–59

Lewis, M *Warm Welcome? Understanding Public Attitudes to Asylum Seekers in Scotland* (Institute of Public Policy Research 2006)

Lillich, R *The Human Rights of Aliens in Contemporary International Law* (Manchester UP 1984)

Lindstrøm, C *European Union Policy on Asylum and Immigration: Addressing the Root Causes of Forced Migration: A Justice and Home Affairs Policy of Freedom, Security and Justice?* (2005) 39 Social Policy and Administration 6, 587–605

Lis, J 'Knesset Passes Bill That Could Put Asylum Seekers in Jail without Trial' Haaretz 10 January 2012

Loescher, G 'The European Community and Refugees' (1989) 65 Intl Affairs 617–636

Loescher, G 'Protection and Humanitarian Action in the Post-Cold War Era' in Zolberg, A and Benda, P *Global Migrants, Global Refugees: Problems and Solutions* (Berghahn Books 2001) 171–205

Loescher, G 'The UNHCR and World Politics: State Interests Versus Institutional Autonomy' (2001) 35 Intl Migration Rev 33–56

Losi, N and Strang, *Intagraref: Local Communities and Refugees, Fostering Social Integration:* Project Report (Institute for International Health and Development 2008). Available at: http://www.eresearch.qmu.ac.uk/1240 (accessed 18 June 2013)

Lubbers, R 'Lubbers Calls for EU Asylum Laws Not to Contravene International Law' (UNHCR Press Release 29.2004). Available at: http://www.unhcr.org/40645bd77.html

Lynn, N and Lea, S 'A Phantom Menace and the New Apartheid': Social Construction of Asylum Seekers in the UK' (2003) 14 Discourse Society 425–452

Make Borders History 'No Border Camp: Ukraine' (August 2007)

Maley, W 'Asylum-Seekers in Australia's International Relations' (2003) 57Aust J Intl Affairs 187–202

Marin, L 'Policing the EU's External Borders: A Challenge for the Rules of Law and Fundamental Rights in the Area of Freedom, Security and Justice? An Analysis of Frontex Joint Operations at the Southern Maritime Border' (2011) 7 J of Contemporary Eur Research 4, 468–487

Marr, D and Wilkinson, M *Dark Victory* (Allen & Unwin 2003)

Martin, M 'The Arab Spring and the Death Toll in the Mediterranean: The True Face of Fortress Europe' (Statewatch Analysis, January 2012). Available at: http://www.statewatch.org/analyses/no-167-arab-spring-med.pdf (accessed 20 March 2013)

Marx, R 'Non-Refoulement, Access to Procedures and Responsibility for Determining Refugee Status' (1999) 7 Intl J Refugee L 383–406

McAdam, J *Forced Migration, Human Rights and Security* (Hart 2008)

McDonough and Tsourdi 'Putting Solidarity to the Test: Assessing Europe's Response to the Asylum Crisis in Greece' New Issues in Refugee Research, Research Paper No 231 (UNHCR 2012)

Medical Justice 'State Sponsored Cruelty: Children in Immigration Detention' (Medical Justice 2010). Available at: http://www.medicaljustice.org.uk/content/view/1420/89 (accessed 23 April 2013)

Medical Justice *Outsourcing Abuse* (Medical Justice 14 July 2008)

Medical Justice *The Second Torture* (Medical Justice 2012)

The Migration Observatory 'Migration to the UK: Asylum' (Briefing, 13 February 2013). Available at: http://www.migrationobservatory.ox.ac.uk/briefings/migration-uk-asylum (accessed 18 February 2013)

Miller, D 'Conclusion: A Theory of Virtualism' in Carrier, J and Miller, D (eds) *Virtualism: A New Political Economy* (Berg 1998) 202

Milner, J 'Recent Developments in International Resettlement Policy: Implications for the UK Programme' in Gelthorpe, V and Herlitz, L (eds) *Listening to the Evidence: The Future of UK Resettlement* (Home Office 2003)

Mink, J 'EU Asylum Law and Human Rights Protection: Revisiting the Principle of *Non-Refoulement* and the Prohibition of Torture and Other forms of Ill-Treatment' (2012) 14 Eur J Migation & L 2, 119–149

Mitsilegas, V 'The Directive on the Reception of Asylum Seekers and Its Implementation in the UK' (1996) 20 IANL 1, 42–45

Mitsilegas, 'Measuring Irregular Migration: Implications for Law, Policy and Human Rights' in Szyszczak, E et al (eds) *Irregular Migration and Human Rights* (M Nijhoff 2004) 29–39

Mitsilegas, V 'A "Common" EU Immigration and Asylum Policy: National and Institutional Constraints' in Shah, P (ed) *The Challenge of Asylum to Legal Systems* (Cavendish 2005)125–144

Mitsilegas, V 'Border Security in the EU' in Baldaccini, A et al (eds) *Whose Freedom, Security and Justice? EU Immigration and Asylum Law and Policy* (Hart 2007) 359–394

Mole, N 'Asylum and the European Convention on Human Rights' (2007) 9 Human Rights Files 12. Available at: http://www.unhcr.org/refworld/pdfid/4ee9b0972.pdf (accessed 16 November 2012)

Mole, N and Harby, C *Immigration, Asylum and Detention* (ECRE, AIRE Centre June 2004)

Monar, J 'Justice and Home Affairs in the Treaty of Amsterdam: Reform at the Price of Fragmentation' (1998) 23 EL Rev 320–335

Morano-Foadi, S and Andreadakis, S 'The Convergence of the European Legal System in the Treatment of Third Country Nationals in Europe: The ECJ and ECtHR Jurisprudence' (2011) 22 Eur J Intl L 4, 1071–1088

Morehouse, C and Blomfield, M 'Irregular Migration in Europe' (Migration Policy Institute 2011)

Moreno Lax, V 'Must EU Borders have Doors for Refugees? On the Compatibility of Schengen Visas and Carriers' Sanctions with EU Member States' Obligations to Provide International Protection to Refugees' (2008)10 Eur J Migration & L 315–364

Moreno-Lax, V 'Seeking Asylum in the Mediterranean: Against a Fragmentary Reading of EU Member States' Obligations Accruing at Sea' (2011) 23 Intl J Refugee L 174–220

Morgades S 'The Externalisation of the Asylum Function in the European Union' (2002) 4 GRITIM Working Paper Series 18

Mori 'Attitudes towards Refugee and Asylum Seekers: A Survey of Public Opinion' (Mori 2002)

Morrison, J and Crossland, B 'The Trafficking and Smuggling of Refugees: The End Game in European Asylum Policy' (UNHCR 2000)

Noll, G *Negotiating Asylum: The EU Acquis, Extraterritorial Protection and the Common Market of Deflection* (M Nijhoff 2000)

Noll, G 'Protection in A Spirit of Solidarity?' in Byrne, R; Noll, G and Vedsted-Hansen, J (eds) *New Asylum Countries? Migration Control and Refugee Protection in an Enlarged European Union* (Kluwer 2002)305–324

Noll, G 'Risky Games? A Theoretical Approach to Burden-Sharing in the Asylum Field' (2003) 16 J Refugee Studies 236–252

Noll, G 'Visions of the Exceptional: Legal and Theoretical Issues Raised by Transit Processing Centres and Protection Zones' (2003) 5 Eur J Migration & L 3, 303–341

Noll, G 'From "Protective Passports" to Protected Entry Procedures? The Legacy of Raoul Wallenberg in the Contemporary Asylum Debate' New Issues in Refugee Research (UNHCR Working Paper 99, December 2003)

Noll, G 'Seeking Asylum at Embassies: A Right to Entry under International Law' (2005) 17 Intl J Refugee L 3, 542–573

Noll, G 'Why Refugees Still Matter: A Response to Hathaway' (2007) 8 Melb J Intl L 536, 89–103

Noll, G; Fagerlund, J and Liebaut, F *Study on the Feasibility of Processing Asylum Claims outside the EU against the Background of the Common European Asylum System and the Goal of a Common Asylum Procedure* (European Community 2002)

Norwegian Refugee Council *Report on the Protection of Internally Displaced Persons, Asylum Seekers and Refugees from Chechnya* (Norwegian Refugee Council April 2005)

Nowak, M *UN Covenant on Civil and Political Rights – CCPR Commentary* (Engel Verlag, Kehl am Rhein 1993)

Nowak, M Interview 'Today Programme' BBC Radio 4 (4 March 2005)

Oakley, S 'Accelerated Procedures for Asylum in the EU: Fairness versus Efficiency' (Sussex Migration Working Paper No 43 University of Sussex, 2007)

O'Dowd, J 'Mutual Recognition in European Immigration Policy' in Goudappel, F and Raulus, H *The Future of Asylum in the European Union* (TMC Asser 2011)73–110

O'Nions, H *Minority Rights Protection in International Law: The Roma of Europe* (Ashgate 2007)

O'Nions, H 'No Right to Liberty: The Detention of Asylum Seekers for Administrative Convenience' (2008) 10 Eur J Migration & L 2, 149–185

O'Nions, H 'What Lies Beneath: Exploring Links between Hate Crime and Asylum Policy in the UK' (2011) 31 Liverpool L Rev 3, 233–257

Oxfam GB *Comment on the Communication from Commission to Council and the European Parliament on the Regional Protection Programmes* (Oxfam 16 October 2005)

Pécoud, A and Guchteneire, P 'Migration without Borders: An Investigation into the Free Movement of People' *Global Migration Perspectives* No 27 (2005)

Pécoud, A and Guchteneire, P 'International Migration, Border Controls and Human Rights: Assessing the Relevance of a Right to Mobility' (2006) 21 J of Borderlands Studies 1, 69–86

Peers, S 'Legislative Update: E Immigration and Asylum Competence and Decision-Making after the Treaty of Lisbon' (2008) 10 Eur J Migration & L 2, 219–247

Peers, S 'Key Legislative Developments on Migration in the EU: SIS II' (2008) 10 Eur J Migration &L 1, 77–104

Peers, S *EU Justice and Home Affairs Law* (OUP 2011)

Peers 'Revised EU Asylum Proposals: "Lipstick on a Pig"' (Statewatch Analysis, June 2011)

Peers, S 'The Frontex Regulation – Consolidated Text After 2011 Amendments' (Statewatch). Available at: http://www.statewatch.org/analyses/no-140-frontex-reg-text.pdf

Peers, S 'The Revised "Dublin" Rules on Responsibility for Asylum-Seekers: A Missed Opportunity' (Statewatch Analysis, June 2012). Available at: www.statewatch.org/analyses/no-173-dublin-III.pdf (accessed 28 March 2013)

Peers, S and Rogers, N (eds) *EU Immigration and Asylum Law Text and Commentary* (M Nijhoff 2006)

Penelope, M 'Resolution 1373: A Call to Pre-Empt Asylum Seekers? (or 'Osama' the Asylum Seeker) in McAdam, J (ed) *Forced Migration, Human Rights and Security* (Hart 2008) 19–62

Phillips, J and Spinks, H 'Background Note: Boat Arrivals in Australia since 1976' Dept of Parliamentary Services, Parliament of Australia (15 July 2011)

Phuong, C 'Protecting Refugees in the Context of Immigration Controls' in Shah, P (ed) *The Challenge of Asylum to Legal Systems* (Cavendish 2005) 33–52

Phuong, C 'Building a Community Return Policy with Third Countries: An Equal Partnership?' in Baldaccini, A et al (eds) *Whose Freedom, Security and Justice? EU Immigration and Asylum Law and Policy* (Hart 2007) 337–358

Pieterse, JN 'Fictions of Europe' (1991) 32 Race and Class 1–10

Pirjola, J 'European Asylum Policy – Inclusions and Exclusions under the Surface of Universal Human Rights Language' (2009) 11 Eur J Migration L 4, 347–366

Pourgourides, C 'The Mental Health Implications of the Detention of Asylum Seekers' in Hughes, J and Liebaut, F (eds) *Detention of Asylum Seekers in Europe: Analysis and Perspectives* (Kluwer 1998) 199–212

Power, M *The Audit Explosion* (Demos 1994)

Power, P 'Australian Attitudes to the Acceptance of Refugees' at 'Racism Revisited' Anti-Racism Leadership and Practice Conference, Murdoch University, Perth, 20 March 2010

Price, M *Rethinking Asylum: History, Purpose and Limits* (CUP 2009)

Pro Asyl *Walls of Shame: Accounts from the Inside: The Detention Centres of Evros* (April 2012). Available at: http://www.infomobile.w2eu.net/files/2012/04/Evros-Bericht_12_04_10_BHP.pdf (accessed 10 July 2013)

Puffett, N 'Anger as Hundreds of Children Deported Alone under EU Rules'(Children and Young People Now, UK National Children's Bureau, 22 June 2010)

Pugh, M 'Drowning Not Waving: Boat People and Humanitarianism at Sea' (2004) 17 J Refugee Studies 66, 50–69

Raitio, J 'A Few Remarks to Evaluate the Dublin System' in Goudappel, F and Raulus, H (eds) *The Future of Asylum in the European Union: Problems, Proposals and Human Rights* (Springer 2011)111–123

Ramji-Nogales, J; Schoenholtz, A and Schrag, P 'Refugee Roulette: Disparities in Asylum Adjudication' (2007) 60 Stan L Rev 295–410

Rawls, J *A Theory of Justice* (Harvard UP 1971)

Refugee Action 'National Asylum Charity Calls for Legal Aid Reform and Greater Access to Justice' (Press Release, 6 August 2012). Available at: http://www.refugee-action.org.uk/news/2012/legalaidreform.aspx (accessed 26 March 2013)

Refugee Council 'Helping Others is part of the British DNA' Press Release (Refugee Council 18 April 2011)

Reslow, N 'The Role of Third Countries in EU Migration Policy: The Mobility Partnerships' (2012) 14 Eur J Migration & L, 4 393–415

Rettman, A 'EU-Ukraine Relations Hit Visa Bump' (EU Observer, 2 October 2006)

Riley, J *Let Them In: The Case for Open Borders* (Penguin Group 2008)

Robinson, V and Segrott, J *Understanding the Decision-Making of Asylum Seekers* (Home Office Research Study 243 2002)

Rodrik, D 'Feasible Globalisations' (Faculty Research Working Papers Series 2029, John F Kennedy School of Government, Harvard University, 2002)

Ronzitti, N 'The Treaty on Friendship, Partnership and Cooperation between Italy and Libya: New Prospects for Cooperation in the Mediterranean?' (2009) 1 Bulletin of Italian Politics 1, 125

Samers, M 'An Emerging Geopolitics of "Illegal" Immigration' (2004) 6 Eur J Migration & L 1, 27–45

Schmeidl, S 'Conflict and Forced Migration: A Quantitative Review 1964–1995' in Zolberg, A and Benda, P (eds) *Global Migrants, Global Refugees: Problems and Solutions* (Berghahn Books 2001) 62–94

Schmitt, C *The Concept of the Political* (University of Chicago Press 1932; reprinted 1996)

Schuck, P 'Refugee Burden-Sharing: A Modest Proposal' (1997) 22 Yale J Intl L 244–297

Schuster, L 'A Comparative Analysis of the Asylum Policy of Seven European Governments' (2000) 13 J of Refugee Studies 1, 118–133

Sen, A 'Population: Delusion and Reality' (1994) 41 New York Review of Books, 15

Shah, P (ed) *The Challenge of Asylum to Legal Systems* (Cavendish 2005)

Simeon, JC 'A Comparative Analysis of the Response of the UNHCR and Industrialised States to Rapidly Fluctuating Refugee Status and Asylum Applications: Lessons and Best Practise for RDS Systems Design and Administration' (2010) 22 Intl J Refugee L 1, 72–103

Singer, P and Singer, R 'The Ethics of Refugee Policy' in Gibney, M (ed) *Open Borders? Closed Societies?* (Greenwood 1988) 112–130

Sivandan, A *Communities of Resistance – Writings on Black Struggles for Socialism* (Verso 1990)

Smith, M 'Warehousing Refugees: A Denial of Rights, A Waste of Humanity' in UN *World Refugee Survey* (2004)

Soguk, N *States and Strangers: Refugees and Displacement of Statecraft* (University of Minnesota Press 1999)

Stana, R 'Testimony before the Subcommittee on Border and Maritime Security, Committee on Homeland Security, House of Representatives' (Border Security Preliminary Observations on the Status of Key Southwest Border Technology Programs, US Government Accountability Office GAO-11-448T). Available at: http://www.gao.gov/products/GAO-11-448T (accessed 7 November 2012)

Statewatch 'EU Buffer States and the UNHCR 'Processing' Centres and 'Safe Havens' (2003) 3 Statewatch Bulletin 2

Statewatch News 'EU Divided over List of "Safe Countries of Origin" – *Statewatch* calls for the list to be scrapped' (Statewatch, September 2004)

Statewatch News 'A Drop of Fundamental Rights in An Ocean of Unaccountability: Frontex in the Process of Implementing Article 26(a)' (15 May 2012). Available at: http://www.statewatch.org/news/2012/may/02-eu-frontex-article26a.html (accessed 3 July 2012)

Statewatch News 'Council Text of Revised Dublin Rules' (April 2012). Available at: http://www.statewatch.org/analyses/no-173-dublin-III.pdf (accessed 28 March 2013)

Statewatch Analysis 'The EU Directive on Reception Conditions: A Weak Compromise' (Statewatch July 2012)

Statewatch Analysis 'The Revised Directive on Asylum-Seekers' Reception Conditions: The Member States Hit Rock-Bottom' (Statewatch, March 2012)

Statewatch News 'Court Annuls Afghan's Dublin II Return to Hungary' (28 June 2012). Available at: http://www.database.statewatch.org/article.asp?aid=31658 (accessed 1 November 2012)

Statewatch News 'Political Agreement on Mobility Partnership: Towards the First Readmission Agreement with An African Country?' (Statewatch, 7 March 2013)

Stefanelli, J N 'Whose Rule of Law? An Analysis of the UK's Decision Not to Opt-in to the EU Asylum Procedures and Reception Conditions Directives' [2011] ICLQ 4, 1055–1064

Stefanelli, J 'A Rule of Law Analysis of the Potential UK Opt-In to the Newly Tabled EU Asylum

Procedures and Reception Conditions Directives' (Bingham Centre for the Rule of Law 2012) Available at: http://www.biicl.org/binghamcentre/eu_asylum (accessed 9 April 2013)

Steiner, N *Arguing about Asylum: The Complexity of Refugee Debates in Europe* (St. Martin's Press 2000)

Stevens, D *UK Asylum Law and Policy* (Sweet & Maxwell 2004)

Stevens, D 'Asylum Seekers in the New Europe: Time for A Re-Think?' in Shah, P (ed) *The Challenge of Asylum to Legal Systems* (Cavendish 2005) 13–33

Storey, H 'Legislative Comment. EU Refugee Qualification Directive: A Brave New World?' (2008) 20 Intl J Refugee L 1, 1–49

Straw, J 'Towards a Common Asylum Procedure' European Conference on Asylum, Lisbon 16 June 2000

Strik, T 'Lives Lost in the Mediterranean Sea: Who is Responsible?' Council of Europe Parliamentary Assembly Migration Committee 29 March 2012 (Council of Europe 2012)

Sullivan, E et al *Testing Community Supervision for the INS: An Evaluation of the Appearance Assistance Program Vera Institute of Justice* (2000 8). Available at: http://www.vera.org/pubs/testing-community-supervision-ins-evaluation-appearance-assistance-program (accessed 22 April 2013)

Sunday Times, Malta 'No Frontex Mission around Malta' (15 May 2011). Available at: http://www.timesofmalta.com/articles/view/20110515/local/No-Frontex-mission-around-Malta.365397 (accessed 18 January 2012)

Sunderland, J *Hate on the Streets* (Human Rights Watch July 2012)

Symes, M and Jorro, P *Asylum Law and Practice* (Bloomsbury Professional 2010)

Taylor, S 'Offshore Barriers to Asylum Seeker Movement: The Exercise of Power without Responsibility' in McAdam, J (ed) *Forced Migration, Human Rights and Security* (Hart 2008) 93–128

Taylor, D 'Britain's Still Locking Up Children' *The Guardian* (23 October 2012)

Teitelbaum, M 'Rights versus Right: Immigration and Refugee Policy in the United States' (1980) 59 foreign Affairs 2–59

Thrändhart, D 'The Political Uses of Xenophobia in England, France and Germany' (1995) 1 Party Politics 3 323–345

Thränhardt, D 'Germany's Immigration Policies and Politics' in Brochmann, G and Hammar T (eds) *Mechanisms of Immigration Control: A Comparative Analysis of European Regulation Policies* (Berg 1999) 29–58

Thielemann, E and El-Enany, N 'Beyond fortress Europe? How European Cooperation Strengthens Refugee Protection' Paper presented at the EU Studies Association's 11th Biennial International Conference, Marina Del Rey Los Angeles, 23–25 April 2009

Tondini, M 'Fishers of Men? The Interception of Migrants in the Mediterranean Sea and Their Forced Return to Libya' (INEX Paper October 2010 Ministry of Interior, Italian Initiatives: Security, Immigration, Asylum, Rome, 14 April 2010) 27. Available at: http://www.interno.it/mininterno/export/sites/default/it/assets/files/19/0844_opuscolo_engl_def.pdf

Tootell, Hughes and Petrasek 'The Relevance of Key UN Instruments for Detained Asylum Seekers' in Hughes, J and Liebaut, F (eds) *Detention of Asylum Seekers in Europe: Analysis and Perspectives* (Kluwer 1998) 183–198

Toshkov, D and de Haan, L 'The Europeanization of Asylum Policy: An Assessment of the EU Impact on Asylum Applications and Recognitions Rates' (2013) 20 J of Eur Public Policy 5, 661–683

Travis, A 'UK Border Agency Computer Failure Leaves Thousands Unable to Travel' *The Guardian* (3 May 2012)

Travis, A 'Torture Victims Held in UK Immigration Detention Centres Launch Legal Action' Guardian Online (22 May 2012)

Trupiano, F Speech before the Italian Parliament's Schengen Committee, Rome (13 October 2009). Available at: http://www.camera.it/_dati/leg16/lavori/stenbic/30/2009/1013/s000r.htm?campo=/_bicamerali/leg15/schengen/resoconti/leg15fr.htm

UK Border Agency *Asylum Performance Measures* (Home Office 2010)

UK Cabinet Office *Migration: An Economic and Social Analysis* (Cabinet Office 1999)

UK Select Committee on Home Affairs 2nd Report *Detention and Removal* (HMSO 2004) part 6

UK Parliamentary Joint Committee on Human Rights *Government Response to the Committee's Tenth Report of This Session: The Treatment of Asylum Seekers* 17th Report of Session 2006–7 HL Paper 134

UK Home Office *Operational Enforcement Manual* (Home Office)

US Committee for Refugees and Migrants *Word Refugee Survey 2006* (US State Dept 2006)

US Dept of State 'Ukraine: Country Report on Human Rights Practices' US 6 March 2007 (US State Dept 2007)

Vachudová, MA 'Eastern Europe as Gatekeeper: The Immigration and Asylum Policies of an Enlarging EU' in Andreas, T and Snyder, P (eds) *The Wall around the West* (Rowman & Littlefield, 2000) 153–172

Van Amersfoot, H 'Migration Control and Minority Policy: The Case of the Netherlands' in Brochmann, G and Hammar, T (eds) *Mechanisms of Immigration Control: A Comparative Analysis of European Regulation Policies* (Berg 1999)135–168

Van Dijk, T *Racism and the Press* (Routledge 1991)

Van Helden, WJ; Van Dorst, PC and Hendriksen, KE 'No Entry: Investigation of the Registration of Foreign Nationals in the Schengen Information System and the Provision of Information in This Connection' Report No 2010/115 17 June 2010, National Ombudsman Netherlands

Van Liempt, I *Navigating Borders – Inside Perspectives on the Process of Human Smuggling into the Netherlands* (Amsterdam UP 2007)

Van Selm, J 'The High Level Working Group: Can foreign Policy, Development Policy and Asylum and Immigration Policy Really Be Mixed?' Paper presented at Conference WIDER, UN University Conference Tampere, 2002

Van der Valk, I 'Right-Wing Parliamentary Discourse on Immigration in France' (2003) 14 Discourse Society 309–348

Vedsted-Hansen, J 'Conditions and Criteria for Determining Asylum' in Goudappel, F and Raulus, H (eds) *The Future of Asylum in the European Union* (TMC Asser 2011), 139–156

Veelke D, 'Expulsion of Illegal Residents (Aliens) with Medical Problems and Article 3 of the European Convention of Human Rights' (2006) 13 Eur J Health L 313–319

Veenkamp, T; Bentley, T and Buofino, A 'People Flow: Managing Migration in a New European Commonwealth' (Demos 2003)

Verkuyten, M 'Immigration Discourses and Their Impact on Multiculturalism: A Discursive and Experimental Study' (2005) 44 Brit J Social Psychology 223–140

Verkuyten, M; De Jong, W and Masson, C 'The Construction of Ethnic Categories: Discourses of Ethnicity in the Netherlands' (1995) 18 Ethnic and Racial Studies 2, 251–276

Vink, M *Limits of European Citizenship: European Integration and Domestic Immigration Policies* (Palgrave Macmillan 2005)

Vrecer, N 'Living in Limbo: Integration of Forced Migrants from Bosnia and Herzegovina in Slovenia' (2010) 23 J Refugee Studies 4, 484–502

Waever, O; Buznan, B; Kelstrup, M and Lemaitre, P *Identity, Migration and the New Security Agenda in Europe* (Pinter 1993)

Walters, W 'The Power of Inscription: Beyond Social Construction and Deconstruction' (2002) 31 Millennium Eur Integration Studies 1, 83–101

Walzer, M *Spheres of Justice: A Defence of Pluralism and Equality* (Martin Robertson 1983)

Waters, T Assessing the Impact of the Rwandan Refugee Crisis on Development Planning in Rural Tanzania, 1994–1996' (1999) 58 Human Organisation 2, 142–152

Weber, L and Gelsthorpe, L *Deciding to Detain: How Decisions to Detain Asylum-Seekers Are Made at Points of Entry* Cambridge Institute of Criminology 2002

Weinar, A 'EU Cooperation Challenges in External Migration' Research Report EU-US Immigration Systems 2011/12 (European University Institute 2011)

Weis, P *The Refugee Convention, 1951: The Travaux Préparatoires Analyzed with a Commentary by Dr. Paul Weis* (CUP, 1995)

West Africa Democracy Radio 'Senegal Appeals to Mauritanian Refugees to End Hunger Strike' (9 July 2012)

White, S *Equality* (Polity 2007)

Wilkes, R; Guppy, N and Farris, L 'Comment on Semyonov, Raijman, and Gorodzeisky, SR, June 2006: Right-Wing Parties and Anti-Foreigner Sentiment in Europe' (2007) 72 American Sociological Rev 5, 831–840

Wilkes, R; Guppy, N and Farris, L 'Usual suspects? Public Views about Immigrants' Impact on Crime in European Countries' (2011) 52 Intl J Comp Sociology 114–131

Wilkinson, R 'Europe: The Debate Over Detention' *Refugees* Magazine (UNHCR Issue 113)

Wilsher, D *Immigration Detention: Law, History, Politics* (CUP 2012)

Woods, T and McAdam, J 'Australian Asylum Policy All at Sea: An Analysis of *Plaintiff M70/2011 v Minister for Immigration and Citizenship* and the Australia–Malaysia Arrangement' (2012) 61 ICLQ 1, 274–300

Wouters, K *International Legal Standards for the Protection from Refoulement* (Intersentia 2009)

Wouters, K and Den Heijer, M 'The Marine 1 Case: A Comment' (2010) 22 Intl J Refugee L 1, 1–19

Young, H; Osman, A; Aklilu, Y; Dale, R and Badri, R *Darfur: Livelihoods under Siege* (Finstein International Famine Centre 2005)

Young, S *Beyond Rawls: An Analysis of the Concept of Political Liberalism* (UP of America, 2002)

Zahn, R 'The EU Lisbon Treaty: What Implications for Anti-Racism?' (European Network Against Racism 2009)

Zieck, M 'Vanishing Points of the Refugee Law Regime' (2005) 1 Ohio J on Dispute Resolution 217–248

Zolberg, A 'The Next Waves: Migration Theory for A Changing World' (1989) 23 Intl Migration Rev 3, 424

Zolberg, A 'The Archaeology of Remote Control' in Fahrmeir, A; Faron, O and Weil, P (eds) *Migration Control in the North Atlantic World: The Evolution of State Practices in Europe and the US: From the French Revolution to the Inter-War Period* (Berghahn Books 2003) 195–222

Zolberg, A and Benda, P (eds) *Global Migrants, Global Refugees: Problems and Solutions* (Berghahn Books 2001)

International Legal Materials

League of Nations

League of Nations, Convention Relating to the International Status of Refugees, 28 October 1933, League of Nations, Treaty Series vol CLIX No 3663

UN

UN Charter 26 June 1945, 59 Stat 1031, TS 993, 3 Bevans 1153, entered into force 24 October 1945

UN GA Universal Declaration of Human Rights, General Assembly Resolution 217 (III) of 10 December 1948 United Nations Economic and Social Council, Summary Record of the twentieth meeting, Ad Hoc Committee on Statelessness and Related Problems, First Session, United Nations doc E/AC 32/SR 20 (1950) 55

Final Act of the UN Conference of Plenipotentiaries on the Status of Refugees and Stateless Persons, Geneva 25 July 1951, D. Available at: http://www.unhcr.org/40a8a7394.html (accessed 12 March 2013)

UN Commission on Human Rights on *Right to Be Free From Arbitrary Arrest, Detention and Exile* 1964 UN Doc E/CN 4/826/Rev1 23–30

UN GA Declaration on Territorial Asylum, GA res 2312 (XXII), 22 UN GAOR Supp (No 16) 81, UN Doc A/6716 (1967)

Vienna Convention on the Law of Treaties May 1969. Entered into force on 27 January 1980. United Nations, Treaty Series, vol 1155, 331

UN Office of the Human Rights Commissioner Optional Protocol to the International Covenant on Civil and Political Rights Adopted and opened for signature, ratification and accession by General Assembly Resolution 2200A (XXI) of 16 December 1966 entry into force 23 March 1976

Human Rights Committee General Comment No 8 *Right to Liberty and Security of Persons* (Art 9) (30 June 1982)

Human Rights Committee *General Comment* No 31 (1984)

UN Convention against Torture and Other Cruel, Inhuman or Degrading Treatment of Punishment UN Treaty United Nations, Treaty Series, vol 1465, 85 (26 June 1987)

United Nations *Convention on the Rights of the Child* 1989 *Treaty Series* vol 1577, 3

UN Office of the High Commissioner for Human Rights *General Comment* 20 (10 March 1992)

UN High Commission on Human Rights Report of the Working Group on Arbitrary Detention UN Doc E/CN 4/1999/63 (18 December 1999)

UN Report of the Human Rights Committee vol 1 (2002–03) UNGAOR 58th session Supp No 40 (A/58/40) Estonia

UN Special Rapporteur on the Human Rights of Migrants, Annual Report 2002 E/CN 4/2003/85

Human Rights Committee *Nature of the General Legal Obligation on States Parties to the Covenant* UN Doc CCPR/C/21/Rev1/Add 13 (2004)

UN High Commissioner for Human Rights Annual Report 2005 27 December 2004 E/CN 4/2005/85

UN Human Rights Council *Report of the Working Group on Arbitrary Detention* 18 January 2010 A/HRC/13/30

UN Human Rights Committee Considers Report of Germany, 19 October 2012. Available at: http://www.ohchr.org/en/NewsEvents/Pages/DisplayNews.aspx?NewsID=12680&LangID=E (accessed 11 December 2012)

UN Office for the High Commissioner on Human Rights, UN 'Crossing Borders: For Millions of People on the Move, Borders Can Be a Dangerous Space' (April 2012)

UNHCR

Statute of the Office of the United Nations High Commissioner for Refugees. General Assembly Resolution 428 (v) of 14 December 1950

Executive Committee

UN EX Com No 6 XXVIII on *Non-Refoulement* 1977 Office on the UNHCR

UN EX Com No 15 *Refugees without an Asylum Country* (1979)

UN EX Com No 30 XXXIV *The Problem of Manifestly Unfounded or Abusive Applications for Refugee Status or Asylum* (UNHCR, 20 October 1983)

UN Ex Com 44 (XXXVII) *Conclusion on Detention of Refugees and Asylum Seekers* 1986 A/AC 96/688

UN EX Com Executive Committee of the High Commissioner's Programme *Note on International Protection* 7 July 1994 A/AC 96/989 UN GA UNHCR

UN Ex Committee Conclusion No 85 on *International Protection* (UNHCR, 1998)

UN Ex Com No 87*Conclusion on International Protection* (UNHCR, 1999)

UN EX Com Executive Committee of the High Commissioner's Programme Standing Committee *Detention of Asylum-Seekers and Refugees: The Framework, the Problem and Recommended Practice* EC/49/SC/CRP13 4 June 1999

UN EX Com of the High Commissioners Programme 52nd Session 'Note on International Protection' A/AC 96/951 13 September 2001

UN EX Com No 93 (LIII) 2002 on *Reception of Asylum-Seekers in the Context of Individual Asylum Systems*

UN EX Com No 99 on *International Protection* (2004)

UN EX Com Standing Committee 'Progress Report on Resettlement' June 2008

UNHCR Handbook on Procedures *and* Criteria *for* Determining Refugee Status *under the* 1951 Convention *and the* 1967 Protocol Relating *to the* Status *of* Refugees HCR/IP/4/Eng/REV 1Reedited, Geneva, January 1992 (UNHCR 1979)

UNHCR *Position on Readmission Agreements 'Protection Elsewhere' and Asylum Policy* (UNHCR August 1994)

UNHCR 'The Concept of "Protection" Elsewhere' (1995) 7 Intl J Refugee L 123, 126

UNHCR *Guidelines on Applicable Criteria and Standards Relating to the Detention of Asylum Seekers* (UNCHR 1999)

UNHCR *Towards Common Standards on Asylum Procedures' Reflections on the Working Document Prepared by the European Commission* (UNHCR 1999)

UNHCR 'Note on International Protection' UN Doc A/AC 96/914 7 July 1999

UNHCR Sub-Commission on Human Rights Resolution 2000/20 *The Right to Seek and Enjoy Asylum* UNHCR 27th Meeting (18 August 2000)

UNHCR *NGO Background Paper on the Refugee and Migration Interface* (UNHCR, Geneva 28–29 June 2001)

UNHCR *Towards a Common Asylum Procedure and Uniform Status Valid Throughout the EU, for Persons Granted Asylum* (UNHCR, November 2001)

UNHCR Declaration of States parties to the 1951 Convention and/or its 1967 Protocol Relating to the Status of Refugees, Ministerial Meeting of States Parties, Geneva, Switzerland, 12–13 December 2001, UN Doc HCR/MMSP/2001/09 (16 January 2002)

UNHCR *Agenda for Protection* UN DOC A/AC 96/965/Add 1 (26 June 2002)

UNHCR Press Release 'Lubbers Calls for "Convention Plus" Approach to New Challenges' 2002

UNHCR Global Consultations Lisbon Expert Roundtable 'Summary Conclusions on the Concept of 'Effective Protection' in the Context of Secondary Movements of Refugees and Asylum Seekers' (UNHCR 9–10 December 2002)

UNHCR Working Paper 'A Revised "EU Prong" Proposal' (UNHCR December 2003). Available at: http://www.unhcr.org/refworld/docid/400e85b84.htm (accessed 21 January 2013)

UNHCR Background Note on the Application of the Exclusion Clauses: Article 1F of the 1951 Convention relating to the Status of Refugees 4 September 2003.

Available at: http://www.unhcr.org/refworld/docid/3f5857d24.html (accessed 7 December 2012)

UNHCR Statistical Yearbook (UNHCR 2005)

UNHCR Advisory Opinion from the Office of the United Nations High Commissioner for Refugees (UNHCR) *on the Scope of the National Security Exception under Article 33(2) of the 1951 Convention Relating to the Status of Refugees* (6 January 2006). Available at: http://www.unhcr.org/refworld/docid/43de2da94.html (accessed 10 December 2012)

UNHCR *Refugee Protection and Mixed Migration: A 10-Point Plan of Action* (UNHCR 2007). Available at: http://www.refworld.org/docid/45b0c09b2.html (accessed 11 June 2013)

UNHCR *Asylum in the European Union: A Study of the Implementation of the Qualification Directive* (UNHCR 2007)

UNHCR *Statement on Subsidiary Protection under the EC Qualification Directive for People Threatened by Indiscriminate Violence* (UNHCR January 2008)

UNHCR *Position on the Return of Asylum-Seekers to Greece under the Dublin Regulation* 15 April 2008 (UNHCR 2008)

UNHCR *Comments on the European Commission's Proposal for A Recast of the Directive Laying Down Minimum Standards for the Reception of Asylum-Seekers COM(2008)815 final 3rd December 2008* (UNHCR 2008)

UNHCR *Directive Laying Down Minimum Standards for the Reception of Asylum Seekers* (UNHCR 2009). Available at: http://www.refworld.org/docid/49ba8a192.html (accessed 28 July 2013)

UNHCR Interview 'Asylum Seekers Pushed Back to Libya' Briefing Paper (UNHCR, 14 July 2009)

UNHCR *Comments on the European Commission's Proposal for Directive of the European Parliament and of the Council on Minimum Standards on Procedures in MS for Granting and Withdrawing International Protection* COM(2009)554 (UNHCR 2010)

UNHCR *Improving Asylum Procedures: Comparative Analysis and Recommendations for Law and Practice* (UNHCR 2010)

UNHCR Statistics 2010. Available at: www.unhcr.org/4dfa11499.html (accessed 27 November 2012)

UNHCR 'Information on National Practice in the Application of Article 3(2) of the Dublin II regulation in particular in the context of intended transfers to Greece' (UNHCR 31 January 2011)

UNHCR Press Release 'UNHCR Calls for More Resettlement Places and Better Support for Resettled Refugee's' (UNHCR 4 July 2011)

UNHCR Press Release 'Fewer Asylum Claims in Australia' (UNHCR 18 October 2011)

UNHCR Press Release 'Asylum Claims in Industrialized Countries Up Sharply in 2011' (27 March 2012). Available at: http://www.unhcr.org/4f7063116.html (accessed 7 November 2012)

UNHCR 'Global Trends for 2011' (UNHCR 2012)

UNHCR *Detention Guidelines* (UNHCR 2012). Available at: http://www.unhcr.org/505b10ee9.html (accessed 27 July 2013)

UNHCR Press Release 'Crossing Borders: For Millions of People on the Move, Borders Can Be a Dangerous Space' (UNHCR 13 April 2012). Available at: http://www.december18.net/article/crossing-borders-millions-people-move-borders-can-be-dangerous-space (accessed 3 July 2012)

UNHCR *Hungary as a Country of Asylum: Observations on the Situation of Asylum-Seekers and Refugees in Hungary* (24 April 2012). Available at: http://www.unhcr.org/refworld/docid/4f9167db2.html

UNHCR 'Asylum levels and trends in Industrialised countries' (UNHCR 2012). Available at: http://www.unhcr.org/4e9beaa19.html (accessed 12 July 2012)

UNHCR 'Finding Durable Solutions' (UNHCR Global Report 2012). Available at: http://www.unhcr.org/51b1d61d0.html

UNHCR Press Release 'Dozens Queue Every Week in Athens to Apply for Asylum' (UNHCR 12 March 2012)

UNHCR Press Release 'As Syria Crisis Continues, UNHCR Urges EU States to Uphold Common Asylum System Principles' (16 October 2012). Available at: http://www.refworld.org/docid/5087d5cc2.html (accessed 20 May 2013)

UNHCR *Global Trends* (UNHCR 2012). Available at: http://unhcr.org/globaltrendsjune2013/UNHCR%20GLOBAL%20TRENDS%202012_V05.pdf (accessed 20 November 2013)

UNHCR Country Operations Profile – Malaysia 2013. Available at: http://www.unhcr.org/pages/49e4884c6.html

UNHCR 'Dublin Regulation'. Available at: www.unhcr.org/4a9d13d59.pdf (accessed 20 March 2013)

UNHCR 'Global Appeal 2013'. Available at: http://www.unhcr.org/50a9f81116.html (accessed 14 13 July)

European Union

Treaties

Consolidated Treaty Establishing the European Community 1997 OJ C 340 10 November 2007 'Amsterdam Treaty'

Consolidated Version of the Treaty on the Functioning of the EU 30 March 2010 OJ C 83/47 'TFEU'

Treaty on the European Union OJ C83/13, 30 March 2010; OJ C326, 26 October 2012 'TEU'

Charter of Fundamental Rights of the European Union 18 December 2000 C 364/01

Cotonou Partnership 2000/483/EC *Agreement between African, Caribbean and Pacific States and the EU*, OJ L317 15 December 2000 10–11

Secondary Sources

Regulations

Reg 574/99 *Determining the Non-EU Member Countries Whose Nationals Must Be in Possession of Visas when Crossing the External Borders of the Member States now Replaced by Regulation 539/2001 of 15 March 2001 Listing the Third Countries Whose Nationals Must Be in Possession of Visas when Crossing the External Borders and Those Whose Nationals Are Exempt from That Requirement* OJ (2001) L 81/1 21 March 2001

Reg 2725/2000 of 11 December 2000 *Concerning the Establishment of 'EURODAC' for the Comparison of Fingerprints for the Effective Application of the Dublin Convention OJ L316, 15 December 2000 0001 - 0010*

Reg 343/2003 of 18 February 2003 *Establishing the Criteria and Mechanisms for Determining the Member State Responsible for Examining an Asylum Application Lodged in One of the Member States by Third-Country Nationals* OJ L 50 25 February 2003 1-10 'Dublin II Regulation'

Reg 377/2004 on *the Creation of an Immigration Officers Liaison Network* OJ L 64/1 19 February 2004

Reg 2007/2004 of 26 October 2004 *Establishing a European Agency for the Management of Operational Cooperation at the External Borders of the Member States of the European Union* OJ L 349, 25 November 2004, 1

Reg 491/2004 of 10 March 2004 *Establishing a Programme for Financial and Technical Assistance to Third Countries in the Areas of Migration and Asylum* AENEASOJ L80/1 18 March 2004

Reg 1987/2006 *On the Establishment, Operation and Use of the Second-Generation Schengen Information System* (SIS II) OJ L381/4 28 December 2006

Reg 562/2006 *Establishing A Community Code on the Rules Governing the Movement of Persons Across Borders (Schengen Borders Code)* OJ 105/1 13 April 2006

Reg 767/2008 of the European Parliament and of the Council of 9 July 2008 *Concerning the Visa Information System (VIS) and the Exchange of Data between Member States on Short-Stay Visas (VIS Regulation)* OJ L218/60 13 August 2008

Reg 439/2010 *Establishing a European Asylum Support Office* OJ L132/11 29 May 2010

Reg 603/2013 of *the European Parliament and of the Council of 26 June 2013 on the Establishment of 'EURODAC' for the Comparison of Fingerprints for the Effective Application of Regulation (EU) No 604/2013* L180/1 29 June 2013

Reg 604/2013 26 June 2013 *Establishing the Criteria and Mechanisms for Determining the Member State Responsible for Examining an Asylum Application Lodged in One of the Member States by A Third Country National* (Recast) 29 June 2013 OJ L 180/31 'Dublin III Regulation'

Conventions

Convention Determining the State Responsible for Examining Asylum Lodged in One of the Member States of the EC adopted 15 June 1990 entered into force 1 September 1997 OJ C254/1 19 August 1997 'Dublin Convention'

The Schengen Acquis – Convention Implementing the Schengen Agreement of 14 June 1985 between the Governments of the States of the Benelux Economic Union, the Federal Republic of Germany and the French Republic on the Gradual Abolition of Checks at Their Common Borders OJ L239, 22 September 2000 0019 – 0062 'Schengen Convention'

Directives

Directive 2000/43/EC of 29 June 2000 *Implementing The Principle of Equal Treatment Between Persons Irrespective of Racial or Ethnic Origin OJ L 180, 19 July 2000 0022 – 0026*

Directive 2001/51/EC of 28 June 2001 *Supplementing the Provisions of Article 26 of the Convention Implementing the Schengen* Agreement of 14 June 1985 OJ L 187, 10 July 2001, 45–46

Directive 2001/55/EC of 20 July 2001 on *Minimum Standards for Giving Temporary Protection in the Event of a Mass Influx of Displaced Persons and on Measures Promoting a Balance of Efforts between the Member States in Receiving Such Persons and Bearing the Consequences of Receiving OJ L212, 7 August* 2001 0012 - *0023*

Council Directive 2003/9/EC of 27 January 2003 *Laying Down Minimum Standards for the Reception of Asylum Seekers* OJ L31/18 6 February 2003 'Reception Directive'

Council Directive 2003/109/EC of 25 November 2003 *Concerning the Status of Third-Country Nationals Who Are Long-Term Residents* OJ L 16, 23 January 2004, 44–53 'Long-term Residents Directive'

Council Directive 2004/83/EC of 29 April 2004 on *Minimum Standards for the Qualification and Status of Third Country Nationals or Stateless Persons As Refugees or as Persons Who Otherwise Need International Protection and the Content of the Protection Granted OJ L304 30 September 2004 0012 - 0023* 'Qualification Directive'

Directive 2004/38 of the European Parliament and of the Council on *the Right of Citizens of the Union and Their Family Members to Move and Reside Freely within the Territory of the Member States* OJ L 158/77 29 April 2004

Directive 2005/85 on *Minimum Standards of Procedures in Member States for Granting and Withdrawing Refugee Status* OJ L 326/13 13 December 2005 'Procedures Directive'

Directive 2008/115/EC on *Common Standards and Procedures in Member States for Returning Illegally Staying Third Third-Country Nationals* OJ L348/98 24 December 2008

Directive 2011/95/EU on *Standards for the Qualification of Third-Country Nationals or Stateless Persons as Beneficiaries of International Protection, for a Uniform Status for Refugees or for Persons Eligible for Subsidiary Protection, and for the Content of the Protection Granted.* OJ L 337/6 20 December 2011

Directive 2013/32/EU of the European Parliament and of the Council of 26 June 2013 on *Common Procedures for Granting and Withdrawing International Protection (Recast)* OJ L 180/60 29 June 2003

Directive 2013/33/EU of the European Parliament and of the Council of 26 June 2013 *Laying Down Standards for the Reception of Applicants for International Protection (Recast)* OJ L180/96 29 June 2013

European Commission

European Commission Decision of 8 July 1985 *Setting up a Prior Communication and Consultation Procedure on Migration Policies in Relation to Non-Member Countries Brussels: Commission of the European Communities* 88/384/EEC, *OJ L183, 14 July 1988 0035 – 0036*

Commission Staff Working Paper 'Revisiting the Dublin Convention: Developing Community legislation for determining which state is responsible for considering an application for asylum submitted in one of the member states' Sec (2000) 21 March 2000, 522

COM (2000) 755 *Towards a Common Asylum Procedure and a Uniform Status, Valid throughout the Union, for Persons Granted Asylum* 22 November 2000

COM (2000) 757 Final *Communication from the Commission to the Council and the European Parliament on a Community Immigration Policy* Brussels 22 November 2000

European Commission Staff Working Paper 'Revisiting the Dublin Convention' March 2000 SEC (2000) 522

COM (2001) 0506 Final *Report from the Commission - Third Report from the Commission on Citizenship of the Union* 7 September 2001

COM (2001) 672 Final on *a Common Policy on Illegal Immigration* 15 November 2001

COM (2001) 720 Final *Development of the Schengen Information System II* 18 December 2001

COM (2001) 743 Final *The Relationship Between Safeguarding Internal Security and Complying with International Protection Obligations and Instruments* Commission Working Paper Brussels 5 December 2001

European Commission Staff Working Paper *Evaluation of the Dublin Convention* 2001 SEC [2001] 756, 13 June 2001, 18

COM (2002) 703 Final *Integrating Migration Issues in the European Union's Relations with Third Countries 3* December 2002

COM (2003) 315 Final *Towards More Accessible, Equitable and Managed Asylum Systems* 3 June 2003

COM (2003) 04 Final *Communication on Wider Europe* (11 March 2003). Available at: http://www.ec.europa.eu/world/enp/pdf/com03_104_en.pdf (accessed 10 June 2013)

COM (2003) 573 *Strategy for the Effective Implementation of the Charter of Fundamental Rights by the EU*. Available at: http://www.europa.eu/legislation_summaries/human_rights/fundamental_rights_within_european_union/dh0004_en.htm (accessed 11 June 2013)

EURACTIV 'EU Divided Over African Asylum Camps' 5 October 2004

COM (2004) 410 Final on *the Managed Entry in the EU of Persons in Need of International Protection and Enhancement of the Protection Capacity of the Regions of Origin: Improving Access to Durable Solutions* 4 June 2004

European Commission 'Visit to Ceuta and Melilla – Mission Report. Technical mission to Morocco on illegal immigration' 7 October– 11 October 2005 EMO/05/380 Brussels, 19 October 2005

COM (2005) 388 Final *on Regional Protection Programmes* 1 September 2005

COM (2005) 184 Final *The Hague Programme: Ten Priorities for the Next Five Years, the Partnership for European Renewal in the Field of Freedom, Security and Justice* 10 May 2005

COM (2007) 299 European Commission *Report from the Commission to the European Parliament and the Council on the Evaluation of the Dublin System* 6 June 2007

COM (2007) 301*On the Future Common European Asylum System*, Green Paper Brussels 6 June 2007

COM(2007) 745 Final on *the Application of Directive 2003/9/EC of 27 January 2003 Laying Down Minimum Standards for the Reception of Asylum Seekers* Brussels, 26 November 2007

COM (2008) 815 Final *Proposal for a Directive of the European Parliament and of the Council Laying Down Minimum Standards for the Reception of Asylum Seekers (Recast)* 2008/0244 (COD)

COM (2008) 68 Final *Examining the Creation of a European Border Surveillance System* (EUROSUR) 13 February 2008

COM (2008) 820 *Proposal for A Regulation of the European Parliament and of the Council Establishing the Criteria and Mechanisms for Determining the Member State Responsible for Examining an Application for International Protection Lodged in One of the Member States by A Third-Country National or a Stateless Person* (Recast) 3 December 208 2008/0243 (COD)

Eurostat Stat/09/175 'Asylum decisions in the EU27' (2008)

COM (2009) 262/4 *An Area of Freedom, Security and Justice Serving The Citizen* 10 June 2009

COM(2011)319 Final *Amended Proposal for A Directive of the European Parliament and of the Council on Common Procedures for Granting and Withdrawing International Protection Status*, Brussels, 1 June 2011 2009/0165 (COD)

COM (2011) 320 Final *Amended Proposal for a Directive of the of the European Parliament and the Council Laying Down Minimum Standards for the Reception of Asylum Seekers (recast)* 1 June 2011 'Commission 2011 Recast'

COM (2011) 549 Final *Annual Report to the Parliament and the Council on the Activities of the EURODAC Central Unit in 2010* 12 September 2011

COM (2011) 680 Final *Smart Borders – Options and the Way Ahead* Brussels 25 October 2011

COM (2011) 907 Final *Progress Report on the Development of the Second Generation Schengen Information System* (SIS II) January 2011 – June 2011 Brussels, 20 December 2011

Eurostat Asylum Statistics 2011 'in Focus' No 48/2011 21 September 2011

European Commission 'EUROSUR: Providing authorities with tools needed to reinforce management of external borders and fight cross-border crime' Memo 11/896 12 December 2011

European Commission 'Common European Asylum System: Better Protection and Solidarity for People Seeking International Protection' Press Release IP/11/665 1 June 2011

European Commission Staff Working Paper *Determining the Technical and Operational Framework of the European Border Surveillance System (EUROSUR) and the Actions to Be Taken for Its Establishment* Brussels, 28 January 2011 SEC(2011) 145 final

European Commission 'EU "Smart Borders": Commission Wants Easier Access and Enhanced Security' Press Release IP/11/1234, 25 October 2011

COM (2012) 254 Final *Amended Proposal for a Regulation of the European Parliament and of the Council on the Establishment of 'EURODAC' for the Comparison of Fingerprints for the Effective Application of Regulation (EU) No [.../...] (Establishing the Criteria and Mechanisms for Determining the Member State Responsible for Examining an Application for International Protection Lodged in One of the Member States by a Third-Country National or a Stateless Person) and to Request Comparisons With EURODAC Data by Member States' Law Enforcement Authorities and Europol for Law Enforcement Purposes and Amending Regulation (EU) No 1077/2011 Establishing a European Agency for the Operational Management of Large-Scale IT Systems in the Area of Freedom, Security and Justice (Recast Version)* Brussels, 30 May 2012, 2008/0242 (COD)

COM (2012) 686 Final Report from the Commission to the European Parliament and the Council Second Biannual Report on the Functioning of the Schengen Area 1 May 2012 – 31 October 2012, 23 November 2012

Eurostat Asylum Statistics 2012 'in Focus' No 8/2012 no date. Available at: http://www.epp.eurostat.ec.europa.eu/statistics_explained/index.php/Asylum_statistics

Eurobarometer 380 'Awareness of Home Affairs' European Commission 2012. Availableat:http://www.aedh.eu/Third-Annual-Report-of-the.html(accessed20 May 2013)

EU Spotlight 'Asylum Applications Continue to Increase in EU' EU Spotlight 28 March 2013

European Commission 'A Common European Asylum System' 2013. Available at: http://www.ec.europa.eu/dgs/home-affairs/what-we-do/policies/asylum/index_en.htm (accessed 1 August 2013)

European Commission 'Migration and mobility partnership signed between the EU and Morocco' Press Release IP/13/513 7 June 2013

Eurostat 'Asylum in the EU27' 48/2013 22 March 2013

European Council

Council Resolution of 30 November 1992 *on Manifestly Unfounded Applications for Asylum* ('London Resolution') (30 November 1992). Available at: http://www.unhcr.org/refworld/docid/3f86bbcc4.htm (accessed 13 July 2013)

Council and Commission Decision of 26 January 1998 on *the Conclusion of The Partnership and Cooperation Agreement between the European Communities and Their Member States, of the One Part, and Ukraine, of the Other Part* 98/149/EC, OJ L 049 19 February 1998 0001-0002

European Council *Responsibilities of Council Bodies in the Field of Justice and Home Affairs Following Entry into Force of the Treaty of Amsterdam* 6166/1/99 Rev 1 (Council of The EU 1999)

European Council *The Schengen Acquis.* 1999/435/EC of 20 May 1999 OJ L 176 10 July 1999

European Council *Council Decision of 28 September 2000 Establishing a European Refugee Fund* 2000 OJ 252/12; [2010] OJ 129/1

European Council *Conclusion for the Reception of Asylum Seekers* Council Doc 13865/00 (Presse 457)

Council Common Position of 27 December 2001 on Combating Terrorism (2001/930/CFSP) OJ L344/90 28 December 2001

EU High Level Working Group on Asylum and Migration *Report to the European Council in Nice* 2001. Available at: http://www.consilium.europa.eu/uedocs/cms_data/docs/pressdata/en/misc/13993.en0%20ann.doc.html (accessed 8 May 2013)

Council of the EU *Modification of the Terms of Reference of the High Level Working Group* 30 May Doc 9433/02

Seville European Council 21 and 22 June 2002, Presidency Conclusions, Brussels 24 October 2002 13463/02

Thessaloniki European Council 19 and 20 June 2003 Presidency Conclusions, Brussels 1 October 2003 11638/03

European Council *The Hague Programme, Strengthening Security and Justice in the European Union* 16054/04 (Council of The European Union 2004)

Council Decision on *the Signing of the Agreement between the European Community and Ukraine on Readmission of Persons* 9312/07 Council of the EU, Brussels 5 June 2007

European Council *European Pact on Immigration and Asylum* 13444/08 Brussels, 24 September 2008

Council of the European Union 'The Stockholm Programme – An Open and Secure Europe Serving and Protecting the Citizens' 17024/09 2 December 2009, [2010] OJ C 115/01 4 May 2010 'Stockholm programme'

Council Decision 2010/252/EU of 26 April 2010 *Supplementing the Schengen Borders Code as Regards the Surveillance of the Sea External Borders in the Context of Operational Cooperation Coordinated by* [*Frontex*] OJ L 111/20 4 May 2010

Council of the EU *Long Term Residents' Directive Extended to Refugees and Other Beneficiaries of International Protection* Press Release 11 April 2011

EU Council Thematic Programme 'Cooperation with Third Countries in the areas of Migration and Asylum' 2011–2013 Multi-Annual Strategy Paper; *EU Readmission Agreements: State of Play* (June 2011)

European Council *Stockholm Programme Mid-Term Review* 15921/12 13 November 2012

Council of the EU *Outcome of Proceedings of High Level Working Group Asylum and Migration on 21 January 2013* 5663/13 22 February 2013

Council of the EU 'EU-Armenia Readmission Agreement' Brussels, 19 April 2013 8630/13 PRESSE 160

Council of the European Union *Joint Declaration Establishing a Mobility Partnership between the Kingdom of Morocco and the European Union and its Member States* 6139/13 Add1 Rev 3 3 June 2013

European Parliament

European Parliament *Presidency Conclusions Tampere European Council* 15 and 16 October 1999. Available at: http://www.europarl.europa.eu/summits/tam_en.htms-tc (accessed 11 November 2012)

European Parliament *Resolution on the Common Immigration Policy* B6-0508/2006 26 September 2006

December No 575/2007/EC of the *European Parliament and the Council Establishing the European Return Fund for the Period of 2008–2013 as Part of the General Programme 'Solidarity and Management of Migration Flows'* OJ L144 6 June 2007

European Parliament *Legislative Resolution 7 May 2009 on the Proposal for a Directive of the European Parliament and the Council Laying Down Minimum Standards for the Reception of Asylum Seekers (Recast)* COM(2008)8015-C6-0477/2008 – 2008/0244(COD)

European Parliament Legislative Resolution 6 April 2011 on *the Proposal for a Directive of the EP and of the Council on Minimum Standards on Procedures in Member States for Granting and Withdrawing International Protection (Recast)* COM(2009) 0554 –C7-0248/2009-2009/0165(COD) Resolution P7_TA(2011)0136

European Parliament, Green Group 26 June 2012. Discussion available at: http://www.greenmediabox.eu/archive/2012/06/26/migration/20120626_migration_en.mp4Lavenex

Economic and Social Committee

COM (2008) 815 Final on *the Proposal for a Directive of the European Parliament and the Council Laying Down Minimum Stands for the Reception of Asylum Seekers* C317/110 23 December 2009, 1.2

European Asylum Support Office

European Asylum Support Office 2011 *Annual Report on the Situation of Asylum in the European Union and on the Activities of the European Asylum Support Offic*e European Union Asylum Support Office 2012

EU Fundamental Rights Agency

The Duty to Inform Applicants about Asylum Procedures: The Asylum-Seekers Perspective (EU Fundamental Rights Agency 2010)

Access to Effective Remedies: The Asylum Seekers Perspective Thematic Report (EU Fundamental Rights Agency 2010)

EU Fundamental Rights Agency *Coping with a Fundamental Rights Emergency: The Situation of Persons Crossing the Greek Land Border in an Irregular Manner* (Fundamental Rights Agency 2011)

EUROSUR

Questioned in the European Parliament, ECRE Weekly Bulletin 29 June 2012

Frontex (European Agency for the Management of Operational Cooperation at the External Borders of the Member States of the European Union)

Frontex Programme of Work 2010, Warsaw. Available at: http://www.frontex.europa.eu/gfx/frontex/files/justyna/pow2010.pdf

Frontex *Fundamental Rights Strategy* 31 March 2011. Available at: http://www.statewatch.org/observatories_files/frontex_observatory/2011-03-31-frontex-fundamental-rights-strategy.pdf

Frontex (2011) *Code of Conduct for All Persons Participating in Frontex Activities*. Available at: http://frontex.europa.eu/assets/Publications/General/Frontex_Code_of_Conduct.pdf (accessed 20 March 2013)

Council of Europe

Committee of Ministers Recommendation (2003) 5 on *Measures of Detention of Asylum Seekers* 16 April 2003 Available at: https://wcd.coe.int/ViewDoc.jsp?id=2121 (accessed 18 November 2013)

Council of Europe Commissioner for Human Rights, Mr Gil Alvaro-Robles Report on visit to the UK 4–12 November 2004 Comm DH(2005)6

Parliamentary Assembly Resolution 1471 (2005) on *Accelerated Procedures in Council of Europe Member States* Council of Europe Available at: http://assembly.coe.int/Main.asp?link=/Documents/AdoptedText/ta05/ERES1471.htm (accessed 18 November 2013)

Parliamentary Assembly Recommendation 1900 (2010) *Detention of Asylum Seekers and Irregular Migrants in Europe* Council of Europe Available at: http://assembly.coe.int/Mainf.asp?link=/Documents/AdoptedText/ta10/ERES1707.htm (accessed 18 November 2013)

Commissioner for Human Rights of the Council of Europe *Report by Thomas Hammarberg Commissioner for Human Rights of the Council of Europe Following His Visit to Turkey on 28 June – 3 July 2009: Human Rights of Asylum Seekers and Refugees (*Council of Europe 2009)

Council of Europe Resolution 1695 (2009) Improving the Quality and Consistency of Asylum Decisions in the Council of Europe Member States C/E 20 November 2009 Available at: http://assembly.coe.int/Main.asp?link=/Documents/AdoptedText/ta09/ERES1695.htm (accessed 18 November 2013)

Parliamentary Assembly *Readmission Agreements: A Mechanism for Returning Irregular Migrants* Council of Europe Doc 21268 17 March 2010

Parliamentary Assembly Resolution *Detention of Asylum Seekers and Irregular Migrants in Europe* 1707 (2010). Available at: http://www.assembly.coe.int/Mainf.asp?link=/Documents/AdoptedText/ta10/ERES1707.htm (accessed 27 July 2013)

Council of Europe *Protocol No 12 to the Convention for the Protection of Human Rights and Fundamental Freedoms* CETS No: 177 4 November 2011

ECtHR *Interim Measure Suspending the Expulsion of the Applicant to Hungary* App 2283/12 11 January 2012

European Committee for the Prevention of Torture and Inhuman or Degrading Treatment or Punishment *Report to the Italian Government on the visit to Italy carried out by the CPT from 27 to 31 July 2009* (Cpt/Inf (2010) 14). Available at: http://www.cpt.coe.int/documents/ita/2010-inf-14-eng.htm (accessed 11 July 2012)

European Committee for the Prevention of Torture, Inhuman or Degrading Treatment or Punishment

European Committee for the Prevention of Torture and Inhuman or Degrading Treatment or Punishment CPT Standards CPT/Inf/E(2002)1 – Rev 2010

Visit reports

CPT/Inf (2006) 11 Poland
CPT/Inf (2006) 41 Greece
CPT/Inf (2007) 40 Ireland
CPT/Inf (2007) 18 of 18 April 2007 Germany
CPT/Inf (2006) 1 of 20 December 2006 Greece
CPT/Inf (2005) 13 21 July 2005 Austria
CPT/Inf (2006) 9 23 February 2006
Report of Special Rapporteur on Torture and Other Cruel, Inhuman or Degrading Treatment of Punishment on His Mission to Greece (10–20 October 2010) A/HRC/16/52/Add 4 21 April 2011
European Committee for the Prevention of Torture and Inhuman or Degrading Treatment or Punishment (CPT) *Public Statement Concerning Greece* (15 March 2011). Available at: http://www.cpt.coe.int/documents/grc/2011-10-inf-eng.htm (accessed 22 April 2013)

Cases

CJEU

Athanasios Vatsouras (C-22/08) and *Josif Koupatantze* (C-23/08) v *Arbeitsgemeinschaft (ARGE) Nürnberg 900*. Joined cases C-22/08 and C-23/08. European Court Reports 2009 Page I-04585
Brahim Samba Diouf v Ministre du Travail de l'emploi et de l'immigration CJEU C-69/10 28 July 2001
Cimade and GISTI v Ministre de L'Intérieur, de l'Outre-mer, des Collectivités Territoriales et de l'immigration Case C-179/11 27 September 2012
Commission of the EC v Hellenic Republic of Greece C128/25 OJ 24 May 2008
European Parliament v Council of the European Union 17 April 2012 Case C-335/10 Unpublished. Available at: http://www.curia.europa.eu/juris/document/document.jsf?text=&docid=121662&pageIndex=0&doclang=en&mode=lst&dir=&occ=first&part=1&cid=14821312 http://www.register.consilium.europa.eu/pdf (accessed 6 November 2012)
European Parliament v European Union C-133/06 6 May 2008
Grzelczyk v Centre Public d'aide Sociale d'Ottignies-Louvain-la-Neuve 2001 Case C-184/99
K v Bundesasylamt C-245/11 6 November 2012
Kadzoev C-357/09 PPU Unreported 30 November 2009
MA, BT, DA v Secretary of State for the Home Department C-648/11, CJEU Press Release No 71/13 Luxembourg, 6 June 2013
Meki Elgafaji, Noor Elgafaji V Stssecretaris Van Justitie C-465/07 [2009] *European Court Reports 2009 Page I-00921*

Metock and Others C-127/08 [2008] ECR I 6241
NS and ME V SSHD C-4110/10, C493/10 CJEU Judgement 21 December 2011
Shamso Abdullahi Case C-394/12. Lodged 27 August 2012

ECtHR

Abdolkhani and Karimnia v Turkey App 30471/08 22 September 2009
Abdulaziz, Cabales and Balkandali v UK App 9214/80, 9473/81, 9474/81 28 May 1985
Al-Skeini and Others v UK App 55721/07 7 July 2011
Amuur v France (1996) 22 EHRR 533
Brogan v UK (1989) 11 EHRR 117
Chahal v UK App 22414/93 15 November 1996;
D v UK [1997] 24 EHRR 423
Dougoz v Greece App 40907/98 6 March 2001
Gaygusuz v Austria App 17371/90 16 September 1996
Gebremedhin v France App 24389/05, 26 July 2007
The Greek Case, 18 November 1969 (1969) 12 YECHR
Hatami v Sweden App 32448/96, ECtHR, 23 January 1997,
Hirsi Jamaa and Others v Italy App 27765/09, 23 February 2012
Hurtado v Switzerland App 17549/90 (1994) Series A No 280-A
Jabari v Turkey App 40035/98, 11 July 2000
Khamroyev and others v Ukraine Communication 26 July 2010
K.R.S. v United Kingdom App 32733/08, 2 December 2008
Koua Poirrez v France App 40892/98 30 December 2003
Litwa v Poland App No 26629/95 4 April 2000
Mayeka and Mitunga v Belgium App 13178/03 12 October 2006
Medvedyev and Others v France [2010] 51 EHRR 39
MSS v Belgium and Greece App 30696/09 21 January 2011
N v Finland ECtHR 26 July 2005 App 38885/02
N v UK [2008] App No 26565/05 27 May 2008
Niedzwiecki v Germany App 58453/00 15 February 2006
Othman (Abu Qatada) v UK App 8139/09 17 January 2012
Peers v Greece App 28524/95 19 April 2001
Petrovic v Austria App 20458/92 27 March 1998
Riad and Idiab v Belgium App 29787/03 and 29810/03 24 January 2008
Saadi v Italy, App No 37201/06, 28 February 2008
Said v Netherlands App 2345/02 2005, 5 July 2005
Saadi v UK App 13229/03 ECHR 29 January 2008, [2008] 47 EHRR
Sampanis and Others v Greece App 32526/05 11 December 2012
SHH v UK App 60367/10 29 January 2013
Soering v UK 161 ECtHR Series A (1989)
Sufi and Elmi v UK App 8319/07 and 11449/07, 28 June 2011
TI v UK App 43844/98 7 March 2000

Tymoshenko v Ukraine App 24987/11 30 April 2013
Uner v the Netherlands App 46410/99 18 October 2006
Vilvarajah and Others v UK App 45/1990/236/302-306 26 September 1991
Willis v UK App 36042/97 11 June 2002
Xhavara v Italy and Albania App 39473/98 11 January 2001,

UN CAT

A v the Netherlands Communication No 91/1997
Abdussamatov et al v Kazakhstan CAT/C/48/D/444/2010 Communication No 444/2010
Agiza v Sweden CAT/C/34/D/233/2003 20 May 2005
Alan v Switzerland Communication No 21/1995
Aydin v Sweden Communication No101/1997
CT and KM v Sweden 2007 CAT 279/2005
Gbadjavi v Switzerland CAT/C/48/D/396/2009 Communication No 396/2009
JHA v Spain No 323/2007 CAT/C/41/D/323/2007 21 November 2008
Kalonzo v Canada CAT/C/48/D/343/2008 Communication No 343/200
Kisoki v Sweden Communication 41/1996
M.*A.M.A et al v Sweden* CAT/C/48/D/391/2009 Communication No 391/2009
Mutombo v Switzerland Communication No13/1993 27 April 1994
P.K. et al v Spain, Communication No 323/2007, UN Doc CAT/C/41/D/323/2007 (2008)
Paez v Sweden Communication 39/1996
Tala v Sweden Communication No 41/1996

Human Rights Committee

A v Australia Communication No 560/1993 CCPR/C/59/D/560/1993
Byahuranga v Denmark HRC 9 December 2004 CCPR/C/82/D/1222/2003
C v Australia No 900/1999 UN Doc CCPR/C/76/D/900/1999 13 November 2002
Celepli v Sweden CCPR/C/51/D/456/1991, 26 July 1994
Ibrahima Gueye et al v France, Communication No 196/1985, UN Doc CCPR/C/35/D/196/1985 (1989)
Van Alphen v the Netherlands No 305/1988 UN Doc CCPR/C/39/D/305/1988 (1990)
Zwaan – de Vries v the Netherlands Communication No 182/1994 UN Doc CCPR/C/OP/2 at 209 (1990)

International Court of Justice

Barcelona Traction Case Belgium v Spain 1970 ICJ Reports 3, 5 February 1980

Inter-American Court

Haitian Center for Human Rights v US Case 10.675 Report No 51/96. Inter-Am. CHR DocOEA/Ser.L/V/II.95 Doc7 Red (1997)

Australia

Plaintiff M61/2010e v The Commonwealth Office (2010) 85 ALJR 133
Plaintiff M70/2011 and Plaintiff M106/2011 v Minister for Immigration and Citizenship [2011] HCA 32 31 August 2011
Karthigesu Rajendran v Minister for Immigration & Multicultural Affairs [1998] 1085 FCA, 1085 FCA, Australia: Federal Court, 4 September 1998. Available at: http://www.unhcr.org/refworld/docid/3ae6b7638.html (accessed 4 December 2012)

Germany

Administrative Court of Berlin, 7 July 2011, 33 K 79.10 A. Available at: http://www.asylumlawdatabase.eu/en/case-law/germany-administrative-court-berlin-7-july-2011-33-k-7910#content (accessed 23 August 2013)

Hungary

Metropolitan Court of Budapest 07/09/2007 *Abdelfatah Saadallah M'hammed v Office of Immigration and Nationality of the Republic of Hungary* 17.K.34.397/2007/8

UK

Islam v SSHD; R v IAT and Anor, ex parte Shah (1999) 2 WLR 1015
R (Do) v Special Adjudicator [2004] 2 AC 323
R (on the application of ZO (Somalia) and others) (Respondents) v Secretary of State for the Home Department, [2010] UKSC 36
R (On Application of EO, RA, CO, OE) v SSHD [2013] EWHC 1236 (Admin)
R (Ullah) v Special Adjudicator [2004] UKHL 26
R v Immigration Officer at Prague Airport and another ex parte European Roma Rights Centre and others [2004] UKHL 55
R v SSHD ex parte Javed, Ali and Ali [2001] EWCA Civ 789
R v SSHD Exp Adan (1998) 37 ILM 1090
R v SSHD exp Adan and Aitseguer [1999] 3 WLR 1274 [2000] INLR 211
R v SSHD ex parte Adam (FC); Limbuela (FC); ex parte Tesema (FC) Conjoined Appeals UKHL [2005] 66
R v SSHD ex p Adan and Aitseguer [2001] UKHL 2 AC 477
R (on Application of Saadi) v SSHD [2002] UKHL 41, [2002] 1 WLR 3131

R v SSHD ex p Robinson [1998] QB 929
R v Uxbridge Magistrates Court exp Adimi [1999] 4 All ER 520
Bugdaycay v SSHD [1987] 1 AC 514
Tekle v Secretary of State for the Home Department [2008] EWHC 3064 (Admin)
Youseff v Home Office [2004] EWHC 1884
R (On the application of EO, RA, CE, OE and RAN) v SSHD [2013] EWHC 1236 Admin
R v Special Adjudicator exp Linsam Kandasamy [1994] Imm AR 333 (QB)
R (On the application of Saadi, Mageb, Osman and Mohammed) v SSHD [2001] EWCA Civ 1512, 4 All ER 961
QD (Iraq) v SSHD [2009] EWCA Civ 620
R *v Secretary of State for the Home Department, ex parte Adam (FC); Limbuela (FC), Tesema (FC) (Conjoined Appeals)*, [2005] UKHL 66, 3 November 2005

United States Supreme Court

Sale, Acting Commissioner INS v Haitian Centres Council 509 US 155 21 June 1993

Index

For Product Safety Concerns and Information please contact our EU representative GPSR@taylorandfrancis.com
Taylor & Francis Verlag GmbH, Kaufingerstraße 24, 80331 München, Germany

www.ingramcontent.com/pod-product-compliance
Ingram Content Group UK Ltd.
Pitfield, Milton Keynes, MK11 3LW, UK
UKHW010958180926
475701UK00004B/446

* 9 7 8 1 1 3 8 2 4 8 1 0 6 *